Th
Sugar Aristocracy

New Historical PERSPECTIVES

New Historical Perspectives is a book series for early career scholars within the UK and the Republic of Ireland. Books in the series are overseen by an expert editorial board to ensure the highest standards of peer-reviewed scholarship. Commissioning and editing is undertaken by the Royal Historical Society, and the series is published under the imprint of the Institute of Historical Research by the University of London Press.

The series is supported by the Economic History Society and the Past and Present Society.

Series co-editors: Professor Elizabeth Hurren (University of Leicester) and Professor Heather Shore (Manchester Metropolitan University)

Founding co-editors: Simon Newman (University of Glasgow) and Penny Summerfield (University of Manchester)

The Glasgow Sugar Aristocracy

Scotland and Caribbean Slavery, 1775–1838

Stephen Mullen

LONDON
ROYAL HISTORICAL SOCIETY
INSTITUTE OF HISTORICAL RESEARCH
UNIVERSITY OF LONDON PRESS

Published by
UNIVERSITY OF LONDON PRESS
SCHOOL OF ADVANCED STUDY
INSTITUTE OF HISTORICAL RESEARCH
Senate House, Malet Street, London WC1E 7HY

Available to download free or to purchase the hard copy
edition at https://www.sas.ac.uk/publications.

ISBNs
978-1-909646-77-3 (hardback edition)
978-1-912702-33-6 (paperback edition)
978-1-909646-93-3 (.epub edition)
978-1-909646-78-0 (.pdf edition)

DOI 10.14296/fyax1274

New Historical
PERSPECTIVES

Cover image: The Port of Glasgow (drawn and engraved by W. H. Bartlett
and J. W. Appleton). Published in William Finden, *The Ports, Harbours,
Watering-Places and Coast Scenery of Great Britain* (London, 1836–42).

To my mother and father

Contents

List of illustrations ix

List of tables xi

List of abbreviations xiii

Maps xv

Acknowledgements xix

Introduction 1

1. Emergence 29

2. Trade and commerce 57

3. A Glasgow-West India house 89

4. 'Wanted, to serve in the West Indies' 119

5. Jamaica 147

6. Grenada and Carriacou 183

7. Trinidad 211

8. Glasgow-West India 'spheres of influence': embedding the profits of Caribbean slavery 253

Conclusion 293

Appendix 303

Bibliography and manuscript sources 313

Index 347

List of illustrations

5.1   James Hakewill, Llanrumny estate, St Mary's, Jamaica (1820–21)   151

6.1   The buildings of Maran estate in the island of Grenada (1822)   193

7.1   Richard Bridgens, 'Protector of Slaves Office (Trinidad), *c.*1833'   217

8.1   Marble busts of James Ewing of Strathleven (1775–1853) and
James Buchanan (1785–1857)   255

List of tables

1.1	Scottish imports and exports, 1755–1827 (official values).	31
2.1	Debtors, and debts owed, to Glasgow-West India elite between 1805 and 1879.	73
2.2	The West India elite's landed estates and borrowing secured upon property, 1775–1840.	76
3.1	The Smith family, wealth on death 1815–83.	111
4.1	Destinations of ships departing from Clyde ports for the West Indies, 1806–34.	140
4.2	Estimated adventurers from the Clyde to the West Indies, 1806–34.	142
4.3	Population of Scotland, by region, 1801–31.	142
4.4	Home residences of individuals departing Greenock for the West Indies in 1774–5, compared to Scottish population.	144
5.1	Wealth on death of Scots in Jamaica in the late slavery era (1775–1838) who died between 1794 and 1857.	170
5.2	Range of wealth on death of Scots in Jamaica in the late slavery era (1775–1838) who died between 1794 and 1857.	170
6.1	Wealth on death of Scots in Grenada in the late slavery era (1775–1838) who died between 1784 to 1858.	199
6.2	Range of wealth on death of Scots in Grenada in the late slavery era (1775–1838) between 1784 and 1858.	199
7.1	Wealth on death of Scots in Trinidad in the late slavery era (1797–1838) who died between 1799 and 1850.	234
7.2	Range of wealth on death of Scots in Trinidad in the late slavery era (1797–1838) who died between 1799 to 1850.	234
7.3	Scottish West India fortunes, by region.	244
7.4	Range of Scottish West India fortunes.	244
8.1	Holdings on the death of 105 Glasgow-West India elites who died between 1800 and 1905.	257
8.2	Range of wealth on death of the Glasgow-West India elites who died between 1800 and 1905.	260

List of abbreviations

ave.	average
BL	British Library
cwt.	hundredweight
GCA	Glasgow City Archives
GH	Glasgow Herald
GUA	University of Glasgow Archives
HCPP	House of Commons Parliamentary Papers
IRO	Island Record Office
J£	Jamaica pound
JNA	National Archive of Jamaica, Spanishtown
£ Scots	Scots pound
LBS	*Legacies of British Slave-ownership* project (which was renamed *Legacies of British Slavery* in 2020)
LOC	Library of Congress
NLJ	National Library of Jamaica, Kingston
NLS	National Library of Scotland
NRAS	National Register of Archives Scotland
NRS	National Records of Scotland
NWGA	NatWest Group Archives
PUL	Princeton University Library
stg.	pound sterling
SUA	University of Strathclyde Archives
TNA	The National Archives of the UK
TRG	The Royal Gazette (Kingston, Jamaica)
UofGSPC	University of Glasgow Special Collections
WCL	William L. Clements Library

Maps

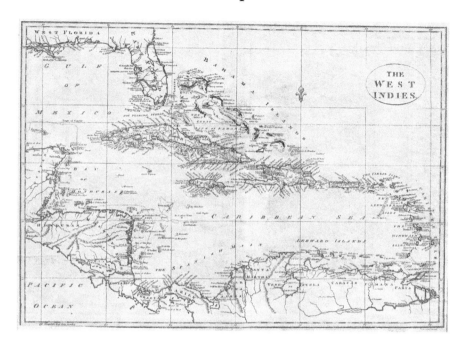

1   Map of the West Indies, 1799 (Clement Cruttwell,
Atlas to Cruttwell's Gazetteer, 1799).

2   A new map of Scotland compiled from actual surveys & regulated
by the latest astronomical observations / by Joseph Enouy. [London]:
Published 12 September 1803 by Laurie & Whittle, 53 Fleet Street
London, [1803]. National Library of Scotland, CC BY 4.0.

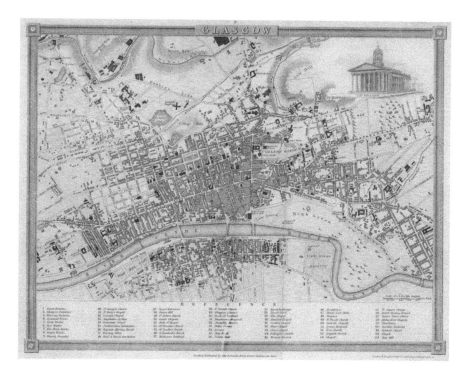

3   Glasgow, drawn and engraved by J. Dower. London: Orr &
Smith, [c.1830]. National Library of Scotland, CC BY 4.0.

Acknowledgements

During my ten-year Glasgow-West India sojourn, I have accumulated many debts. This body of research would not have been possible without an Economic and Social Research Council PhD scholarship awarded by Economic and Social History subject area at the University of Glasgow in 2010 (ES/I902414/1). Funding from the Annie Dunlop Endowment (Scottish History), and a small grant in History, helped support research trips to the United States of America and the Caribbean. A Royal Society of Edinburgh grant allowed a month-long trip to Trinidad in 2016. Postdoctoral employment in the History (2015–19) and Scottish History subject areas (2019–ongoing) at the University of Glasgow allowed me to develop this monograph. Working on the 'Slavery, Abolition and the University of Glasgow' report (2018) was a seminal moment in my development as an historian, transforming my understanding of Atlantic slavery and British capitalism, and how merchant capital continues to influence modern society. This research has contributed to illuminating both the institution and city's historic connections with Atlantic slavery.

My greatest intellectual debt is to my two doctoral supervisors, Simon Newman and Allan Macinnes. The expertise provided by the cross-institutional arrangement (2010–14) embodied the connections between the universities of Glasgow and Strathclyde as well as the connections between Scotland, America and the Caribbean. My external examiner at an enjoyable viva in February 2015, Phillip Morgan, and internal examiner, Mike Rapport, provided excellent advice which shaped the transition from thesis to monograph.

Some of this material has previously been published. An earlier version of Chapter 3 'A Glasgow-West India house' was published as 'A Glasgow-West India merchant house and the imperial dividend, 1779–1867', *Journal of Scottish Historical Studies*, xxxiii, 196–233. A portion of Chapter 2 'Trade and commerce' was published as 'The great Glasgow-West India house of John Campbell, senior, & Co.', in T. M. Devine (ed.), *Recovering Scotland's Slavery Past: the Caribbean Connection* (Edinburgh, 2015), 124–45. A portion of Chapter 7 'Trinidad' was published as 'John Lamont of Benmore: a Highland planter who died "in harness" in Trinidad', *Northern Scotland*, ix,

44–66. I am grateful to Edinburgh University Press for permissions and I am also grateful to NatWest Archives for permission to quote their materials.

Any work developed over many years is dependent upon the generosity of fellow scholars. The intellectual culture and various groups and activities at the University of Glasgow are an important part of scholarly development: I value the advice and comradeship of Ewan Gibbs, Michael Hopcroft, Craig Lamont, Chris Miller, Michael Morris, Arun Sood, Jelmer Vos and Valerie Wright. I appreciate the collegiate support and friendship shown by many scholars of Scotland after I relocated to Scottish History in 2019, especially Dauvit Broun, Catriona M. M. Macdonald and Martin Macgregor. Discussions about the repatriation of capital from the East and West Indies with Andrew Mackillop, in Tennents and elsewhere, improved me as an historian.

I am fortunate to have met several generous scholars in Great Britain, North America and the Caribbean. Eric Graham was an important source of advice as I embarked on a PhD. Mark Freeman was an early mentor and friend: those classes on Mayhew worked better than I thought they would. I am grateful to Nicholas Draper for many discussions since 2010 about slavery, the Atlantic trades and merchant capital. These discussions transformed how I approached this monograph. David Alston is one of the most collegiate historians I know, sharing expertise freely. Karly Kehoe has offered sound advice over several years. John Cairns is a gentleman-scholar, and I am grateful for advice and materials. I thank Tom Devine and Anthony Cooke for transformative works on Glasgow's colonial entrepreneurs. Even if our conclusions do not always align, I learned a great deal from their work. The Royal Historical Society and Institute of Historical Research have put together a superb format in the New Historical Perspectives Series. I am grateful for the feedback and constructive criticism from Penny Summerfield, Alex Murdoch and Nicholas Draper at the initial workshop. This gave me more to think about than I had anticipated but transformed my thinking and ultimately improved this monograph. I am especially indebted to Natalie Zacek, who read each chapter thoroughly and provided great advice, mentoring and friendship as I developed the work.

A project of this nature simply could not be possible without archivists and the generosity of fellow scholars while at home and abroad. Irene O'Brien and all at Glasgow City Archives hold a remarkable and underutilized collection. Staff at the University of the West Indies Mona and St Augustine campuses provided wonderful advice and hospitality for a visiting researcher. In Jamaica, James Robertson of UWI Mona was a superb host and improved my approach to archival work on the island. I was very fortunate to have been introduced to the Ranstons, who became my family in Jamaica. I spent a wonderful time with Emma Ranston in the archives and libraries of greater Kingston and Spanishtown in 2014. In Grenada, John Angus Martin provided much information. I value his polymath's knowledge of the history of the Spice Isle. In Trinidad, I am grateful to Selwyn Cudjoe: my understanding of the modern Caribbean was transformed as we walked and talked in Arima, Port of Spain and Tacarigua. Friends at home have offered unstinting support over many years, and I offer my gratitude in return to Martin Boyle, Paul Cogan and Vincent McGovern.

My greatest debt is to my family: my parents, Stevie and Sylvia. Stephen and Jade, Juliette, Willow Rose and Annabelle Meg have watched this book develop over many years with interest. Over the course of this work, all our lives changed with the passing of my father, Stevie, in February 2016 and grandfather, James Scott, in February 2022. Both taught me a great deal in life, some of which I did not appreciate at the time. Finally, I met my wife, Jade Halbert, at the University of Glasgow, a transformative place, and time, in both our lives.

Introduction

In the spring of 1833, Peter Borthwick, a paid agent of the West India interest, championed the pro-slavery cause at a series of lectures across Scotland. After boisterous debates with abolitionists in Glasgow in February – at the behest of the pro-slavery London Society of West India Planters and Merchants and the Glasgow-West India Association – he arrived at the Edinburgh Assembly Rooms in March 1833. Although full emancipation in the British West Indies was by then a fait accompli, Borthwick hoped to convince the public of the recklessness of immediate abolition and cited economics as the prime factor for the continuation of chattel slavery:

> [I am here to speak] of our brothers and sisters, born at, educated at, reared to manhood at home, and now in the possession of these Colonies, as owners, or rulers, or, in some sort, moral and civil protectors of those beings in bondage. From them, you, the people of Great Britain, draw a revenue of direct income…you have an encouragement to your industry, which is not equalled by any other market…tropical produce…is exported to you in the form of the raw material…it is repurchased by the Colonist…beyond the price he must pay for it in any other market in the world…Then what is your Bristol, your Liverpool, your Manchester, your Glasgow, your Paisley, your Dundee, your eastern end of the great metropolis, even London itself – if you take from them the West India Colonies? Nothing – worse than nothing; one universal scene of beggary and starvation (Cheers).[1]

While Borthwick mounted a defence of resident planters, the entire system was based upon the maritime carrying trades undertaken by merchants who imported tropical produce, exporting goods such as textiles in return.[2] Merchants thus bridged additional factors of production – the landmass of the West Indies, and labour of enslaved people – to create resources for consumption, a process that, according to Borthwick, contributed to the economic development of Great Britain and raised the standard of living of the embryonic manufacturing class. Thus, cotton fields in Grenada and

---

[1] P. Borthwick, *A Lecture on Colonial Slavery and Gradual Emancipation, Delivered in the Assembly Rooms on Friday 1 March 1833* (Edinburgh, 1833), pp. 4–5; I. Whyte, *Scotland and the Abolition of Black Slavery, 1756–1838* (Edinburgh, 2006), pp. 230–1.

[2] J. M. Price, 'What did merchants do? Reflections on British overseas trade, 1660–1790', *Journal of Economic History*, xlix (June 1989), 267–84.

Carriacou and sugar and coffee estates in Jamaica and Trinidad connected with refineries, mills, factories and landed estates in Glasgow, Lanarkshire and elsewhere across Great Britain. While it must have seemed natural to those in attendance that British commerce and industry was powered by the West India trades and, by extension, the labour of 800,000 enslaved men, women and children, exactly how far these connections contributed to economic development, then and now, remains a matter of some debate.

Peter Borthwick situated Glasgow in the appropriate British-Atlantic world context, and contemporary descriptions of the city's West India merchants as the 'sugar aristocracy' are suggestive of their importance.[3] Were the individuals that made these trades possible – transatlantic merchants and young men sojourning to the West Indies to acquire wealth – really so important to the economic and societal development? Despite their grandiose title, contemporary publications condemned the 'sugar aristocracy' to relative insignificance: as entrepreneurs who occasionally generated large fortunes during Glasgow's sugar heyday, *c.*1790 to 1838, yet of lesser overall importance than their commercial predecessors, the 'tobacco lords'. Indeed, prominent antiquary John Guthrie Smith argued Glasgow-West India commerce was a minor enterprise:

> It [the West India trades] probably was never entitled to the consideration it got. Being in few hands, it yielded fortunes that bulked in the public eye, and less showy trades may have been of more real importance…It left behind it no single fortune equal to the largest fortunes left by the tobacco trade.[4]

Since the author's father was a West India merchant who was financially ruined, these views might have been skewed by his own background. Nevertheless, as will be explained below, various historians have argued that the West India trades and/or mercantile investments were incidental to British economic development, thus siding with Guthrie Smith.[5] Such perspectives are part of long-standing debates about Britain's industrial growth and the relative importance of endogenous (such as domestic markets and technology) and exogenous (foreign commerce, including with slavery economies) factors.[6]

---

[3] J. Strang, *Glasgow and Its Clubs* (London and Glasgow, 1857), p. 212.

[4] J. G. Smith and J. O. Mitchell, 'Possil', *The Old Country Houses of the Old Glasgow Gentry* (Glasgow, 1878).

[5] K. Morgan, *Slavery, Atlantic Trade and the British Economy, 1660–1800* (Cambridge, 2000), pp. 59–60.

[6] J. Inikori, 'Capitalism and slavery, fifty years after: Eric Williams and the changing explanations of the industrial revolution', in *Capitalism and Slavery Fifty Years Later: Eric*

This study seeks to understand more about the effects of West India commerce on metropolitan society and economy. At its core, this is a study of mercantile capital in Glasgow which poses several interrelated questions about an era of rapid transformation in Scotland. Who were the 'sugar aristocracy' and how did they come to be? How were West India trades financed and undertaken in Glasgow and abroad? This study goes further, examining the Scots who travelled to the West Indies towards the end of Caribbean slavery and ascertaining how commercially successful they were, if at all. Questions remain: what impact did the direct investments of West India merchants and colonial adventurers have on local economies, as well as the wider effects of such processes on commerce and industry? This study, therefore, takes a new approach to illuminate the world of individuals who acquired West India fortunes (both mercantile and colonial), ultimately assessing, in an Atlantic frame, the interconnections between the colonies and metropole in the late eighteenth and early nineteenth centuries.

Less than forty years after Peter Borthwick's claims, Karl Marx theorized in *Capital* (1867) that state-sponsored colonial expansion and the imposition of chattel slavery were fundamental to the rise of capitalism in Great Britain. The settlement of colonies, and other factors, combined to hasten in 'hot-house fashion, the process of transformation of the feudal mode of production into the capitalist mode, and to shorten the transition'.[7] Merchants had a crucial role within the transformation. Merchant capitalism was said to have had a 'Janus face', parasitically feeding off older modes of production (such as chattel slavery), thus providing access to new markets and the primitive accumulation of capital which underpinned the development of a new capitalist epoch.[8]

From the 1970s, the neo-Marxist world economy school examined flows of global trade and profits on a grand scale. Such theorists take a broad view of the development of metropolitan regions in Europe, arguing that unequal relationships underpinned capitalist development in the imperial core while perpetuating the underdevelopment of colonial peripheries from 1450 onwards.[9] Immanuel Wallerstein was among the most influential in this school,

---

Eustace Williams – A Reassessment of the Man and His Work, ed. H. Cateau and S. H. H. Carrington (New York, 2000), pp. 79–103.

[7] K. Marx, *Capital*, vol. i (London, 1990 edn.), pp. 915–16.

[8] E. Fox-Genovese and E. D. Genovese, *The Fruits of Merchant Capital: Slavery and Bourgeois Property in the Rise and Expansion of Capitalism* (New York, 1983), pp. 6–15.

[9] For example, A. G. Frank, *World Accumulation, 1492–1789* (New York and London, 1978); Frank, *Dependent Accumulation and Underdevelopment* (New York and London, 1979); I. Wallerstein, *The Modern World System II: Mercantilism and the Consolidation of the European World Economy, 1600–1750* (New York, 1980).

viewing capitalism as an interconnected entity, a 'world system' defined by dependency and underdevelopment.[10] Yet, the theory has attracted criticism for the lack of 'systematic statistical underpinning' and, for some historians, colonial commerce was but a small part of European economic activity in the early modern period. Indeed, Patrick O'Brien famously concluded that 'for the economic growth of the core, the periphery was peripheral'.[11]

The view that Atlantic commerce was a significant contributor to British economic activity is also a matter of some debate. It has long been argued that the seventeenth-century Commercial Revolution in England preceded the eighteenth-century Industrial Revolution and thus that domestic demand, rather than overseas trade, powered self-sustained growth.[12] On the other hand, Kenneth Morgan has noted that the Americanization of eighteenth-century British trade underpinned the Industrial Revolution, with foreign commerce an engine of growth. The demand for manufactured goods for export generated growth and reshaped business institutions, banking and commercial strategies. These processes transformed British-Atlantic commerce from a primarily import-led enterprise to one based on the export of a variety of high-value goods.[13] The scale and significance of imports, however, has been questioned. David Eltis and Stanley L. Engerman examined the role of sugar as an 'engine of economic growth' and argued it was not comparable to other domestic industries (echoing the 'small ratios' analysis of the transatlantic slave trade: see below). Thus, for these authors, slavery 'certainly "helped" that Revolution along, but its role was no more than that of many other economic activities, and in the absence of any one of these it is hard to believe that the Industrial Revolution would not have occurred anyway'.[14] While this was a seminal argument, the authors have recently been accused of 'straw man' scholarship by rebutting a claim that no historian makes (i.e. that slavery 'caused' the Industrial Revolution) and critiqued for using the sugar industry as a proxy for the wider Atlantic slave

[10] Wallerstein, *The Modern World System II.*

[11] P. O'Brien, 'Economic development: the contribution of the periphery', *The Economic History Review*, new series, xxxv (1982), 1–18.

[12] R. Davis, *The Industrial Revolution and British Overseas Trade* (Bath, 1979), p .63.

[13] K. Morgan, 'Atlantic trade and British economic growth in the eighteenth century', in *International Trade and British Economic Growth: From the Eighteenth Century to the Present Day, Vol. 5: The Nature of Industrialization*, ed. P. Mathias and J. A. Davis (Oxford, 1996), pp. 14–33.

[14] D. Eltis and S. L. Engerman, 'The importance of slavery and the slave trade to industrializing Britain', *Journal of Economic History*, lx (2000), 123–44.

economy.[15] Nevertheless, Trevor Burnard remains sceptical about the effects of slavery on British economic transformation, arguing the Atlantic trades represented a 'small percentage of European gross national product'.[16]

In contrast to the Eltis-Engerman position, Joseph Inikori argued that commerce with slave-based economies in an Atlantic system dependent on chattel slavery – including Spain and Portugal – had significant multiplier effects not only on English industrialization but also shipping and commercial and financial infrastructure.[17] At a roundtable discussion in 2003, Inikori drew support from Pat Hudson and Nuala Zahedieh but criticism from others.[18] More recent macro analyses provide further support. Knick Harley underlined the importance of the interaction between chattel slavery, the Atlantic economy and British industrialization but claimed that North America, not the West Indies, made the central contribution.[19] Overall, the effects could be substantial. Klas Rönnbäck estimated that direct and indirect economic activities connected with the triangular trade and plantation slavery were equivalent to 11 per cent of Great Britain's eighteenth-century GDP.[20] The two opposing macro analyses of British economic transformation (Eltis-Engerman and Inikori) share a common feature: they are Anglo-centric in focus and their arguments have been accepted as a proxy for overall British economic development.

Chattel slavery was the economic foundation of the North American and the West Indian economies. The system has long been argued to have underpinned the Atlantic trades and British economic growth. Indeed, the publication of Eric Williams' *Capitalism and Slavery* in 1944 established a long-term debate about the overall relationship with British industrialization. Marxisant in tone if not approach, Williams defined an exploitative global relationship. 'Commercial capitalism', according to Williams, was based upon mercantile monopolies and slavery and underpinned the development

---

[15] 'Introduction', in *Legacies of British Slave-Ownership: Colonial Slavery and the Formation of Victorian Britain*, ed. C. Hall et al. (Cambridge, 2014), p. 29, note 33.

[16] T. Burnard, *Jamaica in the Age of Revolution* (Philadelphia, 2020), pp. 217, 225.

[17] J. Inikori, *Africans and the Industrial Revolution in England* (Cambridge, 2002).

[18] J. Inikori and S. Behrendt et al., 'Roundtable', *International Journal of Maritime History*, xv (2003), 279–361.

[19] K. Harley, 'Slavery, the British Atlantic economy, and the industrial revolution', in *The Caribbean and the Atlantic World Economy: Circuits of Trade, Money and Knowledge, 1650–1914*, ed. A. B. Leonard et al. (Basingstoke, 2015), pp. 161–83.

[20] K. Rönnbäck, 'On the economic importance of the slave plantation complex to the British economy during the eighteenth century: a value-added approach', *Journal of Global History*, xiii (2018), 309–27.

of industrial capitalism, which was the foundation for manufacturing.[21] Profits from the slave trade and plantation slavery, commerce with the slave economies, as well as private fortunes of the West India interest and those returned from slavery societies, contributed to the Industrial Revolution in eighteenth-century Great Britain, either in a causal role (strong) or as a significant contributor (weak). In this view, however, the slave economy went into terminal decline after the American War of Independence (1775–83). Caribbean slavery became less profitable thereafter and was of declining importance in nineteenth-century Britain. The abolition of the slave trade in 1807 and emancipation in 1834 were principally due to declining economic conditions rather than humanitarian agitation.[22] For Williams, Atlantic slavery and mercantilism powered industrial capitalism, which in turn destroyed slavery and repositioned Great Britain as a producer of manufactured goods in a new, global nexus.

This study of the Glasgow 'sugar aristocracy' is situated in the orbit of the main Williams thesis – effects on commerce and industry – and another regarding the decline of the West India economy (both of these are discussed in more detail below). These themes have become a 'Williams thesis' in their own right. In an oft-cited section, the main Williams thesis argued that the trafficking in enslaved people, plantation slavery and associated commerce powered the British Industrial Revolution:

> By 1750, there was hardly a trading or manufacturing town in England which was not in some way connected with the triangular or direct colonial trade. The profits provided one of the main streams of accumulation of capital in England which financed the Industrial Revolution.[23]

Yet, overall, Williams did not view Caribbean slavery and associated commerce as a causal factor in industrial change: 'it must not be inferred that the triangular trade was solely and entirely responsible for the economic development. The growth of the internal market…the ploughing-in of profits from industry to generate still further capital and achieve greater expansion, played a large part.'[24] However, Berg and Hudson went further in a recent study which adopted a truly British scope (incorporating

---

[21] E. Williams, *Capitalism and Slavery* (Chapel Hill, 1944), pp. 210–11.

[22] B. L. Solow and S. L. Engerman, 'British capitalism and Caribbean slavery: the legacy of Eric Williams: an introduction', in *British Capitalism and Caribbean Slavery: The Legacy of Eric Williams*, ed. B. L. Solow and S. L. Engerman (Cambridge, 1987), pp. 1–23.

[23] Williams, *Capitalism and Slavery*, p. 52.

[24] Williams, *Capitalism and Slavery*, pp. 105–6.

Scotland), with the authors claiming the Atlantic trades were a 'major causal factor' in the British Industrial Revolution.[25]

Eric Williams provided a broad range of examples underlining how the colonial trades influenced, both directly and indirectly, British industries such as textile production (wool and cotton), sugar refining, rum distillation, pacotille (cheap baubles for trade in Africa) and metallurgical industries production as well as influencing shipping, shipbuilding, insurance and banking.[26] Nuala Zahedieh's study of the copper industry has elucidated Williams' vision of 'commercial capitalism' in England. The demand for copper boilers, coolers and rum stills and other equipment in slave economies made it the 'most dynamic industry' in the British metal industry, thus chaining 'thousands of workers in Cornwall, South Wales, Bristol and London to enslaved labour' while creating vast fortunes for coppersmiths such as William Forbes.[27] Although Forbes had no direct connection to slavery, Williams examined the investments made by those who did – especially the West India interest – thus shifting from macro to micro-economics. Although the effects of direct investments were smaller in relation to the wider, systemic processes, merchants and planters sank slavery-derived fortunes into various enterprises which altered the internal dynamics of eighteenth-century Britain.[28] This study seeks to understand in greater detail how West India commerce, especially direct investments, affected Scottish economic and societal development.

The first stream of Williams' capital accumulation, the trafficking in enslaved people (commonly known as the 'transatlantic slave trade', although this is an increasingly problematic term), has generated a considerable historiography. The horrifying scale seemingly provided compelling evidence to support the manifesto. Modern estimates suggest that European traders forcibly trafficked over 12 million Africans into chattel slavery in the Americas between 1501 and 1875. British ships imported 3.25m people between 1626 and 1808, the second-highest numbers after Portugal.[29] However, the estimates of profits from slave voyages and their relative importance to British economic transformation has been viewed with some

---

[25] M. Berg and P. Hudson, 'Slavery, Atlantic trade and skills: a response to Mokyr's "holy land of industrialism"', *Journal of the British Academy*, ix (2021), 259–81.

[26] Williams, *Capitalism and Slavery*, pp. 57–60, 65–84, 98–102, 104–5.

[27] Williams, *Capitalism and Slavery*, p. 210; N. Zahedieh, 'Eric Williams and William Forbes: copper, colonial markets, and commercial capitalism', *The Economic History Review*, lxxiv (2021), 784–808.

[28] Williams, *Capitalism and Slavery*, pp. 85–98.

[29] Transatlantic slave trade database estimates <https://www.slavevoyages.org/assessment/estimates> [accessed 31 Jan. 2020].

scepticism.[30] Indeed, Engerman's conclusions that the profits of the British trafficking in enslaved people were insignificant has become known as the 'small ratios' argument.[31]

However, this debate has little relevance in a Scottish context. The Royal African Company's trading monopoly from 1660 initially centred the trade in London, which effectively prohibited voyages departing from Scotland before the early eighteenth century.[32] Although port records are not comprehensive for the period between the Union of 1707 and the abolition of the slave trade a century later, just twenty-seven 'triangular trade' voyages have been verified to have cleared Scottish ports between 1706 and 1766. These voyages tended to be economic failures.[33] For comparison, over 1,500 transatlantic slave trade voyages departed from the English port of Bristol alone in the same period.[34] Yet, funded voyages do not tell the full story. Scots were heavily involved in trafficking enslaved people via English ships, and had (as yet unquantified) involvement with such trafficking within British and foreign colonies.[35] Case studies of individuals such as Richard Oswald and John Tailyour reveal they were complicit in trafficking on a horrifying scale, accumulating major fortunes which improved the Scottish countryside.[36] While Scottish slave-traders did accumulate great fortunes from inter-colonial trafficking in enslaved people, and more examples will surely come to light with further research, the systemic effects must have been slight compared to English ports. It was not so much 'small ratios'

[30] Morgan, *Slavery, Atlantic Trade*, pp. 36–48.

[31] S. L. Engerman, 'The slave trade and British capital formation in the eighteenth century: a comment on the Williams thesis', *The Business History Review*, xlvi (1972), 430–43.

[32] W. A. Pettigrew, *Freedom's Debt: The Royal African Company and the Politics of the Atlantic Slave Trade, 1672–1752* (Chapel Hill, 2013).

[33] M. Duffill, 'The Africa trade from the ports of Scotland, 1706–66', *Slavery & Abolition*, xxv (2004), 102–22; S. D. Behrendt and E. J. Graham, 'African merchants, notables and the slave trade at Old Calabar, 1720: evidence from the National Archives of Scotland', *History in Africa*, xxx (2003), 37–61.

[34] Trans-Atlantic slave trade – database <https://www.slavevoyages.org/voyage/database#results> [accessed 15 Sept. 2020].

[35] D. Hancock, 'Scots in the slave trade', in *Nation and Province in the First British Empire: Scotland and the Americas, 1600–1800*, ed. N. C. Landsman (Lewisburg, Pa., 2001), pp. 60–94; S. Schwarz, 'Scottish surgeons in the Liverpool slave trade in the late eighteenth and early nineteenth centuries', in *Recovering Scotland's Slavery Past: The Caribbean Connection*, ed. T. M. Devine (Edinburgh, 2015), pp. 145–66.

[36] D. Hancock, *Citizens of the World: London Merchants and the Integration of the British Atlantic Community, 1735–1785* (Cambridge, 1997); N. Radburn, 'Guinea factors, slave sales, and the profits of the transatlantic slave trade in late eighteenth-century Jamaica: the case of John Tailyour', *William & Mary Quarterly*, lxxii (2015), 243–86.

for Scotland, as tiny. Nevertheless, profits from the trafficking in enslaved people was but one stream of accumulation; the wider, systemic effects of plantation slavery were deemed more important to Britain in general and Scotland in particular.

An assessment of the state of the West India economy, and the origins of the wealth and profits of those involved, is crucial to understanding how slavery influenced British development. The 'golden age' of sugar in the West Indies (a golden age for planters, not the enslaved), according to the traditional view, occurred in the seventeenth century.[37] Noted historian of the British West Indies Richard Pares described the period after the Peace of Paris in 1763 and the outbreak of the American war in 1775 as the 'silver age of sugar'.[38] Plantation profits averaged an annual return of 13.5 per cent on initial investment during this era.[39] With such wealth on offer, it must have seemed natural to presume, as Williams did in *Capitalism and Slavery*, that there was a substantial net in-flow of colonial profits to Scotland and England. But this ran contrary to the wisdom of Adam Smith, professor of logic and moral philosophy at the University of Glasgow, who famously stated that Britain's colonies represented 'mere loss instead of profit' in *An Inquiry into the Nature and Causes of the Wealth of Nations* (1776).[40] Smith criticized the closed mercantile system that created a mutual monopoly between Great Britain and its colonies in the Americas. For Smith, while the Atlantic system was inefficient on a *national* scale, it created vast *private* profits for special interests. One modern account supported this view, arguing that while the British colonies came at a net cost to Great Britain, the real 'winners' of the West India trades were the merchants and planters who organized themselves in powerful lobbying groups.[41]

Furthermore, according to Adam Smith, the overall commercial system was sustained through metropolitan credit.[42] Such agreements between merchants and planters were certainly fundamental to the development of the Atlantic slave economies, although there have been historiographical

---

[37] D. B. Ryden, *West India Slavery and British Abolition, 1783–1807* (Cambridge, 2009), p. 8.

[38] R. Pares, *Merchants and Planters*. Economic History Review Supplement, No. 4 (New York, 1960), p. 40.

[39] Burnard, *Jamaica in the Age of Revolution*, p. 220; 'Et in Arcadia ego: West Indian planters in glory, 1674–1784', *Atlantic Studies*, ix (2012), 19–40, at p. 22.

[40] A. Smith, *Wealth of Nations* (Oxford, 1998 edn), p. 464.

[41] P. Coelho, 'The profitability of imperialism: the British experience in the West Indies, 1768–1772', *Explorations in Economic History*, x (1973), 253–80.

[42] Smith, *Wealth of Nations*, p. 350.

disagreements about the origins of this wealth.[43] Richard Pares initially agreed with Adam Smith: 'since the colonies absorbed as much capital as they could get, they cannot have done much to build up capital in England and thereby to promote the Industrial Revolution…the planters themselves seem to have been recipients of capital rather than sources'.[44] However, at the end of a pre-eminent career cut tragically short, Pares radically shifted position, arguing that the plantations generated their own wealth:

> The profits of the plantations were the source which fed the indebtedness charged upon the plantations themselves. In this sense, Adam Smith was wrong: the wealth of the British West Indies did not all proceed from the mother country; after some initial loans in the earliest period which merely primed the pump, the wealth of the West Indies was created out of the profits of the West Indies themselves, and, with some assistance from the British taxpayer, much of it found a permanent home in Great Britain.[45]

S. D. Smith revisited the house of the Lascelles – the records on which Pares mainly based his conclusions – and cast new light on what he describes as the 'Adam Smith question': did the wealth of the West Indies spring from capital advanced by British merchants, or did wealth accrue by planters reinvesting profits on their estates? Disputing Pares' 'ploughed back profits' thesis, S. D. Smith instead concluded Adam Smith's vision of British riches overflowing into the Caribbean 'was closer to the truth'. In this view, long-term mortgage capital from British merchants underpinned the late eighteenth-century 'sugar-boom' in the West Indies.[46]

The wealth of late eighteenth-century Jamaica provides evidence of the vibrance of the West India economy on the eve of the American Revolution. Richard Sheridan examined the wealth of Jamaican planters and, by drawing up a 'balance sheet of empire', concluded the aggregate wealth of the West Indies was £30 million, with Jamaica comprising 60 per cent (£18 million). Sheridan reasoned that the lucrative West India trade contributed as much as 10 per cent of British national income in this period.[47] Sheridan's

---

[43] J. M. Price, 'Credit in the slave trade and plantation economies', in *Slavery and the Rise of the Atlantic System*, ed. B. L. Solow (Cambridge, 1993), pp. 293–340.

[44] R. Pares, 'The economic factors in the history of empire', *The Economic History Review*, vii (1937), 119–44, at p. 130.

[45] Pares, *Merchants and Planters*, p. 50.

[46] S. D. Smith, 'Merchants and planters *revisited*', *The Economic History Review*, lv (2002), 434–65; *Slavery, Family and Gentry Capitalism in the British Atlantic: the world of the Lascelles, 1648–1834* (Cambridge, 2006), pp. 173–4.

[47] R. Sheridan, 'The wealth of Jamaica in the eighteenth century', *The Economic History Review*, 2nd series, xviii (1965), 292–311, at p. 311.

figures on the extent of trade were disputed as too optimistic.[48] However, by assessing the 'prodigious riches' of Jamaican residents, Trevor Burnard revised upwards Sheridan's capital stock estimates, thus underlining the island's status as the wealthiest British colony at the outbreak of the American Revolution.[49] Yet, it remains unknown how much personal wealth was repatriated to Great Britain. Indeed, Kenneth Morgan's 1996 call for 'firmer evidence' of returned West India fortunes remains open today.[50] While historians have provided colonial estimates of wealth acquired from slavery, especially in Jamaica, much remains to be understood about the profits flowing from the island and the West Indies more broadly to the metropole.[51] Through the inventories generated on the death of Scots in three islands, this study systematically analyses, in a comparative framework, the importance of slavery-generated wealth repatriated to the metropole in the era of supposed decline.

While few historians disagree that Caribbean slavery was still profitable in 1775, the exact date of decline is one of the most important debates in Atlantic world historiography. Some historians have viewed the era after the American War of Independence as a 'bronze or even lead age' for resident sugar planters, although, as will be demonstrated, the view that the West Indies were in economic decline from this point remains contentious.[52] In what has become known as the 'decline thesis', Eric Williams argued the profits from Caribbean slavery declined after 1783, and perhaps as early as 1763, thus following in the footsteps of his mentor, Lowell Ragatz. In *The Fall of the Planter Class in the British Caribbean*, Ragatz located the onset of decline after the Seven Years War (1756–63), but this was qualified. British planter prosperity peaked in 1799, but a glut in sugar production

---

[48] R. P. Thomas, 'The sugar colonies of the old empire: profit or loss for Great Britain?', *The Economic History Review*, xxi (1968), 30–45; R. Sheridan, 'The wealth of Jamaica in the eighteenth century: a rejoinder', *The Economic History Review*, xxi (1968), 46–61.

[49] T. Burnard, 'Prodigious riches: the wealth of Jamaica before the American Revolution', *The Economic History Review*, liv (2001), 506–24.

[50] Morgan, 'Atlantic trade and British economic growth', p. 33.

[51] Burnard, 'Prodigious riches'; C. Petley, *Slaveholders in Jamaica: Colonial Society and Culture during the Era of Abolition* (London, 2009), pp. 22–3; 'Plantations and homes: the material culture of the early nineteenth-century Jamaican elite', *Slavery & Abolition*, xxxv (2014), 437–57, at pp. 440 and 453; R. Sheridan, *Sugar and Slavery: An Economic History of the British West Indies, 1623–1775* (Kingston, 2007 ed.), pp. 369, 375; A. Karras, *Sojourners in the Sun* (Ithaca, 1992), p. 175.

[52] Ryden, *West India Slavery*, p. 8; S. H. H. Carrington is one of the few modern scholars maintaining that the decline of the West Indies originated in 1775. See *Sugar Industry and the Abolition of the Slave Trade, 1775–1810* (Gainesville, 2002).

combined with inefficient agricultural practices and planter debt meant increasingly diminishing profits for 'old Caribbean holdings' from 1763.[53] All historians embrace the general principle of West India decline, yet disagree about causes, the exact starting point and chronology. Seymour Drescher described the abolition of the slave trade as 'econocide' as the trade was still profitable in 1807. Thus, decline did not come in 1783 as Williams contends, but after the Napoleonic Wars.[54]

The view that planting profits entered terminal decline after 1776 has also been challenged. J. R. Ward examined the accounts of twenty British-controlled sugar plantations and concluded that, while profits declined with the American war, profitability rose again in the next decade and depression only arrived in the 1820s.[55] It is now accepted that 'decline' was dependent on date of colonization and stage of development. David Beck Ryden argued the overproduction of sugar in the West Indies and concurrent fall in prices from 1799 initiated decline. The narrative of decline was promoted by vociferous Jamaica planters via the London West India Committee – whose profits *were* diminishing – although planters in newer colonies continued to fare better into the nineteenth century.[56] Indeed, absentee slave owners with interests in British Guiana and Trinidad constituted a 'new and important fraction of "the planter class"' in nineteenth-century Britain.[57] Overall, most historians – even if divided on overall impact – agree on the later chronology of decline. Nicholas Draper dated the origins of decline to the 1820s.[58] Trevor Burnard corroborates the Ward–Draper position.[59] Thus, the process of decline was underway by the 1830s and in all likelihood began during the previous decade.

The importance of Caribbean slavery and its commerce to British industrialization is even more hotly disputed among historians. Based on

[53] L. Ragatz, *The Fall of the Planter Class in the British Caribbean, 1763–1833* (New York, 1928), pp. 286–330.

[54] S. Drescher, *Econocide: British Slavery in the Era of Abolition*, 2nd ed. (Chapel Hill, 2010), pp. 142–61.

[55] J. R. Ward, 'The profitability of sugar planting in the British West Indies, 1650–1834', *The Economic History Review*, xxxi (1978), 197–213, at pp. 210–13.

[56] Ryden, *West India Slavery*; 'Sugar, spirits, and fodder: the London West India interest and the glut of 1807–15', *Atlantic Studies*, ix (2012), 41–64.

[57] N. Draper, 'The rise of a new planter class? Some countercurrents from British Guiana and Trinidad, 1807–33', *Atlantic Studies*, ix (2012), 65–83, at p. 79.

[58] N. Draper, 'Helping to make Britain great: the commercial legacies of slave-ownership in Britain', in *Legacies of British Slave-Ownership: Colonial Slavery and the Formation of Victorian Britain*, ed. C. Hall and N. Draper (Cambridge, 2014), p. 81.

[59] Burnard, *Jamaica in the Age of Revolution*, p. 231.

the assumption of the in-flow of wealth to Great Britain, Eric Williams noted important streams of capital accumulation; national wealth generated via commerce (eg providing the government with income from duties, and the multiplier effects from ancillary industries); and the accumulation of personal fortunes by merchants, planters and sojourners. While historians assessing the importance of slavery to national wealth remain divided, micro-level studies of the personal investments of enslavers suggest a considerable impact. Through examples of prominent absentee West India families such as the Beckfords and the Pennants, Williams traced investments in British institutions and country estates.[60] However, for Williams, the direct investments of the West Indians were but a minor part of the transfer into industry, a position that contemporary Richard Pares agreed with: 'West India millionaires [built]...more Fonthills [i.e. mansions] than factories among them'.[61] Accepting Pares' conclusion in 1992, Pat Hudson was generally sceptical of the importance of the West India interest's *direct* investments in industrial enterprise while maintaining that the slavery system more broadly transformed British industry and commerce.[62] Estimation of the respective proportions of West India fortunes that rested in consumption or industry awaits detailed quantitative assessment but Williams viewed the process as a distinctly eighteenth-century phenomenon. After 1783, Williams envisioned an 'outworn interest, whose bankruptcy smells to heaven in historical perspective'. Decline, therefore, had a transatlantic dimension.[63] Thus, while noting the social, cultural and political prominence of the West India interest in eighteenth-century Britain, the narrative was one of declining economic and political influence, and wider relevance, after 1783.

Nicholas Draper and the historians involved with the *Legacies of British Slave-Ownership* project modified this interpretation by arguing that the patterns illuminated by Williams in the eighteenth century continued into the next. Overall, they concluded that Britain's slave economy was a 'significant contributor' to the remaking of national commerce and to a lesser extent industry (especially cotton and railways) up to the middle of the nineteenth century. Yet, their work underlined the importance of private wealth, as slave owners invested heavily across British society, including in the cultural and political spheres.[64] However, while absentee

---

[60] Williams, *Capitalism and Slavery*, pp. 87–90, 125–34.

[61] Pares, 'Economic factors', p. 132.

[62] P. Hudson, *The Industrial Revolution* (London, 1992), p. 196.

[63] Williams, *Capitalism and Slavery*, pp. 96, 211.

[64] The *Legacies of British Slave-ownership* project situates these arguments among the principal Williams theses rather than a sub-theme about personal investments.

slave owners were vitally important to the infusion of slavery-derived capital into the fabric of British economy and society, colonial merchants represented a more regular channel of slavery wealth into local infrastructure and industry.[65] Since not all slave owners were merchants and vice versa, the study of merchant capital benefits from a focused, regional approach. This study takes up the mantle thrown down by the LBS study, examining Glasgow-West India merchants and their investments up to emancipation and beyond, assessing their relative importance into the Victorian period.

The paid agent of the West India interest, Peter Borthwick, naturally argued the West India colonies were crucial to the development of London and outports along the western seaboard of Great Britain. The importance of mercantile activity to the development of British ports can be gauged through case studies, which will also provide a comparative framework for this study. London, of course, was the premier Atlantic port in Great Britain. With a population approaching 1 million by 1801 (a rise from around 600,000 in the previous century), London stood alone in Britain. Transformed into the leading commercial hub of seventeenth-century Europe, imperial trade initiated 'adaptive innovations'; the accumulation and improvement of capabilities; the improvement and diversification of manufacturing in London and hinterlands; improvement of transport networks; and a major boost in education which 'raised England to technological leadership in Europe'.[66]

Perry Gauci argued the 'ingenuity and courage' of individual merchants underpinned London's spectacular growth after 1660, while noting the importance of large conglomerates such as the East India Company.[67] London remained the premier sugar refinery centre in Great Britain on the eve of the American Revolution.[68] By the 1790s, the West India trades were estimated to be the third highest of London's overseas trade (by value), with substantial mercantile capital sunk into infrastructure such as the West India and London dock companies. Draper concluded the 'slave economy permeated every almost every aspect of London's commercial life', yet, due to the diversified nature of the economy, was not instrumental to the

---

[65] Draper, 'Helping to make Britain great', pp. 79–80.

[66] N. Zahedieh, *Capital and the Colonies: London and the Atlantic Economy, 1660–1700* (Cambridge, 2010), p. 285.

[67] P. Gauci, *Emporium of the World: The Merchants of London, 1660–1800* (London, 2007), pp. 204–5.

[68] C. J. French, '"Crowded with traders and a great commerce": London's domination of English overseas trade, 1700–1775', *The London Journal*, xvii (1992), 27–35, at p. 29.

development of the metropolis (although was not marginal either).[69] Given London's role as a trade hub, West India fortunes were often generated with the intention of removal elsewhere. The Hibbert mercantile dynasty was based in Manchester and London, expropriating wealth from Jamaica which fanned out via the family to philanthropic institutions and country estates in Lancashire, Warwickshire and elsewhere. Prominent Scots, such as Richard Oswald of Auchincruive, implemented a similar business model in the mid-eighteenth century, transferring wealth from the metropole to Ayrshire in Scotland.[70] Yet, while London remained the dominant imperial centre and source of mercantile fortunes, as the eighteenth century progressed the port's relative share of national commerce declined, partially explained by the concomitant rise of three major outports along Britain's western seaboard.

British outports developed various specialisms throughout the eighteenth century. Bristol specialized in the sugar trade, Liverpool in the slave trade and Glasgow in tobacco.[71] Measured by volume and value of trade as well as population size, Bristol was the premier outport at the opening of the eighteenth century. Over the next century, the population rose over threefold from 20,000 to 64,000 in 1801. Initial port specialism in the tobacco trade was superseded in terms of imports by Glasgow in the 1720s and Liverpool in 1738. Similarly, Liverpool took over as the main British slave-trading port in the 1740s. Bristol's merchants increasingly focused on West India trades, and it remained the leading sugar outport for 'virtually all of the eighteenth century'. Liverpool only really challenged Bristol's position as premier English sugar port after 1799.[72] The profits of the slave trade powered Bristol's eighteenth-century 'urban renaissance', and the West India elite invested in land, commerce and industry.[73] David Richardson estimated that 40 per cent of Bristol's income in 1790 was directly connected to slavery-related activities, a figure that does not take into account the multiplier effects of

[69] N. Draper, 'The City of London and slavery: evidence from the first dock companies, 1795–1800', *Economic History Review*, lxi (2008), 432–66.

[70] K. Donington, *The Bonds of Family: Slavery, Commerce and Culture in the British Atlantic World* (Manchester, 2019), pp. 253–82; Hancock, *Citizens of the World*.

[71] J. Price, 'The rise of Glasgow in the Chesapeake tobacco trade, 1707–1775', *The William and Mary Quarterly*, 3rd Series Scotland and America, xi (1954), 179–99, at p. 190.

[72] Morgan, *Slavery, Atlantic Trade*, p. 90; 'Bristol West India merchants in the eighteenth century', *Transactions of the Royal Historical Society*, 6th series, iii (1993), 185–208, at p. 187.

[73] R. Pares, *A West India Fortune* (Bristol, 1950); Morgan, 'Bristol West India merchants', pp. 186, 200–1; M. Dresser, *Slavery Obscured: The Social History of the Slave Trade in an English Provincial Port* (London and New York, 2001).

colonial investment.[74] However, while the concentration on valuable sugar imports generated vast fortunes, such narrow specialization – allied with entrepreneurial failure – hindered regional economic development. Bristol evolved as a consumption centre and, unlike Liverpool and Glasgow, did not develop into an *entrepôt* for foreign trade. Thus, although Welsh industry received a boost, there were few multiplier effects and Bristol was a minor export centre by the mid-nineteenth century.[75]

In 1660, Liverpool was a minor English port with no transatlantic commerce of note. Late seventeenth-century commercial expansion was powered by American and West India merchants and by the mid-eighteenth century, the port was pre-eminent among British outports. The thriving economy promoted, and was in turn stimulated by, population growth and associated urbanization. In 1702, the population of Liverpool was 6,000, rising to 30,000 in 1750 and just over 80,000 in 1801. It reached a remarkable 375,955 in 1851. With the development of commerce, the transport system improved, which helped the growth of new industries and facilitated trade connections with the manufacturing hinterlands of Manchester and Lancashire.[76] The port became the centre of the British slave trade in the mid-eighteenth century, the profits from which could be substantial.[77] But, as Sheryllynne Haggerty noted, the trafficking in enslaved people was only one part of Liverpool's Atlantic economy, and perhaps relatively insignificant compared to the American trades. Voyages were high risk and not always profitable.[78] Beyond the major fortunes made by some of its inhabitants, Jane Longmore doubts whether Liverpool 'derived entirely positive gains from its participation in the slave trade'. While the north-west's industrial production received a boost, Liverpool's own manufacturing base was closely associated with the slave trade, rather than the

---

[74] D. Richardson, 'Slavery and Bristol's "golden age"' *Slavery & Abolition*, xxvi (2005), 35–54, at p. 49.

[75] C. Evans, *Slave Wales: The Welsh and Atlantic Slavery, 1660–1850* (Cardiff, 2010); K. Morgan, *Bristol and the Atlantic Trade in the Eighteenth Century* (Cambridge, 2002 ed.), pp. 219–25.

[76] P. G. E. Clemens, 'The rise of Liverpool, 1665–1750', *The Economic History Review*, xxix (1976), 211–25; Morgan, *Slavery, Atlantic Trade*, p. 88; R. Lawton, 'The population of Liverpool in the mid-nineteenth century', *Transactions of the Historical Society of Lancaster and Cheshire* (1955), 89–120, at p. 93.

[77] D. Pope, 'The wealth and aspirations of Liverpool's slave merchants', in *Liverpool and Transatlantic Slavery*, ed. D. Richardson, S. Schwarz and A. Tibbles (Liverpool, 2007), pp. 164–227.

[78] S. Haggerty, 'Liverpool, the slave trade and the British-Atlantic empire, 1750–1775', in *The Empire in One City? Liverpool's Inconvenient Imperial Past*, ed. S. Haggerty, A. Webster and N. J. White (Manchester, 2008), pp. 17–34.

cotton industry, and when abolition passed in 1807, it destabilized the sector and left a limited workforce unable to shift into other industries.[79]

The direct trafficking in enslaved Africans was arguably of lesser importance to Liverpool's development than either the West India or Virginia trades.[80] Liverpool was the premier British tobacco outport in 1740, but lost this position to Clyde ports for almost a half century afterwards. Liverpool once again became the top outport for tobacco after 1792.[81] As such, the American War of Independence transformed Liverpool's 'empire at home' in an entirely different way compared to Glasgow.[82] The importance of the American market afterwards increased, and Liverpool's West India boom ended in the 1790s. According to S. G. Checkland, the city's 'West India men were really in decline, enjoying the last great flush of prosperity' while the American traders profited from expansion.[83] Despite the relative decline in the city's West India economy, paradoxically, some merchants, such as John Gladstone, became very wealthy by complementing American trading with expansion into Jamaica and British Guiana.[84] While the Liverpool-West India interest were a declining economic force from the 1790s, West India firm Sandbach, Tinne & Company was one of the principal mercantile claimants of slave compensation in Great Britain.[85] By 1834, American traders powered Liverpool's nineteenth-century rise to 'second city' of the British Empire and industrial England's 'main gateway' to the Atlantic world.[86] Overall, in the eighteenth and nineteenth centuries, the systemic effects of

---

[79] J. Longmore, 'Rural retreats: Liverpool slave traders and their country houses', in *Slavery and the British Country House*, ed. M. Dresser and A. Hann (Swindon, 2013), p. 39; '"Cemented by the blood of a negro"? The impact of the slave trade on eighteenth-century Liverpool', in *Liverpool and Transatlantic Slavery*, ed. Richardson, Schwarz and Tibbles, pp. 227–51.

[80] F. E. Hyde, *Liverpool and the Mersey: The Development of a Port, 1700–1970* (Newton Abbot, 1971), pp. 25–42.

[81] J. Price and P. G. E. Clemens, 'A revolution of scale in overseas trade: British firms in the Chesapeake trade, 1675–1775', *Journal of Economic History*, xlvii (1987), 1–43, at pp. 39–40.

[82] S. Hill, 'The Liverpool economy during the war of American Independence, 1775–83', *The Journal of Imperial and Commonwealth History*, xliv (2016), 835–56.

[83] S. G. Checkland, 'American versus West Indian traders in Liverpool, 1793–1815', *The Journal of Economic History*, xviii (1958), 141–60, at p. 142.

[84] S. G. Checkland, 'John Gladstone as trader and planter', *The Economic History Review*, new series, vii (1954), 216–29; *The Gladstones: A Family Biography 1764–1851* (Cambridge, 1971), p. 45.

[85] Draper, 'Helping to make Britain great', 86–7.

[86] J. Kinsey, 'The economic impact of the port of Liverpool on the economy of Merseyside – using a multiplier approach', *Geoforum*, xii (1981), 331–47, at p. 331.

Atlantic trade and merchant capital promoted the development of English ports and their hinterlands, which in turn influenced local commerce, and to a lesser extent industrialization, although the impact varied regionally.

The current English debate about the influence of slavery and the Atlantic trades sets several questions for the incipient historiography of Scottish involvement. Would Scotland have developed at the same rate or within the same timescale in the absence of colonial connections? Scotland had a contrasting trajectory from England, and colonial commerce had a more significant role in its economic transformation. The Scottish nation occupied an anomalous place in Wallerstein's world-systems analysis. It was peripheral to England yet it underwent 'development by invitation' after joining with the imperial core in 1707.[87] Scots were present in colonial America and the English Caribbean from the early 1600s, but the nation did not possess a formal empire of any significance that would have encouraged large-scale transformation.[88] Sharing a monarch with England from 1603, Scots were nominally present in the embryonic English Atlantic world with some trading privileges, yet Scotland was effectively classed as a 'foreign nation' under the terms of the Navigation Acts from 1660.[89] With growing constitutional conflict, exacerbated by the failed Scottish imperial scheme at Darien on the Isthmus of Panama, free trade with the English empire became the lure to coerce Scottish politicians into accepting proposals that led to the Union of Parliaments.[90] For Allan Macinnes, the Incorporating Union of 1707 provided Scots with access to the largest common market in history up to then and opened an array of opportunities for Scots in war, manufactures (both products and markets) and trade in the established English empire.[91] But it was not unrestricted access. Andrew Mackillop has underlined the composite nature of a British empire subsequently governed

---

[87] I. Wallerstein, 'One man's meat: the Scottish great leap forward', *Review*, iii (1980), 631–40.

[88] A. I. Macinnes, 'Scottish circumvention of the English Navigation Acts in the American colonies 1660–1707', in *Making, Using and Resisting the Law in European History*, ed. G. Lottes et al (Pisa, 2008), pp. 109–30; N. C. Landsman, *Scotland and Its First American Colony, 1683–1765* (Princeton, 1985).

[89] D. Dobson, *Scottish Emigration to Colonial America, 1607–1785* (Athens, Ga., 1994); N. Zacek, *Settler Society in the English Leeward Islands, 1670–1776* (New York, 2010), pp. 66–121.

[90] A. I. Macinnes, 'The treaty of union: made in England', in *Scotland and the Union 1707–2007*, ed. T. M. Devine (Edinburgh, 2008), pp. 61–3; D. Watt, *The Price of Scotland: Darien, Union and the Wealth of Nations* (Edinburgh, 2007).

[91] A. I. Macinnes, *Union and Empire: The Making of the United Kingdom in 1707* (Cambridge, 2007), p. 325.

by a miscellany of regulatory monopolistic frameworks.[92] While the British-Atlantic world was open territory to Scots and their trading companies, London-based monopolies such as the East India and Hudson Bay companies administered some zones thereof. Scottish employees infiltrated Asia and Canada via company involvement, although traders, Glaswegians in particular, freely operated in the Caribbean and North America. This invitation did initiate economic development, but, importantly, free trade was offered only in imperial zones already established as slavery societies.

Consistent with the preference of twentieth-century British historians to explain the Industrial Revolution via internal forces, histories of Scottish industrialization in that period also tended to be inward-looking in nature.[93] The trivialization of both mercantile capital and overseas trade in relation to Scottish economic development is exemplified by R. H. Campbell's seminal *Scotland Since 1707: The Rise of an Industrial Society* (1965), a standard university text for many decades. Campbell endorsed a vision of Scottish 'enclave economy' which marginalized the importance of tobacco commerce which supposedly only influenced a small part of the wider economy. He noted 'significant [mercantile] involvement' in the cotton industry, Glasgow banking and the linen industry, although these processes were not deemed of any importance. Instead, the effects of the Atlantic system on Scottish development were of a more 'general and indirect kind', such as repatriated colonial fortunes – although these were reckoned to have little impact on the national economy.[94] Surveys by Henry Hamilton, Christopher Whatley and others acknowledged the importance of transatlantic commerce (albeit ignoring the importance of slavery) yet prioritized internal factors to explain economic transformation.[95]

Historians of Scotland have only recently incorporated transatlantic slavery into surveys of economic development. T. M. Devine's corpus of

---

[92] A. Mackillop, 'A union for empire? Scotland, the English East India Company and the British Union', *Scottish Historical Review*, lxxxvii (Supplement) (2008), 116–34.

[93] Inikori, 'Capitalism and slavery', pp. 51–80. For a recent survey of Scottish historiography and slavery, see S. Mullen, 'Centring transatlantic slavery in Scottish historiography', *History Compass*, xx (2022), 1–14.

[94] R. H. Campbell, *Scotland Since 1707: The Rise of an Industrial Society*, 2nd ed. (Edinburgh, 1992 ed.), pp. 39–43.

[95] H. Hamilton, *An Economic History of Scotland in the Eighteenth Century* (Oxford, 1963); H. Hamilton, *The Industrial Revolution in Scotland* (London, 1966); A. Slaven, *The Development of the West of Scotland 1750–1960* (London and Boston, 1975), pp. 20–6; B. Lenman, *Economic History of Modern Scotland* (London, 1977), pp. 116–18; C. A. Whatley, *The Industrial Revolution in Scotland* (Cambridge, 1997), p. 41; *Scottish Society, 1707–1830: Beyond Jacobitism, Towards Industrialisation* (Manchester, 2000), pp. 220–1.

work bridged the gap between endogenous and exogenous explanations, prioritizing the latter over the former. From the 1970s onwards, Devine emphasized the 'vital contribution' of mercantile investments and the tobacco trade to Scottish economic development, while remaining sceptical that colonial trade in general represented the '*deus ex machina* in the process of [Scottish industrial] change'.[96] However, this position was qualified. Although taking notice of Eric Williams in his early publications, Devine was sceptical about the relevance of the latter's arguments for most of his career.[97] As recently as 2004, he claimed there was 'little evidence' for the claims in *Capitalism & Slavery* and its 'patent exaggerations' had supposedly marginalized the issue of empire in the historiography of economic growth.[98]

There has been an explosion of interest and a notable historiographical shift since then. In 2005, Douglas Hamilton's study of Scots in the Caribbean positively cited Williams in a Scottish context.[99] Five years later, in his last-ever lecture after a forty-year career, Devine apologized ('Mea culpa, mea maxima culpa') for the omission of chattel slavery in his landmark study *The Tobacco Lords*, first published in 1975. In 2011, Devine posed the question 'Did slavery make Scotia great?' which underlined the centrality of chattel slavery to Scotland's economic growth. Invoking Eric Williams' imports/exports/personal profits model, Devine argued three aspects of the transatlantic relationship are of interest in a Scottish context. First, economic growth was rapid from *c.*1760 while dependent on imports of sugar, cotton and tobacco grown by enslaved people. Second, exports of manufactured goods – such as textiles – were shipped from Scottish ports to the Americas, clothing the enslaved. Third, colonial merchants, planters and returned sojourners sunk profits into productive enterprise. In Devine's view, therefore, Scotland provides 'fertile ground' for historians in the Williams school.[100] In 2015, Devine seemingly arrived at a conclusion:

[96] T. M. Devine, 'Sources of capital for the Glasgow tobacco trade, *c.*1740–1780', *Business History*, xvi (1974), 113–29; 'The colonial trades and industrial investment in Scotland, *c.*1700–1815', *The Economic History Review*, xxix (1976), 1–13; 'Colonial commerce and the Scottish economy, *c.*1730–1815', in *Comparative Aspects of Scottish and Irish Economic and Social History, 1600–1900*, ed. L. M. Cullen and T. C. Smout (Edinburgh, 1977), p. 180.

[97] T. M. Devine, *The Tobacco Lords: A Study of the Tobacco Merchants of Glasgow and Their Trading Activities c. 1740–90* (Edinburgh, 1975), pp. 49, 59.

[98] T. M. Devine, *Scotland's Empire 1680–1815* (London, 2004), p. 327.

[99] D. Hamilton, *Scotland, the Caribbean and the Atlantic World, 1750–1820* (Manchester, 2005), p. 196.

[100] T. M. Devine, 'Did slavery make Scotia great?', *Britain and the World*, iv (2011), 40–64; R. Blackburn, *The Making of New World Slavery: From the Baroque to the Modern, 1492–1800* (London, 2010 ed.) pp. 509–81.

'slavery…[was] integral to the weft and woof of the national past from the seventeenth to the early nineteenth centuries'.[101]

The differences between English and Scottish demographic change and economic development mean that the vision of Atlantic commerce powering industrial change, and by extension the Williams thesis, is more persuasive in a Scottish context. First, England's Commercial Revolution evolved from the restoration of the Stuart monarchy in 1660 and thus preceded the Industrial Revolution (c.1760–1830).[102] Yet, rapid economic growth in Scotland only followed after the Incorporating Union of 1707. In contrast to England, Scotland's Commercial Revolution (1730 onwards), Agricultural Revolution (1760s until 1800) and Industrial Revolution (c.1770s–1830) occurred almost concurrently.[103] Second, the Scottish population was relatively small compared to that of England. In 1755, the Scottish population was 1.3m, rising to 2.6m by 1841.[104] Overall, Scots comprised around 14 per cent of the British population between 1801 and 1831.[105] For comparison, the population of the British West Indies in 1829 was almost 800,000 (of which 90 per cent were enslaved people).[106] The relatively small rise in Scottish population between 1755 and 1801 (0.6 per cent per annum) and the low-wage economy, according to Christopher Whatley, meant that the stimulus of overseas trade had more significance than the domestic market.[107] Third, beginning in 1778, Scotland experienced industrial growth at a quicker pace than England, despite starting from a more modest base. Thus, from the 1770s onwards, Scotland witnessed an industrial *revolution* – compared to English evolution – which was inextricably connected with the

---

[101] T. M. Devine, 'Did slavery make Scotia great? A question revisited', in *Recovering Scotland's Slavery Past: The Caribbean Connection*, ed. T. M. Devine (Edinburgh, 2015), pp. 225–45, 246–7.

[102] R. Davis, *A Commercial Revolution: English Overseas Trade in the Seventeenth and Eighteenth Centuries* (London, 1967); *The Industrial Revolution*, p. 63.

[103] P. R. Rössner, *Scottish Trade in the Wake of Union (1700–1760): The Rise of a Warehouse Economy* (Stuttgart, 2008), p. 18; T. M. Devine, 'The transformation of agriculture: cultivation and clearance', in *The Transformation of Scotland: The Economy Since 1700*, ed. T. M. Devine et al. (Edinburgh, 2005), p. 79; Whatley, *The Industrial Revolution*, pp. 6–7, 24.

[104] M. Anderson, 'Guesses, estimates and adjustments: Webster's 1755 "census" of Scotland revisited again', *Journal of Scottish Historical Studies*, xxxi (2011), 26–45, at p. 42; *House of Commons Accounts and Papers*, Vol. II, Session, 19 Aug.–7 Oct. 1841, p. 52.

[105] HCPP (1831) *Comparative Account of Population of Great Britain*, 1801, 1811, 1821 and 1831, p. 409.

[106] J. Cleland, *Enumeration of the Inhabitants of the City of Glasgow*, 2nd ed. (Glasgow, 1832), pp. 220–1.

[107] Whatley, *The Industrial Revolution*, pp. 43–4.

enslaved people of North America and the British West Indies.[108] It seems transatlantic merchants played a proportionately more significant role in the Scottish Industrial Revolution compared to England. And nowhere more so than Glasgow.

Glasgow's Atlantic system was established in the seventeenth century. Granted royal burgh status by the king in 1611, this legal framework confirmed and extended pre-existing trade privileges. Foreign trade was long seen as an economic panacea in the Atlantic port, and the city's merchant fraternity created a vibrant economy.[109] As the river Clyde that passed through what is now the city centre was too underdeveloped to facilitate large-scale maritime commerce, Port Glasgow and neighbouring Greenock on the west coast of Scotland became the favoured satellite outports of Glasgow's merchants.[110] A maritime infrastructure for large ships was not established in Glasgow's boundaries until after 1800.[111] Despite the restricted access under the terms of English Navigation Acts from 1660 onwards, prerogative powers granted to colonial traders encouraged the founding of the city's earliest sugar refineries, which generated the first industrial fortunes.[112] However, at this point, overall trade was small-scale as tax duties and privileges conferred on the select few allowed them to monopolize a lucrative industry.[113]

After the Union of 1707, the markets opened. Early sugar pioneers the McDowalls and Millikens returned to the west of Scotland with slavery-derived wealth from the Caribbean.[114] But the rise in volume of the Virginia tobacco trade was the remarkable story. By the 1740s, Glasgow and Clyde ports (Port Glasgow and Greenock) were the *primus inter pares* in the European tobacco trade. By 1758, more tobacco was imported to Clyde ports than all other British ports together.[115] At the peak of Glasgow's tobacco monopoly, 1770–4, Scottish exports annually to the thirteen American

---

[108] Whatley, *The Industrial Revolution*, pp. 7, 24, 35–6.

[109] T. C. Smout, 'The Glasgow merchant community in the seventeenth century', *The Scottish Historical Review*, xlvii (1968), 53–71.

[110] T. C. Smout, 'The development and enterprise of Glasgow 1556–1707', *Scottish Journal of Political Economy*, vi (1959), 194–212.

[111] G. Jackson and C. Munn, 'Trade, commerce and finance', in *Glasgow, Vol. II: 1830–1912*, ed. W. H. Fraser and I. Maver (Manchester, 1996), pp. 52–5.

[112] T. C. Smout, 'The early Scottish sugar houses, 1660–1720', *The Economic History Review*, xiv (1961), 240–53.

[113] J. Hutcheson, *Notes on the Sugar Industry* (Glasgow, 1901), pp. 32–80.

[114] S. Nisbet, 'That nefarious commerce – St Kitts slavery and the west of Scotland', *Proceedings of Caribbean Studies Conference* (2008), 1–19.

[115] Price, 'The rise of Glasgow', 179–99.

colonies were valued at £298,922 (official values), almost 10 per cent of the overall British total.[116] T. M. Devine's *The Tobacco Lords* examined the Glasgow merchants trading with planters in the Chesapeake region of America between 1740 and 1790. These elite merchants based their commercial success on landed enterprise at home as well as colonial trading, the profits of which underpinned investment in Scottish agriculture and industry. Devine concludes that while direct mercantile investments were limited in number, they were of major significance in developing consumer industries and adding to Scottish exports.[117] Indeed, the tobacco lords' preferred 'store system' – which involved the direct purchase of plantation produce in the colonies – was a 'sophisticated and innovative forward purchasing system' which allowed Glasgow merchants to set purchasing prices of tobacco in Virginia as well as the price of manufactured goods made in Scotland.[118] The exchange of goods promoted an urban economy in Glasgow that developed solely to serve the needs of the planter class.[119] While the direct investments of tobacco merchants were limited, the wider trades were important to regional industrial and commercial development, including banking.

Following the loss of trade with the thirteen colonies at the onset of the American War of Independence, Glasgow's colonial merchants consolidated their existing Caribbean interests. While the American trades did not completely collapse, the West Indies was the main focus of Scotland's Atlantic commerce after 1790.[120] Crucially, West India merchants increasingly imported cotton during the American War and as a result, prices almost halved between 1776 and 1780. Low costs helped increase production at a moment when new technology was available, which stimulated what became large-scale industry.[121] Nevertheless, the role of the West India merchants in Scottish economic transformation has been represented in traditional historiography as a simple addendum to the more lucrative tobacco trade of the previous half-century.[122]

[116] J. Price, 'New time series for Scotland's and Britain's trade with the thirteen colonies and states, 1740 to 1791', *The William and Mary Quarterly*, xxxii (1975), 307–25, at p. 314.

[117] Devine, *Tobacco Lords*, pp. 171–3.

[118] T. M. Devine and P. R. Rössner, 'Scots in the Atlantic economy, 1600–1800', in *Scotland and the British Empire*, ed. J. M. MacKenzie and T. M. Devine (Oxford, 2011), pp. 39–40.

[119] Devine, 'Colonial commerce and the Scottish economy', p. 178.

[120] T. M. Devine, 'The American War of Independence and Scottish economic history', in *Scotland, Europe and the American Revolution*, ed. O. Dudley Edwards and G. Shepperson (Edinburgh, 1976), pp. 61–6.

[121] T. M. Devine, 'The golden age of tobacco', in *Glasgow, Vol. 1: Beginnings to 1830*, ed. T. M. Devine and G. Jackson (Manchester, 1995), p. 171.

[122] Hamilton, *The Industrial Revolution in Scotland*, p. 121.

T. M. Devine's pioneering study of the Glasgow-West India elites in 1978 examined the social background, investments and political influence of over seventy-five Caribbean merchants. While tracing an influx of capital to landed estates and local industry, this study argued that the contribution of West India merchants was unlikely to be a 'decisive influence' on the regional cotton industry.[123] After a thirty-year hiatus in interest, Anthony Cooke examined a smaller group of sixty-four West India merchants of Glasgow with a longer chronological lens, deploying a comprehensive analytical model to trace mercantile investments. Two claims are of relevance to this study here. First, the Glasgow-West India merchant capital was invested in Scottish industry from 1803 (especially cotton) and deemed of significance into the Victorian period (especially railways). Second, the average holdings in Glasgow-West India merchant firms supposedly increased after 1834, suggesting the continued importance of mercantile activities in the post-Emancipation West Indies. According to Cooke, the study developed the 'Williams thesis about the importance of slavery and slave grown products to industrial development in Britain'.[124] Perhaps so, but by including the substantial estates of merchants with principal interests in Mauritius, and others with no connection to Glasgow, Cooke's estimations of the city's West India merchant capital were inflated by including East India fortunes and returned sojourning wealth that improved other areas of Scotland.[125]

[123] T. M. Devine, 'An eighteenth-century business elite: Glasgow West India merchants, 1740–1815', *Scottish Historical Review*, lvii (1978), 40–67 at p. 46.

[124] A. Cooke, 'An elite revisited: Glasgow West India merchants, 1783–1877', *Journal of Scottish Historical Studies*, xxxii (2012), 127–65; 'Glasgow West India merchants, 1783–1877,' Kudos Website <https://www.growkudos.com/publications/10.3366%25252Fjshs.2012.0048/reader [accessed 8 Feb. 2017].

[125] As a study of the Glasgow-West India elite, there were two issues with the Cooke sample. First, individuals with no identifiable connections to Glasgow were included. John Shand, for example, was resident in Jamaica for many years and acquired a sojourning fortune. On his return to Scotland he purchased the estate of Arnhall and the Burn in Kincardineshire in north-east Scotland. He was resident there when he died in 1825. See NRS, SC5/41/1, 'Inventory, last will and testament, codicils, tack of John Shand of Arnhall Esq.', 12 Jan. 1826, pp. 350–452. Second, the Cooke sample cited East India fortunes as originating in the West Indies: the substantial estates of James Richardson who died in 1860 (£213,654) and his son, Thomas Richardson, who died in 1872 (£274,612). Both were partners in a Glasgow merchant house that traded with Mauritius. There is no evidence offered that they ever traded between Glasgow and the West Indies. And in the *c.*1700 shipping adverts of voyages from the Clyde to the Caribbean examined for this study between 1806 and 1834, there is no record of any of their firms shipping from Port Glasgow or Greenock (although the firm only moved to Glasgow from Edinburgh in 1830). Contemporary accounts state that 'the relatively limited supply of West India sugar led to the firm establishing a house in Mauritius' in 1839, which became 'one of the principal houses' on the island. In 1842, the firm sold Mauritius sugars

Instead, this study here a) examines the scale and significance of Glasgow-West India merchant capital via the private fortunes of the city's resident merchants and planters, and b) assesses returned sojourning wealth of Scots in the West Indies in a transatlantic frame, tracing the origins of fortunes and repatriation to Great Britain. This provides a consistent definition of West India fortunes, both mercantile and colonial, with analysis undertaken in a comparative, regional framework.

While Virginia and West India merchants were of great significance to the transformation of the west of Scotland, until fairly recently the influence of absentee slave owners across the country had almost gone unnoticed. Nicholas Draper's *The Price of Emancipation* has radically transformed understanding of Scottish slave ownership on the emancipation of slavery in the British West Indies in 1834.[126] The overall dataset was gathered mainly from a 'Parliamentary Return' which lists all the awards that were finalized by 1838, when 93 per cent of the total compensation of £20 million had been distributed.[127] As such, it represents a census of British slave ownership taken on 1 August 1834. It has been estimated residents of Scotland received c.£2 million of the overall compensation total in what was probably the peak time of Scottish slave ownership. Indeed, Draper demonstrated that Scots comprised just 10 per cent of the total British population, yet those resident in Scotland represented around 15 per cent of all British absentee slave owners in the compensation list (much higher than numbers in Ireland). The high numbers of Scots travelling to the Caribbean, and their propensity to return to the homeland, provides context for this disproportionate over-representation.[128]

---

in Leith, and on his death in 1872 Thomas Richardson still held shares in 'Richardson & Company, Merchants, Mauritius' (£19,262). These large-scale holdings in East India firms and respective fortunes on death have important implications that are discussed in Chapter 8. See J. Craik, J. Eadie and J. Galbraith, 'Thomas Richardson', in *Memoirs and Portraits of One Hundred Glasgow Men who have Died During the Last Thirty Years, and in their Lives did Much to Make the City what it Now is*, vol. ii (Glasgow, 1886), pp. 273–6; Cooke, 'An elite revisited', pp. 142–3, 163; NRS, SC58/42/26, 'Settlement and inventory of James Richardson', 4 April 1860, pp. 393–420; NRS, SC58/42/39, 'Will and inventory of Thomas Richardson', 30 July 1872, p. 969.

[126] N. Draper, *The Price of Emancipation: Slave ownership, Compensation and British Society at the End of Slavery* (Cambridge, 2010).

[127] HCPP 1837–8 (215) 48 *Slavery Abolition Act: An Account of all Sums of Money Awarded by the Commissioners of Slavery Compensation*.

[128] N. Draper, '"Dependent on precarious subsistences": Ireland's slave-owners at the time of emancipation', *Britain and the World*, vi (2011), 220–42; 'Scotland and colonial slave-ownership: the evidence of the slave compensation records', in *Recovering Scotland's Slavery Past: The Caribbean Connection*, ed. T. M. Devine (Edinburgh, 2015), pp. 166–87.

Slave ownership was not always material to the work of West India merchants, although they occupied an integral position within the wider slave economy and acted as conduits of slavery wealth into Scottish society. This study – the first book-length examination of Glasgow's 'sugar aristocracy' – starts with two broad questions in transatlantic context: what did Scots, especially Glasgow merchants, 'give' to the West Indies? And what did the British West Indies (and by extension, slavery and the Atlantic trades) contribute to Scotland, and especially Glasgow, in return? This study, therefore, attempts a new approach: an examination of metropole and colony in a single analytical frame, showing the making of each by the other.

Chapter 1 traces the emergence of Glasgow's West India mercantile elites, revealing this group were much larger than previously recorded. This monograph is centred around a sample of 150 West India merchants in Glasgow who subscribed (either personally or via firms) with the Glasgow West India Association – one of the major pro-slavery lobbying groups in Great Britain – between 1807 and 1834. This chapter traces the social and geographical origins of this group, assessing how the wealth from Caribbean slavery reshaped Glasgow society including through marriage. The 'sugar aristocracy' were an elite group atop the West India community, with an old Jamaica clique at its core, although colonial *nouveaux riches* from new colonies – especially Demerara, Grenada and Trinidad – ensured they dominated local politics. Chapter 2 deals with the financial and commercial networks, including a survey of West India firms: the legal entities that made these trades possible. Much remains to be understood about the Glasgow-West India elite's sources of capital, credit and broader connections with Scottish banking. This study establishes the importance of local sources of start-up finance – including fathers already involved with the colonial trades, amid a nexus of inter-firm mercantile loans – as well as credit sourced from individuals across society and banking institutions which was secured upon landed estates and urban property. Chapter 3 provides a detailed case study of two West India firms, Leitch & Smith and Jas. & Arch. Smith & Co., that operated in Jamaica and Grenada from 1776 until the late nineteenth century. These firms integrated the Atlantic economy into interests in cotton, banking, insurance and landed estates. Chapter 4 examines patterns of recruitment, migration and labour that combined to ship out many thousands of young Scots across the Atlantic. This establishes Glasgow's role as a nineteenth-century Atlantic hub, in which there was a focus on West India commerce which served to reshape the educational systems and labour market. New estimates of Scots departing for the West Indies are provided, establishing a framework to examine colonies with a large Scottish presence. Chapters 5, 6 and 7 present case studies of Jamaica, Grenada and

Trinidad. These three islands were colonized in three consecutive centuries, thus allowing comparisons of Scottish practices of settler-colonialism, presence across each island, levels of wealth accumulation and repatriation. Estimations of fortunes have been established by the systematic analysis of 138 confirmation inventories of Scots lodged in Scottish courts. Together, these chapters revise the pessimistic arguments about the return (or lack thereof) of sojourning fortunes put forward by Alan Karras, placing such wealth repatriation in a comparative framework which allows assessment of impact on Scottish regions. Chapter 8 unravels the life, wealth and death of Glasgow's 'sugar aristocracy' up to the end of Caribbean slavery and beyond. This analysis is based upon over 100 mercantile inventories which reveal personal fortunes as well as patterns of wider investments. As was typical of their counterparts across Great Britain, these merchants purchased landed estates and invested in manufactories, especially cotton mills, but also sunk capital into banks and often took on the role of banking houses, loaning capital within the mercantile community and beyond. While T. M. Devine and Anthony Cooke have viewed the West India elite in terms of industrial investments, this study establishes their importance as a commercial interest. Collectively, this monograph underlines the importance of West India merchants – the trades they made possible and capital they generated – to the development of industry and especially commerce during a period of rapid transformation. Set in the era of supposed decline, this is the story of those who embedded West India commerce into regional societies and economies and, in doing so, made chattel slavery a quotidian feature of life in modern Scotland.

1. Emergence

Soon after arriving in Glasgow in February 1835, the newly appointed sheriff of Lanarkshire Sir Archibald Alison – himself a pro-slavery advocate – surveyed his fiefdom. Given he rented his residence Possil House from the eldest son of John Campbell senior, founder of the great West India house of the same name, Alison had an inside view of Glasgow's mercantile elite.[1] Connecting occupational status with rank and class, he placed the high-earning West India families at the pinnacle of high society:

> The West India merchants then took the lead and considered themselves as the best society in the city: five or six families of that class lived almost exclusively with each other, and rigidly confined themselves to visiting within their own circle. They had in consequence acquired the *sobriquet* of the 'Sugar Aristocracy'.

Cotton masters were next down the social hierarchy, followed by calico printers and iron and coal magnates. Astonished at the 'absence of any old mercantile families in the city', for Alison, the rapid accumulation of fortunes over a thirty-year period had created an unrefined yet socially mobile *parvenu* class. For him, equality in birth, education, accomplishments and especially manners compelled the landed aristocracy and gentry to associate together. But the acquisition of colonial wealth was so rapid that the 'largest fortunes were in vulgar hands', often those who were recently labouring 'at the shuttle, the forge, or in the printfield'. In short, wealth transformed the social standing of some in one or two generations. Thus, according to Alison, while this newly acquired wealth afforded the 'sugar aristocracy' favours at the Royal Exchange and local banking houses, it did not translate into respectability of descent.[2] But who were the 'sugar aristocracy'? How did they come to be? How did they fit within the overall mercantile community in Glasgow? This chapter considers the appropriateness of the 'sugar aristocracy' sobriquet and,

---

[1] C. Hall, '"The most unbending Conservative in Britain": Archibald Alison and pro-slavery discourse', in *Recovering Scotland's Slavery Past: The Caribbean Connection*, ed. T. M. Devine (Edinburgh, 2015), pp. 206–24; J. G. Smith and J. O. Mitchell, *The Old Country Houses of the Old Glasgow Gentry* (Glasgow, 1878), 'Possil'.

[2] Sir Archibald Alison, *Some Account of My Life and Writings: An Autobiography*, vol. i (Edinburgh, 1883), pp. 344–7.

in doing so, broadens understandings about Glasgow's West India merchants and planters during a period of dramatic economic and social change.

Glasgow's sugar era

The inspector general's returns of imports and exports for Scotland provided the estimated values of goods traded with other countries between 1755 and 1827.[3] Table 1.1 provides import and export data for Scottish trade at equal points across the seventy-two-year period, revealing a dramatic upsurge in commerce with Scotland and the Americas in an era of rapid industrialization.[4] Between 1755 and 1827, Scottish imports grew eightfold from £465,411 to £3,948,233 (official values). Incoming trade from the West Indies was the most dynamic force, accounting for 10 per cent of imports in 1755 and rising to over 40 per cent in 1808, an increase by a factor of four in terms of relative share of overall Scottish imports. The export trade, especially of textiles, was the real engine of Scotland's economic growth. Between 1755 and 1827, Scottish exports rose eleven-fold from £535,576 to £6,059,502 (official values). In 1772, the West Indies took less than 4 per cent of Scotland's export trade, rising to almost half by 1808, with exports to the foreign West Indies increasingly important by 1827. Across Scotland's Industrial Revolution, the proportion of exports to Europe and America declined, while the West India trades were the most dynamic force. In some years, the Scottish share of the British export trade to the West Indies was substantial. In 1814, when European trades were restricted due to war, the West Indies received £3,453,979 of Scottish exports (official values). That same year, national exports to the British West Indies were valued at £6,315,000, meaning that over half of British West India commerce by value went through Scottish ports just after the mid-point of the Scottish Industrial Revolution.[5]

Clyde ports (Port Glasgow and Greenock) were the premier outlets in Scotland throughout this period. The American War of Independence (1775–83) dramatically transformed the national relationship with the Atlantic world. The traditional view is that the war initiated a mercantile shift from commodity trade (in tobacco) to manufacturing and export (especially cotton-based textiles) and was a watershed in Scottish economic history.[6]

---

[3]   TNA, CUST 14, 'Ledgers of Imports and Exports, Scotland (1755–1827)'.

[4]   TNA, CUST 14/1a, 14/1b, 14/10, 14/21, 14/39.

[5]   TNA, CUST 14/26, f.98; B. R. Mitchell, with the collaboration of P. Deane, *Abstract of British Historical Statistics* (London, 1962), p. 311. For a useful discussion of the differences with official and current values, see J. J. McCusker, 'The current value of English exports, 1697 to 1800', *The William and Mary Quarterly*, xxviii (1971), 607–28.

[6]   M. L. Robertson, 'Scottish commerce and the American War of Independence', *The Economic History Review*, New Series, ix (1956), 123–31.

Table 1.1 Scottish imports and exports, 1755–1827 (official values).

Scotland					
Imports	**1755**	**1772**	**1791**	**1808**	**1827**
Europe	43.8%	30.3%	50.6%	17.0%	48.5%
Ireland	5.7%	11.6%	17.4%	32.7%	n/a
America	50.5%	47.5%	10.8%	9.6%	18.5%
British N. America	n/a	n/a	n/a	n/a	4.2%
West Indies	n/a	10.6%	20.8%	40.6%	19.6%
Foreign W.I., S. America	n/a	n/a	n/a	n/a	0.5%
Africa	0.0%	0.0%	0.0%	0.0%	0.1%
Asia	0.0%	0.0%	0.0%	0.0%	4.2%
Other	0.0%	0.0%	0.0%	0.0%	4.8%
Total	**100** (£465,411)	**100** (£1,210,263)	**100** (£1,941,630)	**100** (£2,152,583)	**100** (£3,948,233)
Exports	**1755**	**1772**	**1791**	**1808**	**1827**
Europe	62.3%	63.5%	30.1%	15.1%	23.6%
Ireland	12.1%	13.1%	20.7%	20.1%	n/a
America	25.5%	19.4%	20.5%	16.1%	13.5%
British N. America	n/a	n/a	n/a	n/a	7.1%
West Indies	0.0%	3.9%	28.7%	48.7%	20.9%
Foreign W.I., S. America	n/a	n/a	n/a	n/a	12.9%
Africa	0.0%	0.0%	0.0%	0.0%	0.1%
Asia	0.0%	0.0%	0.0%	0.0%	21.7%
Other	0.0%	0.0%	0.0%	0.0%	0.0%
Total	**100** (£535,576)	**100** (£1,560,755)	**100** (£1,296,535)	**100** (£2,817,579)	**100** (£6,059,502)

Source: UK National Archives, CUST 14.

Wartime conditions, at least temporarily, limited Scots' access to markets and Glasgow's tobacco monopoly ended as the Americans afterwards directly shipped tobacco to Europe. Trade in tobacco never again reached more than a quarter of pre-war levels. However, there was no economic collapse, and the West Indies quickly took centre stage in Scotland's Atlantic commerce.[7] Glasgow's resident merchants refocused their Atlantic system to the British West Indies and to sugar, rum and cotton. In 1772, voyages departing from and arriving on the Clyde from the West Indies were around a quarter of all voyages from North America. By 1791, these voyages were almost equal.[8] But this was not a steady increase. The activities of Glasgow's merchants were restricted due to wartime hostilities, associated insurance and freight costs and an increase in privateering. At the end of the war in 1783, however, Glasgow's West India merchants were able to take advantage of well-established mercantile networks, maritime routes and colonial operations, and the growth in commerce ushered in the 'golden age of the Clyde-Caribbean trade'.[9]

Shipping tonnage further illustrates the dramatic rise of the Clyde-Caribbean trades. In 1790, more tonnage from the West Indies (especially Jamaica, Barbados and Grenada) was imported at Clyde ports than from either Europe or America. Examination of commodities landed between 1800 and 1805 underlines the sharp decline of the tobacco trade and the dramatic rise of sugar, coffee and cotton imports.[10] By 1806, Clyde ports had overtaken Bristol as the third largest sugar importer in Great Britain, behind London and Liverpool.[11] And while the tobacco trade was mainly a re-export business, proportionately more sugar reached the domestic market.[12] In 1814 alone, 1,251,092 hundredweight (cwt) of sugar was imported at Port Glasgow and Greenock (an increase of 73 per cent over the 1805 figure); 167,927 cwt of coffee was imported (an increase of 789 per cent) and 1,251,092 gallons of

[7] T. M. Devine, 'The American War of Independence and Scottish economic history', in *Scotland, Europe and the American Revolution*, ed. O. Dudley Edwards and G. Shepperson (Edinburgh, 1976), pp. 61–6.

[8] B. Crispin, 'Clyde shipping and the American War', *The Scottish Historical Review*, xli, Part 2 (1962), 124–34, at p. 133.

[9] T. M. Devine, 'Transport problems of Glasgow West India Merchants during the American War of Independence, 1775–83', *Transport History*, iv (1971), 266–304.

[10] G. Jackson, 'New horizons', in *Glasgow*, Vol. 1: *Beginnings to 1830*, ed. T. M. Devine and G. Jackson (Manchester, 1995), pp. 217–19.

[11] HCPP 1808 (178) *Report from the Committee on the Distillation of Sugar and Molasses*, pp. 244–5.

[12] Crispin, 'Clyde shipping and the American War', p. 131.

rum (increase of 158 per cent).[13] The decline within ten years was dramatic, and 1814 or thereabouts was the peak year of Glasgow's West India era.[14]

Moreover, West India cotton provided the 'spark' for take-off in the first phase of the Scottish Industrial Revolution, with greater multiplier effects on the national economy. In 1778 – a crucial year as the first cotton-spinning mills were established in Scotland – no cotton arrived from America at all, at least according to official statistics, while 216,000lbs arrived from the West Indies (the latter region's cotton remained most important up to 1800).[15] In 1805, a total of 8.42m lbs of cotton was landed at Clyde ports, meaning these were the premier ports in Scotland (99 per cent of Scottish total) albeit only importing a small proportion of the overall British share.[16] As will be explored in a later chapter, cotton had added significance in terms of multiplier effects, as it supplied the mills that provided employment for large swathes of the Scottish population.

Export tonnage at Clyde ports was even more impressive, revealing just how important the West Indies were to Scottish industry in this period. In 1790, just over a quarter of overall exports from the Clyde were destined for the West Indies, greater than the amount bound for North America (17 per cent) or Europe (18 per cent). The predominance of the West Indies was attributed to merchants shipping out manufactured goods, such as textiles, to the plantation colonies.[17] In 1814, the overall value of exports from the Clyde to the West Indies was £2.49m: almost twice as much as to North America and Europe combined. Thus, approximately 72 per cent of Scotland's West India trades went through Clyde ports.[18] The West Indies was the premier trading zone for Glasgow merchants from the American War of Independence to the abolition of plantation slavery in 1834, a period that spanned Scotland's Industrial Revolution.

The 'golden age' of the Clyde-Caribbean trade, however, was short. Great Britain briefly dominated the global trade in sugar after the outbreak of the Haitian Revolution in 1791, although prices declined due to a glut in production. The relocation of the Portuguese Court to Brazil in 1807 and the

---

[13] J. Cleland, *Abridgement of the Annals of Glasgow* (Glasgow, 1817), pp. 354–5.

[14] In 1824 394,896 cwt. of sugar and 11,125 cwt. of coffee were imported at Port Glasgow and Greenock. See *Glasgow Herald*, 6 Jan. 1826, p. 1.

[15] H. Hamilton, *An Economic History of Scotland in the Eighteenth Century* (Oxford, 1963), Appendix VII.

[16] Jackson, 'New horizons', pp. 216, 219; J. Cleland, *The Rise and Progress of the City of Glasgow* (Glasgow, 1820), p. 236.

[17] Jackson, 'New horizons', pp. 217–19.

[18] TNA, CUST 14/26, fo. 98; Cleland, *Abridgement of the Annals of Glasgow*, p. 356.

Argentinian declaration of independence in 1816 opened up new markets in South America, although trade levels fluctuated due to the precarious political situation.[19] The rise of the cotton industry created new profits, although British merchants failed to re-establish a global monopoly over tropical commodities.[20] By the mid 1800s, and perhaps even earlier, the manufacturing class superseded transatlantic merchants as Scotland's agents of economic change.

Methodology

As the Glasgow-West India elites refocused their trading horizons after the American Revolution, they founded new commercial organizations. The individuals that formed the basis of this study were identified through records associated with the West India Club and Glasgow West India Association.[21] The West India Club was a short-lived organization, and predecessor to the more formal Glasgow West India Association. Established in 1807, it evolved into one of the most powerful pro-slavery lobbying groups outside of London. By identifying 150 merchants, merchant-proprietors and absentee planters in Glasgow associated with both bodies in the period 1775–1838, this study revealed the city's West India community was much more numerous than has previously been recorded.[22] But this group were a minority elite

---

[19] Cleland, *Abridgement of the Annals of Glasgow*, pp. 348–9.

[20] A. Cooke, *The Rise and Fall of the Scottish Cotton Industry, 1778–1914* (Manchester, 2010).

[21] This study identified a group of 150 individual West India merchants and planters in Glasgow, who came to prominence at different stages during the city's sugar era between 1775 and 1838. Twenty-four West India merchants and planters were identified in membership lists of a commercial 'West India Club' (1787–91). This group of early Glasgow-West Indians was supplemented and compared with the records of the Glasgow West India Association, a formal lobbying group established to protect the interests of merchants and planters in the city on 22 Oct. 1807. Though the records do not always reveal specific years when all members subscribed, they do list how many joined in 1807, and other names are included between 1807 and 1834. Ninety-five merchants and planters personally subscribed to the Glasgow West India Association between 1807 and 1838 (6 of whom were also members of the West India Club). Others were identified as partners of merchant firms associated with the West India Club or the Glasgow West India Association. See N. Jones (ed.), *Reprint of Jones's Directory for the Year 1787* (Glasgow, 1868), p. 6; J. Mennons, *Jones's Directory for the Year 1789*, p. 69; *Jones's Directory for the Year 1790 and 1791* (Glasgow, 1790), p. 69; J. Strang, *Glasgow and its Clubs* (Glasgow, 1857 ed.), p. 212; GCA, TD1683/1/1, 'Abstract of the Glasgow West India Association (GWIA)', pp. 6–8 and throughout; GCA, TD1683/1/2, 'Minutes of the Glasgow West India Association', 1832–53. Data from the *Legacies of British Slave-ownership* project also informed aspects of this grouping of West India merchants, planters and firms.

[22] T. M. Devine, 'An eighteenth-century business elite: Glasgow West India merchants, 1740–1815', *Scottish Historical Review*, lvii (1978), 40–67; A. Cooke, 'An elite revisited:

within an exclusive mercantile group in Glasgow, comprising around 10 per cent of the city's merchant community (and possibly much less).[23]

Printed, digital and archival sources establish the characteristics of these individuals. Biographical details were initially culled from antiquarian texts and family histories.[24] In some cases, the printed matriculation albums of Old College (now the University of Glasgow) provided detailed information.[25] From this foundation, the commercial rank of individuals in Glasgow was established by examining burgess and guild brethren registrations and the printed subscription lists of the Merchant House.[26] Trade and post-office directories for Glasgow allowed identification of residence status and in many cases provided names of firms that merchants associated with. Wealth and remaining investments on death (as well as family relationships) were established by examining wills and confirmation inventories generated on the death of individuals (which provides the focus of Chapter 8). Shipping advertisements in the *Glasgow Herald* (Chapter 4 provides a thorough analysis of over 1,700 voyages between Clyde ports and the West Indies) confirmed the focus of each merchant firm's colonial trading interests. Annually printed collections of Scottish court cases and comparison with the *London Gazette* and *Edinburgh Gazette* – the preferred broadsheets of the mercantile class – provide further details of colonial activities of firms and individual merchants.

Distinctive groups and personalities came to prominence at different stages across Glasgow's sixty-year sugar era. The listing of the West India Club in trade directories between 1787 and 1792 reveals who among the

---

Glasgow West India merchants, 1783–1877', *Journal of Scottish Historical Studies*, xxxii (2012), 127–65.

[23] Between 1775 and 1838, approximately 10,000 individuals registered burgess and guild brethren in Glasgow, meaning the 150 West India merchants and planters were 1.5 per cent of the overall mercantile community. Between 1768 and 1838, around 1,385 individuals registered with the Merchants House, meaning the West India community was 11 per cent of this total.

[24] Key sources were J. G. Smith, *The Parish of Strathblane and Its Inhabitants from Early Times* (Glasgow, 1886); J. W. Dennistoun et al., *Some Account of the Family of Dennistoun of Dennistoun and Colgrain* (Glasgow, 1906); W. H. Fraser, *The Stirlings of Keir, and Their Family Papers* (Edinburgh, 1858); J. G. Smith, J. O. Mitchell, *The Old Country Houses of the Old Glasgow Gentry* (Glasgow, 1878); J. Craik, J. Eadie and J. Galbraith, *Memoirs and Portraits of 100 Glasgow Men* (Glasgow, 1886); G. Stewart, *Curiosities of Glasgow Citizenship* (Glasgow, 1881).

[25] W. I. Addison, *The Matriculation Albums of the University of Glasgow, From 1728 to 1858* (Glasgow, 1913).

[26] *A List of Matriculated Members of the Merchant's House* (Glasgow, 1858); J. Anderson (ed.), *The Burgesses and Guild Brethren of Glasgow, 1751–1846* (Edinburgh, 1935).

city's mercantile elite transitioned from tobacco to sugar commerce. Significantly, of twenty-four members of the West India Club, over half were previously 'tobacco lords' in Glasgow.[27] Merchants such as John Campbell senior transferred their commercial focus from Virginia to Grenada, joining with a Jamaica clique: the main grouping in the West India Club.[28] Alex Cuninghame (1756–90) of Craigends in Renfrew exemplified the old Jamaica interest.[29] Cuninghame's grandfather acquired Grandvale estate in Westmoreland, which ultimately passed to John Cuninghame on the death of Alexander in 1790. Thus, in the aftermath of the American war, former tobacco merchants collectivized with existing West India merchants and absentee planters in a new commercial grouping. The shift from tobacco to sugar brought considerable commercial disruption in Glasgow. Nine members of the West India Club (including six merchants known to have traded with Virginia) were later made bankrupt. The failure of the co-partners of Glasgow firm Alexander Houston & Co. in 1795 is well-known but this was part of a remarkably frequent pattern of bankruptcy among the city's early West India community.[30] T. M. Devine noted Glasgow's tobacco merchants' diversification into the West Indies averted immediate economic crisis on the outbreak of the American War of Independence,[31] although in reality, the financial rewards were only available to the second generation of West India merchants.

This second generation came to prominence in the abolitionist period, establishing the Glasgow West India Association in 1807. Absentee planters were in the minority but were often prominent, such as John Blackburn, a wealthy returnee from Jamaica. The Jamaica mercantile interest – headed by James Ewing – were the most prominent group in the association. However, the first association committee was composed of individuals from

[27] Thirteen were known 'tobacco lords', including Patrick Colquhoun, Robert Dunmore, James Hopkirk, Alexander Houston, James Somervell and John Riddell. For tobacco credentials, T. M. Devine, *The Tobacco Lords: A Study of the Tobacco Merchants of Glasgow and Their Trading Activities c. 1740–90* (Edinburgh, 1975), pp. 177–84.

[28] Of the 24 members of the West India Club, 13 were partners in firms or had planting interests exclusively in Jamaica.

[29] 'Alexander Cuninghame 11th of Craigends', *Legacies of British Slave-ownership* database <http://www.depts-live.ucl.ac.uk/lbs/person/view/2146650403> [accessed 7 May 2018].

[30] S. G. Checkland, 'Two Scottish West Indian liquidations after 1793', *Scottish Journal of Political Economy*, iv (1957), 127–43; D. Hamilton, 'Scottish trading in the Caribbean: the rise and fall of Houston & Co.', in *Nation and Province in the First British Empire: Scotland and the Americas, 1600–1800*, ed. N. C. Landsman (Lewisburg, 2001), pp. 94–126.

[31] T. M. Devine, 'Glasgow merchants and the collapse of the tobacco trade, 1775–1783', *The Scottish Historical Review*, lii (1973), 50–74.

prominent West India firms with different interests: Robert Dennistoun (St Kitts), Francis Garden (Jamaica), Alexander Campbell of Hallyards (Grenada and Demerara) and Robert Bogle junior (Jamaica) were directors while John Gordon (Jamaica) was appointed chairman. A third group became prominent between abolition and full emancipation in 1838. As noted that year by Colin Dunlop Donald, a lawyer specializing in colonial business and secretary of the association for over forty years, the group by then comprised West India merchants, absentee planters, financiers and merchant-proprietors (merchants who took ownership of Caribbean estates, usually after the defaulting of planters' loans).[32] For example, 'White' Mungo Campbell – who like his father Alexander Campbell of Hallyards was a co-partner in John Campbell, senior, & Co. – took over the running of the firm and registered with the West India Association around 1828. Thus, established West India merchants and their sons joined with newcomers such as George Cole, a Trinidad merchant who migrated to Glasgow to deal with the account of John Lamont, one of the largest planters on Trinidad.

From 1807 to 1838, the Glasgow West India Association was mainly a mercantile body, although some subscribers invested in sugar estates. The Jamaica interest were the most prominent group in the Glasgow West India Association, although the membership overall mainly comprised men who made wealth in newer colonies: Grenada, Trinidad and especially Demerara.[33] The main power within the Association can be measured in director appointments, which reveal the constant influence of the Jamaica interest, although, overall, directors in firms that traded with Demerara, Trinidad and Grenada were more extensive.[34] However, the sheer prominence of the Jamaica interest among the chairmen of the Association confirms this group

[32] GCA, TD1683/1/2, 31 March 1838, pp. 99–100.

[33] Of the subscribers to the Glasgow West India Association between 1807 and 1838, 120 were partners in merchant firms (with a minority owning plantations). Overall, colonial interests were known for 116. Of this group, a select group of 37 were involved with firms who traded with at least 3 colonies, 29 were in firms that traded with 2 colonies, and 50 were in firms who traded with just 1 colony. Thus, merchants with multiple interests were more common. Measuring colonial interests of individuals involved ascertaining each firm's trading connections with individual colonies. Sixty-seven individuals had trade connections with Jamaica. Other merchants: Demerara (40), Trinidad (26), Grenada (23), Tobago (17), St Vincent (17), St Thomas (11), St Kitts (7), New Providence (6), Berbice (5), Antigua (4), St Lucia (2), Guadeloupe (1), St Croix (1).

[34] There were 45 directors of the Association recorded in the Abstract and Minutes between 1807 and 1838. Individuals with interests in Jamaica (21 director appointments); Demerara (16); Trinidad (9); Grenada (7); Tobago (5); St Vincent (4); Antigua, Berbice, St Kitts and St Lucia (1 each).

dominated the organization between 1807 and 1838.[35] Someone in this group was the leading influence. James Ewing was first secretary (1807–10), director (1811, 1825) and chairman (1821–4). In his own words, he held a 'principle share' in the establishment of the Glasgow West India Association.[36] This powerful combination of individuals who controlled the Glasgow-West India trades, as will now be shown, hailed from rural and urbanizing areas of Scotland, and, on occasion, from the Caribbean itself.

Migration and society

In part due to the pull of commercial and industrial opportunities, Glasgow underwent a demographic explosion: between 1755 and 1821, the population rose sharply from 31,700 to 147,000.[37] Individuals migrated to take up commercial occupations in the city. A small minority – sons of elite merchants and planters – originated in the West Indies. William Frederick Burnley was the son of William Hardin Burnley, a Virginian-born merchant in Trinidad and one of the major owners of enslaved people on the island.[38] Burnley was connected through marriage to Glasgow-based merchants the Eccles – themselves sons of a Trinidad-based Irish planter – and it is likely this connection brought him to the city, where he became a senior partner in the merchant firm William Eccles and Co. The Caribbean background of Burnley and the Eccles, however, marked them as unusual among Glasgow's mercantile community.

Over half of Glasgow's West India elite originated from west-central Scotland, with others drawn from the eastern lowlands, the Highlands and the Borders.[39] The most prominent counties were Renfrew, Ayr and especially Lanark.[40] Indeed, the highest proportion (a third of the overall group) of individuals hailed from locations in around Glasgow, such as

---

[35] Of the 11 chairmen identified between 1807 and 1838, 6 had key interests in Jamaica, 2 in Demerara, 2 in Grenada and 1 in St Kitts.

[36] GCA, TD1683/1/1, 'Abstract' fos. 99–101.

[37] T. M. Devine, 'The development of Glasgow to 1830: medieval burgh to industrial city', in *Glasgow, Vol. 1: Beginnings to 1830*, ed. T. M. Devine and G. Jackson (Manchester, 1995), p. 10.

[38] *Merchants House Matriculation List*, p. 9.

[39] Of the 150 individuals identified in this study as being involved with the West India trades in Glasgow, a high proportion of fathers' residences is known (131, or 87%). The most prominent regions in Scotland were: Western Lowlands (78 individuals), Eastern Lowlands (29), Highland-Hebrides (10), Borders (7). A minority of individuals hailed from Trinidad (4) and England (1).

[40] Known fathers' residences in terms of counties in Scotland: Lanark (51), Renfrew (17), Perth (11), Stirling (10), Argyll (9), Ayr (7), Dumfries (4), Dunbarton (3), Fife (3), Forfar (3), Peebles (3), Edinburgh (2), Ross (1) and Inverness (1).

James Ewing, later MP for the city. While a few old families were part of the city's West India elite, the majority were incomers from across Scotland, mixed with a handful from England and the West Indies, who all travelled in search of fortune. Thus, a diverse group was formed into a cohesive Glasgow-West India elite.

As in England, Scottish society was multi-layered and governed by social rank up to 1830 (although 'class' and its associated consciousness eventually superseded rank).[41] Respectability of descent – marked by hereditary titles, landownership and associated political influence – determined rank and order. Eventually, like other European nations, economic resources acted as a 'symbol of social worth that compensated for differences in rank' in elite Scottish society, especially in potential marriage pairings.[42] Wealth gained via colonial activities, therefore, facilitated rapid social mobility and contributed to the reshaping of elite society. In the west of Scotland, the landed aristocracy sat atop the elite pile and comprised notables such as the dukes of Hamilton and Argyll. Distinguished families such as the Lockharts of Lanarkshire and the Houstons of Renfrewshire were lairds: lower in social importance in comparison with the aristocracy, but sometimes equally influential in British politics.[43] The Houstons were representative of a wider influx of landed families who owed their wealth and political influence to sugar plantations in the West Indies.[44] For Katie Barclay, these *arriviste* merchants remained part of a lower gentry (a grouping which also included small landowners such as former tenant farmers).[45] Owing to the rapid changes brought about by colonial wealth, therefore, elite society in the west of Scotland evolved.

Glasgow's elite comprised the landed gentry, merchants, professionals and middling ranks.[46] A wealthy mercantile class sat atop the pile. Most of the gentry – and their sons – lived on landed estates around the west of Scotland but operated as colonial merchants in Glasgow. Once successful, other *parvenu* merchants bought estates and lived in luxurious country

---

[41] S. Nenadic, 'The rise of the urban middle class', in *People and Society in Scotland, Vol. 1: 1760–1830*, ed. T. M. Devine and R. Mitchison (Edinburgh, 1988), pp. 118–19.

[42] K. Barclay, *Love, Intimacy and Power: Marriage and Patriarchy in Scotland, 1650–1850* (Manchester, 2011), p. 81.

[43] A. Slaven, *The Development of the West of Scotland 1750–1960* (London, 1975), pp. 61–2.

[44] Hamilton, 'Scottish trading'.

[45] Barclay, *Love, Intimacy and Power*, pp. 13–18.

[46] R. Carr, *Gender and Enlightenment Culture in Eighteenth-Century Scotland* (Edinburgh, 2014), p. 178; R. H. Trainor, 'The elite', in *Glasgow, Vol. 11: 1830–1912*, ed. W. H. Fraser and I. Maver (Manchester, 1996), pp. 227–64.

houses. The middling orders, likely around 15 per cent of the city's population in 1800, included Church of Scotland ministers. Lower middling groups comprised craftsmen, general merchants, business owners and shopkeepers. Old College professors frequented elite clubs and wielded considerable local status, as did legal and military professionals. Wealth, income and landownership, therefore, did not always determine social rank.[47]

The West India merchants and planters operating in Glasgow between 1775 and 1838 overwhelmingly came from the middling ranks and gentry. None seem to have originated from the aristocracy, instead springing from both old landed gentry and *arriviste* families. The former included 'gentry capitalist' families such as the Stirlings of Keir, who increased their already significant wealth and status through long-term connections with the Caribbean.[48] The latter included the Smiths of Jordanhill, whose transformation from tenant farmers to landed elites coincided with the establishment of a West India firm (as noted in Chapter 3). The writer and illustrator Beatrix Potter compared the *arriviste* mercantile class to 'mushroom lairds', presumably referring to the rapidity with which they popped up across the countryside.[49] Within the already landed ranks who joined the West India trades in Glasgow, the majority were younger sons – who would not normally have inherited their fathers' estate due to the law of primogeniture – although almost as many were first-born sons.[50] Thus, the West India trades of Glasgow provided younger gentry sons with a vocation but also improved existing family estates (as will be discussed in Chapter 8). Most of Glasgow-West India merchants and planters in this study, however, initially hailed from non-landed backgrounds.

Established colonial elites in Glasgow retained involvement with the Atlantic world over successive generations. Of the known fathers of West India merchants and planters, nearly half were previously involved with the colonial trades in the city. At least sixteen were sons of famous Glasgow 'tobacco lords'. For example, James, Robert and Richard Dennistoun were sons of James Dennistoun of Colgrain. Of far greater importance, however,

---

[47] S. Nenadic, 'The middle ranks and modernisation', in *Glasgow, Vol. 1: Beginnings to 1830*, ed. T. M. Devine and G. Jackson (Manchester, 1995), pp. 278–311.

[48] S. D. Smith, *Slavery, Family and Gentry Capitalism in the British Atlantic: The World of the Lascelles, 1648–1834* (Cambridge, 2006), p. 9.

[49] B. Potter, *The Journal of Beatrix Potter from 1881 to 1897* (Harmondsworth, 2012), n.p.

[50] Of this group of Glasgow-West India merchants and planters, 55 of 150 (36%) hailed from a landed background. Of the 55, 41 hailed from families previously involved with the tobacco and sugar trades. Of this group of 55 sons, birth ranks were known in 51 cases; 24 were eldest sons, 12 were second sons, 7 were third sons, 3 were fourth sons, 3 were fifth sons, 2 were sixth sons. Thus, 43 per cent were eldest sons.

was the intergenerational transfer of knowledge, skill and capital to sons from fathers previously involved in the Glasgow-West India trades. Around a third of the group were second-generation West India merchants (thirty-nine of 117 known fathers), a similar proportion to eighteenth-century Bristol merchants.[51] Several notable family West India firms in Glasgow promoted sons into West India commerce. Archibald Smith of Jordanhill, for example, established Leitch & Smith in Glasgow in the 1780s and ultimately groomed his sons to take over the business. The wider importance of family firms will be discussed later in this chapter, while the Smiths of Jordanhill will be discussed in more detail in Chapter 3.

Successive flows of colonial wealth thus created and regenerated an elite mercantile grouping in Glasgow from 1775 onwards. First, capital from the Chesapeake trades created a new cohort of West India merchants who introduced sons across successive commercial generations. Others hailed from a 'middling' background such as the Church, agricultural, military or legal professions.[52] John Hamilton of Northpark, for example, was the son of the Revd John Hamilton, minister of Glasgow cathedral between 1749 and 1780.[53] In rare cases, the privileged status afforded to the clergy provided a path into the mercantile trades. In 1770, Robert Findlay of Easterhill registered burgess (ie a merchant with right to trade – see below) as son of a minister of the gospel in Glasgow. His father, the Revd Robert Findlay of St David's Church, was also professor of Divinity at Old College between 1782 and 1814.[54] While Findlay's background was unusual, the University of Glasgow did have a role in developing West India elites.

Regenerating the elite: education, commerce and marriage

As Glasgow's economic and social structure was transformed in the eighteenth century, Old College prospered. There are two schools of thought regarding the exact relationship with the mercantile elite and the university. On the one hand, a parliamentary commission in the 1820s

---

[51] The occupation of fathers was known for approximately 117 individuals. Of this group of fathers, 60 (51 per cent) were previously involved with colonial trades in Glasgow. The West India trades (39, or 33 per cent of known group) were more important than the Chesapeake trades (16, or 14 per cent). For Bristol data, see K. Morgan, 'Bristol West India merchants in the eighteenth century', *Transactions of the Royal Historical Society*, 6th series, iii (1993), 185–208, at p. 189.

[52] Selected occupations of father's apart from colonial commerce in Glasgow – lairds (10), Church (7), agriculture/farming (6), legal professions (4), shipping (2), maltman (1), military (1).

[53] Addison, *Matriculation Albums*, p. 80.

[54] Anderson (ed.), *Burgesses and Guild Brethren of Glasgow*, p. 69.

concluded young men were 'sent for one or more years to College' before they engaged in commercial pursuits, inferring a close relationship with the mercantile community.[55] Yet, on the other hand, existing studies suggest the links between merchants and Old College were relatively slight. The classic account of Old College students argued that while 50 per cent of matriculants in the period 1800–39 had fathers whose primary occupation was industry and commerce, only 12 per cent of enrolled students were later employed in the same area (leading the author to note that the institution channelled students from commerce to professional occupations).[56]

Elite citizens of the city also believed Old College to be unfit for purpose from the mid eighteenth century. In 1761, the Revd William Thom, minister of Govan, called for a public academy in Glasgow in a series of influential tracts, one entitled 'the defects of a University education and its unsuitableness to a Commercial People'.[57] The city's merchants echoed these criticisms about Old College's arts curriculum. In February 1784, after attending an assembly alongside the city's merchants, Old College student Samuel Rose privately voiced indignation at their stance on a political matter which descended into an attack on the mercantile class:

> What can possibly be expected from a parcel of Merchants, whose every Thought turns upon the <u>one</u> thing needful? Whose acquaintance with Books is confined to the Cash-Book and Ledger? And who have spent their time amongst 'Wool-Packs, Sugar-Kists and Rum Puncheons'? You will think, perhaps, that I hold the merchants in too contemptible a Light. But I do assure you that they return it with a Degree of Interest that frequently amounts to Usury to us poor Book-Worms about the University. To see men who often cannot write their own names who more frequently cannot spell them with propriety, and who sometimes cannot read them after they are written, to see such men on possession of plums, it must naturally excite one's Indignation.

Further, Rose noted, the merchants 'gratified their own ability' at local dinners, regularly comparing the advantages of 'literary, and an illiterate

---

[55] HCPP 1830 *General Report of the Commissioners Appointed to visit the Universities and Colleges of Scotland*, p. 263.

[56] W. M. Mathew, 'The origins and occupations of Glasgow students 1740–1839', *Past and Present*, xxxiii (1966), 74–94.

[57] W. Thom, *The Works of the Rev. William Thom, Late Minister of Govan, Consisting of Sermons, Tracts, Letters* (Glasgow, 1799), pp. 263–302; D. J. Withrington, 'Education and society in the eighteenth century', in *Scotland in the Age of Improvement*, ed. N. T. Phillipson (Edinburgh, 1996), p. 181.

education'. Indeed, they modestly cited themselves as evidence of 'the superior advantage of the latter and hesitate not in giving it the preference'.[58]

Rose's critique and previous historiography, however, underappreciated the strong connections between Old College and the Caribbean over successive generations. Around fifty-eight (39 per cent of the group) West India merchants and planters of Glasgow – a similar number to that of their predecessors, the 'tobacco lords' – are known to have matriculated at Old College between 1737 and 1825.[59] These young lads matriculated aged twelve, on average, leaving the years from sixteen onwards for commercial education. James Ewing, for example, attended Glasgow High School before he matriculated at Old College aged eleven in 1786. He read Latin, Greek and philosophy, and then went into the West India trades with his father.[60] Ewing – unusually among his mercantile peers – went on to author several works, including a history of the Merchants House (a commercial organization explained in detail below).[61] Rose's vision of a generation of illiterate mercantile bean-counters, therefore, was not wholly accurate. Most of the West India elites who matriculated at Old College were themselves sons of colonial traders in the city, and they would have attended with sons of Caribbean planters. Moreover, once successful, the West India elite sent over 100 sons to the institution.[62] Old College was therefore an Atlantic world melting pot in the centre of Glasgow across successive generations and, for many, an important rite of passage before they entered the West India trades.

After education, any budding merchant in Glasgow had to secure the right to trade. In the early eighteenth century, a civic framework regulated entry to the colonial trades in Glasgow.[63] The rank of burgess and guild brethren (B.G.B.) was a privileged position which not only carried great social distinction but conferred the right to trade. After 1605, when a letter of the guildry set out the constitution of the Merchants House and established its prominent position, there were two distinct classes of burgess with protected privileges and related political and judicial powers: the merchant

---

[58] University of Glasgow Special Collections, MS. Gen, 520/58, 'Samuel Rose Papers', 24 Feb. 1784; for context, see R. B. Sher, 'Commerce, religion and the enlightenment', in *Glasgow, Vol. 1: Beginnings to 1830*, ed. T. M. Devine and G. Jackson (Manchester, 1995), pp. 347–50.

[59] Sixty-eight Tobacco lords (40 per cent of an overall group of 163) attended Old College in the period 1728 and 1800. Devine, *Tobacco Lords*, pp. 4–8.

[60] M. Mackay, *Memoir of James Ewing Esq., of Strathleven* (Glasgow, 1866), pp. 18–20.

[61] J. Ewing, *View of the History, Constitution, & Funds, of the Guildry, and Merchants House of Glasgow* (Glasgow, 1817).

[62] S. Mullen, 'British universities and transatlantic slavery: the University of Glasgow case', *History Workshop Journal*, xci (2021), 210–33, at p. 215.

[63] T. C. Smout, *A History of the Scottish People* (London, 1972), p. 147.

rank and craft rank.[64] Entrance requirements for a merchant burgess was especially rigorous, as fines (or fees) were payable at each stage of admission and although they varied over time, they were usually beyond the means of the working poor.[65] The admission of an individual as a 'Burgess Freeman' in the Royal Burgh was controlled by the dean of guild of the Merchants House (as discussed below), who decided worthiness based on their wealth, mercantile training and moral reputation.[66] Individuals had to demonstrate they were worth at least '500 merks' in 'land, heritage and moveable gear', which was double the value set for craftsmen.[67] Registration also included religious considerations based on Scottish Presbyterianism (although strict adherence was not a requirement for entry).[68] While most individuals examined here did register as B.G.B. and it represented an important qualification, in practice, by the early 1800s, it was not an essential pre-requisite for a commercial career.[69] The most common means of entrance for this group studied here was as 'son of a registered burgess and guild brethren', followed 'by purchase'. Several others also took up privileges 'by apprenticeship', through 'nomination' or, in the case of Patrick Colquhoun, as an 'Honorary Burgess'. Others registered after marrying the daughters of burgesses. The wider importance of the marital connections of the West India elite will be explored in more detail below.

Writing of his experiences in Glasgow around 1835, Sir Archibald Alison recounted how he and his wife 'frequently laughed' at the sugar aristocracy's 'rigid and universal adoption of exclusive system'. This associational system was designed to pair off eligible young people of the appropriate rank, sometimes in assemblies and balls, with the intention of continuing family traditions.[70] One study of the Glasgow-West India elite noted the high incidence of marriages within this close-knit community but underestimated how strategic marriage choices created a broad diversity of networks.[71] Wider analysis of the marital connections of West India merchants and planters in

---

[64] Ewing, *View*, pp. 1–12.

[65] Anderson (ed.), *Burgesses and Guild Brethren of Glasgow, 1751–1846*, p. iv.

[66] T. C. Smout, 'The Glasgow merchant community in the seventeenth century', *The Scottish Historical Review*, xlvii (1968), 53–71, at p. 58.

[67] Anderson (ed.), *Burgesses and Guild Brethren of Glasgow, 1751–1846*, p. iv.

[68] GCA, TD1/1246/1, 'Archd Smith burgess ticket of Glasgow', 1779.

[69] I. Maver, 'Power and politics in the Scottish city: town council in the Nineteenth century', in *Scottish Elites*, ed. T. M. Devine (Edinburgh, 1994), p. 125. Of the 150 Glasgow-West India elite examined here, 96 (64 per cent) registered as burgess and guild brethren.

[70] Alison, *Some Account of my Life*, pp. 344–7.

[71] Cooke, 'An elite revisited', p. 132.

Glasgow between 1775 and 1838 reveals eighty individuals married at least once, and a further six married twice or more. At least five died unmarried. Four members of the West India elite married into the peerage of Scotland and England. In May 1804, for example, James Buchanan of Ardenconnell married Lady Janet Sinclair, eldest daughter of the earl of Caithness. These exceptions apart, marriages were generally with daughters of the gentry and middling sorts. West India merchants and planters who hailed from a landed background unsurprisingly tended to marry daughters of other landed families. While it was less common for West India merchants from non-landed backgrounds to marry daughters of landed proprietors, merchants were sometimes propelled up the social ladder.[72]

Transatlantic West India pairings in Glasgow occurred only on an occasional basis, although they provided economic benefits, consolidated commercial connections and no doubt increased the imports of merchant firms. William Frederick Burnley, for example, married Rosina, daughter of James Eccles. Burnley's father – William Hardin Burnley – owned sugar estates in Trinidad, while Rosina's father and uncles ran Robert Eccles and Co., the top Scottish firm on the island. William Frederick Burnley ultimately travelled to Glasgow and became heavily involved in the West India trades. Stana Nenadic has argued the institutions of family and marriage were utilized to reinforce business networks and partnerships and regenerate middle-class status.[73] In these cases, there was an obvious transatlantic dimension to the practice. Marriage also connected mercantile and planting families within Scotland. Charles Stirling of Gargunnock, partner in Stirling, Gordon & Co., married Christian Hamilton, eldest daughter of John Hamilton of Sundrum, who owned two estates in St Mary in Jamaica. On his wedding in 1831, Stirling guaranteed to pay his new wife an annuity of £800 from his half-share of Content estate in St James on the same island.[74]

The Glasgow-West India elites generally married within the west of Scotland mercantile community; this was no doubt rooted in economics. Indeed, Katie Barclay's study of marriage in Scotland underlined that elite families expected the marrying of children to be mutually beneficial for both sides.[75] The daughters of 'tobacco lords' were the most popular choice for

---

[72] Twenty-seven of the known 86 marriages were between partners whose fathers owned land. On the other hand, 14 West India merchants from a non-landed background married daughters of landed proprietors.

[73] Nenadic, 'The rise of the urban middle class', p. 117.

[74] NRS, SC36/51/16, 'Contract of marriage of Charles Stirling of Gargunnock', 29 April 1840, p. 521.

[75] Barclay, *Love, Intimacy and Power*, p. 80.

budding West India merchants.[76] These couplings brought colonial fortunes to the marriage. The daughters of 'tobacco lord' John Alston (1743–1818) were paired with West India merchants: the eldest, Anna Hay, married John Gordon of Aikenhead, Isabella married David Connell and Christian Calder married Richard Dennistoun of Kelvingrove.[77] In this way, partners of three of the top seven Glasgow-West India firms in 1807 – Stirling, Gordon & Co., D&J Connell and G&R Dennistoun & Co. – were brothers-in-law. A high degree of intermarriage between sons and daughters of merchants of similar rank consolidated commercial connections between rival firms. Overall, there were eleven pairings between West India merchants and daughters of other West India merchants. The majority involved partners of firm John Campbell senior & Co. Four of John Campbell senior's sons married into other West India families, as did senior co-partners Alexander Campbell of Haylodge and Alexander Campbell of Hallyards.[78]

Although no other West India families were as connected as the Campbells, marriage was an important mechanism utilized by the Glasgow-West India community in general. The interconnected pairings meant ten of the twenty-nine merchant firms who registered with the Glasgow West India Association in 1807 were directly connected through marriage. But even if this group tended to marry within the west of Scotland mercantile community and among the West India faction in particular, a high number – around forty per cent – of the brides hailed from families with no known colonial connections. Some married daughters of Scottish lairds, such as George Bogle of Rosemount, who took Margaret Buchanan, daughter of Archibald Buchanan of Catrine Bank, as his bride in 1839.[79] Once wealthy, some married into different types of elite families. Patrick Playfair – son of a Perthshire farmer – married Jane Playfair, daughter of the Revd Dr James Playfair principal of St Andrews university. Robert Findlay junior of Easterhill married Mary Buchanan, daughter of John Buchanan of Ardoch, MP for Dunbartonshire (1821–6). Two daughters of the Revd George Rainy, minister in Creich in Sutherland, married West India merchants in

---

[76] Occupations of fathers of the brides were known for 67 marriages. In the west of Scotland: Glasgow 'Tobacco Lords' (12); Glasgow merchants (11); Glasgow-West India merchants (10); Greenock merchants (2); Glasgow cotton, and East India merchant (1 occurrence each). Thus, 56 per cent (38 of 67) of known fathers hailed from within the west of Scotland mercantile community. Other examples: laird with no connection to West India trades (4), Church (3), legal professions (3), politicians (3), surgeon (2), academic (2), and medicine (2).

[77] Smith and Mitchell, *Old Country Houses of the Old Glasgow Gentry*, 'Craighead'.

[78] Smith and Mitchell, *Old Country Houses of the Old Glasgow Gentry*, 'Possil'.

[79] J. Paterson, *History of the Counties of Ayr and Wigtown, Vol. 1: Kyle* (Edinburgh, 1863), p. 692.

Glasgow. The Revd Rainy's son, George Rainy, was a partner in Glasgow firm McInroy, Parker & Co. and these marriages connected Rainy with an other firm, Smith & Browns. Thus, while there was a high degree of intermarriage among the Glasgow-West India elite – especially those of the top rank – it was far from an exclusive caste. Many married daughters of lawyers, bankers, politicians and, on occasion, Church ministers. Marriage consolidated elite connections, but most of the 'sugar aristocracy' also shared the same religious affiliations.

Trust and confidence were crucial for actors involved in Atlantic commerce.[80] Religion was another important tie that connected the West India trades. In Glasgow, however, although Presbyterianism was the preferred faith of most merchants, adherence was not a requirement to commence a West India career. Indeed, detailed examination of the records of St Andrew's-by-the-Green Episcopal chapel and the roll books of the Church of Scotland St George's West parish kirk (latterly known as St George's Tron) reveals the West India elite of Glasgow was not a religiously homogeneous group. By 1780, there were twenty-five churches in Glasgow, mainly of the Established Church of Scotland or of Presbyterian dissent. Moreover, there was a significant Episcopalian presence after the establishment in 1751 of St Andrews-by-the-Green, whose membership was formed mainly of upper middling sorts.[81] West India merchants Patrick Colquhoun, the future lord provost, and William McDowall were managers in the 1780s.[82] It is, however, unlikely a substantial number of West India merchants or planters attended St Andrews-by-the-Green. Although the pew records are incomplete, analysis of the years 1817 to 1837 (at five-year intervals) suggests only a prominent minority (eight) actively worshipped.[83] Episcopalians James Fyffe and Charles Stirling – both partners in Stirling, Gordon & Co. – perhaps shared the same pew in 1827.[84] However, the absence of widespread involvement indicates the Caribbean entrepreneurs tended to their spiritual needs elsewhere.

The West India merchants and planters of Glasgow mainly worshipped in the Established Church of Scotland, although there was an identifiable Episcopalian minority, a pattern of religious affiliation similar to their commercial predecessors. The 'tobacco lords' helped establish St Andrews

<hr>

[80] S. Haggerty, *'Merely for Money'? Business Culture in the British Atlantic, 1750–1815* (Liverpool, 2014), pp. 66–97.

[81] C. G. Brown, *Religion and Society in Scotland since 1707* (Edinburgh, 1997), p. 33.

[82] GCA, TD423/1/1, 'St Andrew's minute book', 1750–1805, p. 27.

[83] GCA, TD423/8/1–2, 'St Andrew's pew rent books', 1817–35; 1836–45.

[84] GCA, TD423/8/1, St Andrew's pew rent books', p. 92.

Parish Church (St Andrews in the Square) in 1756 and worshipped there, although elite merchants gradually relocated westwards in the late eighteenth century. An ecclesiastical resettlement to St George's West parish kirk followed after its establishment in 1807. Examination of the communicants' roll book of the church in the years 1818 and 1823 shows the West India elite were congregation members. Prominent merchant-manufacturers were members of the congregation, including Kirkman Finlay and Henry Monteith. Moreover, over thirty West India merchants and planters were also recorded, including the hierarchy of the Glasgow West India Association: John Gordon, James Ewing, Colin McLachlan, James Connell, William Eccles, Colin Campbell Archibald Bogle et al.[85] As will be illustrated in a later chapter, Scottish Presbyterianism was exported to Kingston, Jamaica, via some of the congregation here. Indeed, John Miller and George Scheviz lived a transient lifestyle across the Atlantic world and worshipped at St Georges in Glasgow as well as establishing the Scots Kirk in Kingston. This mercantile elite also advanced their ecclesiastical cause at home. Several West India merchants who were part of St Georges' congregation – such as Colin Campbell of Jura – donated to the evangelical Dr Thomas Chalmers' scheme for Church extension in 1835.[86] Indeed, the mercantile community of Glasgow 'made as large a contribution to the architecture of our scheme as all the heritors of Scotland put together'.[87] James Ewing was perhaps the most prominent subscriber, and he followed this up by bequeathing over £18,000 to the Free Church of Scotland on his death in 1853 (equivalent to £14.5m relative to average wages in 2020).[88] In 1846, Frederick Douglass's famous 'Send back the money!' speeches criticized the Free Church's acceptance of $3,000 (c.£600) from American slave-owners.[89] Ewing's staggering donation to the Free Church has attracted little attention, yet was thirty times the American monies: the Church's post-Disruption development was powered by wealth derived from West Indian rather than American slavery.

[85] GCA, CH2/818/11–12, 'St George's roll books', 1818, 1823.

[86] T. Chalmers, *Fifth Report of the Committee of the General Assembly of the Church of Scotland in Church Extension* (Edinburgh, 1839), pp. 38–41.

[87] T. Chalmers, *Seventh Report of the Committee of the General Assembly of the Church of Scotland on Church Extension* (Edinburgh, 1841), p. 18.

[88] NRS, SC65/34/7, 'Inventory of James Ewing', 24 Feb. 1854, p. 193. For modern values, see *Measuring Worth* <https://www.measuringworth.com/calculators/ukcompare/> [accessed 2 Oct. 2021]. Relative Wage or Income Growth (Average Earnings), 2020 values have been used.

[89] C. D. Rice, *The Scots Abolitionists* (Baton Rouge and London, 1981), p. 126.

Associational culture and politics

The West India elite were an exclusive group in Glasgow, joined by education, marriage, commercial organizations, merchant firms and religion, with wider connections to elite society across Scotland and the Caribbean. Membership of elite social clubs further consolidated personal and commercial relationships. The associational culture of Great Britain during this period was exemplified by gentlemanly social clubs, sometimes formed for the 'improvement' of members or to endorse national and civic identity. There was an integrative function in all clubs, however, as they took the form of organized social networks in local society.[90] In Glasgow, many colonial merchants frequented clubs. Virginia merchants led an active 'enlightened club life' in literary and political economy societies from the 1740s onwards.[91] The most prominent was the Hodge Podge Club, a literary society ostensibly intended to improve the political debating skills of members. West India merchants and planters – such as John Orr of Barrowfield – were involved even before 1783. After the American war, however, they comprised a sizeable proportion of new members, illustrating the rise of the Caribbean elites in society.[92] Thus, as the Virginia trades and their associational culture faded, West India merchants and planters rose to prominence: many attended social clubs with specific functions.

The Board of Green Cloth was frequented by the 'Burgher aristocracy' in the city, a small, exclusive clique made up of landed interests who dominated commerce and politics.[93] Established *c.*1780, the board met at Buckshead Inn on Argyle Street between October and May. The reprinted minutes describe the activities of an elite whist and supper club in the period; membership was limited to eighteen and admission was decided by ballot, although candidates for admission could be vetoed by any current member. Meetings were held every Tuesday, where the members bet bottles of rum on, for example, the marriages and pregnancies of local gentry wives and daughters. The secretary, Colin Dunlop Donald, attended regularly and he was a conduit of information across the network, given he was secretary of the Glasgow West India Association and his concurrent

---

[90] P. Clark, *British Clubs and Societies, 1580–1800: The Origins of an Associational World* (Oxford, 2000).

[91] Devine, *Tobacco Lords*, p. 9; A. Hook and R. Sher, 'Introduction: Glasgow and the Enlightenment', in *The Glasgow Enlightenment* (Edinburgh, 1995), p. 5.

[92] T. F. Donald (ed.), *The Hodge Podge Club 1752–1900: Compiled from the Records of the Club* (Glasgow, 1900), pp. 59–65.

[93] Trainor, 'The elite', p. 232.

membership in other clubs.[94] Furthermore, the board was frequented by a group of influential individuals connected through kinship and commercial interests. A diverse range of professionals were among the sixty-eight attendees between c.1780 and 1820, such as David Cross of the Thistle Bank, one of the city's provincial banks. Attendance at the club encouraged fraternization among transatlantic entrepreneurs, who represented the largest commercial group. At least twenty-two members of the Board of Green Cloth had West India connections (a third of overall membership), including individuals associated with thirteen elite merchant firms.

The members and associates of the Board of Green Cloth perfectly illustrate how social clubs facilitated a wider network that connected the banks, counting houses and manufactories of Glasgow with the plantations in the West Indies and the Houses of Parliament in London. Five MPs patronized the club and four maintained professional relations with Glasgow West India Association after 1807. As MP for Clyde Burghs, William McDowall (himself an absentee planter) was one of the most important men in Scottish politics in the 1790s. Kirkman Finlay was lord provost of Glasgow (1812–14) and MP for Glasgow Burghs (1812–18). Henry Monteith was Lord Provost of Glasgow (1814–16, 1818–20) and MP for Saltash (1826) and Linlithgow Burghs (1820–6, 1830–1).[95] Another member of the Board of Green Cloth was John Buchanan of Ardoch, MP for Dunbartonshire (1821–6), father-in-law of Robert Findlay junior (1784–1862), a member of the Glasgow West India Association. Another MP in the club, Archibald Campbell of Blythswood, lobbied for pro-slavery interests in the British parliament up to 1831.

Local political appointments further confirmed the elite status of Glasgow's West India class. In the absence of a parliament as in London or the high courts of Edinburgh, Glasgow's elite took up positions in public institutions such as the Merchants House and Town Council, which conferred political influence and associated social status.[96] The idiosyncrasies of the political system of Glasgow prior to the Reform Act of 1832 conferred civic superiority on merchants in the city. Burgess institutions – the Merchants House and the Trade House – dominated the town council, a body with authority to make civic decisions at local and parliamentary

---

[94] C. D. Donald, *Minute Book of the Board of Green Cloth, 1809–1820* (Glasgow, 1891), pp. 10–13.

[95] D. R. Fisher, 'Henry Monteith (?1764–1848), of Westbank, Renfrew Road, Glasgow and Carstairs House, Lanark', in *The History of Parliament: the House of Commons 1820–1832*, vol. iv, ed. D. R. Fisher (Cambridge, 2009), pp. 421–2.

[96] Trainor, 'The elite', p. 231.

levels (since councillors contributed – with other burghs – to the election of an MP for Clyde Burghs).[97] In the town council, however, the Merchants House had a fixed majority of councillors compared to the Trades House, and its members also retained the exclusive privilege of nominating the lord provost. There are two schools of thought regarding the influence of the West India interest in local politics. In 1856, John Strang described the West Indians as a 'limited and united...City aristocracy...who, in the eyes of their fellow-citizens [were] looked up to as the really acknowledged rulers of Glasgow' in commerce and politics.[98] On the other hand, according to T. M. Devine, West India merchants did not form a 'political hegemony', as the town council did not solely represent their views or interests after 1800 (unlike the Virginia traders in the earlier period).[99] The exact nature of the political influence of the West India interest can be gauged via appointments to the Merchants House, the town council and as MPs.

The Merchants House was a commercial organization in Glasgow with responsibilities in important areas of civic life. Its seminal history – written by absentee Jamaica planter and enslaver, James Ewing – describes its three roles: as an assembly that addressed petitions to the crown and parliament, as a charitable association and as an elective body voting on the influential position of dean of guild.[100] Matriculation to the Merchants House conferred status, but also carried an important philanthropic and political role. Around ninety-six West India merchants and planters matriculated between 1768 and 1841, representing under 10 per cent of the overall membership. However, this same group were over-represented as deans of guild. Indeed, of thirty-three deans between 1775 and 1838, twelve were West India merchants and planters (38 per cent). There was only one West India dean between 1775 and 1799, although eleven were appointed (terms covering twenty-two years) between 1800 and 1838. Jamaica merchants and planters were the most prominent single grouping, although merchants with links to newer colonies – especially Grenada – were more numerous overall.[101] The former included James Ewing, and the latter included Archibald Smith and Mungo Nutter Campbell.

The West India elites held similar authority in the office of lord provost of the town council. Of thirty-three lord provosts between 1775 and 1838, twelve (36 per cent) were West India merchants or planters, more numerous than

[97] Maver, 'Power and politics in the Scottish city', pp. 101–2.

[98] Strang, *Glasgow and its Clubs*, pp. 214–19.

[99] Devine, 'An eighteenth-century business elite', pp. 53–4.

[100] Ewing, *View*, pp. 13–18.

[101] *A List of Matriculated Members of the Merchant's House* (Glasgow, 1858), pp. 45–6.

has been recorded in a previous study.[102] Like the dean of guild position, the West India influence increased over the period, with eight members serving (over sixteen years) between 1800 and 1838. Given the frequency of West India appointments as lord provost, they seem to have been much more influential in local politics than their successors, the cotton masters, manufacturers who dominated after 1838 (just five of whom were lord provosts of Glasgow between 1840 and 1912).[103] The rise of a new Caribbean cohort can explain this disproportionate influence. The West India provosts, in general, represented old colonial wealth, epitomized by the dominance of members of the Jamaica interest such as James Ewing, although Demerara merchants became increasingly prominent.[104] Indeed in 1801, by appointment of the town council, Lord Provost Hamilton, whose firm traded with Demerara although he had familial connections with Jamaica, petitioned the king to protect the free port trade in the British colonies. This trade (as will be discussed in Chapter 3) was a relaxation of the mercantilist system and allowed colonial trade with the technically barred French and Spanish West Indies.[105] Thus, as this new group became wealthy and powerful, they used local influence to promote their own agenda in regional and national politics.

Prior to union of 1707, each of the sixty-six royal burghs in Scotland sent a representative to the Scottish parliament, although afterwards they were combined (except for Edinburgh) and limited to just fourteen MPs. Although Glasgow was a major economic force by this period, it became part of the Clyde Burgh with Dumbarton, Rutherglen and Renfrew. In effect, Glasgow only had a quarter share of the MP, and was clearly under-represented compared to population.[106] Nevertheless, of the sixteen MPs for Clyde Burghs between 31 October 1774 and May 1831, five were of the Glasgow-West India elites.[107] William McDowall and Alexander Houston were elected as MPs several times, and both were connected with firm Alexander Houston & Co. Nevertheless, West India merchants and planters seem to have been less prominent in the House of Commons than the

---

[102] Cooke, 'An elite revisited', p. 138.

[103] Cooke, *Scottish Cotton Industry*, p. 186.

[104] Five were Jamaica merchants or planters, others were: Demerara merchants (4), St Kitts (2) and Grenada (1).

[105] R. Renwick (ed.), *Extracts from the Records of the Burgh of Glasgow, 1796–1808*, vol. ix (Glasgow, 1914), p. 230.

[106] F. Montgomery, 'Glasgow and the struggle for parliamentary reform, 1830–1832', *The Scottish Historical Review*, xx (1982), 130–45, at p. 130.

[107] 'Glasgow burghs', *History of Parliament Online* <http://www.historyofparliamentonline. org/volume/1690-1715/constituencies/glasgow-burghs> [accessed 1 May 2018].

cotton masters (although this comparison is made between pre- and post-Reform parliamentary systems).[108] The political influence of the Glasgow-West India elite has therefore been underestimated at regional and national levels. While the Glasgow-West India interest did not form a majority in the Merchants House or town council, they were disproportionately powerful across both, although less powerful than contemporaries in national politics.

Relative political influence in Glasgow – measured by lord provost and dean of guild appointments and chairmen of the Glasgow West India Association – lay with the old Jamaica interest. Paradoxically, as will be explained in a later chapter, the Demerara interest left the highest average fortunes and were the most financially powerful grouping among the Glasgow-West India merchants. Yet, the wealthiest grouping had little interest in city affairs. It is very likely business lifestyles meant they had little motivation for civic duties in the Merchants House or the council. Charles Stewart Parker and partner James McInroy were among the wealthiest Demerara merchants in Glasgow, although they lived outside the city and had diversified their business into Liverpool by the 1820s. The Jamaica interest might have been less wealthy, but they dominated the city's political affairs as well – including the leadership of the city's first pro-slavery lobbying group.

The establishment of the Glasgow West India Association in 1807 provided the merchants and planters with a voice at the highest level of British imperial politics. Membership was comprised of the mercantile elite: James Ewing was the leading influence and initial subscribers included John Campbell senior, Archibald Smith, John Gordon, Robert Dennistoun et al.[109] Anthony Cooke has unconvincingly described the West India merchants and planters of nineteenth-century Glasgow as a 'localised elite' with a modest impact on the national stage.[110] In actuality, members of the association were disproportionately powerful in the national pro-slavery movement and influenced parliamentary affairs up to emancipation in 1834. Its members were over-represented among the standing committee of the London West India Committee, the most powerful body of its type in the Atlantic world.[111] The West India merchants and planters of Glasgow, therefore, promoted their interests and pro-slavery arguments at regional and national levels.

---

[108] Nine cotton masters were MPs between 1840 and 1912. Cooke, *Scottish Cotton Industry*, p. 186.

[109] GCA, TD1683/1/1, 'Abstract of the Glasgow West India Association', pp. 6–8.

[110] Cooke, 'An elite revisited', pp. 138–9.

[111] The University of the West Indies – St Augustine, Alma Jordan Library, SC89 8/9, 'List of standing committees of West India planters & merchants'.

Conclusion

In 1835, Sir Archibald Alison asserted that just 'five or six families' comprised Glasgow's 'sugar aristocracy'. Beyond a handful of strategic marriages, there was no proper aristocratic strand of the Glasgow-West India elite. Instead, the city was dominated by several distinguished families with long-term connections to the Virginia or West India trades who emulated the aristocracy by investing in and bequeathing land. They often intermarried with other colonial families and introduced sons into the business. Alison, therefore, was most likely referring to West India dynasties such as the Bogles of Gilmorehill, the Dennistouns of Colgrain and Kelvingrove, the Stirlings of Keir, the Campbells of Possil and the Smiths of Jordanhill. The latter two families were more *arriviste* than the other examples, but by 1834, all fitted the criteria of 'sugar aristocracy'. And whether or not they were considered part of this upper echelon, all of Glasgow's West India merchants and planters were an elite grouping within the overall mercantile community of the city and Scottish society more broadly.

The West India elite was created in the aftermath of the American War of Independence. Some of its members had longer-term origins as 'tobacco lords' or as scions of old planting families. Economic change after 1783, however, attracted many others to Glasgow in search of opportunity. Most hailed from the west of Scotland, many from other Scottish regions, a few from England and the West Indies. Some were previously landed, others purchased or inherited estates after they became successful. A significant number – mainly from old colonial families – attended Old College, and others sent their sons once they became wealthy. There was a high degree of intermarriage among the sugar aristocracy, and even West India merchants of lower standing married daughters of landed proprietors, politicians, bankers, absentee and resident planters. This was not a religiously homogeneous group but consisted of a mainly Presbyterian faction with an Episcopalian minority. The social clubs further endorsed their status among the elite and encouraged fraternization in the circles they were often married into. While the West India elite were larger than has been understood in previous studies, they only constituted a small proportion of the overall mercantile community. Nonetheless, they were disproportionately powerful as Deans of Guild, Lord Provosts and MPs. An old Jamaica clique retained control, but the rise of a new group involved with second- and third-phase colonies – Grenada, Trinidad and especially Demerara – transformed Glasgow politics. Collectively, they were disproportionately powerful compared to other contemporary merchants. The West India interest were either directly represented as MP for Glasgow Burghs or controlled those who did up to 1832. The West India elite of Glasgow formed their own lobbying group, which rapidly became one of the most powerful outport associations in Great Britain, with strong connections to the London West India Committee. The opportunities in the aftermath of the War of American Independence created a West India elite grouping that radically disrupted society in Glasgow and the west of Scotland more generally. In turn, they influenced local politics, promoting their own agenda locally and further afield in the House of Commons. The Glasgow-West Indians had a voice at the pinnacle of imperial politics via their own Association and the London West India Committee. In short, wealth from the Caribbean had a major impact on the Scottish economy and society and contributed to the transformation of social, political and cultural spheres. The next chapter explores how merchants were prepared for the West India trades and the processes that allowed them to flourish.

2. Trade and commerce

Charles Stewart Parker, and many other West India merchants like him, operated counting houses with multiple employees in the great Atlantic metropolis, Glasgow, towards the end of Caribbean slavery. In 1825, Parker was at the commanding heights of the Glasgow's West India interest. His father, James Parker, from Glasgow, had been resident in Virginia working for 'tobacco lord' Alexander Speirs from 1745, but fled on the outbreak of the American War of Independence. Family tradition alleged that James came home penniless but made a fortune in Glasgow, to be reinvested in colonial enterprise.[1] Charles was sent to Grenada aged eighteen in 1789, eventually establishing a firm with James McInroy, George Parker and Samuel Sandbach.[2] He returned to Glasgow in 1794 and quickly rose up the ranks; by 1825, he was senior partner in McInroy, Parker & Co., which carried on business at Liverpool, Demerara and Glasgow. That same year, he was elected chairman of the powerful Glasgow West India Association. His living arrangements in Scotland were typical of the lifestyle of an elite colonial merchant with business and landed interests. In the late 1820s, Parker lived with his family for seven months of the year on a farm in the Barony parish of Glasgow. During the summer months, he resided in his mansion in Fairlie on the coast of Ayrshire, travelling to Glasgow once a fortnight. He also visited Liverpool three times a year on company business. The merchant house of McInroy & Parker in Glasgow was supervised by Parker and his co-partner James McInroy with the assistance of two clerks. During the seven months he lived in the Barony, he attended his counting house in the Virginia Buildings five days in each a week, spending two or three hours a day at work.[3] In the summer months, Parker was in personal attendance for just three or four hours every fortnight at the counting house. The counting house was in the bustling commercial district, within walking distance of maritime facilities and financial institutions such as the Broomielaw harbour, the Tontine Rooms, the mail-coach office and the Royal Bank at Royal Exchange Square.

---

[1] UofGSPC, MS. Gen 537/46, 'Letter from J. Parker Smith to Mr [J. R.] Anderson. Ryvra, North Berwick', 9 April 1927.

[2] S. Haggerty, *'Merely for Money'? Business Culture in the British Atlantic, 1750–1815* (Liverpool, 2014), p. 31.

[3] *Cases Decided in the Court of Session 1826–1827*, vol. v (Edinburgh, 1827), p. 389.

This chapter offers the first overall survey of Glasgow-West India merchant firms that holistically examines their operations in Scotland and the Caribbean in the late eighteenth and early nineteenth centuries. Previous studies have described the importance of Atlantic merchant enterprise in a British context, noting the importance of Scottish-American traders yet with surprisingly little material about Glasgow-West India firms in the colonial period.[4] This oversight is perhaps explained by the well-developed historiography on Scottish-American firms, with fewer studies focused on their West India counterparts.[5] S. G. Checkland, however, traced the respective bankruptcies of Alexander Houston & Co. in 1801 and Evan Baillie & Co. in 1806.[6] T. M. Devine followed this line of enquiry and outlined that an elite group of partnerships – including Alexander Houston & Co. – dominated Clyde-Caribbean commerce between 1750 and 1815.[7] More recent studies have focused on colonial operations. Douglas Hamilton illuminated the commercial networks in Grenada of Alexander Houston & Co., the premier Glasgow-West India merchant firm in the late eighteenth century.[8] The chapter focuses on the structures and connections that made the West India trades possible in Glasgow, including the firms themselves, preparation for the mercantile trades and trade and communications between metropole and colonies. In doing so, it reveals the legal and commercial structures that underpinned Glasgow's sugar era.

West India merchant houses, Scots law and partnerships

James Morrison, director of a mercantile academy and leading author of commercial works in nineteenth-century Glasgow, defined West India merchants and their firms by geographical focus rather than the commodities in which they traded.[9] This section will focus on a clearly defined group of firms with the strongest connection to the region: the firms who registered

---

[4] S. Chapman, *Merchant Enterprise in Britain: From the Industrial Revolution to World War 1* (Cambridge, 1992).

[5] S. Mullen, 'Glasgow', in *Oxford Bibliographies 'Atlantic History'*, ed. T. Burnard (New York, 2018).

[6] S. G. Checkland, 'Two Scottish West Indian liquidations after 1793', *Scottish Journal of Political Economy*, iv (1957), 127–43.

[7] T. M. Devine, 'An eighteenth-century business elite: Glasgow-West India merchants, 1750–1815', *Scottish Historical Review*, lvii (1978), 53–67.

[8] D. Hamilton, 'Scottish trading in the Caribbean: the rise and fall of Houston & Co.', in *Nation and Province in the First British Empire: Scotland and the Americas, 1600–1800*, ed. N. C. Landsman (Lewisburg, Pa., 2001), pp. 94–126.

[9] J. Morrison, *A Complete Treatise on Practical Book-Keeping*, 3rd ed. (London, 1820), p. xiv.

with the Glasgow West India Association between 1807 and 1834 – that is, between the abolition of the slave trade and the emancipation of enslaved people in the British colonies. On the establishment of the association in 1807, the directors agreed that elite merchant firms should annually subscribe £52 to a 'pecuniary fund', which was double that required of the smaller firms. Thus, the top seven firms in Glasgow were Stirling, Gordon & Co., John Campbell, senior, & Co., George and Robt. Dennistoun & Co., Leitch & Smith, Buchanan, Steven & Co., David & James Connell, and Robert Bogle junior & Co.[10] This chapter is based upon the records of some of these firms, complemented with legal sources and banking records. Colonial records and correspondence with associates in the West Indies – including agents and plantation owners – illustrate Caribbean activities.

In a study of Alexander Houston & Co., Douglas Hamilton attributed the firm's commercial demise to its utilization of a distinctively Scottish store system in the West Indies – that is, one based upon the direct purchase of sugar from resident planters (supposedly identical to the 'tobacco lords' system of direct purchasing of tobacco in Virginia).[11] However, Houston & Co probably operated a classic commission system, providing credit to resident planters in return for trade agreements that guaranteed a set level of imports of sugar on an annual basis. One indenture reveals the co-partners of the firm granted a mortgage of £2,000 sterling to John Buchan, the owner of Cumberland estate in St Vincent, in September 1788. In return, Buchan promised to pay back the principal with interest (5 per cent per annum) and during the repayment period promised to consign 'Sixty Hogsheads of Muscovado Sugars of the Usual and Customary Weight' to the firm in Glasgow.[12] The commission agreements established a revenue system based on interest on long-term mortgages and short-term bills of exchange, as well as the profits from exports and commission on imports such as sugar (secured in repayment agreements), cotton, freight, insurance, customs and port duties. In effect, West India merchants took the role of bankers in the plantation economy and, in addition to normal terms of repayment, often demanded sugar imports in return (although the import agreements were not always legally enforceable).

The West India merchant houses in Glasgow generally operated on a commission system after 1775. These methods were similar to West India firms in London and Bristol after 1750, and in contrast to the preferred direct purchasing

---

[10] GCA, TD1683/1/1, 'Abstract of the Glasgow West India Association', p. 6.

[11] Hamilton, 'Scottish trading', pp. 94–126.

[12] British Library, 'Digitisation of the deed books in Saint Vincent for the slavery era, 1763–1838', EAP688/1/1/3a: Deed book 1788 [Part 1], p. 314 <http://eap.bl.uk/database/results.a4d?projID=EAP688> [accessed 5 April 2017].

of Glasgow's Virginia merchants before 1775. The expansive operations of elite merchant firms sometimes involved diversification into investment in sugar plantations. The largest firms extended capital and export supplies on credit which sustained the plantation system and tied resident planters to long-term consignment plans. Both the commission and store systems depended on young men conducting business in the colonies, although, in contrast, under the commission method the produce was owned by the planters until sold on the British market. Thus, the burden of risk as well as that of the costs lay solely with the planters. However, the system could involve a large outlay of mortgage capital from the merchants to planters and the system required sophisticated communications between colony and metropole.[13]

Scots law offered unique layers of protection for Glasgow-West India merchant firms trading in the colonies. The legal basis for a Glasgow-West India merchant firm was a private partnership, which was defined in a landmark text in 1826 by George Joseph Bell, a Scottish advocate and professor of Law at the University of Edinburgh. Persons of 'sound mind' (ie aged above twenty-one and considered sane) were entitled to enter into a legal contract that established a firm which was given a 'social name'. The firm, recognized as a separate person in Scots law, bestowed upon the partners a preferable right to the funds or stock of the company, which was deemed common property in a trust held by all partners.[14] Many Glasgow-West India firms established separate establishments in the colonies (usually under different but similar names) which transacted on their own terms. In 1814, Reid & McCall pursued the partners of J. T. A. Douglas & Co. for debts owed by Douglas, Reid & Co., their sister firm in Demerara. However, it was decreed that the 'co-partnery…is entirely distinct from the individuals who compose it', and the case was dismissed on the basis that creditors must make a claim against the company in that jurisdiction.[15] In practice, this meant firms managed by Scots in the West Indies could not be pursued in Scottish courts by creditors (such as manufacturers who consigned goods on credit) even if the main partners resided in Scotland.

Studies reveal that Scottish merchant firms also had larger co-partnership structures compared to English firms.[16] Consistent with Bell's opinion on

---

[13] K. G. Davies, 'The origins of the commission system in the West India trade', *Transactions of the Royal Historical Society*, v (1952), 89–107.

[14] G. J. Bell, *Commentaries on the Laws of Scotland and on the Principles of Mercantile Jurisprudence*, 5th ed., vol. ii (Edinburgh, 1826), pp. 621–7.

[15] *Decisions of the First and Second Divisions of the Court of Session, November 1812–1814* (Edinburgh, 1815), p. 644.

[16] Hamilton, 'Scottish trading', p. 120.

the legal basis of firms, large concerns were made possible in Scotland, as they were legally defined as separate entities from co-partners, in contrast to English law, and were able to raise legal action as well as protect rights of co-partners.[17] Thus, large Scottish West India firms provided security for partners by spreading risk, which also promoted the accumulation of capital and improved credit ratings. Other historians have suggested larger partnerships were a means to overcome a shortage of Scottish specie.[18] Whatever the exact reasons, the typically large partnerships in Scottish merchant firms promoted the collectivization of capital and the spreading of risk among individuals.

Partnership structures have been identified for fourteen merchant houses which registered with the Glasgow West India Association and were active between 1807 and 1828.[19] These were long-term concerns, and their size ranged from three to eight partners. The median was both eight and three, meaning smaller firms were as common as larger ones. Glasgow's pioneering West India firms from the 1770s had, on average, four co-partners, although after 1807 the average co-partnership size was 5.5 and even higher for elite firms (6.3).[20] The gradual increase in average partnership size is explained by the rise of family firms. In nineteenth-century Glasgow, all seven of the elite merchant houses had a minimum of two co-partners from the same family. Five of them were dominated by mercantile patriarchs, who introduced at least one son into the family firm.

The rise of the merchant house of John Campbell, senior, & Co. was similar to that of contemporaries Leitch & Smith (see Chapter 3). Both firms were set up by younger sons from minor landed families from just outside Glasgow. John Campbell and Archibald Smith had previously been involved with the Virginia trades but shifted commercial focus to sugar and the Caribbean after Glasgow's Chesapeake tobacco monopoly was ended at the close of the American Revolutionary War in 1783. Both groomed younger sons and male relatives to take over the firm. Similar to Leitch & Smith, the partnership structure of John Campbell, senior, & Co. was

---

[17] T. M. Devine, 'Sources of capital for the Glasgow tobacco trade, c.1740–1780', *Business History*, xvi (1974), 113–29, at p. 122.

[18] D. Hancock, *Citizens of the World: London Merchants and the Integration of the British Atlantic Community, 1735–1785* (Cambridge, 1997), pp. 104–8.

[19] Partnership groupings were identified in co-partner agreements as well as the *London* and *Edinburgh Gazette* and printed Court of Session papers. The 14 firms were Dennistoun, Buchanan & Co., Campbell, Rivers & Co., Campbell, Fraser & Co., D&J Connell, Eason, Alston & Co., Edgar, Lyon & Co., Francis Garden & Sons., G&R Dennistoun, Haddow & Dale, John Campbell, senior, & Co., Leitch & Smith, Robert Eccles & Co, Stirling, Gordon & Co., Wighton, Gray & Co.

[20] Devine 'Eighteenth-century business elite', pp. 65–7.

based on kinship networks which provided the firm with capital, skills and colonial connections. Indeed, of the fifteen co-partners in the firm's business contracts between 1790 and 1848, all but one were men from the same family. And this was with good reason. The consanguineous transfer of power in early modern enterprise limited various risks. Promotion of younger sons and relatives into the family firm kept ownership of the concern within the family, which ostensibly preserved and often increased fortunes. Further, the dangers inherent in setting up new businesses were minimized as succession through kinship relations meant younger male relatives retained existing contacts, customers and suppliers built up over several years. Thus, elite merchant firms recruited from within the direct 'family matrix' and wider familial networks to minimize risk.[21] As Glasgow's sugar era progressed, senior merchants regularly groomed younger relatives for business and occasionally introduced newcomers.

Preparation for a career in a transatlantic sphere of operations

This section outlines how West India merchants were prepared for the trades as young men. In the transatlantic hub of Glasgow, the availability of education, commercial training and apprenticeships attracted many who were destined for a career in the West India trades. As noted in Chapter 1, only just over a third of the Glasgow-West India elite attended Old College (now the University of Glasgow). Despite the public attack by the city's merchants, who mocked the university's classical-based educational provision, the institution retained some prestige. But there was internal criticism from its own staff too. In 1796, former Old College professor John Anderson laid out a vision for a new institution which would provide 'useful learning' in his testament.[22] This legacy established Andersons University – now the University of Strathclyde – which offered vocational learning, specifically in 'mechanic, Arts…Health or Commerce', which was covered in the initial four colleges: Arts, Medicine, Law and Theology.[23] West India merchant Patrick Colquhoun was one of the initial trustees in 1796, although he was resident in London by this point.[24] Other West India merchants such as John Riddell were appointed later that year, and another trustee for over twenty years, William MacNeill, was a partner in West India firm MacNeill,

---

[21] P. Mathias, 'Risk, credit and kinship in early modern enterprise', in *The Early Modern Atlantic Economy*, ed. J. McCusker and K. Morgan (Cambridge, 2000), pp. 16–17.

[22] SUA, GB 249 OB/1/1/1, 'Andersons Institution, minutes, 1796–1799', p. 1.

[23] SUA, GB 249 OB/1/1/1, 'Andersons Institution, minutes, 1796–1799', pp. 11–12.

[24] SUA, GB 249 OB/1/1/1, 'Andersons Institution, minutes, 1796–1799', pp. 3–6.

Stewart & Co.[25] In 1796, the trustees sought to encourage the development of the institution via subscriptions from those 'connected with the trade and prosperity of this City'. The West India proportion of the subscriptions does not seem to be of much importance, but Richard Dennistoun did subscribe three guineas.[26] And there is no clear evidence whether or not merchants and planters attended in significant numbers as there are no systematic matriculation lists available before 1835.[27] Nonetheless, it seems very unlikely there was widespread attendance in what was initially a small-scale institution. There is no mention of commercial training in the initial classes, although a Mathematical Academy taught practical mathematics, including navigation, in 1816.[28] Thus, while Anderson's University eventually emerged as a real alternative to Old College, the West India elite of Glasgow probably received commercial education elsewhere.[29] And, as will be discussed in a later chapter, the main antecedent organization (the Royal Technical College) that became the University of Strathclyde was a beneficiary of a philanthropic fund derived from slavery.

The universities were not the only way into a colonial career and there was an excellent standard of commercial learning in the city. In the 1760s, William Gordon and James Scruton provided such training and this can be considered part of the same movement for 'useful knowledge'. In an essay of 1770, William Gordon – master of an academy in Glasgow – published *The Education of a Young Gentleman Intended for the Counting House*. This work set out his views on the deficiencies of a university education and the theoretical skills deemed pre-requisite for entry to the counting house as well as the practical skills gained in an apprenticeship. Since he was promoting his own private academy, it is unsurprising that Gordon suggested that a mercantile apprenticeship on its own was inadequate as 'the business [of the counting house]…is of such importance, and every moment so precious to the master…he hath no time for attending to the instruction of an apprentice'.[30] Despite his vested interest, Gordon set out a persuasive argument that the

---

[25] SUA, GB 249 OB/1/1/3, 'Andersons Institution and Andersons university minutes, 1810–1830', p. 52.

[26] SUA, GB 249 OB/5/1/2/1, 'Subscription List, 1796'.

[27] SUA, 'Evening Classes', GB 249 OB/9/1.

[28] SUA, GB 249 OB/1/1/1, 'Andersons Institution, minutes, 1796–1799', pp. 91–2; SUA, GB 249 OB/7/1/4, 'Mathematical Academy', 26 Oct. 1816.

[29] R. B. Sher, 'Commerce, religion and the enlightenment', in *Glasgow, Vol. 1: Beginnings to 1830*, ed. T. M. Devine and G. Jackson (Manchester, 1995), pp. 349–50.

[30] W. Gordon, *The Universal Accountant and Complete Merchant*, 3rd ed., vol. i (Edinburgh, 1770), pp. 2–3.

best preparation for apprentice merchants was a period in a grammar school followed by commercial training and a counting-house apprenticeship, the latter of which sometimes attracted high entry fees. While there is no way of ascertaining how many of the merchants took this path, it is important to note the high standard of commercial education available in Glasgow. A later chapter considers the implications of the rise of mercantile academies in the city.

Private training was complemented with the publication of specialist textbooks designed for use in Glasgow. Books authored by James Morrison were illustrated with examples of transatlantic commerce conducted from the city.[31] In *A Complete Treatise on Practical Book-Keeping*, Morrison outlined the operations of a Glasgow-West India commission business undertaken by three partners in the city. According to him:

> Every Merchant should be acquainted with the following branches of Commercial Learning. He should write with ease and correctness; understand Figures and Accounts, and be able to examine Invoices, Accounts – Current, Charter Parties, Polices of Insurance, Bills of Lading, and Bills of Exchange.[32]

West India merchants should precisely understand the nature and quality of their commodities, as well as the aspects of the trade such as the intricacies of insurance and risk of natural disasters, including 'dangerous Navigation, West India hurricanes, [and] enterprizes of the Enemy'.[33] While there was a high standard of training in the city – for those who could pay – around twenty-eight individuals of the Glasgow-West India elite (almost one-fifth of the overall group) travelled to the colonies to gain experience of a more practical nature. Just three travelled to Virginia, which seems surprising given the extent of Glasgow's tobacco monopoly before 1775. The West Indies were the premier region, especially the islands of Jamaica and Grenada. Alexander Campbell, known as 'Marran', later of Haylodge, was in Grenada in 1789 under the supervision of his uncle Thomas.[34] However, that relatively fewer individuals went abroad as youths compared to earlier Virginia merchants suggests that doing so was not a pre-requisite to a West India career.[35] For most West India merchants, the counting houses of

[31] J. Morrison, *The Elements of Book Keeping, by Single and Double Entry* (London, 1813).

[32] Morrison, *A Complete Treatise on Practical Book-Keeping*, p. xiv.

[33] Morrison, *A Complete Treatise on Practical Book-Keeping*, p. xxvii.

[34] NRAS, 2570/116, 'Letter from William Arbuthnot to William Urquhart', 6 March 1789.

[35] Destinations for this group of sojourners among the Glasgow-West India elite: Grenada (10), Jamaica (8), Demerara (3), Virginia (3), Danish West Indies, New Providence, Trinidad, St Lucia (all 1). See T. M. Devine, *The Tobacco Lords: A Study of the Tobacco Merchants of*

Glasgow were their fiefdoms or, more accurately, from the comfort of their landed residences the senior co-partners managed the business undertaken by clerks and apprentices in those little enclaves of transatlantic capitalism.

The typical counting house was a hub that connected employees with the plantation economy of the West Indies and various institutions in Scotland. The counting houses in Glasgow were mainly congregated on or near the Trongate, particularly Argyll Street, the Tontine Buildings, Candleriggs, the Gallowgate and Miller Street. An inventory lodged on the sequestration of one merchant allows the historian to recreate one such business place.[36] In 1837, Daniel Ross' outstanding debts in Glasgow and London exceeded his assets and the firm was wound up. Bankruptcy led to an appraiser evaluating his property for sale in order to appease creditors. Ross was based at Royal Bank Place, a prestigious location in the lane between Buchanan Street and the Royal Exchange. This commercial building was set over three levels. The cellar was sparse, containing only empty boxes, tables and shelving. Up on the ground floor, the warehouse had perhaps been cleared of valuable items. The office was relatively luxurious compared to the other rooms. In more prosperous times – before Ross travelled to the West Indies to escape his debts – he may have sat on the Venetian chair at the mahogany table and looked out to the Royal Exchange. Many commercial discussions could have taken place in this office, with merchants keen to discuss commerce undertaken in partnership with associates in Grenada and Demerara.

The inventory of the adjoining 'counting house' illustrates how such business was undertaken. The two desk stools and a mahogany double desk were undoubtedly reserved for apprentices and clerks. These young men might have warmed themselves at the fire before getting to work on both inward and outward correspondence. The recording of this information into the journal was just as important as calculating figures for the ledger book. The ready reckoner allowed the young apprentices to make quick calculations on discounts and charges, while the Thomson's interest table illustrates just how much their world was based on credit and commission. The padlocked box might have contained bills of exchange for safekeeping. The inventory hints at a functional, commercial space for senior partners and junior clerks, although such establishments acted not only as offices but as training academies and communication hubs. Mail either destined for or newly arrived from the West Indies was placed in the letter box. A desk knife was used to open inward mail while the pewter inkstand held a steady supply

---

Glasgow and Their Trading Activities c. 1740–90 (Edinburgh, 1975), p. 9, for comparative data.

[36] NRS, CS96/4291, 'Daniel Ross and Company, sederunt book', 1837–8.

for the quill pens used by clerks. Before the young men walked along to the mail office in 64 Trongate or the Royal Bank at the west end of Royal Exchange Square, they might have taken an umbrella from the stand to keep out the Glasgow drizzle.

West India merchants – and their clerks – facilitated a two-way flow of information between Great Britain and the Caribbean. Indeed, the service was improved in this period. In 1800, newspapers and letters from the sugar islands came via Liverpool and were delivered to a waiting scrum of merchants in the Tontine Rooms.[37] Daily newspapers also printed the *Tontine List*, which listed mercantile information including arrivals and departures of ships on the Clyde.[38] Personal correspondence was one means of delivering information to the islands, as when Mr Dow, a mason, travelled to Carriacou looking for employment in early 1787 taking with him letters from home.[39] Alexander Houston & Co. used their own fleet of ships to post out letters to Jamaica.[40] However, the official postal service to and from the Caribbean was limited. In 1800, the Glasgow-West India mail service was a monthly occurrence, although it seems that this improved to fortnightly by 1809.[41] That year, the Glasgow West India Association lobbied the secretary of the post office about the Falmouth packet service – deemed to be slower than the London route – and argued that delays in transmitting important commercial information might lead to financial losses.[42] The merchant firms subsequently established their own service. In 1824, the Glasgow agent firm John Cree & Co. collaborated with elite merchant firms in the city to establish the Kingston packet from the Clyde. This efficient arrangement – which connected with the Falmouth packet that left from Jamaica – meant several ships sailed together from Clyde ports at designated times, guaranteeing regular freight and mail between Glasgow and Jamaica.[43] Glasgow-West India mercantile commerce led to innovations in the communications system. This chapter now explores the relationship between commerce, capital and credit.

---

[37] J. W. Hyde, *A Hundred Years by Post: A Jubilee Retrospect* (London, 1891).

[38] 'Glasgow tontine list', *Glasgow Herald*, 4 Feb. 1820.

[39] NRAS, 2570/120, 'John Campbell senior to William Urquhart', 1 May 1787.

[40] NLS, MS. 8795, 'Home letter book of Alexander Houston & Co.', 3 Dec. 1777, p. 138.

[41] Senex, *Glasgow: Past and Present*, vol. iii (Glasgow, 1884), p. 109.

[42] GCA, TD1683/1/1, 'Abstract of the GWIA', pp. 59b–61.

[43] 'Line of packets', *Glasgow Herald*, 1 Nov. 1824, p. 3.

Capitalizing the trades

Given the extraordinary costs, a partnership in a Glasgow-West India firm was an opportunity usually restricted to wealthy younger men. As noted above, the introduction of the younger generation by established merchants was of major importance as a substantial transfer of capital underpinned the rise of the trades. In the case of John Campbell senior & Co., as individuals died or retired, they were replaced by younger family members who were provided with aid to join the business: the number of co-partners remained almost constant throughout the lifecycle of the firm. There were five between 1790 and 1812, six up to 1828 and seven up to 1841. The sharp increase in levels of capital stock underwrote the dramatic rise of the firm: a total of £40,000 was invested in 1790, peaking at £180,000 (among seven partners) in 1828 and declining to £50,000 (among five partners) in 1841.[44] The partnership structure, capital stock and share price of John Campbell, senior, & Co. suggest it was typical of elite firms in Glasgow. For example, in 1806, Dennistoun, Buchanan & Co. had eight co-partners with a capital stock of £175,000. The cost of a share in this firm was just over £2,000 (compared to £1,000 per share in John Campbell senior & Co., as noted below).[45] The capital stock in these two firms exceeded the capitalization of Glasgow firms (*c*.30) trading with the Chesapeake between 1740 and 1789, with the exception of the premier tobacco firm, Alexander Speirs & Co.[46]

Glasgow-West India firms required greater capital than their tobacco predecessors, so where did it come from? The start-up capital for the West India trades in Glasgow was sourced locally, albeit underpinned by wealth derived from slavery economies. The main sources of wealth were three-fold: patrimonial inheritance, marriage 'tochers' (Scots for dowry) and colonial sojourns. The evidence here quantifies the importance of practices previously noted by T. M. Devine.[47] While merchants in London and Bristol hailed mainly from a background in the West India trades, Glasgow's colonial elite evolved across generations, shifting commercial focus from tobacco to sugar, reinvesting capital and increasing wealth.[48] As described in

---

[44] GCA, TD1696, 'Campbell of Hallyards' papers.

[45] University of Glasgow, Special Collections, MS. Murray 605, 'Minute book of Dennistoun, Buchanan, & Co. Glasgow, 1806–42', p. 4.

[46] J. Price, *Capital and Credit in British Overseas Trade: The View from the Chesapeake, 1700–1776* (Cambridge and London, 1980), pp. 151–6.

[47] Devine, 'An eighteenth-century business elite', p. 47.

[48] K. Morgan, 'Bristol West India merchants in the eighteenth century', in *Transactions of the Royal Historical Society*, 6th series, iii (London, 1993), p. 189; R. Sheridan, *Sugar and Slavery: An Economic History of the British West Indies 1623–1775* (Kingston).

the last chapter, over half of the known fathers of the West India elite were previously involved with the colonial trades in Glasgow. Some fathers had been involved with the Virginia trades, although there were twice as many second-generation West India merchants.[49]

The intergenerational transfer of capital, as well as knowledge, skills and contacts, between sugar dynasties was of central importance. Patrimonial support – both *inter-vivos* and post-mortem – provided the most significant source of start-up capital for West India merchants. A sample of probate material of ten mercantile patriarchs who promoted their sons into business – including a lesser rank merchant, David Connell – suggested these cash gifts ranged from £1,250 to £10,000.[50] Inheritance was sometimes offered by fathers for start-up capital before death. In his settlement of 1819 – six years before his death – James McInroy of Lude left explicit instructions for his sons, who were to receive one-third more than their sisters and it to be made immediately available 'in event of marriage or towards an establishment in business'.[51] In time, James Patrick McInroy became a successful West India merchant in his own right. But the commercial passage of rites from youth to merchant was dependent on behaviour. As a nineteen-year-old in 1801, Colin Campbell was warned that the attainment of a co-partnership in the family firm was contingent on his father, John Campbell senior, being of the opinion that his son's conduct 'continues to deserve such transfer being made in his favour'.[52] He evidently behaved himself and inherited four shares worth £4,000 (at £1,000 per share) on 27 January 1803, three weeks after he turned twenty-one.[53] As part of a patrimonial inheritance strategy in his settlement of 1802, John Campbell senior topped up Colin's inheritance with a further £6,000. His other two sons, Thomas and James, were also to be bequeathed £10,000 on his death after deducting 'any sums of money…for the purpose of putting them in business or advancing them in the world and which I may enter as debts against them in my Books'. Thus, on his death in 1807, over half his total wealth passed to his sons, all of whom became successful merchants.[54] As sons were groomed for commercial

---

[49] The occupation of fathers was known for approximately 117 individuals. Of this group of fathers, 69 (51%) were previously involved with colonial trades in Glasgow. Forty-four fathers were involved with West India commerce as merchants and planters (37% of known group) and were more important than the Chesapeake trades (16, or 14%).

[50] Of 10 identified wills and settlements of fathers whose sons went into the West India trades in Glasgow, 9 provided substantial provision for sons – ranging from £1,250 to £10,000 – with 5 wills and testaments explicitly mentioning stock in a West India firm.

[51] NRS, SC49/31/5, 'Inventory of James MacInroy', 8 July 1826, pp. 537–8.

[52] GCA, TD1696, 'Contract of co-partnership', 1801, pp. 4–5.

[53] GCA, TD1696, 'John Campbell senior & Co., minute book', 27 Jan. 1803, p. 3.

[54] NRS, SC36/48/3, 'Inventory of John Campbell senior', 3 Oct. 1808, p. 59.

careers by fathers in the same business, a significant transfer of colonial capital followed commensurate with the extent of the business and personal wealth.

Second, West India merchants, once well-established, consolidated their position with strategic and highly profitable marriages. These pairings connected members of the elite and brought substantial fortunes to the marriage, sometimes from both sets of parents, which eventually trickled down the family line.[55] As noted in the last chapter, the Glasgow-West India elites tended to marry within the mercantile community of the west of Scotland. In this study, occupations of fathers of the brides married to the Glasgow-West India elites were known for sixty-seven marriages. Over half were to daughters of other merchants, especially those involved with colonial trades.[56] Daughters of 'tobacco lords' were the most popular choice, although the children of West India merchants regularly intermarried too. In 1814, Janet Hamilton, daughter of William Hamilton of Northpark, married Colin Campbell, son of West India merchant John Campbell senior and already a co-partner in his father's firm. For her marriage, Janet was gifted £2,000 by her father and £4,000 by her mother, Helen Bogle, herself a daughter of a 'tobacco lord', Archibald Bogle. The tocher was topped up to £6,600 from the residue of Janet's maternal grandfather's estate.[57] In this case, capital generated across successive phases of Glasgow's colonial past flowed through three elite families via inheritance and marriage: from Bogle to Hamilton then resting with Campbell. However, this tocher seems to have been at the higher end of the scale: other examples in this period provided by colonial merchants in Glasgow range from £2,500 to £5,000.[58] Thus, marital gifts among these elites were enough to acquire a share in a West India firm in Glasgow, though it is very likely they more often added to the existing interests of established merchants rather than assisted new starts in business. And since almost a third of the West India elite married

[55] K. Barclay, *Love, Intimacy and Power: Marriage and Patriarchy in Scotland, 1650–1850* (Manchester, 2011), p. 83.

[56] Occupations of fathers of the brides were known for 67 marriages. In the west of Scotland: Glasgow 'Tobacco lords' (12, or 17% of known marriages); Glasgow merchants (11, or 16%); Glasgow-West India merchants (10, or 15%); Greenock merchants (2); Glasgow cotton, and East India merchant (1 occurrence each). Thus, 56% (38 of 67) of known fathers hailed from within the west of Scotland mercantile community. But almost a third had no known connections to West India trades: Laird (4), Church (3), legal professions (3), politicians (3), surgeon (2), university elite (2) and medicine (2).

[57] NRS, SC36/51/8, 'Trust disposition of John Hamilton of Northpark', 6 Nov. 1829, p. 57.

[58] Devine, *Tobacco Lords*, p. 92; 'An eighteenth-century business elite', p. 47; GCA, TD1/18, 'Contract of marriage between John McCall and Isabella Smith', 1 Oct. 1803.

daughters of families with no known connections to the colonial trades, the middling ranks of Scotland also contributed an influx of capital to the Glasgow-West India trades.

The legal supremacy of husbands was entrenched in Scottish matrimonial property law throughout this period, which has implications for the intended use of tochers.[59] Strategies are sometimes revealed in the marriage contracts of the West India elite. Typically paid in cash, they were often placed at the use of the merchant. On his marriage in 1819 over Janet Hamilton (the daughter of former Lord Provost Gilbert Hamilton), John Gordon's marriage contract provided him 'with full power' over his wife's £1,000 tocher.[60] And if women (or their fathers) did not stipulate use for the tocher it automatically became the property of the husband under the Scots law of *jus mariti*, that is, the right of the husband to administer his wife's goods during the marriage.[61] Thus, high-value colonial tochers provided a significant stream of capital for the Glasgow-West India trades, while Scots law often placed the funds in the hands of merchants.

Third, capital from successful sojourns – 'new' colonial fortunes – was invested in West India firms in Glasgow. In 1789, absentee planter William Urquhart of Craigston, who owned a cotton plantation in Carriacou, recommended a potential co-partner to John Campbell senior & Co.:

> Mr Willm Cumine…has been regularly bred to Business when he was a very young man, he first went out to Mr Glassford's Stores in Virginia… he afterwards went out to Jamaica as a Clerk…he has made something considerable during his stay in Jamaica where he was well known & universally esteemed, but as he did not keep his health so well there he wishes…to form some safe connection in Business in this Country and for that purpose he goes to Glasgow to see if he can do anything with his Capital or form any profitable partnership there…I therefore take the liberty of introducing him to you & recommending him to your good offices if you should hear or know of anything that should fall in with his plans. I shall only add that if I did not thoroughly know his worth, integrity & honour, I would not have presumed to recommend him to your services.[62]

[59] A. McCrum, 'Inheritance and the family: the Scottish urban experience in the 1820s', in *Urban Fortunes: Property and Inheritance in the Town, 1700–1900*, ed. J. Stobart and A. Owens (Aldershot, 2000), pp. 152–5.

[60] NRS, SC36/51/7, 'Trust disposition and marriage contract of John Gordon', p. 930.

[61] D. M. Forte, 'Some aspects of the law in Scotland: 1500–1700', in *Marriage and Property*, ed. E. Craik (Aberdeen, 1984), p. 111.

[62] NRAS, 2570/120, 'Letter from William Urquhart', 16 Oct. 1789.

Although unable to employ the budding West India merchant, John Campbell senior's amiable response that Cumine (probably from Aberdeen) was 'very deserving' suggests capital from outside the established mercantile community could make its way into the West India trades in Glasgow.[63] It is unknown if Cumine succeeded, although many others did. As noted above, twenty-eight Glasgow-West India merchants were known to have been in the colonies as younger men. In identifying that over half of Glasgow's West India merchants had direct or familial connections to the colonial trades, mainly West India commerce, this points to the major source of the capital that underwrote the city's Caribbean trades.[64]

Credit and the trades

The provision of credit was instrumental to the West India trades. S. G. Checkland outlined a transatlantic financial system that connected Great Britain and the colonies through West India paper. This paper was used by resident planters as currency to pay merchants and it was drawn on London West India acceptance houses, which guaranteed payment. The capital 'stood at the centre of this web of trade' and linked firms in the outports of Bristol, Liverpool and Glasgow.[65] The merchants then shipped the produce to Great Britain and the proceeds were used to reduce planters' debts. Checkland's study naturally placed London at the centre of the web. Joseph Inikori pointed to the importance of the slave economy in the development of English financial institutions. In doing so, Inikori noted the influence of provincial credit markets, although the Anglo-centric focus of the work ignored the Scottish dimension.[66] This section illuminates the credit that underpinned Glasgow's West India trades, arguing that London finance was a minor influence compared to provincial lenders.

Writing to his attorney in November 1827, Colin Campbell discussed the credit situation in Glasgow. At this point, his firm, John Campbell senior & Co, had begun to restrict their outgoings. Another West India merchant in Glasgow, Colin Campbell of Jura, was aware of the situation

---

[63] NRAS, 2570/122, 'Letter from John Campbell senior', 16 March 1790.

[64] Seventy-seven of the 150 (51%) Glasgow-West India elite had direct or kinship connections to the Atlantic world. Tochers added further colonial capital. Given the occupation of fathers, the rest of the capital is likely to have been sourced from the middling ranks: lairds, military, the church.

[65] S. G. Checkland, 'Finance for the West Indies, 1780–1815', *The Economic History Review*, new series, x (1958), 461–9, at p. 467.

[66] J. Inikori, *Africans and the Industrial Revolution in England: A Study in International Trade and Economic Development* (Cambridge, 2002), p. 360.

and offered credit on high terms, although this did not meet the approval of the partners:

> The House here are well accustomed to similar offers, but they usually reject them, unless the applicants have some claim to a favourable reception, and without any disrespect…if money is wanted & can be applied to legitimate & advantageous purpose, we must try to find it without having recourse to such expensive int[erest]s which are liable to give inconvenience.[67]

Intra-mercantile credit could play an important role in career trajectories. Merchants regularly provided short- and long-term credit to each other: such transactions had a mostly 'beneficial effect', as the advancement of surplus capital promoted enterprise and stimulated the economy.[68] In the evidence here, the Glasgow-West India community loaned to other firms and to individuals, which kickstarted mercantile careers. In turn, creditors collected returns on loans that had been made to usually secure debtors.

It was common for West India merchants to supply credit. Analysis of 105 confirmation inventories generated on the death of the Glasgow-West India merchants (between 1800 and 1903) reveals the nature and extent of the web of mercantile credit in the city (see Table 2.1).[69] Almost half of all inventories on death contained references to over 240 instruments of outlying credit – bills, bonds, promissory notes – totalling £415,123 (12 per cent of the overall wealth held by the Glasgow-West India elite in Scotland). For comparison, the average paid capital of provincial banking companies in Scotland in 1810 was £31,000.[70] In other words, the nineteenth-century Glasgow-West India elite loaned the capital of around thirteen provincial banks, with just over a quarter of the loans made to other West India merchants. The implications of the outlying credit will be fully explored in the final chapter of this study, while this section focuses on one subset of the loans: credit loaned among the Glasgow-West India community (£112,748, or 27.2 per cent of total outlying credit).

The absence of detail in the inventories (interest rates or date of agreements are not always recorded) prevents a comprehensive analysis, but other insights are revealed. On occasion, merchants offered short-term credit to other West India firms. This could take the form of accepting bills

---

[67] GCA, TD1696, 'Private letter book, J. C. Senr. & Co., 1827–1847', p. 49.

[68] R. Olegario, *A Culture of Credit: Embedding Trust and Transparency in American Business* (Cambridge and London, 2006), p. 17.

[69] This study has identified confirmation inventories of 105 West India merchants (active in Glasgow between 1775 and 1838) who died between 1800 and 1903. See Appendix.

[70] C. Munn, *The Scottish Provincial Banking Companies, 1747–1864* (Edinburgh, 1981), p. 105.

Table 2.1 Debtors, and debts owed, to the Glasgow-
West India elite between 1805 and 1879.

Debtors	No. loans	% Total	Value	% Total
West India firms and merchants (Glasgow)	42	17.4%	£112,748	27.2%
Familial loans	26	10.8%	£74,733	18.0%
Industrialists and their firms	25	10.4%	£57,228	13.8%
Unknown	84	34.9%	£54,473	13.1%
Aristocracy	7	2.9%	£44,079	10.6%
Gentry and landowners	15	6.2%	£32,944	7.9%
General merchants and firms	30	12.4%	£26,930	6.5%
West India firms and merchants (abroad)	7	2.9%	£8,199	2.0%
Scottish legal profession	5	2.1%	£3,789	0.9%
Total	**241**		**£415,123**	

Source: National Records of Scotland: Wills, Testaments and
Confirmation Inventories (see Bibliography).

of exchange (effectively a short-term loan, as will be explained below). In 1825, James McInroy accepted bills totalling over £2,800 intended for the firm Robert Bogle junior & Co.[71] In general, however, the pattern was one of wealthy co-partners loaning capital to firms they had personal investments in or firms in which relatives were partners. The partners of Leitch & Smith were especially proficient at utilizing kinship resources to advance the various family firms. Senior partner James Smith of Craighead loaned over £20,000 to his firm – with interest – which was the single largest West India loan identified in this study and one that remained outstanding on his death in 1815.[72]

West India merchants were more likely to take advantage of credit from within the family matrix than other merchants in the Glasgow-West India community with no kinship connections, a process which advanced careers at different stages.[73] Yet, borrowing from other merchants with no familial connections was not unknown. Over a two-year period from 1814, John

[71] NRS, SC49/31/5, 'Inventory of James MacInroy', 8 July 1826, pp. 554.

[72] NRS, SC36/48/9, 'Inventory of James Smith', 9 June 1815, pp. 685–6.

[73] Almost exactly half of all identified intra-mercantile loans were to close kinfolk especially sons, brothers and nephews. For example, John Campbell senior, Archibald Smith of Jordanhill, John Smith of Craigend, Robert Hagart, John Hamilton of Northpark, James Smith of Craighead, Colin Campbell of Colgrain and David Connell were all owed money by family members on death.

Gordon, lead partner in Stirling, Gordon & Co., borrowed over £10,000 from a partner of the same firm, John Stirling of Kippendavie. Later, on 2 May 1826, Gordon loaned over £5,000 on bond to younger men (and partners in a seemingly rival firm) Alexander Campbell and Mungo Nutter Campbell. In later life, Mungo Nutter Campbell loaned credit to the gentry and landowners.[74] Thus, the West India firms of Glasgow were connected by marital and kinship connections which underpinned a web of mercantile capital and credit across, and within, several different firms. In this way, colonial capital was recycled: a process that invigorated the Scottish economy over the long term.

While the above loans seem to have been unsecured, merchants with landed estates or urban properties possessed valuable collateral which allowed more ambitious borrowing. In *An Inquiry into the Nature and Causes of the Wealth of Nations* (1776) Adam Smith famously concluded that:

> A merchant is accustomed to employing his money chiefly in profitable projects, whereas a mere country gentleman is accustomed to employing it chiefly in expense. The former often sees his money go from him and return with a profit; the latter seldom expects to see his money again once he has parted with it. Those different habits naturally affect their temperament and disposition in every sort of business. A merchant is commonly a bold undertaker, a country gentleman a timid one. The one is not afraid to lay out a great deal of capital all at once on the improvement of his land if he has a good chance of raising the value of the land in proportion to the expense.[75]

This high praise is generally regarded as evidence of the influence of colonial merchants upon agricultural 'improvement' in Scotland after 1760.[76] Yet, Smith also noted the practices that underpinned the success: 'mercantile business naturally gives a merchant habits of order, economy and attention, which make him much fitter to carry out any project of improvement with profit and success'.[77]

---

[74] NRS, CC6/5/33, 'Inventory of John Stirling', 14 Sept. 1818, p. 540; NRS, SC36/48/21, 'Inventory of John Gordon of Aikenhead', 11 Aug. 1828, p. 619; NRS, CC9/7/84, 'Inventory of Mungo Nutter Campbell', p. 271.

[75] A. Smith, *Wealth of Nations*, bk. III ch. IV: 'On the different progress of opulence in different nations <https://www.marxists.org/reference/archive/smith-adam/works/wealth-of-nations/book03/ch04.htm> [accessed 5 June 2022].

[76] T. M. Devine, 'Glasgow colonial merchants and land, 1770–1815', in *Land and Industry: The Landed Estate and the Industrial Revolution*, ed. J. T. Ward and R. G. Wilson (Newton Abbot, 1971), p. 205.

[77] Smith, *Wealth of Nations*, bk. III ch. IV.

It is possible to recreate aspects of the West India merchants' 'habits of economy' by examining Scotland's Register of Sasines, as they systematically used land as collateral in credit dealings. Among other things, these records list conveyancing details such as the legal transfers of land, as well as encumbrances secured upon property.[78] Examination of sasines for six counties across the west-central region reveals the extent of West India land-ownership as well as sources of credit. Table 2.2 lists patterns of West India estate ownership alongside credit secured on both landed and urban properties. As will be covered in Chapter 8, seventy-five West India merchants owned 133 landed estates with some owning estates, across multiple counties (see Table 2.2). Between 1775 and 1840, West India proprietors agreed eighty transactions – secured mainly via bonds – worth a total of £298,296 (average £3,728), hereafter described as 'sasine loans'. Thus, West India merchants sourced credit from individuals resident in Scotland (71 per cent), with 20 per cent sourced in England and the remainder from America and the West Indies.

West India commerce was thus embedded across west of Scotland society, although sasine loans were most often secured on property in the Barony of Glasgow. This is unsurprising given the extent of West India merchants living in the district. Patrick Playfair of Dalmarnock was among the top borrowers of all. Playfair's mercantile business was focused on Antigua, and by 1807, he was successful enough to purchase Dalmarnock estate in the Barony. Over the next twelve years, the estate was used as collateral to secure credit of £29,600, including from John Buchanan of Ardoch, a landed MP. In 1816, Playfair took advantage of Caribbean networks and borrowed £6,000 on bond from James Crichton, a sojourner recently returned from Antigua.[79] But not all were secured upon large estates like Dalmarnock. Around 10 per cent by value of the sasine loans was secured upon small urban properties (also mainly in the Barony). Rural estates, as well as urban property, provided security for credit dealings with lenders who helped subsidize Glasgow's West India trades.

As Glasgow-West India elites began to acquire property after 1783, borrowing obviously increased. The peak era for West India proprietary borrowing was the 1810s, with 30 per cent of loans by value secured in this decade alone. This is no coincidence, as there were credit shortages in this

---

[78] As merchants also used urban property and small estates as collateral for lending, a broader approach is required than adopted in the seminal study of colonial landownership (which only analysed estates of 500-plus acres). See Devine, 'Glasgow colonial merchants and land, 1770–1815', p. 207. R. Rodger and J. Newman, 'Property transfers and the register of Sasines: urban development in Scotland since 1617', *Urban History Yearbook*, xv (1988), 49–57.

[79] GCA, T-SA 5/1/2, Glasgow (Barony and Regality) 1809–1820, 7251, 7831, 10748, 12509.

Table 2.2 The West India elite's landed estates and borrowing secured upon property, 1775–1840.

County	W.I. estate owners	No. estates	Credit secured on properties
Argyllshire	5	8	£11,000
Ayrshire	10	12	£17,846
Barony of Glasgow	23	30	£158,300
Dunbartonshire	13	20	£70,550
Lanarkshire	17	21	£8,500
Peebles	2	5	n/a
Perth	3	3	n/a
Renfrewshire	12	14	£32,100
Stirling	11	18	n/a
Wigtown	1	1	n/a
Unknown	1	1	n/a
Totals	75 individuals (98 incidences)	133	£298,296

Source: Abridgements of sasines held in Glasgow City Archives, T-SA 1/1 Argyll (vol. i, 1781–1820; vol. ii, 1821–50); GCA, T-SA 2/1 Ayr (vol. i, 1781–1806; vol. ii, 1806–20; vol. iii, 1821–30; vol. iv, 1831–40); GCA, T-SA 4/1 Dunbartonshire (vol. i, 1781–1820; vol. ii, 1821–30; vol. iii, 1831–40); GCA, T-SA 5/1 Glasgow (Barony and Regality) (vol. i, 1781–1808; vol. ii, 1809–20; vol. iii, 1821–30; vol. iv, 1831–40); GCA, T-SA 6/1 Lanarkshire (vol. i, 1781–20; vol. ii, 1821–30; vol. iii, 1831–40); GCA, T-SA 7/1 Renfrewshire (vol. i, 1781–1807; vol. ii, 1807–20; vol. iii, 1821–30; vol. iv, 1831–40).

period. Banks refused to discount bills during financial crises in Scotland in 1809–12, 1815 and 1818–19, partially due to Napoleon's Berlin and Milan decrees (which closed off parts of Europe to British traders).[80] Bonds secured on land were a more flexible source of credit that has been previously considered. It took West India proprietors eleven years, on average, from purchasing a landed estate to secure credit upon it. However, in the sasine

---

[80] J. Butt, 'The Scottish cotton industry during the Industrial Revolution, 1780–1840', in *Comparative Aspects of Scottish and Irish Economic and Social History, 1600–1900*, ed. L. M. Cullen and T. C. Smout (Edinburgh, 1977), p. 124; S. G. Checkland, *Scottish Banking: A History, 1695–1973* (Glasgow, 1975), pp. 403–5.

loans examined here, 20 per cent of West India proprietors sourced credit secured upon a landed estate the same year they purchased it.[81]

West India proprietors occasionally borrowed from the University of Glasgow (the institution operated as a de facto landlord in the city, also collecting tithe income from agricultural revenues from local parishes).[82] The Register of Sasines also reveals that banks and bankers provided credit (approximately 15 per cent of overall value of sasine loans), including English bankers. In the 1790s, Mark Sprott of London, a prominent stockbroker associated with Coutts, provided £18,000 of credit to elite mercantile families, the Malcolms of Poltalloch and Houstons of Jordanhill.[83] While individuals in London were an important source (15 per cent), over half by value of sasine loans were secured in the west of Scotland. Glasgow was the main source of credit – 28 per cent by value – followed by individuals in Edinburgh (11 per cent). The largest group of lenders hailed in the west of Scotland included other West India merchants (£31,000), trustees of accounts (£26,750), the general mercantile community (£1,695) and 'tobacco lords' (£8,000). Those with capital in Scottish society viewed bonds secured on land as a reliable investment, while West India proprietors were quick to seize the opportunities. A minority of the credit was secured from those involved with the East India Company, such as Major Gen. Thomas Geils, who loaned £900 to John Alston junior of Westerton in 1813.[84] Women, especially widows, were an important credit source (with over 10 per cent of sasine loans by value) for West India proprietors. As women came of age, their inheritance or capital associated with marriage contracts was sometimes loaned to West India proprietors, no doubt with the assumption that lucrative returns would support gentry women across their lives.[85] In this way, a broad section of Scottish society became financially complicit with the integrated West India economy and received income from Caribbean slavery that they would otherwise have had no direct connection to.

---

[81] Bonds secured on landed estates with defined dates of acquisition are known in 44 cases, facilitating the analysis between date of purchase of land with date of credit borrowing.

[82] S. Mullen, 'British universities and transatlantic slavery: the University of Glasgow case', *History Workshop Journal*, xci (2021), 210–33.

[83] GCA, T-SA 4/1/1, 'Dunbartonshire 1781–1820', 744; GCA, T-SA 5/1/1, 'Glasgow (Barony and Regality), 1781–1808', 3188; GCA, T-SA 7/1/1, 'Renfrewshire, 1781–1807', 5348.

[84] GCA, T-SA 4/1/1, 'Dunbartonshire, 1781–1820', 2411.

[85] Alongside nieces Margaret and Janet, Glasgow merchant Laurence Coulter loaned £1,000 to Andrew Houston of Jordanhill in 1789, although, given the failure of Alexander Houston & Co. in the next decade, this was not as secure as they might have imagined. See GCA, T-SA /1/1, 'Renfrewshire, 1781–1807', 2424.

Sasine loans often reveal symbolic transfers: from the Virginia to West India trades, and from commercial to industrial capitalism. In August 1787, Robert Bogle purchased Daldowie estate in the Barony of Glasgow and within three months had secured £4,000 from William Cunninghame of Lainshaw, one of the city's famous tobacco lords.[86] The Register of Sasines reveals the hitherto unknown role of James Watt (1736–1819), the 'great improver' of the steam engine that powered the British Industrial Revolution, as a financier of West India commerce. On 13 May 1793, 'James Watt, Engineer, Heathfield near Birmingham' loaned £8,700 to James Dennistoun junior and James Dennistoun senior, both West India merchants in Glasgow, secured upon Dunbartonshire and Stirlingshire estates.[87] The debt was reconfirmed in his son's name in 1828, almost a decade after Watt's death, identifying this as a long-term debt.[88] Watt was commercially involved with his father's mercantile business in 1760s Glasgow, although his stance towards the abolition of Atlantic slavery in later life remains ambiguous.[89] However, it is now clear he was complicit in the Atlantic slavery economy for most of his adult life. The evidence here reveals he transacted with Glasgow-West India merchants in the 1790s, an era when slavery was increasingly condemned as an odious evil by many in British society. Although Watt is on record as refusing any role in financing the Boulton & Watt firm, it seems very likely that interest from this loan subsidized the famous engineer's final years before he died in 1819. This was a symbolic transfer of profits from Caribbean slavery to the developer of the steam engine – the invention that powered industrial capitalism. These examples underline just how much the West India elite's estates helped embed the profits of Caribbean slavery across British society in general and the west of Scotland in particular.

Financial institutions also played a key role in financing West India merchants. The Royal Bank was a chartered bank located in Edinburgh, although it provided funding for Glasgow's commercial firms throughout the eighteenth century. In 1751, for example, the bank funded twenty-four firms involved with the Chesapeake tobacco trade.[90] As the West India merchants rose to economic prominence after the American Revolution,

---

[86] GCA, T-SA 5/1/1, 'Glasgow (Barony and Regality), 1781–1808', 867, 890.

[87] GCA, T-SA 4/1/1 'Dunbartonshire, 1781–1820', 736. 'James Dennistoun of Dennistoun', Legacies of British slavery database <http://wwwdepts-live.ucl.ac.uk/lbs/person/view/2146642451> [accessed 29 July 2021].

[88] GCA, T-SA 4/1/2, 'Dunbartonshire, 1821–1830', 907.

[89] Heriot-Watt University, for example, claims that 'Watt's feelings on slavery are ambiguous and perhaps changed during his lifetime'. 'Origins of our name: James Watt' <https://www.hw.ac.uk/uk/about/history/origins-of-our-name.htm> [accessed 28 Oct. 2021].

[90] Price, *Capital and Credit*, p. 65.

the commercial relationship similarly developed.[91] The Royal Bank opened its first branch in Glasgow in 1783 and the location in the commercial centre near the Tontine Rooms fostered close relationships with the city's colonial elite. From the bank's point of view, this was fortunate timing, as international developments created opportunity and the Royal Bank ultimately became the premier lenders to the West India merchants of Glasgow.

In early 1793, the ongoing war with Revolutionary France created a run on banks (a sudden withdrawal of finance by customers) in Glasgow which left several institutions in financial difficulty.[92] At this time, West India merchant George McCall noted Glasgow merchants depended on local insurance underwriters due to favourable costs and to limit risk. 'The premiums here I may almost safely say never exceed the merch[ant]s at London, & people here prefer having the Insurance done by Underwriters with whose circumstances they are acquainted rather than send their orders to London.'[93] Although there is little evidence to test his claim, other developments underline Glasgow's status as a commercial hub in its own right. As the news about the run on banks spread quickly among the mercantile community, the crisis rippled across the Atlantic world. In April that year, George McCall informed his future son-in-law, then in London, John Tailyour – a wealthy trafficker in enslaved people just returned to Great Britain – that the Arms Bank of Glasgow (a provincial bank) was in trouble. This had implications for those the bank financed, especially 'foreign traders…[who] pushed business so far beyond their capital' as well as those they supplied. Indeed, McCall dreaded the 'consequences of such numbers of weavers & c. being thrown out of employ[men]t', underlining how much the Glasgow economy depended on Atlantic slavery.[94] Four West India merchant firms were said to be in danger of failure, including John Campbell senior & Co. Around this period, the firm stopped payments to creditors who owned cotton estates in Carriacou (although the firm eventually recovered to become one of the most successful of its type).[95] The Arms Bank was not so lucky and failed alongside another private bank, that of A. G. and A. Thomson. The Royal Bank took advantage of the banking

[91] N. Munro, *The History of the Royal Bank of Scotland* (Edinburgh, 1928), p. 149; Anon., 'The rise of Glasgow's West Indian trade, 1793–1818', *Three Banks Review*, xli (1961), 34–44; Anon., 'An early Glasgow-West Indian miscellany', *Three Banks Review*, xliv (1962), 29–43.

[92] Munn, *Scottish Provincial Banking Companies*, p. 49.

[93] WCL, 'Tailyour family papers', Box 3, 1 March 1793.

[94] WCL, 'Tailyour family papers', Box 3, 27 April 1793.

[95] NRAS, 2570/130, 'William Arbuthnot to William Urquhart', 19 June 1793.

crisis of 1793. With the Thistle Bank, it was reckoned to be the only bank in Glasgow that discounted bills during the crisis.[96]

In the longer term, the Royal Bank came to finance several Glasgow-West India firms, including John Campbell senior & Co. In turn, the Glasgow-West India elites held substantial deposits and stock in the Royal Bank, which underpinned a symbiotic relationship.[97] In his study of Scottish provincial banks, Charles Munn dated the origins of their decline to 1810.[98] By the 1830s, one historian claimed the Royal was the busiest branch outside of London and customer demand for capital on loan has been cited as one reason for its spectacular success.[99] Loans could be long term: the firm of Geo. & Robt. Dennistoun & Co. received £20,000 in a promissory note in January 1821.[100] It seems, however, that the provision of short-term rather than long-term credit was most common. The Royal Bank sometimes provided finance for speculation in the Americas, while the West India magnates relied heavily on the bank for discounts on bills of exchange.[101]

Cash credit accounts were especially important. Analogous to modern overdrafts, they required personal guarantees ratified by the head office in Edinburgh.[102] Examination of directors' minute books reveal West India merchants and related firms were provided with cash accounts of up to £59,000 between 1783 and 1833.[103] The majority (£55,000) was made available to thirteen separate firms: this was a dramatic increase from the mid eighteenth century, when the Royal Bank made available to Glasgow's tobacco firms cash accounts valued at £15,000.[104] Moreover, this seems to have been much more than accounts awarded to cotton manufacturers of the same period.[105] The awarding of cash accounts was closely tied to the status of West India firms and most likely the personal wealth of partners; five of the top seven ranking firms in the Glasgow West India Association

---

[96] WCL, 'Tailyour family papers', Box 3, 27 April 1793.

[97] Of the 105 confirmation inventories of Glasgow-West India elite identified for this study, 27 of 59 investors in Scottish banks (45% of sample) held investments in the Royal Bank (£176,946 of £830,737 overall held in banks, or 21%).

[98] Munn, *Scottish Provincial Banking Companies*, p. 80.

[99] Munro, *Royal Bank of Scotland*, p. 150.

[100] NWGA, RB/12/18, 'Directors minutes', 1820–1824', f.38.

[101] Checkland, *Scottish Banking*, p. 229–30.

[102] Munn, *Scottish Provincial Banking Companies*, p. 48, pp. 115–21.

[103] The analysis here is based on NWGA, RB/12, 'Directors minutes', 1780–1833, vols. xiii–xxi. Thirteen firms were provided with cash accounts, and 6 individuals.

[104] Price, *Capital and Credit in British Overseas Trade*, p. 65.

[105] Checkland, *Scottish Banking*, p. 230.

in 1807 were funded. Cash accounts ranged from the £500 available to Campbell, Rivers & Co. in 1802 to the £6,000 made available to Robert Bogle & Co. in 1818.[106] These accounts were used again and again, meaning the true extent of credit is unquantifiable. However, it does not appear that West India firms were the bank's main customers. A Royal Bank committee in 1818 concluded it was mainly manufacturers – not merchants – who used the high-value cash accounts of between £50,000 and £300,000 per annum, mainly to pay employees.[107]

Commercial reputation was an important indicator of creditworthiness, and the bank implemented a sophisticated intelligence-gathering system. The Royal Bank branch in Glasgow collected information about the 'good credit' of potential customers in the city, which was sent to Gilbert Innes of Stow, a director in Edinburgh.[108] Furthermore, personal obligations – effectively a guarantee to the bank by another individual, thus acting as an assurance of financial health – were required to attain credit. Such obligations evidently had more authority if potential applicants were recommended by others of the same commercial class as they had detailed knowledge of their status.[109] Indeed, in the cash accounts examined with the Royal Bank, West India merchants provided personal obligations. Many of the merchants, such as the Smiths of Jordanhill, relied upon family networks to sign these bonds, while others, such as Haddow & Dale, preferred to rely upon business associates. The credit relationship could extend to the colonies: in March 1829, Robert Bogle 'merchant in Jamaica' was provided with a cash account of £2,000 (which could be accessed by business associates in Glasgow) after an obligation by Hugh Bogle of Calderbank.[110] However, security – either on heritable property or the wealth of nominees – was more important than commercial reputations in acquiring access to credit.

The system of discounting bills of exchange also increased the purchasing power of West India merchants.[111] Munn noted bills of exchange were ubiquitous in eighteenth-century finance and acted as both a document of debt and an instrument of credit.[112] A seller of goods drew up a bill

---

[106] NWGA, RB/12/15, 13 Jan. 1802, n.p.; RB/12/17, 20 May 1818, fo. 98.

[107] NWGA, RB/12/17, 'Directors minutes', 1817 –1820, fo. 136.

[108] NRS, GD113/5/19c/23, 'Glasgow copartnery with N. Morris', Dec. 1810.

[109] Munn, *Scottish Provincial Banking Companies*, p. 117.

[110] NWGA, RB/12/20, 'Directors minutes', 1827–30, fo. 125.

[111] P. Hudson, 'Slavery, the slave trade and economic growth: a contribution to the debate', in *Emancipation and the Remaking of the British Imperial World*, ed. C. Hall, N. Draper and K. McClelland (Manchester, 2014), pp. 40–9.

[112] Munn, *Scottish Provincial Banking Companies*, pp. 121–2.

of exchange payable on a certain date (eg ninety days) which was signed (accepted) by the purchaser and retained by the seller. The purchaser would then sell goods in that period, giving time to credit an account and pay the bill when presented. The practice of discounting bills acted as another form of credit for West India merchants. The bank discounted (or 'bought') bills of exchange before they were mature, for which they paid the value of the bills minus interest and commission. These sums could be substantial. For example, in 1831, MacQueen, McDonnell & Co. discounted bills to a value of £10,000.[113] This practice was not restricted to the Royal Bank. In this period, the Bank of Scotland, which opened a branch in Glasgow in 1802, was the second largest discounter of bills in the west of Scotland.[114] But by 1810, the Royal Bank agency discounted a full-third more bills by value compared to their Bank of Scotland counterparts in Glasgow. Together, they discounted most of the bills in the city.[115]

When ready for payment, the bank presented the bills (sometimes in London or Edinburgh), allowing three days for payment. If the bill went unpaid, it was 'protested', which was the legal process required to ensure payment. In one case in 1810, the Royal Bank of Scotland 'employed' the West India firm of Campbell, Rivers & Co. to 'recover payment and interest on Bill of Exch^e' drawn by L. Nicholls of Trinidad, which subsequently went unpaid. The sum was settled by shipping six hogsheads of sugar to Scotland.[116] The bills of exchange also provided collateral for further loans, and sometimes the bills were 'renewed' – that is, the bank did not call in payment on the payment deadline, which provided an extra credit period for the purchaser.[117] Thus, the system of bills increased the fluid capital in the city in general and of the West India merchants in particular. In summary, colonial merchants, families and the wider community of the west of Scotland largely underwrote Glasgow's sugar era, and the development of a national banking infrastructure was crucial in providing short- to medium-term credit.

Credit and the Glasgow-West India trades: the case of Archibald Smith of Jordanhill

In October 1818, a Royal Bank committee that examined 'Bonds, Debts and Bills lying over at Glasgow' concluded the Glasgow branch received

---

[113] NWGA, RB/12/21, 'Directors minutes', 1830–1833, fo. 45.

[114] R. Saville, *Bank of Scotland: A History, 1695–1995* (Edinburgh, 1996), p. 187.

[115] Checkland, *Scottish Banking*, p. 229.

[116] NRS, GD113/5/19c/19, 'Memo of L. Nicholl, Trinidad debt to Royal Bank', Sept. 1810.

[117] Munn, *Scottish Provincial Banking Companies*, pp. 121–6.

a 'great mass of bills in the course of Trade' from West India merchants.[118] Information on early nineteenth-century Glasgow-West India commerce and the individuals who made it happen can be gleaned from correspondence between Robert Scott Moncrieff, joint agent of the Glasgow agency, and William Simpson, cashier of the Royal Bank in Edinburgh. In 1801, Great Britain had recently occupied Trinidad, and Clyde ports were experiencing unprecedented levels of trade with the West Indies. After the arrival of large fleets in the summer of that year, Moncrieff pointed to the rise in West India commerce and related commercial transactions: 'these cargoes when landed should help them [West India merchants] – What great doings we have here. I really think £1000 now is not more thought of than £100 was when I came here.'[119] The extensive cargoes, however, while profitable for the bank, quickly flooded the sugar market, leading to a sharp decline in prices: 'This may in part account for the increased number of Bills and increased demand for discounts – but the W. Indians...are hanging their Lugs about the price of sugar.'[120] As many ships docked together as a fleet, the demands of customs duties and related charges on merchants was high over short periods, which necessitated the requirement for short-term credit facilities. In one case, one of Archibald Smith's ships arrived and 'will take 10m [thousand] of duties from him'. Since this type of sum could have capitalized a small provincial bank, it is little wonder the demands made by West India merchants were reckoned by Robert Scott Moncrieff to be greater than the Glasgow branch could provide.[121] Nevertheless, for merchants of the proper standing, the Royal Bank provided resolute financial support.

The working relationship with the Royal Bank and the firm of Archibald Smith of Jordanhill provides an example of such banking practices. At the beginning of the nineteenth century, Smith was at the pinnacle of Glasgow's sugar aristocracy. As dean of guild of the Merchant House and leading partner of the well-established firm Leitch & Smith, Smith's impeccable commercial reputation opened doors. He had regular conversations with banking staff about his business affairs and received short-term finance, demonstrated by a note to the Glasgow office which requested an extension of his firm's credit facilities in late 1801:

> You have the last of our London money and as we have near £5000 of sugar
> duty to pay between this & 13th of next month, besides we are obliged to

---

[118] NWGA, RB/12/17, 'Directors minutes', 1817–20, fos. 135–145.

[119] NWGA, RB/837/241, 'Letter from Robert Scott Moncrieff', 8 June 1801.

[120] NWGA, RB/837/279, 'Letter from Robert Scott Moncrieff', 7 July 1801.

[121] NWGA, RB/837/815, 'Letter from Robert Scott Moncrieff', 14 Sept. 1802; Munn, *Scottish Provincial Banking Companies*, p. 105.

renew the bills of some of our sugar buyers. I must ask the favour of yours extending your discounts to £1500 or £2000 & look for two or three weeks until we can get another supply of London money which we look for both from Jamaica and Grenada by first arrivals from thence.

Before forwarding on the application to Edinburgh, Moncrieff added a postscript: 'What can we do but help thru such good People as long as we can'.[122] By way of contrast, the firm of John Campbell, senior, & Co. were refused similar terms two days later: 'we…let them know that we could discount no such sums [£1900] to them as no other asked as much even the Dean [of Guild] only 1500'.[123] Evidently, positions of local civic importance increased reputations. One popular history of Glasgow recounted how Archibald Smith visited the Royal Bank in Glasgow to ensure large-scale bills of exchanges were discounted.[124] The Simpson–Moncrieff correspondence both confirms the anecdotal relationship and outlines how Smith's extensive holdings across four firms provided further commercial leeway:

> Mr Arch Smith has been in with Mr More. He is in good spirits and says by the 1st November all will be right and we shall have more money than we shall know what to do with – it will not be easy to bring my mind to this View of matters – still no appearance of Smith from London – but still the other Parties here say there will be much more than sufficient in other 4 houses to pay all their engagements.[125]

Evidently, Archibald Smith headed an important firm which was represented in London by its associated merchant house, Smith & Lindsay. As a merchant-manufacturer, he also had industrial interests in Scotland as a co-partner in James Finlay & Co, cotton manufacturers. With Finlay, they applied to discount large-scale bills in 1803, and this was ratified by David Dale, first agent of the Royal Bank in Glasgow. Most of the balance (£8,000) was provided by the head office in Edinburgh:

> It appears to me to be of such consequence to the place, and even to the Royal Bank the support of that house as far as it can be done with perfect safety that I had no hesitation in saying to them that although we could not take it upon to us to melt so large a Sum out of our common course, we had little doubt the paper being so unquestionable you would do it.[126]

[122] NWGA, RB/837/514, 'Letter to Robert Scott Moncrieff', 28 Dec. 1801.

[123] NWGA, RB/837/519, 'Letter to Robert Scott Moncrieff', 30 Dec. 1801.

[124] Senex, *Old Glasgow and Its Environs* (Glasgow, 1864), p. 475.

[125] NWGA, RB/837/1202, 'Letter from Robert Scott Moncrieff', 11 July 1803.

[126] NWGA, RB/837/1116, 'Letter to Robert Scott Moncrieff', 16 May 1803.

The relationship between the Smiths of Jordanhill and the Royal Bank lasted over thirty years and encompassed several related firms. Leitch & Smith had access to cash credits of £1,000 and £5,000 in 1789 and 1817 respectively.[127] Co-partners also lodged capital in interest-bearing accounts. In 1821, John Guthrie lodged £10,000 with the bank at 4 per cent interest per annum.[128] However, the main relationship was one of individuals acquiring personal and commercial credit from the bank, a relationship which spanned successive generations of the same West India family. Archibald Smith's son William and his firm Smith & Brown had credit facilities in the 1820s, with obligations given from his brothers, James and Archibald, and uncle, John Guthrie.[129] Similarly, James Smith and the family firm Jas. & Arch. Smith (successor to Leitch & Smith) had credit facilities with the Royal Bank in the same period.[130] The inventory of Archibald Smith confirmed his cosy relationship with the Royal Bank agency in Glasgow. On Smith's death in 1821, a joint agent of the Glasgow office, Robert Scott Moncrieff, owed him £500.[131]

The Smiths of Jordanhill – associated with three separate Glasgow-West India merchant firms and other manufacturing enterprises – had multiple sources of funding. In terms of domestic credit, customers were usually required to maintain accounts with one Scottish bank only. It seems that both Archibald senior and James were untypical as they had credit facilities with other banks than the Royal. Archibald obtained credit from the Thistle Bank in 1801 and James obtained credit from the Bank of Scotland in 1827.[132] Archibald Smith referred to 'London money' in correspondence but it remains unclear if that related to sales from imports or bills of exchange drawn on London merchant firms or banks.[133] However, the long-term loans and large sums of capital held in the firm by partners underpinned the firm's success. The capital came from the merchants themselves – and ultimately from the colonies – but the major fortunes were created with a little support from the banks.

---

[127] NWGA, RB/12/14, 'Directors minutes', 1786–1800, fo. 169; RB/12/17, 'Directors minutes', 1817–20, fo. 62.

[128] NWGA, RB/12/18, 'Directors minutes', 1820–4, fo. 38.

[129] NWGA, RB/12/18, 'Directors minutes', 1820–4, fo. 60; RB/12/19, 'Directors minutes', 1824–7, fo. 202.

[130] NWGA, RB/12/18, 'Directors minutes', 1820–4, fo. 170; RB/12/19, 'Directors minutes', 1824–7, fo. 37.

[131] NRS, CC10/7/4, 'Inventory and settlement of Archibald Smith', 1 Oct. 1821, p. 246.

[132] GCA, TD1/75/2, 'Bond', 1801; GCA, TD1/75/3, 'Bond of credit', 1827.

[133] NWGA, RB/837/514, 'Letter to Robert Scott Moncrieff', 28 Dec. 1801.

West India merchant firms in Glasgow had more substantial connections with Scottish banks – especially the Royal Bank – than has previously been understood. Given the requirement for large-scale credit on a short-term basis, the dramatic rise of the Glasgow-West India trades after the 1790s could not have progressed without major banking facilities. Commission merchants took advantage of the transformation in banking provision in Glasgow due to the timely expansion of national institutions into Glasgow, particularly the Royal Bank. The expansion of Scottish banking houses into Glasgow underpinned the dramatic rise of the city's West India elite and, by extension, Scotland's involvement with Caribbean slavery.

The final word on the importance of the Glasgow banking institutions to West India commerce, and vice versa, comes from the bankers themselves. In February 1833, as the abolition of slavery became inevitable, the Glasgow West India Association 'induced' the Glasgow Chamber of Commerce, banks and banking companies in the west of Scotland to petition for a 'cautious, safe and satisfactory adjustment of the Slavery question'.[134] In March 1833, a petition was sent to Earl Grey, First Lord of the Treasury:

> We, the undersigned, Bankers of Glasgow and the West of Scotland… cannot doubt for a moment…contemplating such an extensive change… [that] His Majesty's Ministers have duly considered the various and manifold consequences…But your Memorialists cannot refrain from stating, that from their knowledge of the financial relations between the colonial trade and the general commerce of the country, any sudden alteration of these relations might produce effects very seriously injurious to commercial credit. And while they hope that every precaution has been taken to prevent that shock [to the] credit of the country…your Memorialists respectfully, but earnestly, entreat His Majesty's Government make such provisions as will avert so destructive a calamity.[135]

This petition invoked a familiar argument that parliamentary interference with West India capital – plantations and resident slaves – would be catastrophic for the British credit system.[136]

These findings further undermine a report by the Royal Bank of Scotland into antecedent institutions and their involvement with slavery in the colonial period. After a transatlantic research process in archives in America, England and Scotland, the authors concluded: 'There is no indication that any RBSG or Citizens predecessors ever directly invested

---

[134] GCA, TD1683/1/2, 'Minutes of the GWIA', pp. 12–15.

[135] Bristol Record Office, SMV/8/3/4/4/7, 'Memorial of bankers of Glasgow', March 1833.

[136] N. Draper, *The Price of Emancipation: Slave Ownership, Compensation and British Society at the End of Slavery* (Cambridge, 2010), p. 82.

in companies or institutions that owned slaves.'[137] By demonstrating that several banking institutions in London – now owned by the RBS Group – were recipients of compensation, Nicholas Draper thoroughly refuted the findings. However, as Scottish banks were noticeably absent from the compensation lists in 1834, Draper contrasted the London position with Glasgow and suggested that Scottish banks had a more indirect role by financing merchants, who in turn financed slave-owners.[138] The findings here confirm this view and suggest the Royal Bank had a key role in the financing of Glasgow firms involved with Caribbean slavery. These firms integrated the Atlantic economy by acting as the conduit between colonial planters and markets, and British banking, industry and commerce, a relationship that will be scrutinized in later chapters.

Conclusion

West India merchant firms in Glasgow were legal entities that enabled wealth creation based on slavery and its commerce, just like others of the same type across Great Britain in the colonial period. The main business was the transportation of commodities back and forth across the Atlantic. But they also served as financial and communication hubs, mercantile academies and prestigious employers and exporters of people. The merchant firms under scrutiny here were located in Glasgow, thus joining the city with satellite ports at Port Glasgow and Greenock further along the river Clyde. Transatlantic commerce connected Scottish banking institutions and manufacturing firms with the West Indies and facilitated a two-way flow of communications and migration. There are several distinctive features that marked Glasgow's development as a commercial hub.

Like English firms, the Glasgow-West India merchant houses operated on a classic commission system which was probably more capital-intensive than that used by the city's tobacco firms before 1783. Start-up capital was mainly sourced within Scotland, although with colonial origins. The structure of the West India merchant firms was defined by Scots not English law, adding a layer of protection to operations in the metropole and the colonies. By defining the firm as a separate legal entity, this regulation limited the exposure of co-partners and protected them from debts taken on in both jurisdictions. West India merchants of Glasgow regularly introduced younger male family members to the firm, which contributed

[137] Citizens Financial Group, Inc. and Royal Bank of Scotland Group, 'Historical research report predecessor institutions research regarding slavery and the slave trade' <https://www.citizensbank.com/pdf/historical_research.pdf> [accessed 2 Aug. 2014].

[138] Draper, *The Price of Emancipation*, pp. 245–6, 258–60.

to the larger-than-average partnership sizes of firms. The family firms were of major importance; the *inter-vivos* and post-mortem distribution of patrimonial inheritance provided an important stream of capital for the Glasgow-West India trades.

Commerce in Glasgow served to modernize the educational system, including the creation of a specialist genre of publications to inform the Glasgow-West India trades. Most West India merchants were probably trained in the city although a minority first went to the colonies, coming home cash rich to sink wealth into partnerships which added more colonial fortunes to the pot. But the availability of capital from within the community does not explain the rise of the Glasgow-West India trades on its own. The advance of the national banking system via agency branches in Glasgow provided a more extensive level of short-term capital than offered to the previous commercial generation. These West India merchants were tied financially to London, but this chapter underlines the importance of Scottish finance provided by Edinburgh-based institutions.

The evidence presented here, therefore, reveals the lifecycle of capital and credit required for the Glasgow-West India trades, at least for elite merchants. Start-up capital mainly came from a mercantile patriarch already involved with the tobacco or sugar trades or from a successful sojourn to the West Indies. Family wealth and connections were important, but not the only definers of success in the Glasgow-West India trades. Once established, a strategic marriage brought a high-value tocher, usually from colonial heiresses or daughters of the middling ranks, to supplement the merchant's interests. On the way up, loans were readily available from other West India merchants, while the national banks with agencies in Glasgow provided high-value credit after 1783. Landed West India proprietors could take advantage of loans from those in British society with no connections to colonial commerce. Once the West India merchants had become wealthy, they loaned capital within their own firms, to younger merchants or to the local gentry or businesses. This model was replicated many dozens of times in Glasgow between 1775 and 1838, explaining the dramatic economic changes during the city's sugar era.

3. A Glasgow-West India house

After the death of his elder brother James in 1815, Archibald Smith looked back on their respective commercial careers during Glasgow's sugar era:

> I had a good right to expect a fair proportion of the money I had been the means of makeing, and I may almost say against his will, he was so extreemly cautious & timid that had I been in the least guided by his advice or followed his views, there would be little to divide... he considered me allways too venturesome, perhaps this was one reason why he entrusted me with so little of his fortune, which I suppose he thought I could not keep.[1]

The merchant firm in which they were co-partners, Leitch & Smith, had brought the family great wealth. James was the owner of Craighead estate in Lanarkshire and worth *c*.£71,000 on death, ranking him among the wealthiest 20 per cent of Glasgow's West India elite. Having purchased Jordanhill estate in 1800, Archibald was also a successful West India proprietor. The correspondence revealed, from Archibald's point of view, that the wealth was based upon high-risk colonial ventures which, as this chapter will show, involved dealings with sugar and cotton planters in the British West Indies. As far as Archibald was concerned, the merchant firm he had established, Leitch & Smith, which operated in Jamaica and Grenada between 1779 and 1824 – and its successor firm up to 1867 – was the main conduit of the family fortune.

In one important way, these merchants were untypical of Glasgow's West India elite: the family were tenant farmers who then improved their standing via the colonial trades. This was a new fortune begotten from the Caribbean. As Archibald Smith's grandson, John Guthrie Smith, revealed, 'when the great West India sugar trade gained a footing in Scotland', the family 'took an early part in it, and prospered exceedingly...principally through the energy of a younger son, Archibald'.[2] In contrast to 'gentry capitalist' landed families such as the Stirlings of Keir, therefore, the Smiths were *arriviste*.[3] The spectacular transformation into elite landowners with multiple estates coincided with the involvement of family members in the

---

[1] GCA, TD1/26/3, 'Letter from Archibald Smith', 11 Aug. 1815.

[2] J. G. Smith, *The Parish of Strathblane and Its Inhabitants from Early Times* (Glasgow, 1886), p. 57.

[3] S. D. Smith, *Slavery, Family and Gentry Capitalism in the British Atlantic: The World of the Lascelles, 1648–1834* (Cambridge, 2006), p. 9.

West India trades across two generations. Robert Smith acquired Craigend in 1660 although the estate was improved in 1734 when Archibald's father James Smith, third laird of Craigend (1708–86), extended what had previously been a minor farm holding.[4] Archibald Smith senior (1749–1821) was thus born into a minor landed family on Craigend estate in Strathblane, just outside Glasgow.[5] As the fourth son, without prospects of landed inheritance, he travelled to Virginia in search of fortune with his three cousins in 1768 and worked as manager of a tobacco store.[6] However, as a large landowner loyal to the crown at the outbreak of the American War of Independence in 1775, he fled and was expropriated. This was a timely return and Smith became a junior partner in Leitch & Smith.[7] The profits acquired by the family's West India pioneers eased the next generation into commerce and underwrote domestic investments. In order to understand this process better, this case study of Leitch & Smith and its commercial successor adopts a transatlantic approach. Colonial deeds, official sources and adventurers' letters illuminate commercial activities and networks in the West Indies, while sources such as wills and confirmation inventories reveal wealth accumulation, investments and dispersal. In doing so, this study reveals an integrated Atlantic economy which facilitated an influx of capital into the west of Scotland.

The family firms: Leitch & Smith (1779–1824) and Jas. & Arch. Smith & Co. (1824–67)

Archibald Smith enjoyed nominal paternal support when establishing Leitch & Smith. On 10 March 1779, his father, James Smith, third laird of Craigend, purchased a Burgess and Guild ticket in Glasgow which helped his son to embark on a mercantile career. As son of a registered burgess, Archibald – alongside his trading partner John Leitch – registered Burgess and Guild brethren the next day.[8] Evidence of start-up capital in 1779 is elusive, although given his father's initial involvement it is possible he chose to assist his ambitious younger son. Within four years of its foundation in 1779, Leitch & Smith was based in the commercial centre of Glasgow

---

[4] Smith, *Strathblane*, pp. 52–7.

[5] J. G. Smith and J. O. Mitchell, *The Old Country Houses of the Old Glasgow Gentry* (Glasgow, 1878), 'Craigend'.

[6] Smith, *Strathblane*, p. 94.

[7] J. Craik, J. Eadie and J. Galbraith, *Memoirs and Portraits of One Hundred Glasgow Men*, vol. i (Glasgow, 1886), pp. 57–8, 285–8.

[8] J. Anderson (ed.), *The Burgesses and Guild Brethren of Glasgow, 1751–1846* (Edinburgh, 1935), p. 113.

at the Trongate.[9] Around a decade later, the firm owned a counting house and merchant lodgings, and had access to a fleet of ships, including the *Pomona, Nestor, Alfred* and *Isabella*, which allowed the transfer of goods and produce across the Atlantic.[10] The counting house itself enabled transatlantic credit exchanges and functioned as a mercantile academy to train the next generation of merchants.

With the establishment of Leitch & Smith, Archibald Smith created a mercantile dynasty that lasted nearly a century. This became the quintessential family firm. John Leitch died around 1805, by which point the Smith family dominated.[11] In October 1807, the co-partners were Archibald Smith senior, John Smith, James Smith, James Smith junior, John Ryburn, John Guthrie, Andrew Ranken and Adam Crooks. Evidently, Archibald's two brothers, John Smith, fourth laird of Craigend (1739–1816), and James Smith of Craighead (d. 1815) had been recruited into the firm by then. John Smith's son, James Smith junior (d. 1836), who inherited Craigend on his father's death, also became a partner. By 1818, John Smith's younger son, Archibald Smith junior (d. 1823), was a co-partner too. His son-in-law, Andrew Ranken, married Hannah Smith in 1809 and was afterwards recruited and loaned money. John Guthrie, a nephew of the Smith family, operated Guthrie & Ryburn, a sister firm in Grenada, which will be discussed below.[12] The partnership structure illustrates the importance of kinship and marital connections to the workings of West India firms, and these relationships underpinned the extension of capital over successive generations.

In time, Archibald Smith senior would also pass on capital and skills to his sons, James (described here as 'youngest'), William and Archibald (described here as 'youngest') who went on to become West India merchants. In contrast to their father's colonial sojourn, the sons followed a typically middling educational path.[13] James attended Glasgow High School and matriculated at the University of Glasgow in 1795. William and Archibald followed in 1798 and 1807.[14] James and Archibald later registered

[9] *John Tait's Directory for the City of Glasgow* (Glasgow, 1783), p. 41.

[10] *Jones's Directory* (Glasgow, 1790), pp. 33, 55.

[11] GCA, T-MJ 80, 'Ledger book of John Leitch', n.p.

[12] Smith and Mitchell, *Old Country Houses*, 'Craigend', 'Craighead'. Smith, *Strathblane*, pp. 57–8.

[13] R. H. Trainor, 'The elite', in *Glasgow, Vol. II: 1830–1912*, ed. W. H. Fraser and I. Maver (Manchester, 1996), p. 244.

[14] W. Innes Addison, *The Matriculation Albums of the University of Glasgow, from 1728 to 1858* (Glasgow, 1913), p. 179, p. 187, p. 229.

as merchant burgesses in Glasgow in 1810 and 1817 respectively before they were given shares.[15] In 1814, Archibald Smith senior gifted his son James £3,000 to 'make up his stock [£8,000] in Leitch & Smith', while Archibald youngest was given a present of over £5,000 on 31 March 1817, consisting of two shares in the West India firm (at £2,000 each) and the rest in profits.[16] James Smith of Craighead was the highest lender of capital to West India merchants and firms in Glasgow, especially within a close kinship matrix. In 1808, William Smith borrowed £2,000 on bond from his uncle. In 1814, James Smith youngest also borrowed £3,000 on bond.[17] There were various other gifts and loans between the partners to younger partners, including to John Guthrie, Andrew Ranken and associated firms, Smith & Browns, and Smith, Hutchison and Co.[18] The extension of capital and credit among the wider kinship group – especially father to son – was a common practice among the firm's co-partners.

The wider Smith family capitalized Leitch & Smith, holding large-scale wealth in shares and stock as well as providing loans to the firm and the younger generation. When John Smith fourth laird of Craigend died in 1816, his inventory listed £46,168 in movable property, with over £37,000 – 81 per cent of his personal wealth – held in stock and profits in Leitch & Smith.[19] When his brother Archibald Smith senior died in 1821, over £42,000 – 90 per cent of his personal wealth – was held in stock and profits.[20] Upon his death in 1815, James Smith of Craighead held £24,000 – a third of his personal wealth – in the firm.[21] The percentage of personal wealth held in the firm by these senior partners was higher than the average held by their peers in this study.[22] Moreover, James Smith loaned £20,000 to Leitch & Smith, which – as noted in the last chapter –was the single largest loan from a merchant to a West India firm identified in this study. Given smaller provincial banks in Scotland worked from paid capital as low

---

[15] Anderson (ed.), *The Burgesses and Guild Brethren of Glasgow, 1751–1846* (Edinburgh, 1935), p. 269, p. 304.

[16] GCA, TD1/1095, 'Daybook extracts'.

[17] NRS, SC36/48/9, 'Inventory of James Smith', 9 June 1815, pp. 685–6.

[18] NRS, SC36/48/11, 'Inventory of John Smith', 24 June 1816, p. 39; NRS, SC36/48/9, 'Inventory of James Smith', 9 June 1815, p. 686.

[19] NRS, SC36/48/11, 'Inventory of John Smith', 24 June 1816, p. 39.

[20] NRS, CC10/7/4, 'Inventory of Archibald Smith', 31 Oct. 1821, pp. 244–5.

[21] NRS, SC36/48/9, 'Inventory of James Smith', 9 June 1815, pp. 685–6.

[22] Forty-three merchants held investments totalling £1,053,967 in West India firms on death, compared to their overall wealth (£2,898,229). Thus, the average held in West India merchant firms was 36% of total wealth.

as £8,000 (and the average starting capital for provincial banks in England was estimated at £10,000), it is no exaggeration to state the success of Leitch & Smith was based upon the collectivization of the wealth of co-partners as rich as several provincial banks.[23] Reinvestment of the colonial fortunes was a key factor in the firm's rise.

The death of Leitch & Smith's senior co-partners – James Smith of Craighead in 1815, John Smith of Craigend in 1816 and Archibald Smith senior in 1821 – removed the firm's main funding sources. The inheritance of James Smith of Craighead's fortune after 1815 was the main cause of the dispute discussed at the opening of this chapter, while Archibald Smith senior's death in 1821 marked the end for Leitch & Smith (disbanded three years after his death).[24] However, Archibald Smith's settlement secured his immediate family's future. James Smith youngest was nominated heir (as was common practice), with £8,000 each to William and Archibald youngest. He left an annuity of £700 to his wife, Isabella (who was also guaranteed the use of Jordanhill mansion in a practice known as 'liferenting') which became a major outlay, since she lived until 1855.[25] With considerable start-up capital and experience of West India commerce, Archibald Smith's first and third sons formed the successor firm of James & Archibald Smith & Co. (hereafter Jas. & Arch. Smith & Co.) in 1824. Second son William established Smith & Browns, which focused on Trinidad. In order to understand how firms generated profits for individuals, this chapter now turns to the colonial end of Leitch & Smith's operations.

Leitch & Smith: Grenada and Carriacou, 1779–1823

After Grenada was subsumed into the British empire under the terms of the Treaty of Paris in 1763, the south-eastern Caribbean island was a prime destination for Scottish adventurers (as will be explored in Chapter 6). One of the early partners of the firm, John Leitch, was in the West Indies in 1781 and Leitch & Smith developed a trade network soon after.[26] The *Isabella* sailed from Glasgow in January 1791 and a specialist trade house, Guthrie & Ryburn, was formed afterwards which became the largest firm on the island by the end of the century.[27] The merchant firm was dominated by a close nexus of family

---

[23] C. Munn, *The Scottish Provincial Banking Companies, 1747–1864* (Edinburgh, 1981), p. 105.

[24] GCA, TD1/26/1–3, 'Letters from Archibald Smith', 1815.

[25] NRS, CC10/7/4, 'Inventory of Archibald Smith', 31 Oct. 1821, pp. 237–44.

[26] D. Hamilton, *Scotland, the Caribbean and the Atlantic World, 1750–1820* (Manchester, 2005), p. 88.

[27] *The Glasgow Advertiser*, 3 Jan. 1791; F. Armytage, *The Free Port System in the British West Indies* (London, 1953), p. 69.

in both Glasgow and the colonies. Guthrie & Ryburn was led by co-partners, John Ryburn and John Guthrie. In 1799, they were respected members of the island community as 'guardians of slaves' in St George's.[28] However, Guthrie returned home in 1800. His colonial partner, Ryburn, brought assets to the firm; he owned land in St George's in 1807,[29] as well as the *Nancy* of Greenock, and had shares in two other ships, the *Pomona* and the *Alfred*.[30] The colonial base in St George's, the commercial centre of Grenada, allowed them to take advantage of the Free Port Acts, legislation which relaxed the strict navigation laws after 1766 and enabled lucrative trade with neighbouring colonies of other European powers. The free ports in the British West Indies allowed foreigners to trade goods which would normally be prohibited. In fact, this was an elaboration of the Navigation Acts, as free ports only accepted foreign imports not in competition with goods produced in Britain or her colonies, while exports were limited to high-value manufactured goods. Thus, in free ports, French and Spanish merchants purchased manufactured goods and paid in bullion or plantation produce. This positive balance of trade created huge profits for British merchants in Grenada.[31]

According to Frances Armytage, Kingston in Jamaica and St George's in Grenada were the 'most flourishing' free ports in 1791, despite the latter only being awarded full privileges after a revision of the system four years earlier.[32] A petition to the Colonial Office reveals Leitch & Smith were pioneers of the Glasgow-Grenada free port trade after the American Revolution. Prior to the revised legislation in 1787, they conducted an informally accepted trade 'chiefly of cotton' with merchants in adjoining Spanish settlements, particularly Trinidad.[33] This was highly lucrative for the Glasgow firm. In 1799, John Guthrie was said to have 'publickally declared' to the collector of customs that profits from a cargo contained in a 'Vessel with Merchandize from home' would be 'five thousand pounds'.[34] However, while Guthrie later admitted the trade was 'very advantageous', he disputed the profit level and stated it was £5,000 Grenada currency (around £3,250 stg.).[35] In any case, the profitable trade with slave-based economies in Spanish America provided markets for Glasgow merchants as well as payments in bullion.

---

[28] TNA, CO101/42, 'Persons appointed as guardians of slaves', 1805, p. 22.

[29] W. Snagg (ed.), *The Laws of Grenada and the Grenadines* (Grenada, 1852), pp. 147–8.

[30] D. Dobson, *Scots in the West Indies, 1707–1857*, vol. ii (Baltimore, Md., 2006), p. 98.

[31] Armytage, *Free Port System*, p. 70.

[32] Armytage, *Free Port System*, p. 68.

[33] TNA, CO101/26/83, 'Memorial', 8 June 1786, p. 354.

[34] TNA, BT1/18/1, 'Letter to Governor Green', 13 Feb. 1799, pp. 13–14.

[35] TNA, BT1/18, 'Guthrie & Ryburn to Governor Green', 23 Feb. 1799, p. 22.

The partners of Leitch & Smith concurrently developed a portfolio of investments in Scotland that effectively connected colonies with the metropole. In 1799, Leitch & Smith joined with a group of merchants in Glasgow to fund a 'cotton wool adventure' which paid annual dividends.[36] This involved the purchase of new world cotton for import to Glasgow. This was part of a longer-term strategy. Leitch & Smith were trading cotton with the Spanish in Grenada before 1786 and were still importing cotton into Glasgow from Jamaica and Grenada in the 1820s.[37] The organization used English ports to land produce, particularly Liverpool. The *Diana* arrived from Berbice on 19 April 1810 and the *Caesar* arrived from Demerara in July 1813.[38] By the early nineteenth century, then, Archibald Smith senior was one of the most influential cotton merchants in Glasgow. At an exclusive meeting on 10 February 1803, he was present alongside other luminaries such as Archibald Campbell, Kirkman Finlay and James Dennistoun. According to them, cotton required for the Glasgow manufactures was 'chiefly the product of foreign independent Countries, or of Colonies of other European powers', and the high duty on such imports created an 'artificial scarcity'. Subsequently, they sought the repeal of the government duty in order to enhance industry and increase 'the productive power and wealth' of Scotland.[39] Thus, the Glasgow merchant rhetoric demanded a relaxation of the monopoly conditions which had initially allowed them to flourish in favour of boosting profits from cotton manufacturing.

While this was not clarion call for Adam Smith's free trade, the move was consistent with Eric Williams' view that merchant-manufacturers sought to undermine orthodox mercantilism in the nineteenth century once the profits from trade with British West India colonies were in decline.[40] The firm also invested in cotton firms. James Finlay & Co. was the largest producer of textiles in Scotland in the early nineteenth century, with three cotton mills at Ballindalloch, Catrine and Deanston. Leitch & Smith were partners from 1792 until 1823, while Archibald was involved on his own account.[41] In 1797, the capital stock was valued at £30,000, with Leitch &

---

[36] GCA, TD1/76, 'Business record', Feb. 1800.

[37] TNA, CO101/26/83, 'Memorial and petition from the merchants of Saint Georges', 8 June 1786, pp. 345–58; *GH*, 22 July 1822; *GH*, 12 Aug. 1822.

[38] *The Lancaster Gazette and General Advertiser*, 21 April 1810; *The Liverpool Mercury*, 2 July 1813.

[39] *The Morning Post*, 1 Mar. 1803.

[40] E. Williams, *Capitalism and Slavery* (Chapel Hill, 1944), p. 57.

[41] C. Brogan, *James Finlay & Company Limited: Manufacturers and East India merchants, 1750–1950* (Glasgow, 1951), p. xvii.

Smith holding £5,000 and Archibald Smith £1,000 of the total. This made Leitch & Smith the second largest shareholder and their account current suggests they bought and sold produce and finished goods.[42] By investing in cotton manufactories, the firm and its partners connected the 'forward linkages' under the staple theory of economic growth which Richard Sheridan argued fuelled the British Industrial Revolution.[43] Alongside John Campbell senior & Co., Leitch & Smith were the major mercantile shippers from Clyde ports (see Chapter 4), and both firms' cotton enterprise underpinned the Scottish Industrial Revolution.

The gains were not without risk, however, as the Scots were residents of a colony in a state of growing turmoil. Among the wave of rebellions that swept the Caribbean in the aftermath of the uprising on Saint Domingue in 1791, the Franco-Grenadian free people of colour led by Julien Fedon joined forces with their black slaves to overthrow the British regime in favour of revolutionary France. The violent uprising began on 2 March 1795 and continued for sixteen months; around 7,000 enslaved people were killed as well as forty-eight British hostages, including Alexander Campbell. The sugar mills, buildings and rum works were obliterated on 100 estates and the total loss to the island's economy was £2.5 million sterling between 1795 and 1798.[44] In order to rebuild the colony, the British government passed two acts that provided £1,500,000 'for the purpose of making Loans to persons with or trading to the Islands of Grenada and St Vincent'.[45] Although they were eligible, Leitch & Smith did not take loans, suggesting that even if the firm owned any property, it remained undamaged.[46] More importantly for the firm, their associates were present during the lucrative restoration of the plantation economy.

In 1817, the speaker of the House of Assembly in Grenada, George Munro, pleaded with the British government and condemned the merchants who had taken advantage of ruined planters:

> A bill indeed was passed, and an issue of exchequer bills was made in May 1795 intituled 'For Relief of the Grenada Planters and Merchants connected with that Island and St Vincents'. But to the latter only, it was a boon; to

---

[42] GUA, UGD91/1/4/1/3/1 'Ledger of James Finlay and Co.', 1792–1800, pp. 105–6.

[43] R. Sheridan, *Sugar and Slavery* (Kingston, 2000), p. 475.

[44] E. Cox, 'Fedon's rebellion, 1795–96: Causes and consequences', *Journal of Negro History*, lxvii (1982), 7–19, at p. 15.

[45] (HCPP) 1801 (98) *Report on the Petition of the Proprietors of Estates in the Island of Grenada*, p. 11; HCPP 1801–2 (43) *An Account of the Loans Advanced, in Exchequer Bills and Cash, to the Planters and Merchants Interested in the Islands of Grenada and St. Vincent's*.

[46] The University of the West Indies – St Augustine, Alma Jordan Library, SC89 6/3, 'Minutes of the Board of Commissioners for the Issue of Exchequer Bills', 1795–7.

the former it was the reverse; it was calculated to save the merchant; to save merchants who must thus have become bankrupts if no such insurrection had happened; but more completely to subjugate them the planters. The merchant, supported by his numerous creditors and connections in Great Britain, only could command the personal security there the act required, and to them it was granted; and in respect to a few individuals, to a most enormous amount; but the ruined planter was stripped of his counter security by the same hand that held out this impotent relief. If any benefit had been meant to him, even by way of loan, Government was well aware his estate, in the plight it stood, was the only security he could give, and none other should have been exacted of him. The estates of course became more deeply encumbered than they had previously been and fell very generally into the hands of the mortgagees, merchants in England.[47]

Munro's testimony points to vast profiteering in Grenada, and although evidence of Leitch & Smith's participation in such activities in the late eighteenth century remains elusive, the firm operated in Grenada throughout these years. In 1807, the co-partners initiated a policy designed to consolidate their interests in the West Indies. At a meeting in October that year, they agreed on a transatlantic 'house of trade' system to lease sundry land and slaves, which was probably a renewal of a previous agreement. Across the Atlantic, the colonial business in Grenada was regulated by nominating power of attorney to John Lindsay, Daniel Brady and William Mitchell. By this point, the firm had expanded into Jamaica (as discussed below) and nominated Robert Smith and Thomas Huie of Kingston as representatives.[48] In the same period, several co-partners of Leitch & Smith were founder members of the influential pro-slavery lobbying group the Glasgow West India Association in 1807 and were among the top seven company subscribers, indicating its elite status. The mercantile strategy of Leitch & Smith strengthened their connections with the West Indies just as the Glasgow-West India interest reacted to the abolition of the slave trade in 1807.

With increasing prominence in Glasgow, the co-partners of Leitch & Smith expanded in the West Indies and minimized risk by recruiting known employees. Newspapers in Glasgow in this period listed various

---

[47] HCPP 1821 *House of Commons Papers*, 14, 'Correspondence between Lord Bathurst and the Colonies', 12 April 1817.

[48] Grenada Supreme Court, St George's, Grenada, Registry of Records, Grenada Deeds (GD), M2, 'Power of Attorney', 19 April 1808, pp. 489–93. The author is grateful to Jim Smith of Florida for drawing his attention to these sources which were acquired from Microfilms held at the Family History Library <http://www.familysearch.org/eng/library/fhlcatalog/printing/titledetailsprint.asp?titleno=574884> [accessed 13 May 2011]. In April 2014 and May 2016, the author examined the originals, which are held in Grenada Supreme Court Registry, St George's, Grenada.

employment opportunities in Grenada. As will be argued in Chapter 4, the recruitment and shipping of young Scots was a commercial business. However, Leitch & Smith only recruited a small number of employees via public advertisement in Glasgow for plantations in the West Indies.[49] Instead, they recruited adventurers of the correct sort based on established networks, essentially adopting a closed recruitment policy. As well as John Guthrie, Archibald also secured employment for his elder brother James Smith (later of Craighead). Crucially, he was entrusted with conveying profits to Glasgow:

> I took him into the concern four years after its commencement [ie 1783] when he was idle, merely to give him employment. The business in Grenada was begun before he went there & which he rather check'd than promoted the only good he did was remitting the money regularly.[50]

The senior co-partners of the firm also handpicked young merchants from outside the Smith family circle and trained them prior to departure. A series of letters that travelled by the packet on the ships *Pomona*, *Ardent* and *Nestor* illustrates the working of the trade house in St George's and the preparation of young adventurers in Glasgow. The Kirk family of Kilmarnock were kin of Adam Crooks, a co-partner in Leitch & Smith. This connection allowed two brothers, Robert and Adam Kirk, to embark on a colonial career. A commercial handbook published for use by 'men of business' in commercial Glasgow suggested firms employed groups of individuals as a risk-averse policy:

> In the West Indies…merchants who establish factors there, find it necessary to settle two, three or more, in the same house, that, on the case of the death of one, there may still be a sufficient number known to their business, to carry on the affairs of the house till the vacancy is supplied.[51]

By training and employing the Kirk brothers simultaneously, Leitch & Smith adopted a similar risk-averse policy and one that was to prove a wise decision.

Adam travelled to Grenada in 1811 into the care of Guthrie and Ryburn and immediately connected with an established network of Scots: 'there is so many young men…for here you have a general acquaintance with every Body'. Thomas Gregory and Adam Pringle from Ayr were 'kind of cronies',

---

[49] Between 1806 and 1834, Leitch & Smith advertised just 11 jobs in Grenada and Jamaica in the *Glasgow Herald*. For example, see 'For St George's, Grenada', 14 Jan. 1814, p. 3.

[50] GCA, TD1/26/3, 'Letter from Archibald Smith', 11 Aug. 1815.

[51] W. Gordon, *The General Counting House, and Man of Business* (Edinburgh, 1766), p. 379.

while John Todd from Kilmarnock travelled from Carriacou to see Adam Kirk soon after his arrival.[52] While Adam began his career in Grenada, his brother Robert remained in Glasgow for commercial education prior to embarkation. In the counting house in 1812 he was 'keept very close at work attending French and Spanish classes'.[53] These classes were international in focus and the practical skills allowed transactions with the resident French plantation owners on Grenada as well as the Spanish cotton merchants of Trinidad. The Glasgow merchant house took full advantage of the increase in free port trade from St George's from 1808 to 1815. Indeed, the value of Guthrie & Ryburn's exports in the first eight months of 1813 was $144,240, which was seven times greater than every other trade house in Grenada together. Some of the export goods had been sourced from the East Indies and Manchester, although almost half by value ($71,250, or £16,047) were sourced in Glasgow.[54] Perhaps to assist with the increasing business, the parent firm Leitch & Smith purchased over one acre of 'land covered with water' in the Carenage harbour area in St George's sometime between 1807 and 1814, allowing the transfer of stock and refitting of ships. The land was acquired at auction from the trustees of Alexander Houston and Co. for £290 sterling.[55] This was to prove a canny investment and was sold in 1830 to Kirk & Todd in Grenada for £1,500.[56] The merchant firm connected metropole and colony in various ways, extracting wealth and encouraging the Scottish economy.

A ship captain, Mr Mcilven, recounted to Adam Kirk's father in January 1812 how his son was 'Commander in Chief in the shop' in St George's and 'had entirely put down flogging' to an extent that 'the poor black fellows' were 'extraordinary taken' with him.[57] Adam's brother Robert, eventually a key part of the Glasgow enterprise, served a longer apprenticeship and in 1814 was still working in the store.[58] On 22 February 1812, Leitch & Smith purchased enslaved men Louis, Alexis Brutus and Sampiere from Walter McInnes of the island of Martinique, a French colony, although under British control in 1812.[59] They probably became workers attached to the store, or crew on the firm's

---

[52] NRS, GD1/632/2, 'John Kirk to Adam Kirk', 22 Feb. 1811; NRS, GD1/632/4, 'Adam Kirk to John and James Crooks', 26 June 1812.

[53] NRS, GD1/632/3, 'John Kirk to Adam Kirk', 20 Feb. 1812.

[54] NA, CO101/53, 'Abstract of exports', 1813, pp. 70–1.

[55] GD, Y4, 'Indentures for parcel of land', 20 June 1814, pp. 156–64.

[56] GD, L5, 'Indentures for Carenage', 19 April 1830, pp. 614–20.

[57] NRS, GD1/632/3, 'John Kirk to Adam Kirk', 20 Feb. 1812.

[58] NRS, GD1/632/6, 'Adam Kirk to Marion Crooks', 24 July 1814.

[59] GD, P2, 'Purchase of slaves', 19 Dec. 1812, pp. 46–7.

schooner *Betsy* that traded along the Spanish Main.[60] They also released at least two enslaved people from their chattel status in this period. In 1817, a 'Negro woman slave named Mary with her infant mulatto son James' were freed for the 'good Causes and Considerations' of Leitch & Smith.[61] While it is possible they sold enslaved people in the free port prior to 1807, the purchase and manumission described here represent the only direct trafficking in the available evidence concerning Grenada. Instead, Leitch & Smith primarily advanced capital to planters although, as was common practice, the firm accepted estates as security with literally hundreds of enslaved people (including infants only days old) as human collateral in such business dealings.

There is, however, no evidence the co-partners of Leitch & Smith took direct ownership of plantations in Grenada. Nevertheless, they extended capital and export supplies on credit which sustained the system and tied resident planters to long-term consignment plans under the commission system. A series of indentures from 1810 illustrate the process which allowed absentee Scottish merchants in Grenada to gain a stranglehold of the plantation economy. Leitch & Smith advanced Ferdinand De Creeft and his wife a mortgage on 9 October 1810. The repayment of the principal loan was made annually over the next three years with interest, which was typically 5 per cent. The credit agreement tied the plantations to Leitch & Smith for the duration of the mortgage and permitted future loans and advance of stock, while the sugar and all produce (except cocoa and molasses) were consigned to Scotland. As collateral, the De Creefts put up Columbia, a sugar plantation with sixty-six slaves, as well as a coffee and cocoa estate named Pyrrhenees, both in the parish of St Andrew.[62] Leitch and Smith were repaid with interest by 1819.[63] A reprinted *Reference to the Plan of the Island of Grenada* listed F. De Creft as the proprietor of Columbia in St Andrew in 1824, indicating he was a successful plantation owner over the long term.[64]

As well as mortgages secured on plantations, Leitch & Smith also advanced short-term credit in the form of bond loans and bills of exchange. The extension of credit brought more consignments of produce to Glasgow and in order to deal with the increasing business they appointed three new attorneys in October 1816.[65] John Lindsay was retained while resident merchants, William Kirkland and Robert Kirk, were added to the Smith

[60] NA, CO101/52, 'Guthrie and Ryburn to Governor Ainslie', 5 April 1813, pp. 19–20.

[61] GD, R2, 'Manumission', 8 Sept. 1817, pp. 154–5.

[62] GD, Z4, 'Indentures', 29 Jan. 1816, pp. 257–67.

[63] GD, A5, 'Indentures', 6 March 1820, pp. 872–5.

[64] G. Smith, *Reference to the Plan of the Island of Grenada* (London, 1882), p. 8.

[65] GD, R2, 'Power of attorney', 23 May 1817, pp. 22–4.

payroll. The two Kirk brothers had contrasting fortunes. Adam died on Grenada on 8 December 1816, while Robert, after completing a five-year apprenticeship, was promoted to a senior position, which he held for over twenty years.[66] A subsequent power of attorney in April 1818 recruited more individuals; Lindsay, Kirk and William Mitchell, a resident planter, were nominated, with a further six persons required. The colonial remit had shifted since 1807. In order to pursue outlying debts, attorneys were instructed not only to manage 'mercantile affairs and Business', but also to supervise with the 'collecting and receiving debts' as well as 'carrying in suits at Law or in Equity'.[67] Thus, the organization broadened their trading operations and reinforced an efficient debt recovery strategy. Just as the Grenada business developed from 1779, the firm's metropolitan operations had expanded too: the extension of capital to another merchant firm in Glasgow in 1800 initiated further trade and commerce with planters, although with less lucrative returns.

'The Jamaica business', 1800–67

This section traces the relationship between the Glasgow-West India house of Robert Mackay and Co., the absentee owners of two Jamaica plantations, and their preferred financiers, Leitch & Smith. The Caribbean economy was based on the extension of credit from Great Britain and there were frequent court cases, bankruptcies and foreclosures leading to merchants assuming control upon default on debts. Leitch & Smith and their mercantile successors were involved in at least five court cases in the 1820s and 1830s concerning debts in the Caribbean, most of which concerned Iter Boreale and Heywood Hall. The two estates, located in the northern parishes of St George and St Mary, were acquired after Robert Mackay and Co. foreclosed mortgages with previous proprietors. In 1800, Archibald Smith senior advanced £25,000 to Mackay and Co., secured with a bond agreement. The loan ensured all plantation produce was consigned to Leitch & Smith, who took 2.5 per cent commission on sales of sugar imported from the estate.[68] The capital injection also marked the decline of one Glasgow-West India merchant house and the rise of another. The estates remained heavily encumbered with annuities paid in London, however, and Henry Glassford (son of 'tobacco lord' John Glassford) was appointed trustee around 1790.[69]

---

[66] NRS, GD1/632/8, 'Sarah Kirk to John Kirk', 30 March 1817.

[67] GD, S2, 'Power of attorney', 29 June 1818, pp. 312–16.

[68] GCA, TD1/1081/1, 'Contract and bond of Robert Mackay', Oct. 1800, pp. 2–3.

[69] GCA, TD569/1, 'Opinions of counsel', 1808.

Part of his remit involved the regulation of operations, which included attracting investment capital.

A legal document based on the estate accounts of Iter Boreale and Heywood Hall outlines the practicalities of the Glasgow-West India trade.[70] Sugar was the most valuable commodity and Iter Boreale was the more productive plantation of the two. The produce was transported in two ships on bi-annual journeys: 383 hogsheads of sugar were shipped from both plantations in 1820. Leitch & Smith sold the sugar to local refiners, such as James McNair, who purchased part of the July shipment on the *Pomona*.[71] The raw muscovado was refined in Glasgow sugar houses and sold in local shops or re-exported to Europe. The provisions of the initial loan also guaranteed imports of high-quality Jamaica OP (over-proof) rum, and ninety-four puncheons were sent in 1820. That triple-distilled Jamaican rum was high quality was reflected in the price, which was 4s 9d a gallon compared to 3s 5d for the Leeward Island version in 1810.[72] Leitch & Smith imported rum from Jamaica at least from 1801, when it was sold to Hugh Milliken and Co. in Glasgow.[73] Manufactured goods were exported to Jamaica in 1820, adding a level of integration with their manufacturing interests. Commission at 0.5 per cent interest was charged on drafts and payments.

The trading privileges were protected by provisions of the loan, which placed the burden of risk on the absentee owners. However, the available evidence suggests this became a costly investment that was not repaid. After Robert Mackay and Co. went bankrupt around 1818, Leitch & Smith provided working capital at the behest of Henry Glassford. While it was in the interests of attorneys of the plantations to maintain accurate accounts and maximize profits, the highest costs in the next two years were for draft bills drawn in Jamaica.[74] The purchase of island provisions, lumber, salaries for bookkeepers and carpenters as well as the hiring of slave labour constituted the highest costs. Indeed, correspondence in 1820 between Leitch & Smith and Patrick Cockburn, an accountant in Edinburgh in charge of the Mackay estate, suggests the plantations required more resident slaves to produce large sugar crops.[75] There was also a high level of legacies served on the plantations, some of which were only cleared in 1856. The Iter Boreale annuities were historic

---

[70] GCA, TD1/1081/2, 'States respecting the affairs', 1820.

[71] NRS, CS96/4260, 'Raw sugar book', 1820.

[72] *The Edinburgh Monthly Magazine and Review*, i (Edinburgh, 1810), p. 140.

[73] NRS, CS96/4361, 'Imports book', 13 Oct. 1801, p. 5.

[74] B. W. Higman, *Plantation Jamaica, 1750–1850: Capital and Control in a Colonial Economy*, (Kingston, 2008), pp. 94–112.

[75] The National Library of Jamaica, MS. 707/2, 'Letter from Leitch & Smith', 28 Sept. 1820.

debts paid in London, sometimes to family members of past owners.[76] In 1819, the costs of attorney drafts and annuities alone were over £1,000 more than the total proceeds from both estates in 1820.

The activities in Grenada were evidently rewarding to Leitch & Smith, and initially so too was the business in Jamaica: 'the agency of these estates was very profitable for many years, indeed was the best account in their books'.[77] However, in 1818 they assumed de facto ownership of the Jamaican plantations – in contrast to Grenada – and in the next two years a balance of over £18,000 became due.[78] As trustee of the estate of Robert Mackay & Co., Henry Glassford assumed legal responsibility for outstanding debts, including the outstanding balance and the initial investment of £25,000.[79] A business history of the Jamaican plantations – written in 1867, perhaps by Archibald Smith youngest – described how the Glasgow firm had sunk all 'proceeds of these estates' from 1800 back into them, as well as a 'large additional sum'. When Henry Glassford died on 14 May 1819, Leitch & Smith were ranked on his estate for debts upwards of £45,000.[80] After his death, trusteeship was transferred to accountants Patrick Cockburn and Charles Selkrig, although Leitch & Smith retained trading privileges and ownership. They eventually raised a court case in order to pursue over £50,000.[81] The account was passed on to James and Archibald Smith, who were paid a dividend of £15,572 and concurrently took ownership of both plantations before slavery was finally abolished in the British West Indies in 1834.[82] This chapter now turns to James and Archibald Smith youngest: the inheritors of the family business towards the end of Caribbean slavery.

The transfer of power: Jas. & Arch. Smith & Co., 1824–67

In July 1822, Robert Kirk closed the business of Leitch & Smith in Grenada and mooted travelling to another island.[83] Instead, he remained on the island under the employment of successor firm, Jas. & Arch. Smith & Co., which was formally established on 5 April 1824. The firm subsequently became significant merchant financiers, investing a minimum of £61,175

---

[76] GCA, TD1/1081/1, 'List of Iter Boreale annuitants'.

[77] GCA, TD1/1081/1, 'Iter Boreale and Eden estate', 7 March 1867.

[78] GCA, TD1/1081/2, 'States respecting the affairs', 1820, p. 6.

[79] GCA, TD1/1081/1, 'State of Henry Glassford affairs', Feb. 1820.

[80] GCA, TD1/1081/1, 'Iter Boreale and Eden estate'.

[81] NRS, CS44/9/45/6, 'Summons', 1 Dec. 1821.

[82] GCA, TD1/1081/1/1, 'State of the dividends'.

[83] NRS, GD1/632/13, 'Sarah Kirk to Marion Crooks', 14 July 1822.

across the Caribbean, mainly in Grenada between 1829 and 1832. While Jas. & Arch. Smith & Co. consisted of only three co-partners, the personnel and strategy in Grenada remained unchanged. They inherited the business interests of Leitch & Smith and the smaller structure streamlined profits into fewer hands. At a meeting in Glasgow on 12 February 1827, James and Archibald Smith and Robert McCunn made an agreement to trade in Grenada and 'all foreign West India islands except the Islands of Jamaica'. Taking advantage of established networks in Scotland and Grenada, the Smiths appointed the Kilmarnock adventurers John Todd and Robert Kirk as attorneys alongside William Scott Kirkland to support operations in Carriacou.[84] Todd temporarily returned to Glasgow in 1827, perhaps to meet with the Smiths to receive instructions for the next investment cycle.

As the abolitionist movement gathered pace, the Smiths increased the extension of credit and laid out over £54,000 in a five-year period after 1827. This level of credit is comparable to the top lenders in Barbados between 1823 and 1843, the merchant house of Daniel, a 'major force' who provided £62,694 in mortgages to planters.[85] The Smith investment cycle was large-scale and ambitious in a period which Richard Pares suggested abolition provided an ideal excuse for merchants to decline credit.[86] In the years leading up to emancipation, many West India merchant houses across Great Britain were threatened with insolvency. Foreign competition and overproduction of sugar meant fluctuating prices, and uncertainty over debt repayment made conditions increasingly volatile. Ten merchant firms across Great Britain went bankrupt in 1831 alone.[87]

The Smith strategy would therefore seem at first to be high risk. However, all loans after 1827 were secured with mortgages on plantations and they added security after 1829 by strictly limiting credit to British planters. In the post-1829 sample, the Glasgow-West India merchant house set mortgages at 5 per cent interest, which was the legal British rate up to 1854. By adhering to the usury regulations and by demanding payment in sterling in London and Glasgow, they placed the terms of credit in the British system which meant disputes could be settled in metropolis courts with greater prospects of success.[88] Furthermore, they had the option of legal action against executors of individuals resident in the West Indies but whose wills were

---

[84] GD, V2, 'Power of attorney', 11 Sept. 1829, pp. 42–6.

[85] K. M. Butler, *The Economics of Emancipation: Jamaica & Barbados, 1823–1843* (Chapel Hill, 1995), p. 66.

[86] R. Pares, *A West India Fortune* (Bristol, 1950), p. 261.

[87] Butler, *Economics of Emancipation*, p. 66.

[88] Pares, *West India Fortune*, p. 258.

proved in Scotland. Leitch & Smith had previously raised a court case in Edinburgh in 1821 against the executors of the will of Andrew Rome, a Scottish merchant-planter resident in Carriacou. Rome was 'in the practice of sending home to them rum and sugar, the produce of his estate to be sold on commission by them and he drew bills on them from time to time'.[89]

The Smiths had a long-term trading relationship with another Scot, William Stuart from Inverugie in Aberdeenshire. Stuart was a resident planter in Grenada in 1816, although he returned to Scotland and eventually entered into mortgage agreements with Jas. & Arch. Smith & Co. in 1829. They took over his extensive debts and Stuart put up three estates, Mount Hardman, Grande Ance and Morne Delice, as well as 430 enslaved people as security. Some of the enslaved people that were placed as collateral were registered to Stuart's other plantations, Mount Moritz in St George, and Diamond in St Mark. This was to prove important on emancipation in 1834. The interest on the mortgage was charged at 5 per cent,[90] and they gained supply privileges and consignment rights to Grand Ance, the largest sugar and cotton estate in Grenada, spread over 1,237 acres.[91] The principal loan was scheduled to be paid in stages at the Royal Exchange in London by 1834, as well as an additional advance which took the outstanding Stuart debt to over £24,000.[92]

The Glasgow merchant house continued to loan large sums in Grenada, including to their Scottish representatives, Kirk & Todd, who started business on their own account. They sold the merchant store at Carenage to their former attorneys in April 1830,[93] marking the beginning of a new relationship. Kirk and Todd subsequently borrowed capital from the Smiths in June 1830, which allowed them to take over the mortgage of David McEwan.[94] Jas. & Arch. Smith & Co. also continued with company policy of increasing sugar imports through large mortgages. The honourable George Paterson – originally from Old Rayne, Aberdeen – was a former governor of Grenada. By 1832, he was a resident planter who owned two plantations, Marli and Union, in the parish of St Patrick. He transferred a large mortgage to Jas. & Arch. Smith & Co. and, as part of the repayment agreement, he consigned sugar bi-annually each March and August. In a profitable arrangement, Jas. & Arch. Smith & Co. charged for shipping and organized the export of 'stores, supplies, goods, wares and merchandize'.

[89] NRS, CS44/38/29, 'Condescendence for Leitch & Smith', 1822.

[90] GD, L5, 'Indentures', 9 Sept. 1829, pp. 174–217.

[91] Smith, *Reference to the Plan of the Island of Grenada*, p. 3.

[92] GD, L5, 'Indentures', 4 Jan. 1830, pp. 392–405.

[93] GD, L5, 'Indentures', 19 April 1830, pp. 614–20.

[94] GD, M5, 'Indentures', 21 Oct. 1830, pp. 124–53.

While they also promised to pay bills of exchange drawn in the colonies and assumed responsibility for the disposal of the sugar in Glasgow, the burden of risk was firmly on Paterson until it arrived, as 'the dangers of the seas and the Kings enemies only and always expected'.[95]

In the absence of merchant correspondence or company ledgers, it is impossible to reach definitive conclusions on the extent of their commission business or the profits emanating from them. However, although it is a small dataset of loans, it is useful to make some observations, especially as 'much remains to be learned about plantation finance...during the years leading up to Emancipation in 1834'.[96] Indeed, there is no comparative sample of loans provided by Scottish firms in the West Indies. This study identifies Leitch & Smith and their successors as significant merchant financiers in Grenada, with loans of over £84,000 in both short- and long-term credit to individual planters. They also loaned to their own merchant attorneys, Kirk & Todd. The Glasgow merchant house was well situated to take advantage of restoration of Grenada: they operated in the colony, before 1783 (although the sample of loans analysed here begins in 1810) and were pioneers of the free port trade. Their trade house was the largest on the island, and the Guthrie declaration suggests they acquired large-scale capital from this. However, the peak years were before 1793, and the British capture of Trinidad in 1797 marked an exodus of free port traders to the new colony, as it was closer to the Spanish Main. The decline in the Grenada free port trade was dramatic after 1816.[97] Thus, the mortgage agreements were part of a diversification strategy designed to increase the commission business within Grenada.

The evidence suggests the Smiths preferred to undertake colonial business with Scottish compatriots. Indeed, they utilized known networks not only for recruitment in Glasgow and the Caribbean, but also for business opportunities. The mortgages secured on Jamaican plantations were loaned to Scots, including a Glasgow-West India merchant house. Of the twelve transactions in Grenada and Carriacou, the majority were with individuals with Scottish surnames and six individuals or trustees have been identified as Scots. The Smiths were specialists in acquiring trade rights from plantations through the extension of long-term loans. Significantly, the six mortgages and largest bill of exchange in Grenada were not intended to consolidate existing debt, but instead were the lure that attracted new correspondents. For example, in 1817 a loan was provided to James Bain, who purchased

[95] GD, N5, 'Indenture', 1 Aug. 1832, pp. 261–70.

[96] Smith, *Gentry Capitalism*, p. 171.

[97] Armytage, *Free Port System*, pp. 123–4.

Belmont plantation from Thomas Townsend. Most of the Smith loans were to planters indebted to other lenders, a strategy in sharp contrast to the merchant house of Pinney based in Bristol, who stopped taking on clients with outstanding mortgage debt in 1815 due to the depressed conditions.[98] The strategy allowed the Smiths to increase their share of the sugar trade, which they consolidated through monopolistic practices.

The Smiths controlled planter debt by imposing strict demands that tied the import of plantation produce to the repayment of mortgages, thus increasing their consignment business. Although these conditions of trade were not legally enforceable, similar agreements were written into the deeds of at least four planters with mortgages secured on multiple large sugar plantations. The Glasgow house maintained control of outstanding loans and account current through sales of sugar and cotton, which were imported in regular shipping runs. While the merchant house of Pinney in Bristol struggled to undertake two voyages per year in the 1790s,[99] Leitch & Smith insisted on bi-annual voyages in at least one mortgage in Grenada (and the bond agreement in Jamaica). It is significant that the Smiths did not foreclose any mortgages in Grenada. Three of the six planter mortgages were fully repaid. Another was reduced through compensation and the largest bill of exchange was also cleared. Although it is certain they had bad debts in Grenada, it is impossible to identify them through the available sources. Nonetheless, the evidence suggests they maintained an efficient approach to debt recovery, enforced by trusted attorneys primed for lawsuits in the colonies and supported by the threat of court action in the metropolis.

When plantation slavery was abolished in the British West Indies on 1 August 1834, the British government compensated enslavers for the loss of their chattel property – that is, the lives of men, women and children. A fuller discussion will be undertaken in the final chapter, but this section reveals the Smith family were involved in at least nine compensation claims for enslaved people in the West Indies, most of which arose from the outlying debt in Jamaica and Grenada. However, as merchant financiers advancing capital, this was a complex process. Jas. & Arch. Smith & Co. remained the main creditor of the bankrupt estate of Robert Mackay and Co. in 1834. John Ryburn, previously of Grenada, was involved as a trustee, suggesting he had been appointed as an agent by Jas. & Arch. Smith & Co. A deal was struck in 1836 between Edinburgh accountants and trustees Charles Selkrig, Patrick Cockburn and John Bell, who claimed the compensation for the

---

[98] Pares, *West India Fortune*, p. 307.

[99] Pares, *West India Fortune*, p. 227.

slaves on Heywood Hall and Iter Boreale. The compensation was intended for creditors of the bankrupted Robert Mackay and Co. while the Smiths assumed ownership of the two plantations, which were valued at £23,550.[100]

In Grenada, the co-partners of Jas. & Arch. Smith & Co. made six compensation claims and received £12,573 for 480 enslaved people.[101] The first two claims were small (four and seven slaves), perhaps for the workers attached to the store and the ship. However, the four largest claims were for slaves on Mount Moritz, Morne Delice, Mount Hardman and Grand Ance, plantations owned by William Stuart, a mortgagee since 1829. It is very likely that Stuart reached an agreement to take this total from his outstanding mortgage, and the partners of Jas. & Arch. Smith & Co. claimed compensation on the human property which formed the collateral of the credit agreements. The family of Archibald Smith claimed around £15,000 in slave compensation, placing them among the elite West India families who received large-scale awards, such as the Campbells and the Bogles of Gilmorehill.[102]

As will be outlined in the final chapter, there was a large-scale exodus of Glasgow-West India merchants from the Caribbean after 1834, but in this case, the Smiths were only able to partially extricate the firm. The co-partners tried, and failed, to auction Iter Boreale and Heywood Hall 'with the services of the Apprentices' in the Royal Exchange sales rooms in Glasgow in early 1837.[103] However, they advanced credit secured with a mortgage on Eden estate in Jamaica from James Geddes in 1845,[104] and were still importing sugar to Glasgow a year later.[105] Power of attorney on Iter Boreale and Heywood Hall was subsequently devolved to several individuals, and Iter Boreale was eventually offered to William Hosack as a cattle pen for £1,000 in 1853. The Smiths also assumed control of Eden estate after the previous owner, James Geddes, died in 1846 but lamented the fact that it had provided no profits, unlike Iter Boreale in the past.[106] Two of the estates in Jamaica were still in

[100] GCA, TD1/90, 'Conveyance deeds', 1837.

[101] HCPP 1837–8 (215) 48 *Slavery Abolition Act: an account of all sums of money awarded by the Commissioners of Slavery Compensation*, p. 98, p. 312.

[102] See A. Smith, *Legacies of British Slave-Ownership* database <http://wwwdepts-live.ucl.ac.uk/lbs/person/view/42021> [accessed 23 Aug. 2021; 'William Smith of Carbeth Guthrie', *Legacies of British Slave-Ownership* database <http://wwwdepts-live.ucl.ac.uk/lbs/person/view/28824> [accessed 19 Dec. 2018].

[103] *Caledonian Mercury*, 18 June 1836.

[104] GCA, TD1/1081/1, 'Iter Boreale and Eden estate'.

[105] *The Scottish Jurist*, vol. xxi (Edinburgh, 1849), p. 369.

[106] GCA, TD1/1081/1, 'Iter Boreale and Eden estate'.

their possession in 1867, revealing the Smith family were connected to the Caribbean for over eighty-five years, during which time a flow of profits underwrote investments across the west of Scotland.

Investing slavery's profits

In the antiquarian text *The Parish of Strathblane* (1886), John Guthrie Smith pointed to the decline of his paternal family's wealth: 'the fortune, and for those times it was a very large one, gradually melted away till it finally disappeared', noting the Smith family's seat, Craigend Castle, was sold in 1851.[107] The evidence here supports the view of a rise and fall in a family fortune, although John Guthrie Smith's views probably would have been skewed by his father William's relatively small fortune (see Table 3.1). On death, the co-partners of Leitch & Smith and Jas. & Arch. Smith owned personal wealth valued at around £269,449, with average holdings (£29,944) over a third lower than the average wealth of the Glasgow-West India elite.[108] Yet, these averages obscure the considerable differential between the first- and second-generation merchants. The initial partners left the largest fortunes. James Smith of Craighead died in 1815 worth over £71,000.[109] John Smith of Craigend left a fortune of over £46,000 in 1816.[110] Archibald Smith senior's personal fortune was valued at £47,000 on his death in May 1821.[111] Yet their sons left, on average, much less (£19,262). Although this level of wealth placed them comfortably over the average wealth of the Scottish middling ranks in the 1820s, the downwards pattern can be contrasted with the firm of John Campbell senior & Co.[112] The direct paternal line of John Campbell senior left increasingly large fortunes as profits were retained, diversified and reinvested, culminating in one of the largest fortunes of Scotland in the colonial period. By compiling biographies and tracing investments in

[107] Smith, *Strathblane*, pp. 52–7.

[108] 105 inventories were identified for the Glasgow West India merchants in this study. They left a total of £4,806,712 (ave. £45,778) compared to the 9 Smith co-partners (total holdings £269,449, ave. £29,944).

[109] NRS, SC36/48/9, 'Inventory of James Smith of Craighead', 9 June 1815, pp. 685–6.

[110] NRS, SC36/48/11, 'Inventory of John Smith of Craigend', 24 June 1816, p. 39.

[111] NRS, CC10/7/4, 'Settlement and inventory of Archibald Smith of Jordanhill', 31 Oct. 1821.

[112] A. McCrum, 'Inheritance and the family: the Scottish urban experience in the 1820s', in *Urban Fortunes: Property and Inheritance in the Town*, ed. J. Stobart and A. Owens (Aldershot, 2000), pp. 149–71, at pp. 156–7; S. Mullen, 'The Great Glasgow–West India house of John Campbell Senior & Co.', in *Recovering Scotland's Slavery Past: The Caribbean Connection*, ed. T. M. Devine (Edinburgh, 2015), pp. 124–45.

life (where possible) and inventories on death, this section explains factors underpinning the relative decline of the Smiths of Jordanhill.[113]

All senior partners of Leitch & Smith inherited or purchased landed estates in Scotland. As eldest son of the laird of Craigend, John Smith inherited the estate from his father in 1786, afterwards building a new house on the land. On his death in 1816, his son James Smith junior set about constructing Craigend Castle, a country pile more befitting a West India merchant.[114] The Atlantic trades also propelled younger sons into the landed ranks. James Smith purchased Craighead in 1800, the same year as his younger brother Archibald also bought an estate. After the commercial demise of Alexander Houston & Co., the pre-eminent sugar merchants in Scotland, the estate of Jordanhill, including a mansion house and 285 English acres of land, was sold by auction at the Tontine Coffee House on 7 May 1800.[115] On 10 September 1800, Archibald Smith paid £16,500 for the estate.[116] He later estimated that Jordanhill had cost almost £30,000 including improvements.[117] In order to announce his rise from merchant to laird, he modestly commissioned a coat of arms adorned with the Latin motto 'Macte' ('well done').[118] Archibald Smith senior's estate on death, however, reveals the shortcomings of using confirmation inventories as sole indicators of commercial success. His personal property was valued at £47,000. However, his overall estate (that is, movable *and* heritable property, the latter consisting of land and buildings) was valued that same year at £81,494. The estates of Jordanhill (£22,000) and Whiteinch Farm (£13,000) were the most valuable assets.[119] Thus, with a total estate (including heritable property) of over £80,000, Archibald Smith epitomized the very successful – although not the wealthiest – Glasgow-West India elite.

Other partners invested in land too. On his return from Grenada in 1800, John Guthrie purchased the estate of Carbeth in Strathblane. He improved so much of the surrounding area that he was described as 'the maker' of

---

[113] Further research into the wider Smith family has facilitated a more detailed, comparative approach than in the author's earlier article on which this chapter is based, 'A Glasgow-West India merchant house and the imperial dividend, 1779–1867', *Journal of Scottish Historical Studies*, xxxiii (2013), 196–233.

[114] Smith, *Strathblane*, p. 55.

[115] *The Edinburgh Advertiser*, 15 April 1800.

[116] GCA, TD1/100, 'Ledger of Archibald Smith, 1799–1803', p. 70.

[117] GCA, TD1/1095, 'Daybook extracts', 1800–1817.

[118] GCA, TD1/1246/4, 'Patent of Arms', 4 June 1802.

[119] GCA, TD1/1096, 'Estate of the late Arch. Smith'.

Table 3.1 The Smith family, wealth on death 1815–83.

First name	Surname	Year of death	Landed estate	Method	Wealth on death
James	Smith	1815	Craighead	Purchase	£71,027
John	Smith	1816	4th of Craigend	Inheritance	£46,168
Archibald	Smith snr.	1821	Jordanhill	Purchase	£47,017
Archibald	Smith jnr.	1823			£20,682
John	Guthrie	1834	Carbeth	Purchase	£8,977
James	Smith jnr.	1836	5th of Craigend	Inheritance	£19,591
James	Smith ygst.	1867	Jordanhill	Inheritance	£17,727
William	Smith	1871	Carbeth Guthrie	Inheritance	£4,639
Archibald	Smith ygst.	1883	Jordanhill	Inheritance	£33,671
Total					£269,499

Source: National Records of Scotland: Wills, Testaments and Confirmation Inventories (see Bibliography).

the village of Carbeth.[120] This ultimately passed to William Smith. Another partner, Andrew Ranken, purchased Ashburn in Gourock (although he was bankrupted before he died in 1851). Thus, West India profits improved the Smith family seat of Craigend while two younger sons, a nephew and the son-in-law of the firm's senior partner joined the landed ranks. The co-partners of Leitch & Smith thus operated at the pinnacle of the regional economy, accumulating extensive wealth, and investing across the west of Scotland. Like their contemporaries, the 'tobacco lords', the partners based their success on exploitative methods of trade in the colonies which created vast profits to be invested in landed enterprise and industry in Scotland.

None of the first generation of the family owned industrial investments on death, although it is certain they disposed of some as they aged. John Smith inherited the family seat of Craigend but held considerable capital in the firm and was owed up to £9,000 in bond loans.[121] He can be described as a West India proprietor lender. The origins of his brother James Smith of Craighead's fortune lay in employment in Grenada from 1783. He also became a West India proprietor lender whose colonial wealth was invested in the firm and landed enterprise in Scotland. His inventory on death reveals – in addition to loans to Leitch & Smith – other loans mainly on bond to various individuals

---

[120] Smith, *Strathblane*, pp. 41–4.

[121] NRS, SC36/48/11, 'Inventory of John Smith of Craigend', 24 June 1816, pp. 39–40.

between 1803 and 1814.[122] The interest on major outlying loans in Scotland – the rates of which are not defined in the sources – was a supplementary source of income. According to his brother Archibald, he was averse to risk-taking, which explains his preference for supplying credit within the family.

Archibald Smith senior was a speculative West India mercantile investor. Having arrived back in Glasgow in 1779 – more likely penniless but with commercial knowledge – he founded Leitch & Smith, which became the source of the family wealth. Throughout his life, he continued with risky investments in Scotland. Glasgow's first banks were established by tobacco merchants and, similarly, Archibald Smith sunk investment into savings banks and insurance schemes. He bought four shares for a total of £1,000 in Glasgow Fire Insurance Society in 1803 and was voted a director.[123] With James Ewing, Smith was involved with the establishment of the first Provident Bank in Glasgow in 1815 and the family still had outstanding subscriptions on its winding up in 1851.[124] As noted above, Smith held investments in cotton firm James Finlay & Co. in 1797. He also expanded into textile production by employing handloom weavers.[125] In 1799, he established Smith, Hutchison and Co., which became one of the great Glasgow linen houses.[126] On Archibald's death in 1821, he held no shares in insurance, banking or manufacturing firms, but had provided credit to his son's firm, Smith & Browns, among others.[127]

Case study comparisons thus reveal Glasgow-West India merchants were involved in a range of activities across the Scottish-Atlantic world, drawing capital from the colonies for speculative investment at home, which was governed by the entrepreneurial tendencies of each individual. The accumulation of colonial wealth improved the co-partners' social standing, while local political appointments publicly affirmed their elite status. Archibald Smith senior was one of the original subscribers of the Chamber of Commerce in 1783, and chairman in 1815. He was also the dean of guild of the Merchants House, 1799–1800. John Guthrie was dean of guild of the Merchants House in 1814–15 and Adam Crooks was deputy chairman of the Chamber of Commerce in 1829. Archibald Smith, John Guthrie and Adam Crooks were founder members of the influential lobbying group the

---

[122] NRS, SC36/48/9, 'Inventory of James Smith of Craighead', 9 June 1815, pp. 685–6.

[123] GUA, UGD 71/1/5, 'Glasgow Fire Insurance Society', May 1803.

[124] J. Cleland, *The Rise and Progress of the City of Glasgow* (Glasgow, 1840), p. 64; *GH*, 5 Sept. 1851.

[125] GCA, TD1/107, 'Day book'.

[126] Craik, Eadie and Galbraith, *Memoirs and Portraits*, pp. 173–6.

[127] NRS, CC10/7/4, 'Inventory of Archibald Smith of Jordanhill', 31 Oct. 1821, pp. 244–7.

Glasgow West India Association in 1807. In time, both Archibald Smith senior and youngest were appointed director and chairman. As discussed in Chapter 1, influential positions consolidated elite reputations in the city.

In financial terms alone, the next generation were not as successful. When Archibald Smith junior, the son of John Smith of Craigend, died in 1823, he was worth over £20,000 (the vast majority of which was held in the merchant firm) but more still was held in mortgages secured on enslaved people:

> At the time of his decease, his share of certain sums of money secured over certain plantations in the colonies…by mortgages or otherwise and held by the said concern of Leitch and Smith which it is impossible to value at present…being heritable Colonial property.[128]

When his brother James Smith junior (who had inherited Craigend from his father) died in 1836, he was worth over £19,500. Leitch & Smith had been disbanded by then and Smith had moved away from the West India trades. Instead, his inventory revealed significant cash in the bank, as well as outstanding bond loans to firms associated with cousins, Smith, Hutchison & Co., and Jas. & Arch. Smith & Co. He had also invested in Glasgow Waterworks. With no direct investments in West India trades, James Smith junior of Craigend symbolizes the wider family's movement away from colonial to domestic enterprise.[129]

Archibald's Smith's three sons, however, retained interests in the West Indies. The glorious histories of Glasgow portray James Smith youngest of Jordanhill as having limited involvement in the family West India business.[130] However, James had a major financial interest in Leitch & Smith and was a leading influence in the successor firm. He might be described as a West India merchant *dilletante*, utilizing profits to support an elite lifestyle centred around cultural pursuits in the west of Scotland. James Smith ostensibly devoted himself to science, literature and gentrified activities. A statement of his wealth in April 1832 confirmed he was part of the 'very wealthy merchant elite' who maintained an estate and townhouse. Yet in 1832, he held £7,800 in Leitch & Smith – suggesting it was still owed debts – and £15,200 in Jas. & Arch. Smith & Co. Smith's main income came from West India shares and stock. The most valuable investments were Jordanhill and Whiteinch – which he had inherited from his father – as well as his library and house in

---

[128] NRS, SC36/48/19, 'Inventory of Archibald Smith', 10 Aug. 1824, pp. 145–6.

[129] NRS, SC36/48/25, 'Inventory of James Smith of Craigend', 15 Dec. 1836, pp. 726–7.

[130] G. Stewart, *Curiosities of Glasgow Citizenship* (Glasgow, 1881), p. 237; Craik, Eadie and Galbraith, *Memoirs and Portraits of One Hundred Glasgow Men*, vol. ii, p.286.

George Square.[131] His pastimes were symbolic of his gentrified lifestyle. As the 'father of yachting on the Clyde', he owned sailing ships from 1806.[132] From 1830 until 1839 he was president of Anderson's University (now the University of Strathclyde) and was a significant donor to the Andersonian Museum. As president of the Glasgow Dilettanti Society, he had a keen interest in fine arts, exemplified by his extensive painting collection at Jordanhill, which was valued (with furniture) at £3,000.[133] James had no industrial investments on his death in 1867 or in two subsequent inventories which revised his estate.[134] In 1867, his interests in the organization including two Jamaica plantations were deemed to be of 'no value'.[135] It is very likely the costs of an elite lifestyle drained the fortune to the extent he left much less than his brother Archibald. Neither was able to extricate the firm from the West Indies. Instead, on James Smith's death in 1867, they were left with the shell of a merchant firm whose only assets were plantations in Jamaica that could not be disposed of after years of unprofitability. Moreover, James inherited Jordanhill, and with that came the responsibility for the upkeep of his mother, Isabella Smith, who died in 1855, having lived to the grand old age of 100.[136] James Smith's high-consumption lifestyle was entirely based upon the family West India fortune and his successor firm, the profits from which declined after emancipation. The firm, Jas and Arch. Smith & Co., disbanded soon after the death of James Smith. Unlike the Campbells of Possil, the Smiths of Jordanhill's fortune declined in two generations.

The third son of Archibald Smith senior, however, inherited his father's business acumen and was the exception to this pattern of relative failure. Indeed, Victorian histories of Glasgow describe Archibald Smith youngest as an 'excellent man of business'.[137] He was the most successful financially of his siblings and can be considered a second-generation West India speculator who invested West India profits across Victorian Scotland. In the 1820s and 1830s he was the senior partner in Jas. & Arch. Smith & Co.

---

[131] GCA, TD1/1096, 'Statement', April 1832; S. Nenadic, 'The Victorian middle classes', in *Glasgow, Vol. 2: 1830–1912*, ed. W. H. Fraser and I. Maver (Manchester, 1996), p. 283.

[132] Craik, Eadie and Galbraith, *Memoirs and Portraits*, p. 285.

[133] GCA, TD1/1096, 'Remarks on paintings at Jordanhill'; 'Statement of James Smith, April 1832'.

[134] NRS, SC58/42/34, 'Inventory of James Smith', 28 Aug. 1876, pp. 941–79; NRS, SC58/42/52, 'Additional inventory of James Smith', 28 Jan. 1886, pp. 935–8.

[135] NRS, SC58/42/34, 'Deed of settlement of James Smith', 31 Oct. 1867, pp. 977–8.

[136] NRS, SC36/48/41, 'Inventory of Isabella Smith', 9 Oct. 1855, p. 845. Mrs Smith was worth £2,177 when she died.

[137] Craik, Eadie and Galbraith, *Memoirs and Portraits*, p. 286.

and made commercial investments much like his father; he was named as a director of Beacon Fire Insurance Company of London and Edinburgh in 1826.[138] On his brother's death in 1867, Archibald Smith youngest inherited the family interests and the estate income was £5,899 per annum. Although the estate was heavily burdened, the main annual source was £3,000 from the Monkland Iron and Steel Company who mined Jordanhill estate. The investment in land from the initial fortune meant the family profited from successive stages of industrialization in Scotland.[139] He speculated in railway shares and left personal wealth of over £33,000 when he died. Owning shares in Scottish railways as well as in banks in Scotland and England, his holdings were typical of the West India elite who lived into the latter half of the nineteenth century.[140] As one of the oldest surviving members of the Chamber of Commerce, Archibald Smith maintained a public role before he died aged eighty-eight in 1883. Thus, as one of the last remaining elite Glasgow-West India merchants, he ensured the Smiths of Jordanhill saw out the city's sugar era.

Conclusion

In *An Inquiry into the Nature and Causes of the Wealth of Nations* (1776), Adam Smith was unequivocal that credit from the metropolis overflowed to the British West Indies, which drained the mother country. At the end of a pre-eminent research career examining the private papers of merchants and planters, including the Lascelles and the Pinneys, Richard Pares (after initially agreeing with Adam Smith) radically shifted position:

> The money came, in the last resort, from the planters themselves. The factors charged high interest – even, on occasion, compound interest. They paid it to themselves on the planters behalf, without any order from him, and they made sure of having it, whoever else went short. The money which was received from one planter was lent again, either to him or another planter... Thus, it was the planter who was paying, so to speak, for his own enslavement. The profits of the plantations were the source which fed the indebtedness charged upon the plantations themselves. In this sense, Adam Smith was wrong: the wealth of the British West Indies did not all proceed from the mother country; after some initial loans in the earliest period which merely primed the pump, the wealth of the West Indies was created out of the profits of the

---

[138] Glasgow Herald (hereafter *GH*), 26 June 1826.

[139] GCA, TD1/22, 'Statement of Archibald Smith', 1873.

[140] NRS, SC65/34/26, 'Inventory of Archibald Smith', 7 April 1883, pp. 295–310.

West Indies themselves, and, with some assistance from the British taxpayer, much of it found a permanent home in Great Britain.[141]

Thus, for Pares, the merchants ensured the profits of the sugar trade were repatriated through monopolistic practices which subsequently assisted the development of Great Britain. Richard Sheridan, also citing the Lascelles accounts, argued that surplus in the account current of planters managed by metropolis merchants was invested in Great Britain, indicating a 'capital in-flow'.[142] More recently, after detailed analysis of the remaining material concerning the Lascelles, S. D. Smith suggested that 'Adam Smith's image of an overflowing of British riches into the Caribbean was closer to the truth'.[143] The sources sampled here do not allow detailed tracing of the 'ontogeny of debt',[144] but in their own words, the Smiths provide evidence that reveals their family fortune originated in the West Indies. The Smith fortunes came from West India planters themselves – in Grenada especially, although less wealth flowed from Jamaica – which was ploughed back into the firm, providing the capital that was ultimately invested (and lost) in Scotland.

This study has examined Leitch & Smith and their commercial successors and illuminated the operations that connected Scotland and the West Indies. Between 1800 and 1866, over £149,000 was extended to a merchant house in Grenada (4 per cent of the total), a Glasgow-West India merchant house for working capital on Jamaica plantations (35 per cent) and individual planters across both colonies (61 per cent). Clearly, the Smiths were powerful merchant financiers who operated a long-term commission system based on the extension of capital, similar to the English-West India merchant houses like the Pinneys, who had £80,000 of outstanding debt in the Caribbean in 1819.[145] Indeed, the Smiths were exceptions to the view that merchants in Glasgow were less inclined to become bankers to plantation owners, in contrast to those in London.[146] In fact, the opposite was true: the elite West India houses of Glasgow also took on a de facto role as bankers with mainly Scottish planters in the West Indies. This adds a new dimension to the vision of British credit flowing into the colonies.

[141] R. Pares, *Merchants and Planters*. The Economic History Review Supplement, No. 4 (New York, 1960), p. 50.

[142] Sheridan, *Sugar and Slavery*, p. 295.

[143] Smith, *Gentry Capitalism*, p. 173.

[144] S. D. Smith, 'Merchants and planters revisited', *The Economic History Review*, lv (2002), pp. 434–65.

[145] Pares, *West India Fortune*, p. 181.

[146] R. Pares, *Merchants and Planters*, p. 49.

On the other hand, in Archibald Smith senior's own words in 1815, he 'had been the means of making' the fortune.[147] Indeed, he fashioned a family dynasty based initially on the Grenada business, as Leitch & Smith dominated the profitable free port trade on the island. Based on John Guthrie's statement, this seems to have been the most profitable branch of the business. The firm supplied credit to planters after 1800 and maintained an efficient system protected by a series of risk-averse methods based on established networks of kith and kin. In Jamaica, the firm acquired the trade from plantations which was their most valuable account up to 1818. Thus, the sugar and cotton plantations of the Caribbean primed the pump and – with support from Scottish banks – allowed the accumulation of capital for investment and diversification in Scottish land, industry and commerce. This boom time coincided with the purchase of the estates of Jordanhill, Craighead and Carbeth, while the family seat of Craigend was much improved. Moreover, capital was sunk into textiles, banking, insurance and eventually heavy industry. Thus, the Smiths converted the profits from commodity trades to property in Scotland and collected the imperial dividend where others – such as Alexander Houston & Co. – ultimately failed. When considering the long-term solvency of the firm and the investments of merchants in life and wealth on death, it seems a profitable business underpinned high personal incomes and wealth of co-partners, up to a point.

The study also reveals different types of mercantile spenders: investors in land, speculators in commerce, lenders of large-scale credit and high-consumption lifestyles. The senior partners left the largest fortunes, loaned regularly and invested wisely. The sons who inherited business interests bequeathed lesser personal wealth. However, by contrasting the investment patterns of Archibald Smith's sons, explanations for the decline in the family fortunes become apparent. James Smith youngest of Jordanhill spent freely on non-entrepreneurial investments in Scotland, while Archibald youngest diversified into Scottish industry such as railways. Thus, while the Jamaica business seemingly took some of the family fortune back, by diversifying his investments, Archibald Smith youngest was able to grow his inheritance and acquire substantial personal wealth. In this way, despite a relative decline, the accumulation of West India fortunes boosted the family's status and, in the process, reshaped the Scottish economy and society throughout the eighteenth and nineteenth centuries.

---

[147] GCA, TD1/26/3, 'Letter from Archibald Smith', 11 Aug. 1815.

4. 'Wanted, to serve in the West Indies'[1]

On the morning of 11 January 1833, John Kennedy departed from the port of Greenock aboard the ship *Glasgow* destined for Jamaica.[2] Born in Glasgow, he was the son of Gaelic poet and accountant Duncan Kennedy who hailed from Argyll in the Scottish Highlands. Aged nineteen, Kennedy engaged for Jamaica with dreams of easing his family's financial worries. Given his later debts to the Glasgow firm Robert Bogle & Co., Kennedy most likely engaged for Kingston in the firm's counting house on 49 Queen Street, near Glasgow's Royal Exchange.[3] By this time, the exchange had replaced the Tontine Rooms as the city's commercial headquarters and was home to the pro-slavery lobbying group, the Glasgow West India Association. Kennedy must have been aware of the West India merchants who sold valuable sugar from the exchange's sample room. The opulence of the building would have reminded him of the wealth on offer in the West Indies. As the voyage had been advertised in the *Glasgow Herald* before the New Year, Kennedy was undoubtedly aware Bogle's ship was preparing to depart from Greenock in early January.[4] On the day, he probably travelled in a small barge (a gabbart) to the larger vessel docked further along the Clyde basin in the deep-water port. At 2pm on 11 January, the *Glasgow* cleared the port of Greenock. With a 'heavy heart' and residing in the 'miserable steerages' of the ship, John Kennedy set off on the long journey to Jamaica. As the ship cleared the Tail O' the Bank at Greenock, he wore trousers and a heavy coat – warm clothes for a Scottish winter – which held out the cold as they sailed past the island of Great Cumbrae before crossing the Irish Sea towards Cork and the Atlantic Ocean. As the ship approached the latitude of the Canaries, the air became warmer and Kennedy wished for more appropriate clothing. Crossing the Atlantic in just thirty-one days – 'as quick a passage as the ship

---

[1]   The advertisement placed by John Campbell senior & Co., looking for labourers to transport to Tobago and Grenada in 1812. *GH*, 18 May 1812, p. 3.

[2]   The author is grateful to James Brown for providing a copy of this privately held correspondence. See J. Brown, 'Duncan Kennedy: from Gaelic poet to Glasgow accountant', *Scottish Local History*, lxxxviii (2014).

[3]   *The Post Office Directory, for 1832–33* (Glasgow, 1832), p. 62.

[4]   *GH*, 21 Dec. 1832, p. 3.

ever made' – the *Glasgow* arrived at the Windward Islands on 12 February 1833, eventually reaching Kingston a week later.

Kennedy enjoyed the luxury of a good education and kept a journal on the voyage. To keep the promise made to his father before departure, he immediately wrote a letter home in a fine copperplate script. Without clothing such as pantaloons, tight trousers and jackets required for employment in the tropics, he was woefully underprepared. Even more troubling was his lack of funds. He only possessed £3 sterling and had to draw a bill – repayable from his first salary – to cover the costs of the carriage from Kingston to his destination in St Thomas-in-the-Vale, close to Spanishtown. Since he was drafted at once into the island militia, he was also without the funds required to purchase a red coat and blue feather of the Light Infantry as well as a horse, saddle and bridle. He was, however, thankful for his connections with the influential West India merchants and planters of Glasgow. His father's acquaintance George William Hamilton, cousin of Archibald Bogle, provided a letter of introduction to Henry Lowndes, temporary attorney of the Bogle plantations while Hamilton was back in Scotland. Lowndes was a nephew of prominent Glasgow planter, John Blackburn, who owned Wallens estate in St Thomas-in-the-Vale. Kennedy was delighted to be quickly appointed as a bookkeeper on the Hyde estate in the same parish on 1 March 1833. The position meant Kennedy could repay debts. Although not under the impression 'a fortune can be made easier in Jamaica than at home', he understood a reputable person of good conduct could make rapid progress on the island. Kennedy had already promised to send home half his salary of £42 per annum, which, they all hoped, would end his and the family's hardships.

The typicality of John Kennedy's narrative will be analysed in this and further chapters. As an educated young man of Highland stock, he went to Jamaica in the hope of easing his family's penury. A beneficiary of patronage from Glasgow merchants, a letter of introduction to a Scottish planter secured his first start on the island. Nevertheless, he took on debts which afterwards vexed him and would have taken him months to repay. Exactly how Kennedy fared is unknown. It is probable he died in Jamaica – he left no will or inventoried wealth in Scotland – perhaps after supporting his family for some years but having failed to realize a large fortune. This chapter takes a broad approach, first by tracing flows of Clyde-Caribbean labour, recruitment and migration and illustrating the processes that facilitated Kennedy's journey – and that of many others like him – to the West Indies during Glasgow's sugar era, 1775–1838.

Scottish imperial adventurers

There was a long tradition of mobile Scots emigrating in search for advancement. Indeed, the extent of seventeenth-century outward migration to Ireland, Poland and Scandinavia from Scotland could have been the highest per-capita rate in Europe.[5] After the Union of 1707 opened up the British empire, migrants from the Scottish Lowlands and Highlands departed in high numbers. It is estimated that around 90,000 Scots migrated to North America between 1700 and 1815.[6] Levels of outward migration were influenced by both 'push' factors in Scotland and 'pull' factors from the colonies.[7] Indeed, adverse economic conditions led many to leave the country, although numbers remained paradoxically high even after the increase of employment opportunities due to the growth of domestic industry.[8] Scottish emigration to settler colonies – especially North America – was thus large-scale and has been the subject of a well-developed historiography. Migration to the West Indies, however, particularly after 1800, has received less scholarly attention, mainly due to the paucity of official sources.[9]

Scots were pervasive across the British West Indies, despite not possessing formal colonies. Even before the Incorporating Union of 1707, imperial commentators envisioned Scots as ideal emigrants to bolster military presence and labour power in the colonies, and the Union's passage enabled what has been described as the 'harnessing of Scotland' to enhance the English empire.[10] Although a relative latecomer to the Americas, England established control over a range of colonies – in an era of expansionist conflict between the dominant European powers – which became known as the British empire by 1708.[11] What became the Thirteen Colonies of North America began with the establishment of Virginia in 1607. Further south, the tropic of Cancer

---

[5] T. C. Smout, N. C. Landsman and T. M. Devine, 'Scottish emigration in the early modern period', in *Europeans on the Move: Studies on European Migration, 1500–1800*, ed. N. Canny (Oxford, 1994), pp. 76–112.

[6] Smout, Landsman and Devine, 'Scottish emigration in the early modern period', pp. 97 and 104; B. Bailyn, *Voyagers to the West: A Passage in the Peopling of America on the Eve of the Revolution* (New York, 1986), pp. 11–12.

[7] R. H. Campbell, 'Scotland', in *The Scots Abroad: Labour, Capital, Enterprise, 1750–1914*, ed. R. A. Cage (London, 1985), pp. 7–8.

[8] T. M. Devine, 'The paradox of Scottish emigration', in *Scottish Emigration and Scottish Society*, ed. T. M. Devine (Edinburgh, 1992), pp. 1–15.

[9] Scottish migration to the Caribbean hardly features in modern works. For example, T. M. Devine, *To the Ends of the Earth: Scotland's Global Diaspora* (London, 2011).

[10] A. I. Macinnes, *Union and Empire: The Making of the United Kingdom in 1707* (Cambridge, 2007), pp. 195–7.

[11] J. Oldmixon, *The British Empire in America*, 2 vols. (London, 1708).

defined the edge of the European peace treaties, which allowed open conflict in the frontier 'beyond the line'.[12] In turn, the Caribbean became a crucible of European maritime wars as the English took advantage of the declining strength of the Dutch, French and Spanish empires.

For B. W. Higman, the British West Indies were created in three phases of colonial expansion and shaped by voyages of settlement, emigration and trade in conjunction with colonial spoils of war.[13] In the first phase of the English colonization, the islands of Barbados (1625) and Jamaica (1655) were settled mainly by English colonists, although bolstered with Scots adventurers and indentures who also swept into the Leeward Islands of St Kitts (1623), Nevis (1620), Antigua (1632) and Montserrat (1632). For Scots on the make after the Union of 1707, second-phase colonies were unrestricted and opportunities increased after the Treaty of Utrecht in 1713 and especially after the Seven Years War (1756–63). Under the terms of the Treaty of Paris, Great Britain acquired Dominica, Grenada, St Vincent and the Grenadines and Tobago (the 'ceded islands'). Third-phase colonies – added after victories in the French Revolutionary and Napoleonic Wars (1793–1815) – included Trinidad (1797) and St Lucia (1803). Demerara, Berbice and Essequibo were taken from the Dutch and merged to become British Guiana in 1831. These colonies attracted significant British investment capital at the beginning of the nineteenth century as new fortunes were made.[14]

Scots took full advantage of rampant imperial expansion in what became the British West Indies. The motives of transient migrants to the West Indies were, of course, rooted in economics. In November 1837, the advocate Lord Corehouse passed judgment in a case regarding inheritance, domicile and jurisdiction at the Court of Session in Edinburgh:

> Persons going to the East or West Indies from this country, with the view of making a fortune, have for the most part a fixed intention of returning home when their fortune is made. I know but of one instance of a gentleman who realised a large fortune, and who had retired from public service, but who resolved to end his days [in the Indies].[15]

---

[12] R. S. Dunn, *Sugar and Slaves: The Rise of the Planter Class in the English West Indies, 1624–1713* (Chapel Hill, 1972), p. 3.

[13] B. W. Higman, *Slave Populations of the British Caribbean, 1807–1834* (Baltimore, 1984), pp. 43–4.

[14] J. R. Ward, 'The British West Indies in the age of abolition, 1748–1815', in *The Oxford History of the British Empire: The Eighteenth Century*, vol. ii, ed. P. J. Marshall (Oxford, 1998), p. 415; N. Draper, 'The rise of a new planter class? Some countercurrents from British Guiana and Trinidad, 1807–33', *Atlantic Studies*, ix (March 2012), 65–83.

[15] *Decisions of the Court Session from 12 November 1837 to 12 July 1838* (Edinburgh, 1839), p. 81.

The Corehouse observation reveals the *mentalité* of Scots in the West Indies – major wealth accumulation and rapid return – a learned opinion that is, of course, consistent with modern historiography. The role of Scots across the West Indies was first noted by Richard Sheridan and their motives explored in Alan Karras' classic study of the temporary economic migrants he described as sojourners.[16] Jamaica was an obvious destination for wealth accumulation, according to one contemporary Scot who viewed the island as a 'constant mine, whence Britain draws prodigious riches'.[17] The prospect of wealth attracted Scottish and English adventurers to the West Indies who sought to acquire wealth before returning home.[18] This goal was shared with counterparts who travelled to the East Indies, although, ironically, West India fortunes – even though derived from enslaved labour – were deemed the more acceptable in nineteenth-century Britain. The latter were perceived to be based upon landownership and natural produce, while the former were seemingly accumulated from 'murky sources' such as usurious speculation in shares, contracts or luxury items.[19]

The impact of both imperial streams look to have been profound, and Andrew Mackillop claimed Scots in the West Indies secured one of the greatest per capita returns.[20] T. M. Devine argues that returned West India capital was a prime source for Scotland's eighteenth-century agricultural improvement.[21] While the supporting evidence is not comprehensive, there is growing consensus that an in-flow of capital from West India sojourners was invested in land and built heritage across Scotland. Thus, instead of the loss of labour and enterprise that departed permanently for white settler communities in North America, presumably taking capital with them,

[16] R. Sheridan, 'The role of Scots in the economy and society of the West Indies', *Annals of the New York Academy of Sciences*, ccxcii (1977), 94–106; A. Karras, *Sojourners in the Sun* (Ithaca, 1992).

[17] C. Leslie, *A New History of Jamaica* (London, 1740), p. 337.

[18] D. Hamilton, *Scotland, the Caribbean and the Atlantic World, 1750–1820* (Manchester, 2005); A. O'Shaughnessy, *An Empire Divided: The American Revolution and the British Caribbean* (Philadelphia, 2000).

[19] A. Mackillop, 'The Highlands and the returning nabob: Sir Hector Munro of Novar, 1760–1807', in *Emigrant Homecomings: The Return Movement of Emigrants, 1600–2000*, ed. M. Harper (Manchester, 2005), pp. 236–7.

[20] A. Mackillop, '"As hewers of wood, and drawers of water": Scotland as an emigrant nation, *c.*1600 to *c.*1800', in *Global Migrations: The Scottish Diaspora since 1600*, ed. A. McCarthy and J. M. MacKenzie (Edinburgh, 2016), p. 36.

[21] T. M. Devine, 'Did slavery make Scotia great? A question revisited', in *Recovering Scotland's Slavery Past: The Caribbean Connection*, ed. T. M. Devine (Edinburgh, 2015), p. 238.

Caribbean sojourning provided an acceptable means – by contemporary standards – to accumulate wealth which subsequently enriched Scotland, at least in theory.[22]

The sojourning mentality therefore poses several questions for historians of Scotland and the Caribbean. How many of these persons travelled? How were they educated or trained in Scotland prior to departure? How much private wealth did they accumulate while there? How many returned and what was the impact at home? The subsequent chapters of this monograph answer these questions by examining Scots in the plantation economies of the British Caribbean. First, this chapter identifies Glasgow as the premier Scottish-Atlantic commercial hub. The perception and attraction of West India fortunes are traced, as well as the business of emigration, and estimates of shipping and emigration. This chapter offers the first estimates of migration for the pivotal years between the abolition of the slave trade (1807) and the abolition of plantation slavery (1834). This framework lays the foundations for chapters focused on Scots in Jamaica, Grenada and Carriacou, and Trinidad: colonies acquired in the first, second and third phases of British imperialism in the West Indies.[23] The reality is that very few sojourners to the British West Indies accumulated great wealth, with most dying in situ, and even those that were successful were only able to repatriate, in general, low-to-medium returns if they managed to get home at all, which was unlikely.

West India fortunes in the Scottish imagination

At the opening of what might be considered Glasgow's sugar era, Sir John Sinclair published *The Statistical Account of Scotland* ('the Old Statistical Account'). Sinclair wrote to over 880 Church of Scotland ministers to survey parishes across Scotland, collating information from 1790 onwards. Responsible for various civic and ecclesiastical duties in communities, ministers were best placed to answer questions in local parishes, including population and prominent citizens, agriculture, education, work and wages.[24] A subsequent volume, *The New Statistical Account*, was published

---

[22] A. Murdoch, 'Hector McAllister in North Carolina, Argyll and Arran: family and memory in return migration to Scotland in the eighteenth century', *Journal of Scottish Historical Studies*, xxxiii (2013), 1–19.

[23] As well as levels of Scottish outward migration, availability of source material was a consideration in choosing these colonies; Jamaica is recognized as holding the best archive collection in the region. See K. E. Ingram, *Manuscript Sources for the History of the West Indies* (Kingston, 2000).

[24] R. L. Plackett, 'The old statistical account', *Journal of the Royal Statistical Society*, series A (general), cxlix (1986), 247–51.

in 1845. The statistical accounts are unique sources for illustrating life in late eighteenth- and early nineteenth-century Scotland. The compilers noted the 'West Indies' in over half of all thirty-four Scottish counties, suggesting that the region was a regular feature of everyday life.

The statistical accounts reveal, first, that the effects of West India fortunes were well-known across Scotland, and, second, that many young men regularly migrated to acquire more. Successful returnees and their fortunes became famous in local communities. In 1793, the Revd Thomas Henderson noted: 'this parish [Dryfesdale in Dumfries] has produced several eminent, learned men who have travelled to the East and West Indies, and successfully obtained fortunes'.[25] These men often became prominent notables. In 1794, the Revd John Hutcheon noted two major success stories in the parish of Fetteresso in Kincardine. First, 'Mr. Silver, a native of this district, made a purchase of the estate of Netherby, on his return from the West Indies, where he built a genteel modern dwelling-house.' Second, 'Mr Mackie, lately from the West Indies, made a purchase of the lands of Sketraw, in 1788, where he has built a very good dwelling house and made very great improvements.'[26]

In addition to private wealth acquisition, returned West India fortunes often improved the local environment as well as the standard of living of the local population. In the united parishes of Logie and Pert in the county of Forfar in 1793, the Revd Alexander Peter was dazzled by the 'increase both of splendour and luxury in many places of the neighbourhood occasioned chiefly by the influx of wealth from the East and West Indies'.[27] That same year, three ministers in Inverness noted the increasing prosperity of the burgh was due to 'great influx of money from the East and West Indies'.[28] Ministers noted almost twenty examples of philanthropy from West India adventurers to provide alms for the poor and bequests for schools, or to universities. Often these were large-scale and lived long in the public memory. In 1732, Dr Gilbert Ramsay, late rector of Christ Church in Barbados, bequeathed around £5,000 to fund students of divinity and a professor of Oriental Languages at Marischal College. This bequest remained well-known enough to be commented upon a half-century later.[29] In 1786, John Erskine Esq. of the parish of St James, Jamaica, left £5,000 'for the benefit of ten poor families...[and] to be divided among eight poor

---

[25] Sir John Sinclair, *The Statistical Account of Scotland*, Dryfesdale, Dumfries, vol. ix (Edinburgh, 1793), p. 432.

[26] Sinclair, *Statistical Account of Scotland*, Fetteresso, Kincardine, vol. xxi, pp. 593–4.

[27] Sinclair, *Statistical Account of Scotland*, Logie Pert, Forfar, vol. ix, p. 51.

[28] Sinclair, *Statistical Account of Scotland*, Inverness, Inverness, vol. ix, p. 617.

[29] Sinclair, *Statistical Account of Scotland*, Birse, County of Aberdeen, vol. ix, p. 119 and p. 127.

boys...which has proven highly advantageous to the charity'. This was reported by *The New Statistical Account* well over a half-century later.[30] In 1794, a minister reported how a Mrs Elizabeth Farquharson of Jamaica, originally of Tulloch in Aberdeenshire, bequeathed £400 'for the benefit of the poor here, and the like sum to keep school and schoolmaster in these parishes', which was noted thirty years after her death.[31] In 1831, an endowed school, Bathgate Academy, was established from a bequest of c.£14,000 by John Newlands, 'a native of the parish, who, after being bred a carpenter, left Bathgate at an early age and proceeded to Jamaica'.[32]

After the abolition of plantation slavery, one parochial school in Rogart in Sutherland retained a considerable reputation for educating young men who went to the West Indies. The Revd John Mackenzie noted graduates had found employment 'on plantation estates in the West Indies' and were 'reported to be persevering and industrious'. The 'small remittances frequently made to poor relatives afford a pleasing proof that they are prosperous'.[33] Unrepresentative success stories like the above glared in public for decades. West India fortunes were widely known across the country, which compelled skilled and educated young men to cross the Atlantic. Thus, the prospect of major slavery fortunes encouraged large-scale migration from across Scotland (and not the Highlands exclusively) to high-risk environments.[34]

West India migration, and the fortunes that came back in return, were well known to late eighteenth-century Scots. In 1792, the Revd John McKill of Durisdeer in the county of Dumfries noted 'several of the natives have gone abroad likewise in the mercantile line, and some of them have been very successful in the West Indies'.[35] And this was mainly young men. When writing the statistical account for Kells in the country of Kirkcudbright in 1792, the Revd John Gillespie noted: 'Several young men of spirit go to the West Indies as planters and merchants'.[36] Knowledge of successful wealth accumulation must surely have encouraged others to follow, which decreased the numbers

---

[30] J. Gordon (ed.), *The New Statistical Account of Scotland*, Montrose, Forfar, vol. xi (Edinburgh, 1845), p. 290.

[31] Sinclair, *Statistical Account of Scotland*, Glenmuick, Aberdeen, vol. xii, p. 221.

[32] Gordon, *New Statistical Account of Scotland*, Bathgate, Linlithgow, vol. ii, pp. 164–5.

[33] Gordon, *New Statistical Account of Scotland*, Rogart, Sutherland, vol. xv, p. 56.

[34] D. Alston, '"You have only seen the fortunate few and draw conclusions accordingly": behavioural economics and the paradox of Scottish emigration', in *Global Migrations: The Scottish Diaspora since 1600*, ed. A. McCarthy and J. M. MacKenzie (Edinburgh, 2016), pp. 46–63.

[35] Sinclair, *Statistical Account of Scotland*, Durisdeer, Dumfries, vol. iv, pp. 462–3.

[36] Sinclair, *Statistical Account of Scotland*, Kells, Kirkcudbright, vol. iv, p. 264.

of men of working age. In 1795, the Revd Dr John Scott bemoaned there were no more than four servants who had been born in the parish of Twynholm in Kirkcudbright. For 'seventeen young men, if not more, within these few years, have gone to England, America and the West Indies, in the mercantile line'.[37] The perception of colonial wealth in full public view across Scotland naturally pulled young men across the Atlantic in search of more, while the lack of opportunities pushed thousands away from their homeland forever. This became a self-perpetuating cycle of declining opportunity: young men migrated from Scotland in search of fortunes and most died abroad, a process which, in some cases, constrained the development of local economies.

Thomas Somerville, the minister of Jedburgh, was ultra-pessimistic when he summarized the fate of Scots in the West Indies in 1814:

> Of all these, few returned to their native country – Jamaica in particular, from the number who died there, was long known by the name of 'the grave of Scotland;' – and of those who did return, few added to the stock of national wealth.[38]

This lament was not simply rhetorical. White mortality rates in Jamaica have been described as higher than almost anywhere else (except West Africa) in the British empire. The average life expectancy for migrants was 12.5 years. Urban mortality in 1780s Kingston was 51 per 1,000 people (5.1 per cent): twice the comparative rates in England.[39] Sometimes the smaller islands had occasionally higher rates. On 14 December 1828, one commentator in Tobago noted 'out of a resident population…not exceeding 256 Whites, the deaths since February 1826 are 73!' This would suggest thirty-six deaths per year, a mortality rate of 14 per cent.[40] These abstract percentages mask the human dimension. In 1818, forty-three men arrived in Tobago from Scotland and only two were still alive in 1825 (a master carpenter remained on the island, but the other had given up and returned to Europe).[41] One historian noted that of sixteen young men who departed from the Scottish Highlands for Demerara and Berbice in early 1800, only one was still alive

---

[37] Sinclair, *Statistical Account of Scotland*, Twynholm, Kirkcudbright, vol. xv, p. 91.

[38] T. Somerville, *My Own Life and Times, 1741–1814* (Edinburgh, 1861), p. 359.

[39] T. Burnard, '"The countrie continues sicklie": white mortality in Jamaica, 1655–1780', *Social History of Medicine*, xii (1999), 45–72, at pp. 50 and 62.

[40] *Beinecke Lesser Antilles Collection at Hamilton College*, M534, 'Scraps &c. In the tropics from 1824 to 1831', fo. 83 <https://beinecke.hamilton.edu/> [accessed 23 Oct. 2021].

[41] *Beinecke Lesser Antilles Collection at Hamilton College*, M534, 'Scraps &c. In the tropics from 1824 to 1831', fo. 11.

eighteen months later.[42] With so few of the outward bound living long lives, a Scottish doctor in Dominica, Jonathan Troup, commented in 1789 about the hopelessness of the quest for wealth: 'One man only makes a fortune in W Indies out of 500', while it could take twenty years to accumulate 'more than £3,–4,000'.[43] If these rates are representative of the Scottish sojourning experience overall, the vast majority would have been dead before they managed to acquire any substantial fortune at all.

The micro-effects of West Indian emigration on Scottish development remains little understood, but the impact was not always positive in economic terms. On occasion, the departure of colonial adventurers was said to have contributed to the decline of a local parish. In 1792, the Revd Dr Alexander Duncan noted the population in the parish of Smallholm in Roxburgh had decreased six-fold in ninety years, with just 100 remaining in 1790. Emigration of young men, including to the West Indies, was a contributory factor, especially as 'many of [them] never return'. As labour became scarce, wages went up and farmers relocated from the area.[44] While West India success stories – usually men with great fortunes – were well-known across Scotland throughout the slavery period and continue to attract the attention of historians, the failures were publicized less often. With profits in the public eye, and deaths on estates out of sight across the Atlantic, outward migration dramatically increased. Clyde ports, and the colonial merchants who facilitated the Atlantic trades, are normally viewed as the source of Scotland's commercial wealth that underpinned industrialization in west-central Scotland, but the insatiable demand for educated men, skilled labour and capital also contributed to the under development of other regions.

Recruiting for the plantation economy

In the aftermath of the Treaty of Paris in 1763, one author in the *Scots Magazine* suggested unscrupulous merchants offered young lads passage to the West Indies. The servitude that followed invariably led to a premature death, which subsequently deprived the nation of labour:

> Every year we see advertisements offering encouragement to persons to go to Jamaica & *c*. These persons enter into indentures, binding themselves for three or four years. This is a custom worthy the attention even of the legislature, not only as by it the country is deprived of many useful hands, but also as these persons are deceived into perpetual slavery. Young men void

---

[42] Alston, 'You have only seen the fortunate few', p. 46.

[43] A. I. Macinnes and L. G. Fryer, *Scotland and the Americas, c.1650–c.1939: A Documentary Source Book* (Edinburgh, 2008), p. 216.

[44] Sinclair, *Statistical Account of Scotland*, Smallholm, Roxburgh, vol. iii, p. 218.

of experience are easily prevailed upon to enter into these engagements: they hear of fortunes made in those distant parts; but they do not know, that one in ten doesn't live, and that the lives of those who go from Britain to the West Indies cannot be computed at above three years. This demand, though the country is less able to supply it, is rather increasing than diminishing.[45]

In times of full employment in Scotland, high wages were the lure to entice skilled employees. In 1791, a representative of the merchant firm Stirling, Gordon & Co. revealed the previous Scottish bookkeeper they sent to Jamaica was paid £30 sterling per year, although improved terms would now have to be offered, as it was more difficult to 'tempt' new recruits due to the scarcity of labour in Scotland that year.[46] Medicinal incentives were offered too. Partners of Alexander Houston & Co. offered a cooper, William Allason, an indenture contract in Grenada based on incremental wages that rose from £20 to £35 across the four-year period. Half of Allason's medical bills were also to be covered.[47] For young men in search of fortune, the offer of a guaranteed start with high wages and medical care must have been extremely alluring. Yet, most did not live long enough to reach the peak wage point.

The labour of many young men was retained for set periods in the Caribbean through indentured contracts signed in Scotland. The contract provided assisted passage, although it would also have tied young lads to positions for several years – usually three.[48] Indentures offered in Glasgow effectively tied young adventurers to long-term occupational positions in the West Indies. The indenture system – based on an advance in wages to cover passage – prevented the desertion of skilled personnel in the colonies. The importance of indentures is revealed in correspondence from Spencer Mackay, a Scots merchant-proprietor in Demerara in the late 1790s:

> The young man Mr Hill arrived here two days ago…I would never have a young man in this part of the world without indentures, I…mentioned 2–3 years. I…never intended bringing people out to the W. Indies at my risk without some security over their future services.[49]

These contracts became synonymous with Scots in the West Indies. One French traveller in Tobago in the 1810s was astonished at the widespread rise

---

[45] *Scots Magazine*, xxvi, 1 June 1764, 314.

[46] GCA, T-SK 16/10/87, Letter to Charles Stirling, 16 Oct. 1792.

[47] NLS, MS. 8795, Home letter book of Alexander Houston & Co., 29 Nov. 1777, p. 133.

[48] The indentured contracts in this study could be 2 to 4 years in length, although 3 years was the average duration.

[49] The University of the West Indies, Mona, Jamaica, West Indies and Special Collections, MS.1798–1800, Journal of Spencer Mackay, 22 Aug. 1798.

of the 'thirty-six months Scotch' who arrived as 'bands of...poor devils... in tatters' but soon 'found the means to make considerable fortunes in many of the West India islands and to monopolize all the lucrative places'.[50] Although conditions were undoubtedly grim for some Scots and most died abroad, some survived to accumulate great wealth.

James Buchanan was the son of a farrier near the Trongate at Glasgow. Moses Steven and James Buchanan (no relation), both partners in the merchant firm Dennistoun, Buchanan & Co., had their horses fitted at this blacksmith, thus introducing the younger son to Glasgow's colonial elite. In 1800, young Jamie travelled to the West Indies with a letter of recommendation from both partners addressed to George Wilson, representative of the firm in Grenada:

> Sir, by the 'Louisa', a young man goes to you, as an assistant. He is...clever; but it is a doubt whether he is to turn well or ill out. Mr Stiven is of the opinion that this namesake of mine will cut no ordinary figure in the world. He thinks he will either be the cleverest fellow, or the greatest blackguard in the West Indies; but take no notice, he is neither the one nor the other at present.[51]

This letter – which commented on Buchanan's intelligence, his character as well as his father's reputation – effectively endorsed the young lad as an able worker and ensured he was provided with employment by a stranger in the West Indies. As will be demonstrated in a later chapter, Buchanan eventually became one of the wealthiest Scottish returnees from the colonial West Indies.

Glasgow was the premier Scottish-Atlantic trade hub, with many Scots in temporary residence while in transit to the West Indies, often taking advantage of educational opportunities to acquire the skills for the plantation economy. Correspondence between George Oliphant of Kinloch, absentee owner of Grange plantation in Jamaica, his attorney John Wedderburn based in Westmoreland and James Somervell, a merchant in Glasgow, reveals much about Clyde-Jamaica emigration in the 1770s. Over a two-year period, Kinloch regularly sent young men from Perthshire to be shipped out by Somervell, Gordon & Co., his preferred merchant firm in Glasgow.[52] This was a classic patronage service provided by an elite absentee planter to sons of friends, neighbours, tenants and local landowners. In a two-year period, Scots attorney John Wedderburn received so many in

[50] J. F. Dauxion Lavaysse, *A Statistical, Commercial and Political Description of Venezuela, Trinidad, Margarita and Tobago* (London, 1820), p. 355.

[51] G. Crawford, *A Sketch of the Rise and Progress of the Trades' House of Glasgow* (Glasgow, 1858), pp. 265–9.

[52] NRS, GD1/8/36, Letter book of George Oliphant of Kinloch, p. 19, pp. 36–7, p. 56.

Jamaica that it was 'difficult to find a place for them to live on'.[53] At least some of these lads were educated prior to departure. On one occasion, Kinloch asked Somervell to improve the writing skills of a young man while he was waiting on a ship.[54] Somervell, however, advised that formal training was the best preparation for the plantation economy: 'You may give him proper advice…to be put to school immediately to Learn writing, arithmetic, bookkeeping & Navigation.'[55]

Glasgow's commercial academies provided the training in skills which could be adapted for careers across the Atlantic world. From the 1760s onwards, teachers such as William Gordon and James Scruton offered commercial education in the city, and 'useful learning' became a large-scale enterprise by the nineteenth century.[56] By 1838, nine mercantile academies were established around the commercial centre: the highest concentration of such institutions in Scotland. Academies in Glasgow provided the highest standard of commercial training in Scotland. In a two-year period after 1836, over 1,600 male and female students (aged between eight and twenty-five) attended classes taught by teachers who in some cases had connections with local firms. One had worked in mercantile houses for ten years before he opened a school in 1829.[57] The curriculum was broadly similar: writing, arithmetic, as well as mercantile accounts and bookkeeping. Several made use of specialist textbooks that illustrated examples of transatlantic commerce conducted from Glasgow like those authored by James Morrison.[58] The usual duration for students was one to four years, although J. McCall's academy in the city offered a short-term course which many students attended for just one quarter. School fees ranged in price: a bookkeeping course in McDougall's mercantile academy was just over £2 a course, while attendance at J. McCall's academy cost from sixteen shillings per quarter-term.[59] These costs compared favourably

---

[53] NRS, GD1/8/36, Wedderburn to Kinloch, 20 March 1774, pp. 73–4.

[54] NRS, GD1/8/36, Kinloch to Somervell, 18 December 1773, p.56.

[55] NRS, GD1/8/36, Somervell to Kinloch, 20 Aug. 1773, pp. 23–4.

[56] D. J. Withrington, 'Education and society in the eighteenth century', in *Scotland in the Age of Improvement*, ed. N. T. Phillipson (Edinburgh, 1996), pp. 197–8.

[57] There were at least 1,612 pupils taught in the 'Mercantile Academies' in Glasgow in 1836–7, comprising 1,068 males and 544 females. See HCPP 1841 (64) *Answers Made by Schoolmasters in Scotland to Queries Circulated in 1838, by Order of the Select Committee on Education in Scotland*, pp. 520–40.

[58] J. Morrison, *The Elements of Book Keeping, by Single and Double Entry* (London, 1813).

[59] HCPP 1841 (64) *Answers Made by Schoolmasters in Scotland*, p. 522.

to attendance at the nearby University of Glasgow.[60] Although not all of the learners in these academies would have been subsequently employed in transatlantic commerce, the excellent standard of education ensured the merchants had a large pool of candidates to choose from. This chapter now turns to open recruitment in the premier Atlantic hub.

The Glasgow-Atlantic world labour market

A survey of the *Glasgow Herald* between 1806 and 1834 reveals the nature and extent of Clyde shipping to the West Indies (see below for more details). The top merchant firm shippers between 1806 and 1834 were, in order of importance, John Campbell, senior & Co. (186 voyages or 9 per cent of an overall total of 1,742 voyages), John Cree, Stirling, Gordon & Co., Leitch & Smith, Robert Bogle & Co., J. T. & A. Douglas & Co. These firms were the most successful Glasgow-West India merchant houses of the period, except for shipping agents John Cree & Co. There were regular ships destined for the West Indies from Clyde ports, averaging around one a week in the period under examination. The production cycles of the plantation economy promoted specific types of departures at crucial times. Merchant firms mainly recruited towards the end of the year – September, October and November – which ensured young men travelled to the West Indies with the winter fleet, providing skilled labourers for the crop season in January.

The *Glasgow Herald* advertisements also reveal recruitment strategies of West India firms.[61] The Glasgow-West India labour market was seemingly limited in the early nineteenth century. There were few positions available, with around only 300 relevant advertisements over a twenty-eight-year period, around eleven per year (on average). In the context of the estimated numbers of Scottish adventurers in this period (discussed below), this was a very small minority. Nevertheless, these advertisements provide insights into the top recruiters, the social demographics of the desired personnel and the skills and trades in demand in the plantation economy.

---

[60] *General Report of the Commissioners Appointed to visit the Universities and Colleges of Scotland, October 1830* (Reports from Commissioners, Session 14 June–20 Oct. 1831, xii), p. 259.

[61] This study identified almost 300 job openings in the West Indies placed by Glasgow merchant firms in the *Glasgow Herald* newspaper between 1806 and 1834. In the 10-year period after 1806, over 200 positions were advertised. The peak year was 1806, with 42 jobs on offer. However, such offers became increasingly rare in the 1820s, with only 5 jobs advertised on average each year. By 1832, no jobs were publicly advertised at all. Almost half the jobs offered were for Jamaica (129 jobs), with positions in Grenada (66), Demerara (40), St Vincent (16), Trinidad (14) and Tobago (8) also on offer.

West India merchant firms usually opted to recruit young lads 'brought up in the country',[62] although middle-aged men (aged thirty to thirty-five) were, on occasion, required for supervisory roles such as foremen. In 1816, for example, the firm D&J Connell advertised an indentured position in Jamaica for 'middle-aged man of experience as an overseer on a Gentleman's Estate in this Country, to take a similar charge in that Island'.[63] Thus, young men – probably with no marital ties – would have been preferred for the Caribbean. The open recruitment of firms aimed to entice agricultural workers and skilled tradesmen. Of the almost 300 jobs identified in the advertisements, the positions that were most in demand were: carpenters (89), overseers (32), coopers (29), blacksmiths (26), planters (20), masons (17), engineers (13) and coppersmiths (10). Trade skills were prioritized over educational qualifications. Only one advertisement in the *Glasgow Herald* – looking for experienced ploughmen – requested a 'tolerable education'.[64] However, a good commercial education would have improved the chances of gaining employment with firms or in the plantation economy.

Overseers and planters were much in demand – no doubt destined to supervise enslaved peoples cultivating and processing the sugar cane – and for those experienced in husbandry to work on cattle pens adjacent to many plantations. This would have been the starting position for many Scots lads who were able to transfer farming experience directly to the plantation economy. Evidently, these advertisements were designed to recruit reliable men of lower rank from agricultural backgrounds. As noted in the statistical accounts, these processes sometimes drained local economies of agricultural labour and skilled tradesmen.

The building of the colonial infrastructure required skilled carpenters, which was the occupation desired most by recruiters in Glasgow. Many were to be employed as house or mill carpenters on estates, perhaps working in planters' houses or windmills. Flexible tradesmen who could work as both carpenters and wheelwrights were particularly well regarded.[65] Others were required to have experience in 'country work' such as the making of carts, wheels or roofing.[66] Experienced carpenters could be employed as foremen in shipping yards, thus taking Scottish shipbuilding skills to the West Indies. Manufacturing skills were in no less demand. Blacksmiths, coppersmiths, masons, plumbers, tilemakers and bricklayers would have ensured the

[62] *GH*, 14 Jan. 1814, p. 3.

[63] *GH*, 6 Dec. 1816, p. 4.

[64] *GH*, 15 Aug. 1819, p. 3.

[65] *GH*, 6 Oct. 1806, p. 4.

[66] *GH*, 17 Feb. 1823, p. 3.

plantation was in working order. Such tradesmen were perceived to sit atop a Scottish-Atlantic labour hierarchy, well above the common indentures. In July 1771, James Dallas, writing from Jamaica, bemoaned his father's decision to allow his brother to go to Dominica as an indentured labourer:

> I assure you it will be a stain & reflection on his name which all his merit be if ever so great will never be able entirely to wipe off, besides the many hardships it will daily subject him to, had he been bred a mason, Carpenter, Copper or Blacksmith, he might have not only got bread, but in time acquired a fortune in the West Indies – in his present situation he will be subject to every Insult, temptation and difficulty which can render Human life in some degree miserable.[67]

Tradesmen were held in higher esteem due to their skills and higher earning potential and this had reputational consequences. In early 1787, Mr Dow, a mason, travelled to Carriacou looking for work where – according to one experienced Glasgow merchant – there was 'not the least doubt of his getting employment and doing very well if he keeps his health'.[68] Trade skills acquired in Scotland were in high demand in the plantation economy and individuals had the opportunity to make great wealth, a conclusion that will be tested in future chapters.

Other tradesmen with specific skills dealt with plantation produce. Young Scotsmen bred in distilleries were sometimes required in Jamaica, no doubt destined to learn the secrets of producing OP (over-proof) rum.[69] The merchants also recruited coopers to produce hogsheads which facilitated the storage and transportation of the semi-refined muscovado sugar and rum. The advertisements also provided some insight into the increasing influence of new technologies. The increasing dependence on steam-power by sugar planters as the nineteenth century progressed promoted further skilled emigration. Engineers were required to operate steam engines that served to power mills to crush the cane with more efficiency as well as for transportation. In September 1830, for example, Robert Eccles & Co. required two engineers for Trinidad to operate the steamboats that would have taken hogsheads of sugar onto the large sea-going vessels waiting in the Gulf of Paria to depart for the Clyde.[70] With steam engines shipped out from Great Britain – including the Boulton-Watt version after 1803

---

[67] NRS, GD314/109, 'James Dallas, Whitehall, St. Mary's, Jamaica to his father in Edinburgh', 1 July 1771.

[68] NRAS, 2570/120, John Campbell senior to William Urquhart, 1 May 1787.

[69] GH, 18 Sept. 1829, p. 3.

[70] GH, 24 Sept. 1830, p. 3.

– these engineers were part of a steam-revolution that transformed sugar production during Caribbean slavery's amelioration era.[71]

The targeting of skilled migrants was also intended to improve infrastructure and labour capabilities on the islands. Merchant firms also attracted recruits from outside known networks via newspaper advertisements and certificates were required to testify to the specialist skills of tradesmen. In October 1828, Robert Eccles & Co. required for Trinidad a blacksmith 'acquainted with Horse shoeing and Country Work in general, who can produce testimonials of his having served a regular apprenticeship to the Trade, and of being sober and industrious'.[72] Such endorsements of reliability created trust which was crucial given the employees were soon to be left to their own devices across the Atlantic.[73]

Although advertisements offering agricultural and manufacturing positions were restricted to those with the appropriate experience and recommendations, it is noticeable that offers of commercial positions were even rarer. Of the almost 300 jobs advertised in the *Glasgow Herald* between 1806 and 1834, only three of these – two bookkeepers and one clerk – offered an immediate start in jobs related to finance. In October 1806, Stirling, Gordon & Co. required a young man 'thoroughly acquainted with books to act as a Clerk' for Jamaica. Certificates of good character were required, and liberal encouragement was promised.[74] These positions were not usually openly recruited; instead, such roles were filled by trusted individuals from known networks. For example, in 1778, representatives of Alexander Houston & Co. knew of a 'clever lad' in Scotland to be employed as a clerk in a store in Grenada.[75] As factors and agents in the West Indies dealt with accounts, the issue of trust was paramount, meaning strangers – however well recommended – were unlikely to be immediately employed in positions dealing with finance and remitting profits. Other elite merchant firms in Glasgow also recruited from within the direct 'family matrix'

[71] J. Tann, 'Steam and sugar: the diffusion of the stationary steam engine to the Caribbean sugar industry 1770–1840', *History of Technology*, 19 (1997), 63–84; J. R. Ward, *British West Indian Slavery, 1750–1834: The Process of Amelioration* (Oxford, 1988), p. 52, p. 93, p. 98, pp. 100–1, pp. 241–2, p. 251.

[72] *GH*, 3 Oct. 1828, p. 3.

[73] D. Hamilton, 'Transatlantic ties: Scottish migration networks in the Caribbean, 1750–1800', in *A Global Clan, Scottish Migrant Networks and Identities since the Eighteenth Century*, ed. A. McCarthy (London, 2006), p. 53.

[74] *GH*, 6 Oct. 1806, p. 4.

[75] NLS, MS. 8795, Home letter book of Alexander Houston & Co., 12 Dec. 1777, pp. 147–8, p. 187.

and close networks in order to minimize risk.[76] As demonstrated in the chapter on Leitch & Smith, the firm employed James Smith – the brother of the principal co-partner – as their representative in Grenada and he had responsibility for remitting money home. Closed recruitment from kinship networks minimized the risk of dishonest dealings across the Atlantic and kept wealth within the family at the same time.

As the nineteenth century progressed, the importance of the indentured system decreased. Of almost 300 positions advertised by the merchant firms in the *Glasgow Herald* between 1806 and 1834, only around half were explicitly advertised as indentured contracts. There were very few by the 1830s, when it was very likely the merchant firms' recruiting role became obsolete due to the declining use of the indentures in the West Indies.[77] For most of the period under consideration here, indentured contracts offering an immediate start would have been the most desirable way for young men to travel to the West Indies. But many others – even the majority – who departed from Clyde ports would have travelled under their own accord towards an uncertain future.

To the West Indies

Many Scots travelled to Glasgow to secure passage on ships docked in the Clyde at Greenock and Port Glasgow. Shipping movements were well known: local newspapers contained advertisements of departing ships and the Tontine List detailed both arrivals and departures from specific islands.[78] For those paying their own fare, passage could be agreed directly with captains on ships or by visiting merchants' counting houses congregated on or near the Trongate at Argyle Street, the Tontine Rooms, Candleriggs, the Gallowgate, Miller Street and Queen Street.[79] The merchant firms advertised their voyages weeks in advance, notifying the public about the availability of 'freight and passage' to specific colonies. Some made a point of referring to the 'superior accommodation' in the cabin and steerage as well as reasonable terms, no doubt hoping to entice more passengers than

[76] P. Mathias, 'Risk, credit and kinship in early modern enterprise', in *The Early Modern Atlantic Economy*, ed. J. McCusker and K. Morgan (Cambridge, 2000), p. 16.

[77] M. Guasco, 'Indentured servitude', 'Atlantic history', in *Oxford Bibliographies*, ed. T. Burnard (New York, 2011).

[78] *GH*, 4 Feb. 1820.

[79] *The Glasgow Directory, 1806–1808* (Glasgow, 1806).

their rivals.[80] Personal introductions might be required for those seeking passage in cabins and there were high costs involved.[81]

The process of transporting adventurers can be traced in merchant correspondence. In October 1810, John Campbell, senior, & Co. advertised in the *Glasgow Herald* for a 'mason, cooper, house carpenter and some overseers… who want to serve in the West Indies under indentures for three years', who would travel on the imminent voyage of the *Susannah* to Grenada.[82] At the request of planter John Urquhart later that year, the firm arranged for Adam Reid from Aberdeen to travel to Carriacou via Port Glasgow aboard the ship. Urquhart put up the initial costs of £24 4s 10d (to be repaid by Reid), which included £21 for steerage on the ship, £1/16s for 'sea bedding and board' and carriage expenses to Port Glasgow.[83] In August 1821, Stirling, Gordon & Co. and James Ewing & Co. charged Mr Jeffrey £36 for the cabin and John Orr £21 for steerage on their jointly owned ship, *The Hamilla*, which departed from Greenock for Jamaica.[84] By means of comparison, the standard steerage fare was around six months' wages for an adult male cotton mill spinner in Glasgow.[85] Indentured contracts obviously guaranteed passage, although other young men worked on the outward ships or had fares advanced by merchant firms.[86] It seems most likely that most young men arriving in the West Indies had debts preventing early return to Scotland. Owing to a paucity of sources, exactly how many travelled to the West Indies will never be known. This monograph, however, offers new estimates.

In a period of almost continual war with America, France and Spain up to 1815, wartime conditions affected shipping from the Clyde. During the period of the American War of Independence (1775–83), the ubiquity of enemy shipping in the Atlantic initially prevented the development of Clyde-Caribbean commerce. Much of the conflict was contested in the Atlantic and the Caribbean, meaning shipping departures were restricted by the convoy system, which had implications for operating costs especially

---

[80] *GH*, 2 Jan. 1824, p. 3.

[81] NLS, MS. 8795, Home letter book of Alexander Houston & Co., 18 Oct. 1777, p. 56, p. 59.

[82] *GH*, 19 Oct. 1810, p. 4.

[83] NRAS, 2570/40, 'Letter from John Campbell senior', 15 Dec. 1810.

[84] GCA, T-SK24/18/2, 'Account current with Stirling, Gordon & Co.', 1821.

[85] In a sample of 29 cotton mills in the Glasgow area, the average wage of adult males was around 21 shillings a week, which was regarded as high remuneration (£44s per month or £50 per annum). See J. Cleland, *Enumeration of the Inhabitants of the City of Glasgow and County of Lanark for the Government Census of 1831*, 2nd ed. (Glasgow, 1831), p. 291.

[86] NLS, MS. 8795, Home letter book of Alexander Houston & Co., 6 Oct. 1777, p. 21, p. 107.

insurance.[87] However, a cease in hostilities – such as the temporary peace with France in 1802–3 – freed up shipping and opened European export markets. In January 1802, Glasgow's sugar merchants were said to be in favour of the French resuming trade with Jamaica, thus driving up sales and maximizing prices.[88] A clause of the Treaty of Amiens in March 1802 also ceded Trinidad to Great Britain, which opened up commercial opportunities to the merchants of Glasgow, although staff at the local branch of the Royal Bank of Scotland expressed surprise at what they regarded as a risky investment.[89] Thus, the spoils of war created opportunities for investment and the long-term peace with America and France cleared the way for the development of Clyde-Caribbean commerce. Many chose to migrate.

Any study of emigration is much the better with an estimation of numbers, although such a task in this context presents methodological issues. There are two issues: West India islands were not individually classified in Scottish port statistics before 1840, and there are no reliable figures of voyages (or systematic passenger lists) leaving for specific colonies.[90] However, Clyde ports were the main departure point. In 1787, of the seventy-seven outward voyages to the region from Scotland, almost 90 per cent (sixty-seven) left from Port Glasgow and Greenock, the city's satellite ports. Of the seventy voyages landing in Scotland from the West Indies, sixty-four docked in the same two ports.[91] In this period, Port Glasgow specialized in tobacco imports from North America, while Greenock received more West India voyages.[92] This trend continued into the nineteenth century. Data compiled just after the abolition of slavery provides a benchmark of emigration statistics. In 1841, a total of 2,104 emigrants were recorded leaving British ports for the West Indies. Of this total, 366 departed from Scottish ports (17 per cent of the British total). Of the Scottish figure, 264 left via Clyde ports (72 per cent of Scottish total): Glasgow (98 individuals), Greenock (147), Port Glasgow (19). For comparison, 1,259 individuals left London, 479

[87] T. M. Devine, 'Transport problems of Glasgow West India Merchants during the American War of Independence, 1775–83', *Transport History*, iv (1971), 266–304.

[88] NWGA, RB/837/521, Letter from Robert Scott Moncrieff, 2 Jan. 1802.

[89] NWGA, RB/837/664, Letter from Robert Scott Moncrieff, 24 May 1802.

[90] M. Harper, *Emigration from North-east Scotland: Willing Exiles*, vol. i (Aberdeen, 1988), p. 29.

[91] HCPP 1787 *An Account Of The Quantities of Sugar, Rum, Cotton, Coffee, Cocoa, Indigo, Ginger, Aloes, and other Goods, Imported into the Several Ports of Great Britain, from the British Sugar Colonies, from Christmas 1786 to Christmas 1787 Inclusive*, p. 83.

[92] B. Crispin, 'Clyde shipping and the American War', *The Scottish Historical Review*, xli, part 2 (Oct. 1962), 126–7.

left Liverpool, ninety left Aberdeen, and eleven left Leith.[93] Thus, official sources suggest as much as 90 per cent of Scottish-West India shipping, and around three-quarters of all emigrants, went through Clyde ports.

In the absence of official statistics, however, voyages to the West Indies between 1775 and 1838 can only be estimated from unofficial sources such as shipping advertisements: this approach defines current understandings concerning eighteenth-century estimates of Scots travelling to the Caribbean in the slavery period. Newspaper evidence suggests an increase in nineteenth-century Clyde-Caribbean trade and shipping. The *Glasgow Herald* reveals over 1,700 individual voyages were advertised to depart for the West Indies from Clyde ports between 1806 and 1834 (see Table 4.1).[94] It is possible this data is an underestimation of actual voyages, and even so, the advertised numbers of ships indicate a dramatic increase from the previous half-century.[95] For example, between 1806 and 1834, Jamaica was the main destination and the 615 advertised voyages from Clyde ports to the island in this twenty-nine-year period (an average of twenty-one per year) exceeds Alan Karras' estimates of 569 for the same ports in the period 1750 to 1800 (an average of eleven per year).[96]

While Jamaica was the favoured port of call, as the nineteenth century progressed new colonies became increasingly popular destinations. Voyages to the other first-phase colonies of Antigua, Barbados and St Kitts represented a small proportion (under 5 per cent) of the destinations in the advertisements. This reflects the relatively minor importance of trade between Scotland and the classic English settler colonies. Indeed, the destination of St Thomas – then part of the Danish West Indies – was a more popular destination than these three colonies together, although this probably reflects the island's status as a first landfall in the Leeward Islands. Of far more importance were the second- and third-phase colonies subsumed into the British West Indies after the Union of 1707. The advertisements seem to reveal an increase in trading activities with the newer colonies, especially Demerara, Grenada and

[93] HCPP *Accounts and Papers of the House of Commons: Revenue, Population, Commerce*, vol. lvi (1843), p. 315.

[94] This period was chosen for analysis due to the availability of sources in an era in which Glasgow's connections with Caribbean slavery were most pronounced. The *Glasgow Herald* is complete in these years, allowing a comprehensive survey of over 2,000 editions for this period.

[95] For example, in 1814, 147 ships left Port Glasgow and Greenock for the West Indies (although it is possible that not all offered passage), while only 68 advertisements of commercial ships offering passage were counted in the *Glasgow Herald*. See J. Cleland, *Abridgement of the Annals of Glasgow* (Glasgow, 1817), pp. 354–5.

[96] Karras, *Sojourners*, pp. 43–5.

Table 4.1 Destinations of ships departing from Clyde ports for West Indies, 1806–34.

Destinations	1806–10	1811–20	1821–30	1831–4	Total
Selected colonies					
Antigua (1st phase, BWI)	2	8	6	12	**28**
Barbados (1st phase)	3	6	8	6	**23**
Berbice (3rd phase)	10	19	11	2	**42**
Demerara (2nd phase)	29	125	154	61	**369**
Grenada (2nd phase)	17	37	34	13	**101**
Jamaica (1st phase)	96	271	193	55	**615**
Martinique (French)	3	3	N/A	N/A	**6**
New Providence (US)	4	8	1	N/A	**15**
St Kitts (1st phase)	N/A	11	16	1	**28**
St Thomas (Danish)	N/A	58	56	41	**154**
St Vincent (2nd phase)	9	33	38	10	**90**
Tobago (2nd phase)	6	21	10	1	**39**
Trinidad (3rd phase)	6	53	112	47	**218**
Other	7	8	0	1	**14**
Voyages to all colonies	**192**	**661**	**639**	**250**	**1742**

Source: *Glasgow Herald*, 1806–34.

Trinidad. Demerara was the second most important destination after Jamaica throughout the period, replacing it as the principal destination by the early 1830s. Trinidad was the third most popular destination, with voyages more than doubling in a ten-year period after 1820. As new colonies opened up, shipping numbers increased compared to the previous half-century.

This monograph now enters the realm of speculative history to provide tentative estimates of adventurers who departed from Clyde ports to the West Indies. Historians have estimated eighteenth-century departures from Scotland. Alan Karras examined over 1,000 advertisements of ships leaving for Jamaica and the Chesapeake from Glasgow, Edinburgh, Leith and Aberdeen during the period 1750–1800. Working on the assumption of five passengers per ship (and some from English ports), Karras estimated 6,000 Scots travelled to Jamaica during this period.[97] However, based on

[97] Karras, *Sojourners*, pp. 43–5.

Trevor Burnard's analysis of passengers arriving in Jamaica by ship (average of 7.39 per ship), Douglas Hamilton revised the Karras figures upwards: it seemed most likely that 10,800 Scots arrived in Jamaica during the period 1750–99 and, by extension, between 17,090 (7 per ship) and 20,800 (9 per ship) Scots departed for the West Indies in the same period.[98] While these historians provided estimates of Scottish adventurers travelling to first- and second-phase colonies of the British West Indies, there has been no complete analysis including the third-phase colonies settled after 1800.

As shipping advertisements in the *Glasgow Herald* dramatically increased between 1806 and 1834, the obvious inference is outward passengers did too. But not all ships would have left, while some could have carried few passengers. On the other hand, many would have been at full capacity while leaving the Clyde. Based on the assumptions of passengers per ship noted above, between 8,700 and 15,600 departees (300 to 540 per year) could have left the Clyde for the West Indies during the period 1806–34 (see Table 4.2). These figures facilitate new estimates of Scots departing for the West Indies between 1750 and 1834. Phillip Morgan estimated 34,000 Scots travelled to the West Indies in this period, but this appears too low.[99] Based on estimates derived from the Clyde shipping data, this study suggests between 37,000 and 46,000 Scots departed for the West Indies (from both Scottish and English ports) during the period 1750 and 1834.[100] This was around half the level of Scottish emigration to North America between 1700 and 1815, and around 3 per cent of the Scottish population in 1801 (see Table 4.3).[101]

---

[98] T. Burnard, 'European migration to Jamaica, 1655 to 1780', *William & Mary Quarterly*, 3rd series, liii (1996), 769–96, at p. 774; Hamilton, *Scotland, the Caribbean*, pp. 22–5.

[99] P. Morgan, 'Foreword', in *Recovering Scotland's Slavery Past*, ed. T. M. Devine, p. xiv.

[100] New Scottish estimates for 1800–34 are based upon the data for Clyde shipping between 1806 and 1834, which suggests between 12,194 (7 per ship) and 15,678 (9 per ship) individuals departed. Estimates for 1800 –1805 are added (7 per ship is 420 per year, or 9 per ship is 540 per year) to provide an overall Clyde estimate of 14,714–18,918 individuals departing between 1800 and 1834. Twenty-eight per cent is then added to allow for individuals from other Scottish ports (this proportion is based on the 1841 data discussed above), which provides a Scottish total of 18,833–22,158. Five point six per cent is then added to allow for Scots departing from English ports. Added together, this suggests between 19,987 (7 per ship) and 25,571 (9 per ship) Scots departed Great Britain for the West Indies between 1800 and 1834. Add this range to the Hamilton totals of 17,090 (7 per ship) and 20,800 (9 per ship) for 1750–99. See Hamilton, *Scotland, the Caribbean*, p. 23. This study therefore provides overall estimates of between 37,077 and 46,371 Scots departing Great Britain for the West Indies in the period 1750 and 1834.

[101] Smout, Landsman and Devine, 'Scottish emigration in the early modern period', p. 98, p. 104.

Table 4.2 Estimated adventurers from the Clyde to the West Indies, 1806–34.

Destinations, 1806–134	Total voyages	5 per ship	7 per ship	9 per ship
Selected colonies				
Antigua (1st phase, BWI)	28	140	196	252
Barbados (1st phase)	23	115	161	207
Berbice (3rd phase)	42	210	294	378
Demerara (2nd phase)	369	1845	2583	3321
Grenada (2nd phase)	101	505	707	909
Jamaica (1st phase)	615	3075	4305	5535
Martinique (French)	6	30	42	54
New Providence (US)	15	75	105	135
St Kitts (1st phase)	28	140	196	252
St Thomas (Danish)	154	770	1078	1386
St Vincent (2nd phase)	90	450	630	810
Tobago (2nd phase)	39	195	273	351
Trinidad (3rd phase)	218	1090	1526	1962
Other	14	70	98	126
Total	**1,742**	**8,710**	**12,194**	**15,678**

Source: *Glasgow Herald*, 1806–34.

Table 4.3 Population of Scotland, by region, 1801–31.

Population	1801	%	1811	%	1821	%	1831	%
Borders	184,834	11.6%	207,368	11.5%	233,981	11.2%	245,740	10.4%
West Lowlands	329,771	20.6%	412,491	22.8%	511,178	24.4%	628,528	26.6%
East Lowlands	584,777	36.6%	647,719	35.9%	731,881	35.0%	817,973	34.6%
Highlands-Hebrides	283,226	17.7%	306,589	17.0%	347,062	16.6%	368,498	15.6%
North-east	193,858	12.1%	208,102	11.5%	239,116	11.4%	269,846	11.4%
Far north	22,609	1.4%	23,419	1.3%	30,238	1.4%	34,529	1.5%
Total	**1,599,075**		**1,805,688**		**2,093,456**		**2,365,114**	

Source: HCPP (1841) *Accounts of Population and Number of Houses according to Census, 1841, of Each County in Great Britain*, p. 6.

West India sojourners intended to return with wealth, however, in contrast to North American migration. In theory, Caribbean sojourning should have had a more significant effect on the economic development of Scotland, especially as there was relatively limited capital compared to its southern neighbour. However, there are almost no surviving emigration records showing the characteristics of those who departed from Scotland for the West Indies, never mind those who returned. Nevertheless, Douglas Hamilton has argued – based on a register of emigrants, which provides rare data on journeys from Greenock to the West Indies in September 1774 and July 1775 – there were two main differences in the patterns of emigration to the West Indies and mainland American colonies. First, he noted migrants to the Caribbean were mainly young, single males. Second, Hamilton argued that these skilled migrants intended to 'follow their employment'. That is, the migrants were not escaping destitution but instead had elected to seek more profitable opportunities in the West Indies.[102]

Further examination of these sources provides details of occupational status as well as place of home domicile. The records reveal thirty-four Scotsmen travelled to the British West Indies from Greenock in September 1774 and July 1775. The average age was twenty, the eldest was thirty-four and the youngest fifteen. This group who crossed the Atlantic – thirty to Jamaica and four to Antigua – testified as to their occupations, and the high incidence of those intending to enter mercantile rather than planting occupations seems to be significant. Almost 80 per cent described themselves as merchants and clerks. While it is possible some, such as the sixteen-year-old James McLean, characterized themselves as merchants in anticipation of new employment rather than based on previous experience, most sought employment in the mercantile line. The remainder described themselves as planters, a farmer, a land surveyor, a blacksmith and a wright. Francis Stewart, who was on his way to Antigua, was the solitary 'gentleman'. It seems very likely these ships carried mainly lower- and middling-rank men.[103]

While one can speculate on previous experience and occupational aspirations, former residences are definitely known for thirty-four of these Scotsmen, which provides a rare insight into regional migration from Scotland to the Caribbean (see Table 4.4). Forty per cent of this group of the outward bound hailed from the Western Lowlands. By contrast, just under 10 per cent hailed from the Eastern Lowlands and 5 per cent hailed from the Borders. Almost half of the outward bound departed from the Highlands

---

[102] V. R. Cameron, *Emigrants from Scotland to America, 1774–1775* (Baltimore, 1990), pp. 45–6, p. 80; Hamilton, *Scotland, the Caribbean*, p. 25.

[103] Cameron, *Emigrants from Scotland*, pp. 45–6, p. 80, p. 87.

Table 4.4 Home residences of individuals departing Greenock for
the West Indies in 1774–5, compared to Scottish population.

Residences: region	No	%	Scottish population, 1801	%
Borders	2	5.88%	184,834	11.6%
Western Lowlands	14	41.18%	329,771	20.6%
Eastern Lowlands	3	8.82%	584,777	36.6%
Highland-Hebrides	7	20.59%	283,226	17.7%
North-east	7	20.59%	193,858	12.1%
Far north	1	2.94%	22,609	1.4%
Total	34		1,599,075	

Source: V. R. Cameron, *Emigrants from Scotland to America, 1774–1775* (Baltimore,
Md., 1990), pp. 45–6, p. 80; HCPP (1841) *Accounts of Population and Number
of Houses According to Census, 1841, of Each County in Great Britain*, p. 6.

(20 per cent), north-eastern Scotland (20 per cent) and Caithness (2 per
cent) combined. Given the relative decline in the Highland population as
a proportion of Scottish society in this era (see Table 4.3), the implications
of this relatively high outward migration from the Highlands are significant
and will be explored more fully in a later chapter. A transient class of young
men from across Scotland with agricultural, manufacturing and especially
commercial skills internally migrated to Glasgow and the outports before
travelling to the West Indies in the hope of employment. Exactly how many
succeeded in Jamaica, Grenada and Trinidad will be addressed next.

Conclusion

Scots were a highly mobile group of people before, during and after the
slavery period. The perception of quick riches in the West Indies attracted
many young men who hoped to return in a wealthier position, a general
mentality that has implications for studies of Scotland and the Caribbean.
Glasgow was the premier Atlantic trade hub and attracted migrants from
across Scotland. Some were beneficiaries of patronage, offering privileged
starts in the colonies. Many more were recruited by merchants via open
recruitment. Scots were offered attractive incentives to go the West Indies
including indentured contracts and assisted passage, high wages and
sometimes even medical care. Many were recruited in Glasgow – often
through advertisements placed by planters and merchant firms – for
positions in the plantation economy. Some of these young men were
educated, although commercial academies – the best in Scotland – involved

relatively high costs. Nevertheless, the merchants and planters of Glasgow had a large pool of candidates to recruit from on an annual basis. Practical experience gained by lads on the farm and skilled craftsmen was much in demand, as it was transferable to the West Indies. Partners in merchant firms less often recruited employees from kith and kin networks to work in trusted roles dealing with finance and commerce. This was a professional – mainly skilled or educated – class of men who travelled to take up important positions in medicine, trade and commerce. What is clear is that education, skills and experience acquired in Scotland opened up many possibilities in the plantation economy.

The merchants and planters of Glasgow were the main agents – both recruiters and shippers – of Scottish emigration to the West Indies. Passage was readily available from Glasgow in the 1800s. Some paid their own way, others secured indentured contracts, but many would have travelled under their own risk or with high debts, which prevented an early return. It is very likely that many thousands of Scots landed in the British West Indies towards the end of Caribbean slavery, especially in Jamaica, although Grenada and Trinidad became favoured locations. As will now be revealed in the next three chapters, many young men succeeded and were able to accumulate and repatriate large fortunes to Scotland, while many, even most, failed in their quest.

5. Jamaica

For several months in late 1786, Robert Burns, then a failing farmer but later Scotland's national bard, mooted crossing the Atlantic to become, in his words, a 'poor negro-driver' in Jamaica to escape his multiple woes. In 1783, Robert and his brother Gilbert took over Mossgiel farm in Mauchline, Ayrshire, although it remained 'very unprofitable' three years later.[1] Burns' private life was also in disarray: the father of Jean Armour had reportedly initiated legal proceedings due to an out of wedlock pregnancy. Yet, Burns was a literate young man with a growing reputation as a poet. Dr Patrick Douglas, an Ayrshire landowner and absentee planter, attempted to recruit him as a 'book keeper' on the Ayr Mount estate in Portland. Burns was offered a reported salary of £30 per annum, although he had to fund his own passage to Jamaica. To meet these costs, *Poems, Chiefly in the Scottish Dialect*, which became the famous 'Kilmarnock edition', was published on 31 July.[2] The literary success that followed secured the cost of passage and, in Burns' own words, 'as soon as I was master of nine guineas [£9 9s], the price of wafting me to the torrid zone, I took a steerage passage in the first ship that was to sail from the Clyde'. He subsequently booked three separate voyages: the *Nancy* from Greenock for Savanna-la-Mar on 10 August 1786; the *Bell* from Greenock for Port Morant at the end of September; and the *Roselle* from Leith to Kingston on 23 December. Later correspondence reveals Burns was aware of his probable fate: 'a victim to that inhospitable clime, and gone to the world of spirits!'[3] Anticipating an early grave was not merely fatalistic pessimism. As outlined in the last chapter, mortality rates in Jamaica were very high and, in all likelihood, Burns would have been dead from yellow fever within three years. Fortunately, he did not board a ship for Jamaica.

---

[1]   Details of Burns' voyages have been culled from two sources: Robert Burns, 'Letter lvi – to Dr Moore, Mauchline', 2 Aug. 1787 <https://www.gutenberg.org/files/9863/9863-h/9863-h.htm> [accessed 19 Jan. 2021]. And a 'Narrative by Gilbert Burns of his brother's life' <http://www.robertburns.org/encyclopedia/NarrativebyGilbertBurnsofhisBrothersLife.674.shtml> [accessed 19 Jan. 2021].

[2]   C. McGinn, 'The Scotch bard and "the planting line": new documents on Burns and Jamaica', *Studies in Scottish Literature*, xliii (2017), 255–66, at p. 258.

[3]   Robert Burns, 'Letter lvi – to Dr Moore, Mauchline', 2 Aug. 1787.

One scholar argued that Burns made a rational economic choice to call off in December 1786, rather than showing principled opposition to chattel slavery, simply because a 'better offer came along'.[4] Instead of crossing the Atlantic to Jamaica, Burns travelled to Edinburgh to chase his literary ambitions and quickly became a national sensation. The 'Kilmarnock edition' grossed c.£91 sterling, of which Burns, in his own words, 'pocketed, all expenses deducted, nearly twenty pounds'. A second edition, *Poems, Chiefly in the Scottish Dialect* (Edinburgh Edition), was published in April 1787. From this, Burns earned £700 sterling and 100 guineas (£105) for the sale of the copyright.[5] In all, Burns made £825 from both editions; it would have taken a bookkeeper on Ayr Mount estate around twenty-seven years to earn a similar sum. Subsequently taking up a literary career,[6] Robert Burns has become synonymous with Caribbean slavery for *not* crossing the Atlantic. The irony is that he has become shorthand for those who *were* resident in Jamaica, most of whom remain unknown in the modern British imagination.

This chapter addresses that lacuna by examining Scotsmen who did cross the Atlantic for Jamaica. Large numbers were present in supervisory and managerial positions on the island, bringing with them Scottish Presbyterianism, which led to the construction of St Andrew's Scots Kirk in Kingston in 1813.[7] Although a British rather than a distinctively Scottish phenomenon, many young adventurers sought rapid wealth and a quick return to live in luxury, sometimes as absentee owners of sugar estates.[8] Sojourning and absenteeism were different forms of economic pursuits, but they both served to extract wealth from Jamaica.[9] Yet, while the activities

---

[4] McGinn, 'Scotch bard', p. 265.

[5] N. Leask, *Robert Burns and Pastoral: Poetry and Improvement in Late Eighteenth-Century Scotland* (Oxford, 2010), p. 102.

[6] M. Morris, *Scotland and the Caribbean, c.1740–1833: Atlantic Archipelagos* (New York and London, 2015), pp. 98–141.

[7] S. Mullen, 'The Scots kirk of colonial Kingston, Jamaica', *Records of the Scottish Church History Society*, xlv (2016), 99–117.

[8] Alan Karras and Douglas Hamilton both examined 'sojourning' (ie transient economic migration with hope of quick wealth accumulation in the colonies followed by a departure to the homeland) in a Scottish-Atlantic world context. See A. Karras, *Sojourners in the Sun* (Ithaca, 1992) and D. Hamilton, *Scotland, the Caribbean and the Atlantic World, 1750–1820* (Manchester, 2005). Andrew O'Shaughnessy sees sojourning as a British, not simply a Scottish, practice; see *An Empire Divided: An American Revolution and the British Caribbean* (Philadelphia, 2000), pp. 3–33.

[9] Trevor Burnard views sojourning as analytically different from absenteeism (ie individuals not resident in Jamaica but living in Great Britain and dependent on the plantation economy for income); see T. Burnard, 'Passengers only', *Atlantic Studies*, i (2004), 178–95, at p. 181. For accounts of absentees, see D. Hall, 'Absentee-proprietorship in

of Scots in Jamaica are increasingly well known, a lot less is known about the wealth these men acquired, and the effects on the Scottish economy and society.

Acquired during Oliver Cromwell's 'Western Design' in 1655, Jamaica was a classic first-phase English settler colony. By 1713, it had superseded Barbados as the premier sugar-producing island in the British empire, and just sixty years later produced more of the commodity than all other islands combined.[10] Historians have long noted the wealth of those who owned the estates, and Trevor Burnard has revealed the 'prodigious riches' of the eighteenth-century Jamaica plantocracy.[11] However, by the 1800s, while great wealth could still be made in new colonies Berbice and Demerara-Essequibo, this was generally no longer the case in Barbados and Jamaica.[12] The increased demand for African slaves in the late eighteenth century meant the economy remained vibrant.[13] However, from around 1805 up to emancipation, due to a combination of economic conditions and political factors in the West Indies and Europe (including the abolition movement), the fortunes and influence of Jamaica's planters were on the wane.[14]

If Jamaica was in decline, Scots continued to flourish more than most. Like other minorities on the island such as the Sephardic Jews, Scots operated in networks, and although ethnicity did not automatically confer trustworthiness, these groupings served to increase the transatlantic flow of capital, goods and people.[15] In a seminal study of Scottish networks, Alan Karras attempted to trace 'whence sojourners came, where they went, what they did after they arrived, and how they fared', an approach

the British West Indies to about 1850', *Jamaican Historical Review* (1964), 15–35; R. Sheridan, *Sugar and Slavery: An Economic History of the British West Indies, 1623–1775* (Kingston, 2007 ed.), pp. 385–7.

[10] N. Zahedieh, 'Trade, plunder, and economic development in Early English Jamaica, 1655–89', *The Economic History Review*, xxxix (1986), 205–22.

[11] T. Burnard, 'Prodigious riches: the wealth of Jamaica before the American Revolution', *The Economic History Review*, liv (2001), 506–24.

[12] T. Burnard, *Planters, Merchants, and Slaves: Plantation Societies in British America, 1650–1820* (Chicago, 2015), p. 126.

[13] A. Reid, 'Sugar, slavery and productivity in Jamaica, 1750–1807', *Slavery & Abolition*, xxxvii (2016), 159–82, at p. 173.

[14] T. Burnard, 'Et in Arcadia ego: West Indian planters in glory, 1674–1784', *Atlantic Studies*, ix (2012), 19–40.

[15] N. Zahedieh, 'Defying mercantilism. Illicit trade, trust, and the Jamaica Sephardim, 1660–1730'. Paper delivered at the British Group of Early American Historians, University of Cambridge, 1–4 Sept. 2016.

subsequently extended across the West Indies by Douglas Hamilton.[16] Karras argued that Scots in Jamaica became increasingly wealthy as the eighteenth century progressed, although he was pessimistic as to whether British capital invested in West India property (land and enslaved people) was ever converted to profits in Scotland without costly legal action in colonial courts.[17] Hamilton was more optimistic and noted an unquantified number of wealthy Scots returned to both Scotland and England and afterwards purchased landed estates, established educational facilities and invested in the Scottish cotton industry.[18] Allan Macinnes' study of the colonial activities of the Malcolms of Poltalloch underlined Hamilton's view of a capital in-flow model to Great Britain. From 1750, Jamaica profits – siphoned through London from 1786 – directly improved their estates in Argyll, Scotland.[19] Beyond case-study approaches, the impact of Jamaica fortunes, if they were ever repatriated to Scotland at all, has been little studied. This chapter rectifies this, first by surveying adventurers who travelled to the island after 1775 and then by unravelling how they lived, worked, became rich, repatriated and ultimately dispersed slavery-derived capital in Scotland and elsewhere throughout the nineteenth century.

Scottish adventurers in Jamaica

Jamaica was essentially a rural society, with most of the population resident along the coast. In 1788, the island's total population was 254,184, including a small white population (18,347; 7 per cent), free people of colour (9,405; 4 per cent) and large numbers of enslaved people (226,432; 89 per cent).[20] By the early 1800s, the white population had risen to 20,000–25,000, while the enslaved population dramatically increased to 354,000: a result of increased trafficking by British ships during the era of 'gradual abolition'. Both enslaved and free labourers mainly worked on sugar and coffee plantations or on the adjoining cattle pens that provided livestock for the plantation economy.[21] Kingston was the island's main trade hub, overtaking

---

[16] Karras, *Sojourners*, p. xiii.

[17] Karras, *Sojourners*, p. 60, p. 175.

[18] Hamilton, *Scotland, the Caribbean*, pp. 195–216.

[19] A. I. Macinnes, 'Commercial landlordism and clearance in the Scottish Highlands: The case of Arichonan', in *Communities in European History: Representations, Jurisdictions, Conflicts*, ed. J. Pan-Montojo and F. Pedersen (Pisa, 2007), pp. 47–64.

[20] TNA, CO137/88, 'Colonial office: Jamaica, original correspondence, 1788', fo. 173.

[21] C. Petley, *Slaveholders in Jamaica: Colonial Society and Culture during the Era of Abolition* (London, 2009), pp. 5–6.

Figure 5.1 James Hakewill, 1778–1843, British, Llanrumny Estate,
St Mary's, Jamaica, between 1820 and 1821, watercolour on moderately
thick, slightly textured, cream wove paper. Yale Center for British Art,
Paul Mellon Collection, B1977.14.1960Dhh. Public Domain.

Port Royal and Spanishtown in the early 1700s.[22] The island's wealthiest residents, especially merchants and planters, lived in its burgeoning urban sprawl, many of whom had a key role developing Jamaica's domestic and external economy.[23] One traveller to late eighteenth-century Kingston observed many upwardly mobile Scottish merchants thriving in the bustling commercial hub:

> There are some extensive merchants in Kingston, Spanish Town, Montego Bay, &C. a few of whom are English and Irish, but ten times the number of Scotch; they all in general live elegantly; it is not thought strange for a

[22] J. Robertson, *Gone is the Ancient Glory: Spanish Town, Jamaica, 1534–2000* (Kingston, 2005), pp. 78–9.

[23] T. Burnard, '"The great mart of the island": the economic function of Kingston, Jamaica in the mid-eighteenth century', in *Jamaica in Slavery and Freedom*, ed. K. Monteith and G. Richards (Kingston, 2002), pp. 225–41.

peasant's son from Glasgow, or Aberdeen, in the space of four of five years, to commence merchant, and in a few years afterwards to make a pretty independence; or if he enters the planting line, to succeed as well; to get possession of slaves.[24]

These merchants not only helped to drive the prosperity of Kingston but promoted commercial relations between Jamaica and Scotland, introducing kith and kin to the island and connecting institutions located across the Atlantic.

Overall, *Glasgow Herald* shipping advertisements suggest over 600 voyages departed from the Clyde for Jamaica during 1806 and 1834. The most prolific merchant firm shippers were, respectively, Stirling, Gordon & Co, followed by James Ewing & Co., Leitch & Smith and Robert Bogle & Co. The latter firm was based in Kingston over many years. At least from 1797, Robert Bogle acted as an agent for Scottish planters in Jamaica, at times ensuring the wealth of deceased planters on the island was returned to Glasgow.[25] The firm also diversified into planting, which provided opportunities for well-connected Scots. As part of wider trading across the West Indies, the firm scheduled, on average, around one voyage between the Clyde and Kingston every year. The most important stopping points for Glasgow ships in Jamaica were located on the north and west of the island, particularly Falmouth, Savannah-Le-Mar and Montego Bay. However, the single most popular destination was Kingston, with almost half the ships departing from the Clyde arriving in the port.[26] Based on estimates in Chapter 4, it is possible these ships carried 3,000–5,500 people. Given the high mortality rates and extensive opportunities across the island, incomers would have little trouble finding exploitative opportunities.[27] And still they arrived.

Ascertaining the true number of Scots in Jamaica in any given era is problematic. Notwithstanding the anecdotal nature of the evidence, several eyewitnesses described a sizeable Scottish community. In 1774, for example, planter-historian Edward Long famously quantified the Scottish diaspora on the island:

[24] J. B. Moreton, *West India Customs and Manners* (London, 1793), p. 64.

[25] *Reports of Cases Decided in the Supreme Courts of Scotland*, vol. xix (Edinburgh, 1847), p. 279.

[26] Of the over 600 voyages advertised to Jamaica in the *Glasgow Herald* between 1806 and 1834, almost 300 were scheduled for Kingston and around 200 were set for Falmouth, Montego Bay and Port Antonio.

[27] T. Burnard, '"The countrie continues sicklie": white mortality in Jamaica, 1655–1780', *Social History of Medicine*, xii (1999), 45–72; V. Brown, *The Reaper's Garden: Death and Power in the World of Atlantic Slavery* (Cambridge, Mass., 2008), p. 236.

Jamaica, indeed, is greatly indebted to North Britain, as very near one third of the [white] inhabitants are either natives of that country, or descendants from those who were. Many have come…every year, less in quest of fame than of fortunes; and such is their industry and address, that few of them have been disappointed.[28]

Given that Jamaica's white population ranged from between 12,000 to 15,000 before the American War of Independence, Long imagined that around 4,000-5,000 Scots were resident on the island in the early to mid 1770s – although, in general, his eighteenth-century estimations are disputed.[29] Empirically informed estimates suggest the Scottish proportion lies somewhere between a tenth and one-third of white Jamaican society.[30] There are modern estimates of numbers of Scots on the island at various times, although none are authoritative.[31] While the exact figures will never be known, the sheer number of Scots on the island astonished one visitor in 1824 who claimed that 'the majority of the Planters here are Scotchmen'.[32] Even if an exaggeration, Scots probably *were* over-represented on Jamaica, since they comprised only around 14 per cent of the British population between 1801 and 1831.[33]

The presence of just so many Scots helped shape Jamaican society. Scots established and frequented secular bodies and ecclesiastical institutions with

[28] E. Long, *A History of Jamaica*, vol. ii (London, 1774), p. 287.

[29] Burnard, 'Passengers only', pp. 179–84. Trevor Burnard previously estimated Jamaica's white population was 10,000–12,000 before 1775. See 'European Migration to Jamaica, 1655–1780', *The William and Mary Quarterly*, 3d ser., 53 (1996), p. 772. However, Prof. Burnard has advised this author he now estimates Jamaica's white population in 1775 to be closer to 15,000.

[30] S. Mullen and S. Newman, 'Scotland and Jamaican Slavery: the problem with numbers', *Centre for the Study of the Legacies of British Slavery blog*. <https://lbsatucl. wordpress.com/2021/11/12/scotland-and-jamaican-slavery-the-problem-with-numbers> [accessed 15 Nov. 2021].

[31] Eric Graham suggests as many as 6,000 Scots were on the island in the mid 1770s (this estimate is not unrealistic); see 'The Scots penetration of the Jamaican plantation business', in *Recovering Scotland's Slavery Past: The Caribbean Connection*, ed. T. M. Devine (Edinburgh, 2015), p. 82. A recent popular history claimed 'Best estimates calculate this population ['of young Scottish men'] never dipped much below 20,000, but in the late 1700s and early 1800s could have been much higher. They accounted for about a third or perhaps half of Jamaica's white residents'. See K. Phillips, *Bought and Sold: Scotland, Jamaica and Slavery* (Edinburgh, 2022), p. 31. Phillips' estimates of both proportion and absolute numbers of Scots on the island are far too high – the population estimate exceeds the island's entire white society *c.*1775 – and are not supported by documentary evidence.

[32] NLS, MS. 17956, 'Journal of [unknown] of Banffshire', 15 Jan. 1824, p. 24.

[33] HCPP (1831) *Comparative Account of Population of Great Britain, 1801, 1811, 1821 and 1831*, p. 409.

a Caledonian dimension. In the 1790s, members of the St Andrews masonic lodge in Kingston led the annual celebrations dedicated to the patron saint of Scotland, which included a procession down to the local Anglican church.[34] Despite increasing numbers of Scots flooding into the eighteenth-century West Indies, there were no Presbyterian kirks whatsoever in the region. The first was probably established in the Bahamas in 1809.[35] Before then, the Anglican Church offered a temporary compromise in Kingston and most likely elsewhere, although the need for a place of worship in line with the faith of their homeland became more pronounced as more Scots arrived. Although the first attempt to construct a kirk in Kingston in the 1780s was unsuccessful, increasingly tolerant attitudes towards the practising of dissenting faiths in early nineteenth-century Jamaica allowed Scots to establish their own institution.[36]

The minutes of the St Andrews Scots Kirk, now held in the Jamaica National Archives, reveal that a petition was lodged with the Mayor and Aldermen in Kingston to establish a Presbyterian place of worship in December 1813.[37] Over 200 men and firms, mainly based in Kingston, simultaneously subscribed over £8,000 Jamaican currency (c.£5,700 stg.). Many of the initial subscribers based in Kingston hailed from Glasgow, such as George Scheviz, who was named on the kirk's first committee with fellow Glaswegian, John Miller.[38] The prominent Glasgow firm Bogle & Co. also contributed £200. Nephews and representatives of the Bogle family, George William and Robert Hamilton, subscribed individually too. Subscriptions were also received from Scots in the parishes of St Mary, St Andrew and especially St Thomas in the East. Thus, with the establishment of the Scots Kirk, Kingston became a hub of Scottish ecclesiastical activity, promoting a two-way transatlantic flow of people and capital from Glasgow to Jamaica.

'Toil and care under the scorching sun'

Writing home in 1791, James Smith, a Scottish overseer in the parish of Trelawney in Jamaica, reminisced about his homeland and, in doing so, revealed the *mentalité* of his compatriots on the island:

[34] Moreton, *West India Customs*, p. 34, p. 64.

[35] A. M. Jones, 'Race, religion, and the Scottish empire: St. Andrew's Kirk, Nassau, ca. 1810–1852', *International Journal of Bahamian Studies*, xxvi (2020), 1–12.

[36] TRG, 28 Jan.–4 Feb. 1815, p. 10; M. Turner, *Slaves and Missionaries: The Disintegration of Jamaican Slave Society, 1787–1834* (Illinois, 1982), p. 20.

[37] JNA, 5/20/2/1, 'St Andrews Scots Kirk minutes', 1814, n.p.

[38] JNA, 5/20/2/1, 1814, n.p.

I had…no word from Old Scotland – Ungrateful Country – but you gave me Birth, for that reason your Soil your Inhabitants your Climate your Religion are all dear to me. I believe sir it is the secret wish and propensity of every man who travels from his Native Land to return with the fruits of his Industry and marks of his prudence, to close his Days amongst endearing Relations and mingle his Dust with Native ground. This is my dearest Wish and this has been the Motive for these 8 years toil and care under the scorching sun.

Smith further elaborated on the 'toil and care' on Roslin estate, which, he hoped, would make him wealthy and enable a return home. From an annual wage of £120 local currency (£85 stg.), he had purchased three enslaved people to be hired out for jobbing work. This arrangement, Smith reckoned, would allow him to annually save the equivalent of a year's salary for his eventual return to Scotland.[39] Although we cannot determine if Smith succeeded in his quest, there is much evidence testifying to Scots as exploiters in Jamaica, revealing a comprehensive picture of their lives.

This chapter is centred around a group of 119 Scotsmen known to have been resident in Jamaica between 1775 and 1838, towards the end of Caribbean slavery.[40] Wills and probate inventories (held in Jamaica National Archives and Island Record Office) reveal occupational roles and wealth levels, while a later section provides further information on repatriated fortunes and investments in Great Britain (based upon wills and confirmation inventories registered in Scottish courts). This diverse group hailed from

---

[39] GCA, TD1710, 'Letter from James Smith', 10 Nov. 1791; This study uses a conversion formula contained in a contemporary source: 'To change West India currency into Sterling multiply by five and divide by seven. For sterling to currency, multiply by seven and divide by five'. See NLJ, MS. 132, 'Letterbook of Georgia estate', vol. i, p. 1. For an account of jobbing slaves in Jamaica, N. Radburn and J. Roberts, 'Gold versus life: jobbing gangs and British Caribbean slavery', *The William and Mary Quarterly*, lxxvi (2019), 223–56.

[40] This study identified wills and probate inventories for 119 Scotsmen who were known to be resident in Jamaica (1775–1838). Twenty-nine Scots were identified from Jamaican based probate data, and 90 from wills and confirmation inventories in Scottish archives. In Jamaica, material was gathered from Island Record Office (hereafter IRO), vol. lvi (1792) up to vol. cxiv (1833) and the JNA 1B/11/3, Probate inventories, vol. lxxvii (1791–2)–vol. cl (1833). For the sample of Jamaica sources, a distinctive methodology was followed. First, volumes of wills – held in the Registrar General's Department (IRO) in Twickenham Park – were examined for persons with Scottish surnames. Locations in Scotland were sometimes named, or individuals were linked to Scottish places through contemporary sources such as the *Edinburgh Magazine*, which listed deaths of Scots abroad. Second, residences were also sometimes named in complementary probate inventories – held in the Jamaica Archives at Spanishtown – which complemented the wills. For Scottish-based sources, wills and confirmation inventories in the National Records of Scotland were randomly identified via *Scotland's People* website by searching 'Jamaica' as a keyword in 'Description'. Individuals with property over £20 were included in the sample.

regions across Scotland. Highlanders were prominent in Jamaica, although not overly numerous, comprising just over 10 per cent of this group. Urban dwellers from the Central Lowlands – Edinburgh and especially Glasgow – were the most extensive group of Scots on Jamaica.[41] This section, therefore, examines Scots on Jamaica within a comparative framework.

Given the regularity of ships to southern Jamaica from the Clyde, it is no surprise Kingston was the premier destination for these Scots. Other favoured parishes included Hanover and Trelawney in the north-west of the island, Westmoreland on the south-west coast and St Thomas in the East.[42] It is well known these Scots abroad bonded together. After residents of St Thomas in the East made a further contribution to the Scots Kirk in 1823, a newspaper reported that 'it is gratifying to see a community of Scotch people, congregated together in a foreign land…testifying their attachment to the worship of their fathers, and country'.[43] Scots not only operated in networks in Jamaica but in 1793 one commentator J. B. Moreton noted an entrepreneurial spirit matched their inclination for patronage:

> The Scotch are more enterprising, partial, and friendly to each other than other nations; besides in general they are well educated young men; I never knew a raw lad from the country, who had not a letter of recommendation to his Excellency, or to some Mac or other; upon delivery of which he was taken notice of, and immediately put into some business.[44]

If these Scots were more enterprising and had better connections on Jamaica, is this reflected in patterns of wealth accumulation?

Richard Sheridan noted the disproportionate wealth of Scots on Jamaica, albeit based upon the seminal yet unreliable method of sampling local records using Scottish surnames. In 1754, individuals in Jamaica with Scottish surnames owned around a quarter of taxable land. Moreover, of all inventories of over £1,000 in a five-year period (1771–5) in Jamaica, around 20 per cent had Scottish surnames, but this same group owned a remarkable 40 per cent of overall wealth in the island. In the same period, merchants in

---

[41] Of this group of Scots in Jamaica, 101 family residences in Scotland are known. Prominent Scottish regions include the Western Lowlands (37 individuals), the Eastern Lowlands (24), north-east (15) and the Highland-Hebrides (13). Important locations included Glasgow (18), Edinburgh (9), Argyll (8), Ayrshire (7), Aberdeen (6), Dumfries (4), Banff (4).

[42] Of this group of Scots in Jamaica, 85 residences are known. Favoured locations include Kingston (21), St Thomas in the East (12), Trelawney (9), St Ann (6), Hanover (6), St Elizabeth (5), Westmoreland (5), St Elizabeth (5), St Mary (5).

[43] *TRG*, 14–21 April 1827, p. 19.

[44] Moreton, *West India Customs*, p. 64.

Jamaica with Scottish surnames owned as much property on their deaths as English and Welsh merchants combined and double the levels of Sephardic Jews.[45] How was this wealth earned and extracted? This section addresses these questions through analysis of wills and probate inventories of Scots – verified through place names – who died leaving property in Jamaica 1790–1838 (hereafter known as 'Jamaica inventories').[46] These sources reveal much information about individuals, but the limitations must be noted. Most males in Jamaica did not leave a will and testament, and those who did obviously hailed from the propertied class.[47] Moreover, inventories usually evaluated personal property only, meaning that estate ownership is rarely included in any valuation. Perhaps more importantly in the context of this study, the inventories do not include individual debt.[48] Nonetheless, Jamaican probate material reveals occupations, tentative levels of wealth on death and the remittance strategies of Scottish adventurers in Jamaica.

Merchants naturally congregated around the bustling trade hub of Kingston, in a career that could bring great wealth in a short period.[49] Indeed, of the top eight inventories left by Scots on Jamaica examined here, five were individuals based in Kingston. For example, on William McMurdo's death at thirty-seven in July 1795 – assuming he arrived on the island around twenty years before – he accumulated capital of over £35,000 in Jamaican currency (c.£25,000 stg.) in that period.[50] His property consisted mainly of enslaved people and he was owed over £19,000 in 'good' debts.[51] The death of another prominent merchant, James Waddell Esq., in Jamaica on 18 November 1825 was announced early the next year in *Blackwoods Magazine*.[52] Waddell's house in Temple Lane was filled with expensive books, wine and furniture. His considerable business, based in the

---

[45] Sheridan, *Sugar and Slavery*, p. 369, p. 375.

[46] The wills are now held in IRO in Twickenham Park, Jamaica; sources consulted: Wills, vol. lvi (1792)–vol. cxiv (1833). The inventories are held in Jamaica National Archives in Spanishtown; sources consulted: 1B/11/3, Probate inventories, vol. lxxvii (1791–2)–vol. cl (1833).

[47] T. Burnard, 'Inheritance and independence: women's status in early colonial Jamaica', *The William and Mary Quarterly*, 3rd series, clviii (1991), 93–114, at p. 96.

[48] Petley, *Slaveholders in Jamaica*, p. 21.

[49] Burnard, 'The great mart of the island', pp. 225–41.

[50] It should be noted that the Jamaican inventories were recorded in island currency. The sterling value is around 70% of the total. Alan Karras inferred McMurdo's fortune was over £35,000 sterling instead of Jamaican currency. See Karras, *Sojourners*, p. 182.

[51] JNA, 1B/11/3/84, Inventories, 1796, fo. 90.

[52] IRO, Wills, 1825–6, vol. cvi, p. 113; *Blackwood's Edinburgh Magazine*, vol. xix (Edinburgh, 1826), p. 627.

parish of St Andrews, stretched across the island. He owned several enslaved people with an overall value of £1,000 (some of whom had his surname) and outlying loans.[53] His son was educated at the prestigious Edinburgh Academy in 1824 and was resident in Scotland on his father's death.[54] Even merchants outside Kingston acquired relative fortunes. Daniel McKenzie operated a modest store in Clarendon peddling goods such as axes, knives and masons' hammers as well as carry combs and brushes. Most of his estate (£3,700 stg.) consisted of small debts owed to him by individuals to whom he advanced credit.[55]

The inventories reveal how the Scots plantocracy lived and died.[56] Duncan McLachlan was a mid-level planter owning thirty-three enslaved people on his mountain plantation in St Andrew, Castle Lachlan, as well as livestock in the adjoining cattle pen, Dunad (probably named after the Iron age hillfort of the same name in Argyll, Scotland).[57] The McLachlan inventory reveals basic but functional accommodation: the plantation house was furnished with a couch, two desks, looking glasses and some old books. The planters' main business was agriculture and exploitation, and McLachlan's saddle and harness show supervisory work was undertaken on horseback in the cane fields. The spying glass for surveillance, a pair of pistols and an old sword betray the planters' constant fear of a slave uprising. McLachlan also enjoyed the estate produce and had a puncheon of rum, sugar and coffee in the big house when he died. Perhaps he swigged rum while looking over the enslaved workforce on the mountain estate and reminisced about the glens and cairns of Argyll. McLachlan left post-mortem instructions to manumit and 'set free a certain negroe woman called Johanna McLachlan', probably his daughter with an enslaved woman on the plantation. William Smith, his nephew in Kingston, was appointed executor to carry out his wishes. McLachlan advised Smith to get out of Jamaica and return to the 'west of Scotland or near relations in the Highlands' to purchase a farm. His brother, Dr McLachlan, was appointed executor in Glasgow and annuities were left to their sisters in the city, Catherine and Elizabeth Smith. McLachlan also made ample provision for his niece, Elizabeth, who was bequeathed an

---

[53] JNA, 1B/11/3/142, Inventories, 1826, fo. 66.

[54] *The Edinburgh Academy Register* (Edinburgh, 1914), p. 28.

[55] JNA, 1B/11/3/84, Inventories, 1796, fo. 45.

[56] For a study of consumption patterns of planters in Jamaica, see C. Petley, 'Gluttony, excess, and the fall of the planter class in the British Caribbean', *Atlantic Studies*, ix (2012), 85–106.

[57] JNA, 1B/11/3/77, Inventories, 1791–2, fo. 179.

annuity of £20 while she remained unmarried and £400 if she wed.[58] Thus, capital from the plantation economy of Jamaica occasionally seeped into the west of Scotland.

The occupational description of planter requires some qualification. B. W. Higman's work on plantation management hierarchies notes that in the absence of the estate owner the attorney had overall legal responsibility and managed operations assisted by overseers and bookkeepers.[59] Many individuals in this study were referred to as planters, although they were overseers with little property, while others were rentiers of jobbing slaves. Some, however, owned large estates and hundreds of resident enslaved people. The career of one Scot contextualizes the trajectory from overseer to attorney and eventually enslaver. The letter-books of the Georgia estate in Trelawney – owned by the Gordon family of Cairness – reveals the upward career trajectory of one well-connected Scot in Jamaica. When he left for Great Britain in July 1812, the attorney of the Gordon family, Francis Graham, devolved the management of Georgia estate to another Scot, George William Hamilton. This was not a lower-rank sojourner. He was descended from Glasgow's 'sugar aristocracy' on both maternal and paternal lines. His father, John Hamilton, West India merchant and thrice lord provost of Glasgow (1800–12), was married to Helen Bogle, sister of Robert Bogle of Gilmorehill, who operated the Glasgow merchant firm Bogle & Co. Like many other sons of West India merchants, George William Hamilton and his brother Robert attended the University of Glasgow before entering commerce. [60] However, instead of joining the family firm, both travelled to Jamaica, where George William became known for his 'liberal education and gentlemanly demeanour', while his elevation on the island was attributed to his 'great interest' at home.[61]

The records of Georgia estate after 1812 illustrate initial challenges faced by the young overseer in his formative period. In October 1812, he took charge of the plantation and supervised the planting of the sugar crop for the coming year.[62] This was a temporary position, however, and Hamilton soon stepped up the economic ladder. By June 1817, he was the attorney for his relations, the Bogle family, in Vere, Jamaica, which involved supervising

[58] IRO, Wills, 1790–1, vol. lvi, fo. 135.

[59] B. W. Higman, *Plantation Jamaica, 1750–1850: Capital and Control in a Colonial Economy* (Kingston, 2008), p. 31.

[60] W. I. Addison, *The Matriculation Albums of the University of Glasgow, from 1728 to 1858* (Glasgow, 1913).

[61] B. McMahon, *Jamaica Plantership* (London, 1839), p. 65.

[62] NLJ, MS. 132, 'Letterbook of Georgia estate', vol. i, pp. 122–39.

groups of slaves on plantations. Deeds lodged in Kingston reveal Hamilton became a slave owner on his own account. In September 1829, Robert Page conveyed twenty-seven enslaved people to Hamilton, who may have been employed afterwards in jobbing work on estates.[63] By 1830, Archibald Bogle in Glasgow had conveyed two plantations in trust to his cousins then resident in Jamaica: George William Hamilton, the planter, and Robert, the merchant in Kingston. The two brothers accepted the task of revitalizing the fortunes of Phillipsburgh and Palmetto Valley estates – both St Thomas-in-the-Vale – by 'keeping down the contingencies…[and] to pay over the entire clear net proceeds'.[64] In this period, Hamilton was at the centre of the major network of nineteen attorneys whose influence stretched across the island, which, according to one contemporary, was detrimental to conditions of the enslaved. Hamilton tasked large numbers of overseers – described by a contemporary as 'the worst planters' – to produce good sugar crops, but his policy of non-interference meant conditions for the enslaved – even by the standards of the time – were reputedly barbaric.[65] George William Hamilton was one of the leading influences on the development of St Andrews Scots Kirk in Kingston. On emancipation in 1834, he was a large-scale claimant of compensation, collecting over £11,500.[66] He died in Edinburgh in 1857, leaving a fortune of over £8,700, much of which went to family including his wife, a free mixed-race woman named Martha Hamilton, resident in Spanishtown.[67] Hamilton was one of the select few to 'mingle his dust' in his native land and is buried in the Necropolis, the prestigious graveyard of Glasgow's mercantile elite.

Others died before they accumulated fortunes. Alexander Reid from Banffshire died in Jamaica on 3 November 1827. As the overseer on Tryall estate in Hanover, his inventory reveals possessions required for agricultural work. He owned three horses and a riding saddle, a pair of pantaloons, a black hat and a red coat. He had a writing desk, a liquor case and a silver and gold watch. He was owed a salary of £90 local currency from Tryall estate.[68] These types of activities were a risky and often fruitless business,

---

[63] IRO, Jamaica deeds, 1829, 'Conveyance to uses', vol. dccix, fo. 139.

[64] IRO, Jamaica deeds, 1830, 'Conveyance of land in trust', vol. dcclxv, fos. 262–264.

[65] Higman, *Plantation Jamaica*, pp. 73–4; McMahon, *Jamaica Plantership*, pp. 165–6.

[66] 'George William Hamilton', *Legacies of British Slave-ownership* <http://www.ucl.ac.uk/lbs/person/view/14412> [accessed 23 May 2016].

[67] NRS, SC70/4/58, 'Deed of settlement of George William Hamilton', 12 June 1858, pp. 362–99; SC70/1/99, 'Add. inventory', 14 Dec. 1858, p. 367.

[68] JNA, 1B/11/3/144, Inventories, 1828, fo. 215; D. Dobson, *Scots in the West Indies*, 1707–1857, vol. i (Baltimore, 1998), p. 117.

and many other Scots died in even more impecunious conditions than Reid. However, many others survived to repatriate fortunes.

In his magnum opus, *A History of Jamaica*, Edward Long commented on the artisans from the north of Scotland, particularly stone masons and mill wrights, as 'remarkably expert, and in general are sober, frugal and civil'. According to Long, these qualities were instilled by 'the good education, which the poorest of them receive [which is] a great influence on their morals and behaviour'.[69] Scots tradesmen were evidently noted for their skills and industry, allowing them to attain a level of income on the island that far exceeded the available remuneration at home. Writing home to a cousin in Edinburgh, one Andrew Taylor enquired about a carpenter back home: 'I should advise him very much to come out to this country if he is not married a carpenter here can commonly get a salary of...£100 to £120 sterling a year' which was five times the wage of carpenters in Glasgow.[70] As well as the high wages on offer, tradesmen could accumulate profits from the exploitation of skilled enslaved labour.

On 10 September 1797, the death of the Scottish carpenter James Riddoch Esq. in Montego Bay was announced in the *Edinburgh Magazine*.[71] He was a carpenter in St James parish in the north-west of the island, which bordered the Scots enclave Westmoreland. On his decease, most of his estate (worth £4,650 stg.) was held in enslaved people. Riddoch owned numerous gangs including valuable 'carpenter slaves' such as Suphax. He also had several 'open accounts', no doubt with local planters for carpentry work on plantations. Riddoch may have travelled from Scotland with carpentry skills and set about training enslaved people to undertake manual work. Other Scots tradesmen in this study – surveyors, shipwrights and masons – made use of skilled enslaved labour. Enslaved people in Jamaica were apprenticed to tradesmen in Jamaica, which effectively meant their labour created more profit in the plantation economy. Lauchlan McLean, a native of Coll and wealthy shipwright in Kingston, owned several enslaved people that had been apprenticed to work in his business. One bellow-blower named Scotland was worth a mere £5, no doubt due to limited productivity in his advanced years. A shipwright, Big Chester, was far more important

---

[69] Long, *History of Jamaica*, vol. ii, p. 288.

[70] NLJ, MS. 706, 'Letter from Andrew Taylor', 8 May 1819. The daily wage of joiners and house carpenters in Glasgow in 1819 was 2d or 40 shillings (£2) per month for a 10-hour day, 5 days a week. Thus, wages were most likely around £24 per annum. See J. Cleland, *Statistical Tables Relative to the City of Glasgow*, 3rd ed. (Glasgow, 1823), p. 132.

[71] JNA, 1B/11/3/86, Inventories, 1797, fo. 43; *The Edinburgh Magazine or Literary Miscellany*, vol. ix (1797), p. 79.

to the operation and was valued as such (£140 Jamaica currency).[72] Masons and carpenters also utilized slaves in semi-skilled labouring gangs.[73] As these life stories show, Scots were involved at all levels in the plantation economy: as planters, merchants and tradesmen.

Wealth on death was identified for nineteen Scots in Jamaica archives: planters (5), merchants (5), doctors (3), carpenter (2), surveyor (1), shipwright (1), overseer (1) and mason (1). Merchants left the highest-value estates, followed by planters.[74] James Waddell's extensive mercantile dealings, for example, allowed him to accumulate a fortune of £47,857 sterling.[75] The total value left by those with identified inventories (19) was J£336,106 (£240,076 stg.). Removing 15 per cent (£36,011) for liabilities, the average value estate was £10,740 sterling.[76]

Comparisons with other studies support the view that on average Scots held higher-valued estates on death in colonial Jamaica compared to the general white population. Richard Sheridan noted the average wealth of individuals who died in Jamaica in 1771–5 with personal property valued at at least £1,000 was £2,656 sterling.[77] Trevor Burnard's study of the wealth of Jamaica on the eve of the American Revolution estimated the personal wealth of white colonists in 1774–5 was on average £2,710 sterling (after removing 15 per cent for liabilities).[78] In the nineteenth century, Christer Petley's sample of over 200 inventories of free whites in Jamaica from 1807 to 1834 revealed an average personal estate of c.£5,000 sterling.[79]

---

[72] The inventory of Lauchlan McLean suggested he had property worth over £7,100 sterling; see JA, 1B/11/3/148, Inventories, 1831–2, fo. 37. It is probable this was the same Lauchlan McLean who died on 15 Oct. 1829 at the age of 43, 'a native of the island of Coll' in Scotland who had a monumental inscription in Kingston Parish Church. See J. H. L. Archer, *Monumental Inscriptions of the British West Indies from the Earliest Date* (London, 1875), p. 112.

[73] For example, the inventory of Roderick McKenzie, a mason in St Thomas in the East, on 8 July 1813 establishes he owned male slaves worth £1,060, no doubt employed as a labouring squad. See JA, 1B/11/3/122, Inventories, 1813, fo. 42.

[74] In this study, merchants (5) left a total of £138,704 stg. (ave. £27,740); planters (5) left a total of £52,607 (ave. £10,521); doctors (3) left a total of £31,553; (ave. £10,517). The median was £4,357 stg. and the range was £49,618 stg.

[75] JA, 1B/11/3/142, Inventories, 1826, fo. 66

[76] For rationale on liabilities in eighteenth-century Jamaica, see Burnard, 'Prodigious riches'.

[77] Sheridan, *Sugar and Slavery*, p. 370.

[78] Burnard, 'Prodigious riches', p. 517.

[79] C. Petley, 'Plantations and homes: the material culture of the early nineteenth-century Jamaican elite', *Slavery & Abolition*, xxxv (2014), 437–57, at p. 440, p. 453.

Evidence culled from studies that adopt the admittedly unreliable surname analysis suggests that Scots in eighteenth-century Jamaica were wealthier than their average counterparts. Among his study of individuals who left property worth more than £1,000 in Jamaica in 1771–5, Richard Sheridan noted seventy-seven individuals with Scottish surnames were worth a total of £891,916, meaning the average personal property of those presumed to be Scots was £11,583 sterling.[80] Alan Karras reported lower average wealth than Sheridan, although those with Scottish surnames left increasingly large amounts in late eighteenth-century Jamaica, with an average of £3,284 in 1778, rising to £4,669 in 1796.[81] Yet, the evidence from Jamaica archives identified here (19 Scots who died in Jamaica 1790–1838; mean value £10,740 stg.) is closer to the Sheridan estimate, which suggests Scots retained estates with a relatively higher average value on death, and remained wealthier than their counterparts in white Jamaican society towards the end of Caribbean slavery. While fortunes were still available to Scots in Jamaica during the early 'decline' era, the largest estates consisted mainly of enslaved people and debts which, as noted by Karras, would have made early relocation difficult. Moreover, identifying levels of capital held by Scots on death in Jamaica does not reveal the levels of profits repatriated to Scotland and the effects, if any. This chapter now examines how the 'prodigious riches' were repatriated before tracing the impact at home.

Inter-vivos and post-mortem wealth repatriation

In tracing the careers of Colin and Alexander Maclarty, two Scottish medical doctors in Jamaica, historian Alan Karras pessimistically dismissed their chances of remitting wealth to eighteenth-century Scotland. Karras was 'unclear how successful Colin Maclarty was' and suggested that many Scots remained in eighteenth-century Jamaica because it was 'almost impossible' to convert capital and credit in Jamaica into profits without court action.[82] Thus, the Maclarty case seemed to support Karras' position that Jamaica wealth could not be extracted easily. In reality, however, Maclarty returned to Scotland and claimed compensation for enslaved people in 1834.[83] He was a highly successful adventurer who acquired landed property in Scotland. A court case reveals he owned the estate of Keilcolmkeill in Argyllshire, houses in Campbelltown and Chester Vale plantation in Jamaica.

---

[80] Sheridan, *Sugar and Slavery*, p. 370.

[81] Karras, *Sojourners*, p. 175.

[82] Karras, *Sojourners*, p. 60.

[83] N. Draper, 'Possessing people: absentee slave-owners within British society', in *Legacies of British Slave-ownership*, ed. C. Hall, N. Draper et al. (Cambridge, 2014), p. 44.

He also bequeathed £3,000 each to his two daughters.[84] Maclarty had in fact accumulated capital in Jamaica, which was invested in land in Scotland, which passed to beneficiaries. This was not uncommon, yet this vision of unsuccessful Scots in Jamaica has become accepted orthodoxy. Leading economic historian of Scotland, Bruce Lenman, positively cites Karras to argue that few Scots in the West Indies lived to achieve their aspirations of acquiring great wealth.[85] It is perhaps unsurprising this view endures, since there is relatively little known about the few that did succeed. By examining *successful* Scots in Jamaica, this chapter redresses the imbalance – first by examining strategies of returning wealth in life and death. Even if Karras was correct about Scots in eighteenth-century Jamaica, this group repatriated dramatically more wealth after 1800.

Scots in nineteenth-century Jamaica developed both *inter-vivos* and post-mortem strategies that facilitated wealth repatriation to their homeland. Advertisements in the island's newspapers reveal how resident merchants attempted to recover money before they departed from the island.[86] Planters were able to convert plantation produce into capital easily. Many planters in this study were in credit with Glasgow-West India merchants demonstrating how plantation profits were transferred to Scotland. Lower-rank adventurers also repatriated wealth via the merchant firms of Glasgow. The letters from Andrew Taylor reveal much about the repatriation of profits to Scotland and the mentality behind it. As overseer on York estate in Trelawney in May 1819, some of his earnings were sent home to his cousin via bills of exchange which were deemed safe, as they 'cannot be lost'. In one case, he advised drawing the bill on Stirling, Gordon & Co., merchants of Glasgow, as they were the 'most [secure] house in North Britain'.[87] In a letter in 1827, he sent money to his cousin – who by this point was economically dependent on him due to the 'hard times' in Scotland – and contrasted his own position in Jamaica: 'I want for nothing'.[88] Taylor underwent a series of upward promotions across plantations in Trelawney and took up 'a very healthy situation' on Georgia estate in 1826. At this point, he had been in Jamaica at least seven years and offered some emotional comfort, matched by an economic guarantee, to his cousin, who had despaired in an earlier letter that he would not see him again:

---

[84] *Cases Decided in the Court Session, July 20 1863–1864*, 3s, V.II (Edinburgh, 1863–4), p. 489.

[85] B. Lenman, 'Review: Michael Morris, Scotland and the Caribbean, c.1740–1833', *Eighteenth-Century Scottish Studies Society Newsletter*, xxxi (2017), p. 24.

[86] 'The Subscriber', *Jamaica Mercury*, 1 Oct. 1779.

[87] NLJ, MS. 706, 'Letter from Andrew Taylor', 2 May 1827.

[88] NLJ, MS. 706, 'Letter from Andrew Taylor', 1820.

Be assured that should anything happen to me in this Country that I have regulated my affairs so far with certain individuals which I can depend on as will let you know my end I cannot promise you a fortune but I have a little and I have no person hear to leave anything too therefor I consider you most deserving of what I may leave behind. But there is no knowing the reverses of fortune & how things turn out.[89]

Thus, Taylor was in Jamaica principally to improve his own position, although his wealth was naturally bequeathed to his family. In the event of his decease, trusted associates – essentially operating as executors – would send his small fortune to Scotland. However, it seems there was no requirement for this, as Taylor left the island in February 1832. His last letter describes a picturesque tour through the Bay of Honduras and the Gulf of Mexico up to the United States en route home to Edinburgh.[90]

Of those who died in Jamaica, many had large fortunes waiting to be remitted to Great Britain. Planters sometimes bequeathed profits to family in Scotland in the form of annuities (a sum of money from the yearly profits), which provided an annual income long after the death of the planter concerned.[91] Others left more substantial legacies. In 1801, James McPherson, a planter in St George, left his plantation and resident slaves to his sister and brother in Inverness, on the condition that the enslaved people were not disposed of but retained for the 'benefit and advantage of the family'.[92] This presented issues, as family members were afterwards responsible for estates they most likely had no experience of running. Planters sometimes resolved these issues by leaving instructions for associates to sell their property in Jamaica and to remit the wealth to Scotland, although this depended on trustworthy individuals carrying out instructions.

Capital was often sent home via transatlantic merchants. Elite adventurers in this study – planters, merchants and doctors – appointed West India merchants based in Glasgow as executor or trustee. Both roles involved the gathering and disposition of the estate, although trusteeship involved taking legal responsibility for the property. Executors were appointed merely to ensure the property was distributed based on the direct wishes of the testator. For holders of West India property, appointing merchants in Glasgow as executors was a logical step. In some cases, planters had open accounts with merchants with whom they had built up trusted commercial

---

[89] NLJ, MS. 706, 'Letter from Andrew Taylor', 16 June 1826.

[90] NLJ, MS. 706, 'Letter from Andrew Taylor', 8 April 1832.

[91] *Decisions of the First and Second Divisions of the Court of Session, from November 1810 to November 1812* (Edinburgh, 1813), pp. 129–34.

[92] IRO, 'Wills', 1802, vol. lx, p. 8.

relationships over many years. Furthermore, testators had estates consisting of assets (land and enslaved people) that had to be sold: the merchant firms had the expertise to dispose of such property and remit profits home. It is very likely testators assumed they could rely on an honest disposition of proceeds; merchant firms who defaulted on the legal distribution of testators' estate would have damaged their commercial reputation. Glasgow merchants were known to advertise in local newspapers looking for relations of dead Scotsmen as much as twelve years after their deaths.[93] However, if executors were based in Jamaica, the distance from the source of the fortune to the beneficiary and the differing legal systems meant the risks of dishonest practices were far more likely.[94] Indeed, one bookkeeper, Benjamin McMahon, described the role of executors in his memoirs of plantation life and noted a contemporary saying: 'When a man dies in Jamaica, he is ruined forever'.[95] There was legal process to address dishonesty, although it was generally a protracted and costly process.

A transatlantic legal case in November 1820 provides further insight into the role of an executor on the island. Excessive fees had been charged by one executor, Mr Samson, on a deceased planter's estate, meaning the beneficiary, Miss Oliver of Leith, Edinburgh, received far less than her due. Preparing for a legal challenge, a lawyer's firm in Great Britain requested advice from Robert Hamilton – the brother of George William Hamilton – who was described as a 'highly respected gentleman of Jamaica...now in Glasgow'. The subsequent nine-point questionnaire answered by Hamilton revealed executors were entitled to 6 per cent of the total estate before any payments were made to beneficiaries (fees which had been overcharged in the Oliver bequest). The legal firm then asked for the professional opinion of a solicitor in Kingston who was to be appointed as power of attorney to collect and remit the correct sum to Miss Oliver and other beneficiaries.[96] Much can be taken from this source. First, it behoved any executor to gather as much as possible from the deceased's estate to raise their own fee, although some were unethical and did not remit the true sum. Second, legal process allowed inheritors in Scotland – if they were financially able to do so – to pursue individuals across the Atlantic.

As well as merchant firms, some adventurers left instructions that remitted proceeds to banks in Scotland for subsequent distribution to heirs. Alexander

[93] *The Glasgow Journal*, 22–9 Sept. 1763, p. 4.

[94] For a pessimistic view of the remittance of capital by executors in Jamaica, see Brown, *The Reaper's Garden*, pp. 102–7.

[95] McMahon, *Jamaica Plantership*, p. 227.

[96] NLJ, MS. 708, 'Questionnaire proposed to Mr R. Hamilton', 10 Nov. 1820.

Milne, a planter who died on his Castle Gordon estate in St Thomas in the East in 1823, originally hailed from the east coast of Scotland. His death in 1823 was advertised in the *Edinburgh Annual Register*.[97] Like many other Scots in Jamaica, he imported luxury goods from Scotland which maintained his connection with his homeland; for example, his library contained copies of Walter Scott's *Rob Roy* (1817) and *Ivanhoe* (1820).[98] There was a thriving trade in Scottish books on Jamaica; subscribers ordered publication of titles back home to be delivered via Scottish publishers in Kingston. Gaels on the island were also known to subscribe to dictionaries published in Great Britain.[99] Like those Scots who sent money home, Milne left instructions on where his fortune was to be sent. His last will and testament ensured his plantation and twenty resident slaves should be sold 'to the highest & best bidder or to the best advantage and if possible, to a good humane Master' after his decease. The capital was to be remitted to Scotland and lodged on with 'the Royal Bank of Scotland in Edinburgh, upon interest and that on account and benefit of my sister, Sarah Milne' in Kirkcaldy.[100] Taken together with the remittance of profits in life and the legal framework that transmitted wealth on death, Caribbean adventurers enriched Scotland for well over a century, and increasingly so after 1800.

Scots-Jamaica fortunes

This section traces the fortunes of ninety Scots who were known to be in Jamaica between 1775 and 1838 and left property in Scotland on death, principally through their confirmation inventories (hereafter 'Scottish inventories'). This group died between 1794 and 1857; that is, during and after the era of 'decline'.[101] Thus, in contrast to the above estimates from Jamaica archives, this section measures wealth repatriated mainly from nineteenth-century Jamaica. The limitations of these legal sources must be noted. Assessing the value of real property in Jamaica – land and enslaved people – was outside the capacity of the appraisers and they were not normally given

---

[97] *The Edinburgh Annual Register for 1823*, vol. xvi, parts 1–3 (Edinburgh, 1824), p. 474.

[98] JA, 1B/11/3/124, Inventories, 1823, fo. 124.

[99] *TRG*, 3–10 March 1827, p. 19; Sheila Kidd, 'Gaelic books as cultural icons: the maintenance of cultural links between the Highlands and the West Indies', in *Within and Without Empire: Scotland across the (Post)colonial Borderline*, ed. C. Sassi and T. van Heijnsbergen (Newcastle, 2013), pp. 46–60.

[100] IRO, 'Wills', 1823, vol. ciii, p. 111.

[101] Of these 90 Scots with Scottish inventories who died between 1794 and 1857, only 3 died before 1800. They left a total of £1,545, which is almost incidental compared to the overall total of £701,506.

a value. The inventory of James Anderson, a carpenter who died in Jamaica in 1830, acknowledged it provided only a partial valuation, as 'it is reputed that the deceased had left property or effects in Jamaica but the Executrix [in Scotland] does not know if this be true and cannot therefore condescend on the value of them'.[102] Similarly, the value of heritable property in Great Britain – landed estates and dwellings – was not included. These snapshots, therefore, systematically underestimate the value of the deceased's property. On the other hand, the Scottish inventories reveal verified personal wealth levels on death, and investments in Great Britain. The associated wills and testaments, discussed below, also reveal property transmission strategies which benefited family, friends and often complete strangers over successive generations.

Given Jamaica's reputation as 'the grave of Scotland', it is unsurprising some settled their affairs before departure.[103] About to travel to the West Indies in January 1817, John Donald had the foresight to draw up a will and testament, as he was dead in just over two years.[104] There was a historical and legal precedent for this practice. In the early modern period, Scots destined for Europe arranged settlements before leaving, as, in case of early decease, distance added complications to recovering inheritance. Indeed, some fortunes were simply forfeited when family members did not have the appropriate networks abroad to administer estates or the means to pursue costly legal action.[105] The Atlantic world presented similar issues, although some adventurers that travelled without sorting their affairs arranged them in Jamaica. This presented further issues due to the nature of colonial property and the idiosyncrasies of the Scottish legal system. While in Jamaica, William Rae ensured his will was written up with a codicil in the 'Scotch form' to ensure dissemination of his estate in England, Jamaica and Scotland.[106] Scots were the only residents of the West Indies who required knowledge of a triple legal system (British, colonial and Scots law), knowledge that facilitated sophisticated strategies that ensured the desired transmission of property across the Atlantic world.

In *Capitalism & Slavery* (1944), Eric Williams famously argued the onset of the American Revolution in 1776 initiated the 'decline' of the West India

---

[102] NRS, SC70/1/46, 'Inventory of James Anderson', 11 May 1832, p. 857.

[103] T. Somerville, *My Own Life and Times, 1741–1814* (Edinburgh, 1861), p. 359.

[104] NRS, SC70/1/20, 'Inventory of John Donald', 23 Oct. 1819, p. 80.

[105] S. Murdoch, 'The repatriation of capital to Scotland: a case study of seventeenth-century Dutch testaments and miscellaneous notarial instruments', in *Back to Caledonia: Scottish Homecomings from the Seventeenth Century to the Present*, ed. M. Varricchio (Edinburgh, 2012), p. 36.

[106] PUL, C1222, Rae Family Estate Collection: Box 1/Folder 6, 'Case and opinion regarding William Rae's will', 19 July 1837, p. 2.

economy (although it is now generally accepted 'decline' did not set in until the 1820s).[107] Williams had little to say about the repatriation of sojourning capital, although his vision of a declining West India economy after 1776 inferred decreasing personal fortunes. In similar fashion, Alan Karras doubted whether wealth acquired in eighteenth-century Jamaica was ever converted to profits in Scotland.[108] While Karras may have been accurate for eighteenth-century Jamaica, the wealth extracted by Scots from Jamaica increased exponentially after 1800. In this sense, Scots seem to have been the exception to accepted orthodoxies around the accumulation of personal wealth in the plantation economy: fewer and smaller fortunes were acquired before 1800, yet wealth levels increased dramatically afterwards, with many more Scots acquiring larger fortunes which they successfully returned to Scotland.[109] The evidence from the Scottish inventories underlines how increasingly large wealth derived from slavery in nineteenth-century Jamaica contributed to the development of rapidly industrializing Scotland.

The Scottish inventories reveal this group of ninety Scots in the late-slavery era Jamaica left property valued at a total of £701,506, an average of £7,794 (see Table 5.1). Known occupations included: planters (20), merchants (10), doctors (5), overseers (3), Guinea factors (3), carpenters (2), house wright (1), coppersmith (1), carpenter (1). The highest average wealth was owned by resident traffickers in enslaved people (average £35,296) and it should be noted these three individuals were part of large Kingston firm Taylor, Ballantine & Fairlie (discussed below). Merchants represented the second highest average fortunes (£21,194), followed by planters (£12,491)and doctors (£6,862). Scots retained a major role in planting, although their commercial success in nineteenth-century Jamaica was based upon a diversification of interests.

Based on average wealth on death (£7,794), these Scots in Jamaica were relatively high earners. These average fortunes were worth around a quarter more than the average fortunes (£5,804) of the middling ranks in Glasgow and Edinburgh in 1822–4.[110] And if compared to modern values, the average

---

[107] E. Williams, *Capitalism and Slavery* (Chapel Hill, 1944); T. Burnard, *Jamaica in the Age of Revolution* (Philadelphia, 2020), p. 231.

[108] Karras, *Sojourners*, p. 60, p. 175.

[109] The author's forthcoming chapter, 'The Scottish extraction of wealth from Jamaica' in the collection (provisionally titled 'Williams@75' edited by Trevor Burnard, Andrew O'Shaughnessy and Laura Sandy), is based upon a sample of Scottish inventories left by 119 Scots present in Jamaica 1750–1834. Between 1750 and 1799, the average was £183 sterling, while the average between 1800 and 1834 rose to £6,837 (a 3,636% increase).

[110] A. McCrum, 'Inheritance and the family: the Scottish urban experience in the 1820s', in *Urban Fortunes: Property and Inheritance in the Town*, ed. J. Stobart and A. Owens (Aldershot, 2000), pp. 156–7.

Table 5.1 Wealth on death of Scots in Jamaica in the late
slavery era (1775–1838) who died between 1794 and 1857.

Home Scottish region	Inventories	%Total inventories	Wealth	%Total wealth
Borders	7	7.8%	£92,247	13.1%
Western Lowlands	33	36.7%	£210,463	30.0%
Eastern Lowlands	21	23.3%	£266,843	38.0%
Highlands-Hebrides	3	3.3%	£36,306	5.2%
North-east	10	11.1%	£26,847	3.8%
Far north	0	0.0%	£0	0.0%
Unknown	16	17.8%	£68,800	9.8%
Total	90		£701,506	

Source: National Records of Scotland: Wills, Testaments
and Confirmation Inventories (see Bibliography).

Table 5.2 Range of wealth on death of Scots in Jamaica in the late
slavery era (1775–1838) who died between 1794 and 1857.

Decile	Range	Inventories	Average	%Total wealth
Top	£100,000–150,000	1	£133,361	19%
Second	£75,000–£99,999	1	£76,169	11%
Third	£50,000–£74,999	0	n/a	n/a
Fourth	£25,000–£49,999	7	£34,195	34%
Fifth	£10,000–£24,999	7	£15,115	15%
Sixth	£7,500–£9,999	5	£8,884	6%
Seventh	£5,000–£7,499	5	£5,743	4%
Eight	£2,500–£4,999	10	£3,673	5%
Ninth	£500–£2,499	23	£1,331	4%
Tenth	£20–£499	31	£204	1%
Total		90		

Source: National Records of Scotland: Wills, Testaments
and Confirmation Inventories (see Bibliography).

wealth was enormous. Indeed, £7,794 in 1825 – a mid-point of dates of death – is equivalent to £6.91m (relative to the worth of average earnings in 2020).[111] Caution is required, however. Most of the assets in Jamaica were held in few hands. Just sixteen individuals (17 per cent of the overall group) left fortunes of £10,000 or more, owning approximately 80 per cent of the assets (Table 5.2). Within this elite, two exceptional fortunes accumulated by two individuals, John Shand and William Rae, represented a third of the overall total. Indeed, with assets valued at over £133,000 on his death in 1826, absentee planter John Shand of Fettercairn in Aberdeenshire was among the richest men in Great Britain.[112] The bottom half of this group by decile (74 individuals or 82 per cent of the sample) owned approximately 20 per cent of the total assets.[113] There was major inequality in levels of wealth, and most were relatively poorer.

While great fortunes of £100,000-plus could be generated in Jamaica during the 'age of decline', these were exceptional cases. Scottish inventories suggest that even for *successful* Scots in Jamaica, themselves a small proportion who crossed the Atlantic, the repatriation of small- to medium-sized fortunes of under £500 (and often much less) was most common. In general, those who survived the high-risk environment could expect a modest fortune at best if they survived. Even so, £200 in 1825 was still a major sum, equivalent to £177,000 in modern values (relative to the worth of average earnings in 2020).[114]

Not all returned to enjoy the spoils. Almost as many of this group died in Jamaica as managed a successful return home. Even so, this is a remarkably high proportion of absenteeism (49 per cent). There was a noted Scottish departure from Jamaica after 1800, as Scots returned home with their profits.[115] In 1829, representatives of St Andrew's Scots Kirk in Kingston noted their fee-paying congregation had decreased by half, which was attributed 'to the deaths and departures from this island of many opulent

---

[111] For modern values, see *Measuring Worth* <https://www.measuringworth.com/calculators/ukcompare/> [accessed 27 Oct. 2021]. Relative wage or income worth (average earnings), 2020 values has been used here.

[112] NRS, SC5/41/1, 'Inventory of John Shand', 1826, pp. 350–453.

[113] This group of 90 Scots in Jamaica left property in Great Britain valued at £701,506. The mean estate value was £7,794, median £1,607 and range was £133,331.

[114] For modern values, see *Measuring worth* <https://www.measuringworth.com/calculators/ukcompare/> [27 Oct. 2021]. Relative wage or income worth (average earnings), 2020 values have been used here.

[115] Of the sample of 90, 41 Scots died in Jamaica and 44 died in Scotland. Two died in England and 2 died at sea (and 1 unknown).

Presbyterians'.[116] The reason for this departure is unknown, but perhaps these Scots anticipated the end of plantation slavery and chose to return. Significantly, the average fortunes of those who died on the island were around 40 per cent smaller than the fortunes of those who died in Scotland.[117] Obviously, wealthier people would have found it easier to return. However, it seems very likely that the under-reporting in Scottish inventories of the main assets – land and enslaved people – of those who died on the island partially explains this discrepancy, but many did not own such property in the first place. Prior to overseer Adam Johnston's death in St Elizabeth in 1796, his total assets – the £30 worth of cotton he had shipped to Scotland – would barely have covered his own return journey home.[118]

Yet, many Scots died in Jamaica while asset rich in Great Britain. Almost a quarter of the group who died in Jamaica owned personal property valued at £5,000 or more, a sum that would have placed them among the middling ranks had they returned.[119] Scots in the West Indies may have been sojourners in theory, but they were commercial adventurers in practice, which meant lifestyles dictated their plans. Wealth levels did not always dictate a return home, and some even became permanent residents. William Rae epitomized the Scottish plantocracy whose colonial sojourn evolved into permanent residence. Living on the island for over fifty years, Rae entered business as a merchant in Kingston soon after arriving on the island in the 1780s.[120] He afterwards came into ownership of coffee and sugar estates, cattle pens and urban property in Kingston and Port Royal. On his death on 7 May 1837, he possessed property in England, Jamaica and Scotland valued at over £76,000, the largest identified estate of any Scot who died in Jamaica.[121] This example complicates the vision of avaricious Scottish sojourners resident in Jamaica in the hope of gaining quick wealth and a rapid return home. While more Scots overall died in Jamaica than became wealthy, even *successful* adventurers who accumulated substantial property in Great Britain were not certain to immediately return home.

[116] *Votes of the Honourable House of Assembly of Jamaica in a Session, 3 November 1829 – 20 February 1830* (Kingston, Jamaica, 1830), pp. 87, 224, 233.

[117] Of the 41 who died in Jamaica, the overall value of property was £243,400 (average £5,936 per inventory). Of the 44 who died in Scotland, the overall value of property was £423,164 (average £9,617 per inventory).

[118] NRS, CC8/8/130, 'Inventory of Adam Johnston', 12 March 1796, pp. 667–9.

[119] Of this group of Scots who died in Jamaica, 17 had fortunes of £1,000 or more, and 10 had fortunes of £5,000 or more. William Rae was worth £76,169 when he died in Kingston.

[120] PUL C1222, Box 1/ Folder 9, 'Memorial for the executors of the late William Rae', 17 Nov. 1837.

[121] NRS, SC70/1/55, 'Inventory of William Rae', 21 July 1837, p. 783.

The wealth of Scots in Jamaica was repatriated across Great Britain. Assets held in Scotland were worth almost 15 per cent less than those in England, and a lesser amount remained in the West Indies (including held in Kingston merchant firms). Indeed, over half of the overall personal wealth was held in England (twenty-six individuals owned assets in England valued at £378,290).[122] But most of the wealth in England was held by just three individuals, revealing the tendency of elite Scots to repatriate capital through English port cities, especially London. William Rae owned English property valued at over £50,000 on his death in 1837, including major sums held by merchants in Liverpool who imported his produce, as well as investments in English railways. London merchants owed James Fairlie over £40,000 on his death in 1819. John Shand owned an incredible £122,000 in 3 per cent government consols in 1826.[123] It is possible Shand invested after his return to Scotland, although in any case, the financial returns on offer in London were much more attractive than provincial opportunities. Shand's case is consistent with what Robert Morris has described as the 'property cycle'. Property made distinctive contributions to capital formation at different stages in life, and the investments of individuals became less risky as they aged.[124] In Shand's case, he initially held investments in West India property but ultimately consolidated his fortune by transferring the fortune to more secure government stock.

Scots in Jamaica with assets in England were also more likely to own land in Scotland, hinting at the existence of colonial landed ranks integrated with the London moneyed interest. Indeed, the substantial English investments of elite Scots in Jamaica give support to aspects of the 'gentlemanly capitalism' thesis.[125] In this case, Scots in Jamaica, mainly merchants, planters and 'Guinea factors', invested in the national debt, revealing a flow from colony to the metropolis that added to the wealth of London.[126] On the other hand, the inventories suggest numerically more Scots in Jamaica – those

---

[122] Of the £701,506 left by 90 Scots in Jamaica, a total of £378,290 (53.9%) was held in English assets, £278,152 (39.6%) was held in Scottish moveable property and £49,073 (6.9%) remained in West India property.

[123] NRS, SC5/41/1, 'Inventory of John Shand Esquire', 12 Jan. 1826, pp. 350–452; NRS, SC70/1/55, 'Inventory of William Rae', 21 July 1837, pp. 782–7; NRS, SC36/48/15, 'Inventory of James Fairlie', 19 Nov. 1819, pp. 728–47.

[124] R. J. Morris, 'The middle class and the property cycle during the Industrial Revolution', in *The Search for Wealth and Stability*, ed. T. C. Smout (London, 1979), pp. 91–114.

[125] P. J. Cain and A. J. Hopkins, *British Imperialism, 1688–2000*, 2nd ed. (Singapore, 2002), pp. 87–103.

[126] Eight individuals owned £160,269 in 3% consols and government stock (22% of the overall total wealth). Another owned an East India bond of £2,200.

of lesser means – did not repatriate wealth through London. Even if most of the wealth went via England in general and London in particular, large sums *were* directed to Scotland, adding support to Andrew Porter's vision of a 'Scottish blend of commerce' independent of London.[127]

This chapter now turns to the transatlantic dispersal of Scots-Jamaica fortunes. Scots in Jamaica held considerable property in merchant firms and banks. Merchant houses operating a commission system carried the produce of planters to market and converted sugar, rum, coffee and cotton to sterling. Slave-traders in Kingston sometimes deposited their profits with London agents. Indeed, over half of the finance in merchant houses was held in firms located in Liverpool and London.[128] 'Guinea factor' James Fairlie held the exceptional account of over £40,000 in London merchant firms, especially Fairlie Bonham and Company.[129] If most of the wealth was retained in England, the majority of accounts were held with Glasgow merchant firms.[130] Stirling, Gordon & Co. was the preferred option for Scots in Jamaica, underlining Trelawney overseer Andrew Taylor's opinion of the firm's financial integrity. On his death in 1825, John Black, owner of Elderslie Hedge in Trelawney, Jamaica, held over £20,000 in account current with Stirling, Gordon & Co., a fund that possibly contributed to the purchase and upkeep of his landed estate Ardmarnoch in Argyll from around 1820.[131] Scots with wealth in Jamaica shipped through ports of Clyde to family residences scattered across Scotland, confirming the city of Glasgow's role as a commercial hub whose firms circulated profits across the nation.

If the merchant firms carried tropical produce across the Atlantic and converted sales into profits in Great Britain, banks also held interest-bearing capital over the long term. It was common for Scots in Jamaica to repatriate capital to Scottish banking institutions.[132] Accounts with values of £1,000 and under were typical, although returned adventurer John Miller of Muirshiel held an exceptional account of £16,000 in the Clydesdale and Western Banks on his death in 1854.[133] These accounts were more likely

---

[127] A. Porter, '"Gentlemanly capitalism" and empire: the British experience since 1750?', *The Journal of Imperial and Commonwealth History*, xviii (1990), 265–95, at p. 277.

[128] Twenty-seven Scots held £139,563 in British merchant firms. Six individuals held £75,084 in English firms.

[129] NRS, SC36/48/15, 'Inventory of James Fairlie', 19 Nov. 1819, p. 730.

[130] Eighteen individuals held £56,368 in Glasgow merchant firms.

[131] NRS, SC70/1/35, 'Inventory of John Black', 1826, p. 304.

[132] Around a third of this group (31 individuals, 34% of the overall group) held accounts worth £52,577 (average £1,696) in Scottish banks.

[133] NRS, SC36/48/41, 'Inventory of John Miller', 16 July 1855, pp. 685–92.

to be held in Edinburgh-based banks with Glasgow offices.[134] That few accounts were held in the provincial banks, such as the Thistle and Ship Banks, underlines the deep connections that Scots in slavery societies had with the Edinburgh financial system. Two returned adventurers, however, set up their own provincial bank in the west of Scotland in 1802. After the Bank of Scotland withdrew its Kilmarnock branch in 1801 and the Royal Bank refused to step in, Patrick Ballantine and John Fairlie established the Kilmarnock Banking Company a year later.[135] This group were part of the triumvirate of wealthy returned slave-traders in Scotland who made their wealth via Kingston-based firm Taylor, Ballantine & Fairlie and sunk their wealth into banking institutions and landed estates. This underlines the mutually beneficial relationship between the West Indians and Scottish banks – the institutions provided credit to Glasgow-West India merchants and planters who dealt with Scottish planters in Jamaica. In return, merchants, planters and commercial adventurers deposited slavery fortunes in Scottish banks, which could be used as interest-bearing capital in loans to manufacturers and merchants, especially across Scotland.

The merchant firms and banks may have been the means of transmitting capital, but the ultimate investment for many Scots in colonial Jamaica was the landed estate at home. Among this group of *successful* Scottish adventurers with assets, only a minority had achieved the dream of land. Yet it was a very sizeable minority. Around one-third of the overall group were associated with heritable property in Great Britain: under 15 per cent owned or were resident in landed estates, while a higher proportion owned urban and semi-rural properties.[136] The Scottish estates associated with this group were located in the Central Lowlands, especially Ayrshire. The north of Scotland was popular too, including John Shand's estate in Kincardineshire, although only one returnee had a Highland estate, John Black in Ardmarnoch in Argyll. That some of this group died on the island

---

[134] Of the 35 identified accounts, the majority were held in Edinburgh-based institutions: Bank of Scotland (6), The Royal Bank (4), Commercial Bank (3) and the British Linen Bank (7).

[135] C. Munn, *The Scottish Provincial Banking Companies, 1747–1864* (Edinburgh, 1981), pp. 59–60.

[136] Thirteen of this group of Scots in Jamaica (14% of the overall group) owned or were resident in landed estates in Scotland (12) or England (1) on death. While most were purchased directly, 2 returnees – John Robertson of Gartincaber and Thomas McQuiston Angus of Turnberry Lodge – were listed merely as residents, not owners. Another was likely acquired via inheritance. Taylor Cathcart of Pitcairlie and Orbiton on Fife hailed from a gentry family and his wealth from Jamaica likely added to a 'gentry capitalist' fortune. Of the 13 landowners, 4 died in Jamaica, 9 died in Scotland. Another 17 individuals (19% of the overall group) owned or were resident in urban or small rural properties across Scotland.

while in possession of a Scottish estate reveals that if possible, individuals invested in land prior to a return. Before he died in 1825, John Black collected rentier income from tenants on Ardmarnoch (which he owned outright) and ultimately bequeathed the freehold to his nephew, John McIvor.[137] But most estates were purchased directly after returning to Scotland. John Tailyour was part of a triumvirate associated with the Kingston firm Taylor, Ballantine & Fairlie who returned to live in sprawling landed estates in Scotland.[138] Writing to Tailyour from Kingston in December 1796, his former co-partner, James Fairlie, wished him well in his hunt for an estate and revealed he also hoped to 'find such a situation on his return'.[139] Fairlie ultimately built a mansion on Bellfield estate in Ayrshire and was worth over £46,000 when he died in 1819.[140] The other partner, Peter Ballantine bought and improved the estate of Castlehill in Ayrshire and was worth over £26,000 in movable property when he died in 1810.[141]

The case of John Tailyour reveals how colonial wealth revitalized one landed family's fortunes. After Tailyour's return to Scotland in 1792, Glasgow merchant George McCall scouted suitable landed estates for his future son-in-law in the west of Scotland.[142] Instead, Tailyour purchased his father's former estate Kirktonhill in Montrose by 1798.[143] Much of his fortune was ultimately sunk into heritable property, eventually dwarfing his personal estate. On his death in Scotland in 1816, Tailyour's personal estate in Great Britain was valued at over £33,000 (£8,937 in Scotland, and £24,625 in England). By including both heritable and movable property, it is very likely Tailyour was worth over £108,000 in 1811.[144] For Scots in Jamaica, land in Scotland was evidently of some importance: for reasons of prestige, to elevate themselves to the landed ranks with political influence, to live an independently profitable life or to regain lost family estates. Lesser properties such as farms or urban dwellings provided secure incomes and

---

[137] NRS, SC70/1/35, 'Inventory of John Black', 1826, pp. 303–8.

[138] N. Radburn, 'Guinea factors, slave sales, and the profits of the transatlantic slave trade in late eighteenth-century Jamaica: the case of John Tailyour', *The William and Mary Quarterly*, lxxii (2015), 243–86.

[139] GCA, TD248/2, 'Letter book of Jas. Fairlie (1783–1815)', 10 Dec. 1796, n.p.

[140] NRS, SC36/48/15, 'Inventory of James Fairlie', 19 Nov. 1819, pp. 729–46.

[141] NRS, SC36/8/5, 'Inventory of Patrick Ballantine', 18 Aug. 1811.

[142] WCL, Tailyour Family Papers, Box 3, 'George McCall to John Tailyor', 28 Nov. 1793.

[143] WCL, Tailyour Family Papers, Box 5, 'George Oswald, Edinburgh, to John Tailyor Esq. at Craigo, Montrose', 14 Feb. 1798.

[144] NRS, CC20/7/8, 'Inventory of John Taylor', 11 Feb. 1816, pp. 647–81. WCL, Tailyour Family Papers, Box 8, John Tailyour Account Journal, Kirktonhill 1805–13, p. 150.

solid investments. Albeit a sizeable minority, it must be recognized that adventurers like John Tailyour were unrepresentative. For most Scots in colonial Jamaica, and even those who managed to return, the dream of a sprawling landed estate remained just that.

Furthermore, it is also striking just how little of the overall wealth was invested in British industry. Just six in this group held substantial investments in industry in Great Britain (£70,739, or 10 per cent of overall wealth). Investments were made in English and Scottish railways, and manufactories in Scotland. As William Rae was the exceptional case, holding most of these industrial investments (over £27,000) in English railways, this group invested just c.£43,000 in Scottish industry.[145] Instead, Scottish adventurers in Jamaica mainly held profits in institutions that facilitated the transatlantic flow and dispersal of capital such as merchant firms in Glasgow, Edinburgh banks and, on occasion, landed property in Scotland. There seems to have been no large-scale influx of sojourning capital to Scottish industry: ultimately these fortunes passed to the families of those concerned and, less often, to nominated philanthropic institutions.

Reshaping Scottish society and transatlantic families

While great Jamaica fortunes were conspicuous in Scottish society, how they were disbursed was less apparent. This section – based upon sixty-seven wills and testaments lodged in Scottish courts by Scots resident in Jamaica 1775–1838 – traces the pathways of Jamaica wealth. On occasion, these great fortunes were reported in the local press. When Dr James Black, sometime surgeon in Jamaica, died in October 1834, his fortune was reported to be £18,000.[146] Black's fortune passed to family members but £200 was bequeathed to each of the Glasgow Royal Infirmary, Lock Hospital, the Magdalene Asylum and the 'School for Instruction of Deaf and Dumb', as well as to establish a fund to provide annual payments to 'faithful domestic servants' in Glasgow.[147] These types of substantial schemes were not uncommon: around 10 per cent of the wills and testaments examined revealed examples of philanthropic and charitable donations. Some donations were sizeable and were designed to improve local conditions – education, health and living standards – of the urban poor and working

---

[145] NRS, SC70/1/55, 'Inventory of William Rae', 21 July 1837, pp. 782–3.

[146] 'Dr James Black's Will', *The Reformers Gazette*, 28 Feb. 1835.

[147] NRS, SC36/51/12, James Black, 11 Dec. 1834, p. 43; see also *Decisions of the Court of Session: from 21 December 1831 to 28 July 1836* (Edinburgh, 1836), p. 471.

classes across Scotland over successive generations.[148] However, most of the Jamaica fortunes were bequeathed to close relations. Kinship ties, not patriotic altruism, governed where fortunes eventually rested.

Ann McCrum noted that the principal historical beneficiaries of testamentary bequests in nineteenth-century urban Scotland were, unsurprisingly, the immediate family.[149] This pattern was generally also the case in this study, although the legal status of the property and sometimes even the heirs was unusual. In Scotland, heritable property included land, estates and buildings, while movable included investments, shares and money. In Jamaica, enslaved people were classed as real estate – analogous to heritable property – alongside the plantations to which they belonged.[150] Many Scots in Jamaica thus owned a distinctive type of chattel property that did not easily convert to capital in Scotland. Many on the island, therefore, developed bespoke inheritance strategies for family both in Jamaica and in Scotland, with specific types of bequests dependent on the sex, residence, age and legal status of heirs. In Jamaica, heirs were often formerly enslaved peoples themselves (partners, or illegitimate children sometimes described as 'reputed'), while inheritances could consist of estates and resident enslaved people. Heirs in Scotland were sometimes bequeathed estates in Jamaica, although it was more common for this group to receive movable property that had already made its way across the Atlantic.

The wealth of some Scots, however, remained in Jamaica. The owner of Kendall estate in Hanover, John Blyth, had purchased the plantation with money from his father-in-law John Buddle on the understanding it would pass to his daughter, Mary Blyth née Buddle. His will – written up in Spanishtown in August 1836 – ensured just that.[151] Transatlantic inheritance strategies were more common, however. After he returned to Glasgow in 1840, William Dobbie bequeathed Glenhead plantation to Mary Dobbie, 'a woman of colour' in Jamaica, although the residue of his estate went to Alexander, his nephew in Dunipace, Scotland. Thus, Dobbie rid the family of the by then unprofitable estate, while its profits remained in Scotland.[152] But legacies to partners were often designed to improve their life chances in

---

[148] In 1815, returned merchant Alexander Forbes of Aberdeen left £100 to the Kirk Session of Mortlach, the interest of which was to be paid annually to poor householders sharing his name. NRS, CC1/6/78, 'Inventory of Alexander Forbes', pp. 21531–53.

[149] McCrum, 'Inheritance and the family', p. 149.

[150] Reports of Cases Decided in the Supreme Courts of Scotland, vol. xvi (Edinburgh, 1844), p. 126.

[151] NRS, SC70/1/56, 'Inventory of John Blyth Esq.', 18 April 1838, pp. 672–5.

[152] NRS, SC36/51/16, 'Trust disposition of William Dobbie', 14 May 1840, pp. 568–73.

Jamaica. Approaching death in 1801, John McPherson, a Scottish resident of St Thomas in the East, resolved to sort his Jamaica family's affairs. His last will and testament manumitted his 'woman slave named Eleanor Jean McPherson for…her long & faithful service'. The testament left instructions to purchase another enslaved woman to ensure an income for the soon to be freed Eleanor. Most of his capital went to his 'well beloved son', also John McPherson, who was to be taught carpentry. Nevertheless, McPherson's estate followed a familiar pattern, as the residue was left to his sister's family in Scotland.[153]

Daniel Livesay's study of mixed-race Jamaicans reveals a picture of island society governed by race. Most illegitimate children born into slavery in early nineteenth-century Jamaica – as many as 80 per cent – remained enslaved.[154] Thus, only a minority of fathers – white European men – manumitted children born to enslaved women. Livesay's study paints a grim picture for most mixed-race children in Jamaica in which only around 20 per cent were freed from enslavement. Of this minority, few received any other support. However, a small elite group were sent to Great Britain for education or an apprenticeship in trades. Those who remained eked out a living in Jamaica – if they were lucky – as artisans or in small pens or estates.[155]

Broadly consistent with these estimates, around one-third of the group of the wills or testaments of Scots in Jamaica referred to illegitimate children.[156] The terms 'reputed' or 'natural' (meaning illegitimate) were commonly used for children, although some were described using overt racial descriptors such as 'mulatto' or 'quadroon'.[157] A small minority of fathers provided their children with passage off the island. Around late 1802, John Finlay of Killearn travelled to Jamaica 'animo revertendi' ('with intention to return'). While resident in St Elizabeth he fathered a 'reputed son', William Finlay, with a 'mulato…Cecil Allison' whom he was 'uncertain whether of free condition or otherways'. Children born of enslaved mothers usually took the unfree status of the mother, and John Finlay's will of September 1804 ensured his son's freedom. The settlement also made provision for his son's

[153] NRS, CC8/8/132, 'Testament testamentary of John McPherson', 15 Dec. 1801, pp. 526–34.

[154] D. Livesay, *Children of Uncertain Fortune: Mixed-Race Jamaicans in Britain and the Atlantic Family, 1733–1833* (Chapel Hill, 2018), pp. 2–3.

[155] Livesay, *Children of Uncertain Fortune*, pp. 24–6.

[156] Of the 67 identified last wills and testaments associated with Scotsmen known to have been in Jamaica between 1775 and 1838 and lodged in Scottish courts, 23 (34%) referred to a total of 44 illegitimate children.

[157] Now offensive terms, 'mulatto' described an individual of mixed origin in the West Indies (usually White European fathers and African mothers). A 'quadroon' was one-quarter African ancestry.

passage to be educated in Scotland. As his appointed executor, prominent Glasgow-West India merchant Archibald Smith of Jordanhill was to make such provisions for William Finlay as he 'may see fit and proppar deuring the time of his education' in Glasgow. The son was to be paid £500 sterling once he reached twenty-one.[158] These types of post-mortem bequests of capital to illegitimate children, however, were rare. On occasion, absent fathers improved the life chances of 'reputed children' through educational provision or by sending them to Great Britain. However, the major bequests – landed estates, shares in firms and banks – were almost exclusively reserved for immediate and wider families in Scotland. In other words, most of the Scots-Jamaica fortunes identified in this study remained within Scotland. Kinship arrangements governed the flows of repatriated slavery-derived wealth which effectively underpinned the development of some Scottish regions throughout the period of this study.

Conclusion

This chapter reveals a distinctive Clyde-Caribbean system of commerce. Thousands of skilled and educated Scotsmen, mainly hailing from central Scotland, departed from Clyde ports and flooded into the West Indies, especially Jamaica, in search of wealth. Attracted by the prospect of opportunities and wealth not on offer at home, Scots continued to arrive in Jamaica towards the end of Caribbean slavery, confirming it as the premier Caledonian colony in the region.

Disproportionately high numbers of upwardly mobile young men worked in merchant houses and in supervisory and managerial positions on estates throughout the island, but were especially concentrated in Kingston, Westmoreland and St Thomas in the East. Fortune-building was an uncertain business, taking many years in an environment in which lives were cut short due to disease. In general, this was a high-risk environment that generally provided low to medium returns. But while it was difficult to acquire and repatriate wealth, it was not impossible.

The Scottish diaspora in Jamaica were, in general, exceptions to Eric Williams' vision of a plantation economy in 'decline'. Evidence tentatively suggests Scots in eighteenth-century Jamaica accumulated higher-value estates on death compared to the general white population, perhaps as a result of patronage within kith and kinship networks. Wealth and property brought political influence in the Jamaica assembly which helped bring a Caledonian dimension to the island, evidenced by the construction of the Scots Kirk in 1813. To what extent this wealth was repatriated before 1800

---

[158] NRS, SC36/48/1, Inventory of John Finlay, 17 Jan. 1805, pp. 541–4.

remains unknown, but it is clear that many Scots continued to acquire great personal wealth after the American Revolution, especially post-1800, which they successfully repatriated.

Yet, this study complicates the vision of Scots sojourners aiming for rapid wealth and a quick return to Scotland. Some permanently resided in Jamaica – such as William Rae – or on a long-term basis, such as George William Hamilton. There is no doubt Scots were a transient group in general, and many hoped for a quick sojourn but, in practice, fortune-building could take many years. Scots were commercial adventurers on the island, accumulating wealth and acquiring property and associated political power that allowed them to shape the civic life of Jamaica.

Elite Scots funnelled capital through English ports but the majority – those of lesser means – transmitted fortunes via Glasgow merchants, sometimes to rest in Scottish banks. And by utilizing British, colonial and Scots law, they ensured fortunes arrived home after death. On occasion, mixed-race children and former partners make an appearance in the wills and testaments lodged in Scottish courts by this group of Scots in Jamaica, but these sources, especially confirmation inventories, provide compelling evidence of the slavery-derived capital that seeped into certain Scottish regions, thus improving the life chances of family at home and wider society in general through philanthropic and educational bequests.

6. Grenada and Carriacou

Some months after the abolition of plantation slavery in the British West Indies in 1834, Duncan Cameron contacted the colonial office in London to enquire of his brother's circumstances. Exactly a half-century before, his brother Alexander had walked out of his local village in Fort William in Scotland and was never heard of again. Duncan, however, received news that someone of the same name had died in Grenada 'leaving a considerable sum of money' which was lodged in Chancery Court. Without the means to travel to Grenada, or any contacts to make enquiries, in desperation Cameron wrote to the authorities with several questions. First, could they confirm that an Alexander Cameron died in Grenada between 1814 and 1834? Was this person from Glenloy in Fort William? Was the deceased a seafarer and trader? The correspondence was marked with a blunt response: 'this office is not in possession of the means of answering'.[1] This was a typical story throughout the period of British slavery: untold numbers of young Scotsmen missing abroad with family members unaware of their fate but hoping for fortunes derived from slavery in return.

Since the south-east Caribbean was one of the most popular destinations for Scots after 1750, many hundreds of Scots ended their days in Grenada. In life, Douglas Hamilton illuminated the activities of Scottish sojourners in colonies such as Grenada. For Hamilton, commercial networks provided opportunities in the form of jobs and advancement, as well as economic security which facilitated credit through partnerships: 'utilising the kinship and local connections, Scots on the plantations extended their links throughout the West Indies, purchasing land, engaging attorneys, managers, overseers and bookkeepers, and welcoming new arrivals…The networks almost uniformly, were based on pre-existing bonds.'[2] Hamilton further illuminated the commercial networks in Grenada of both the Glasgow-West India merchant firm Alexander Houston and Co. and the Baillies of Dochfour, a model that evolved from Checkland's work on the respective bankruptcies of Alexander Houston and Co. in 1801 and Evan Baillie and

---

[1] TNA, CO101/78, Despatches: Offices and Individuals, 1834, fo. 402.

[2] D. Hamilton, *Scotland, the Caribbean and the Atlantic World, 1750–1820* (Manchester, 2005), p. 78.

Co. in 1806.[3] Hamilton followed up with a study of the Caribbean operations of Alexander Houston and Co. in Grenada. In 1796, the firm were owed as much as £343,935, probably from planters in the Windward Islands, although they went bankrupt in 1800 due to the illiquidity of their assets.[4] Mark Quintanilla has detailed the trading network and commercial demise of Alexander Bartlet and Co. in 1778,[5] and added understanding about the mercantile empire of Alexander Campbell prior to his murder during Fedon's Rebellion in Grenada in early 1795.[6] These studies have focused on individuals or firms that failed, sometimes violently.

Other historians have focused on individuals with more longevity. In a detailed micro-study of the Johnstones of Dumfriesshire and their imperial careers, Emma Rothschild documented the lifecycle of ownership of Westerhall plantation in Grenada across three generations. In an example of successful 'economic lives', Alexander Johnstone was the largest owner of slaves and most prosperous absentee landowner in Grenada in 1779, while ownership passed to his brother James in 1783.[7] David Lambert's historical geographical approach documented the imperial career of James MacQueen in Grenada from 1797, when he was employed as overseer on Westerhall the plantation owned by the Johnstones of Dumfries. MacQueen later became famous as the demagogic editor of the pro-slavery newspaper, the *Glasgow Courier* and chief propagandist of the British West India interest.[8]

That Scots were both pervasive and prominent across Grenada is now well-known, but questions remain: essentially, how advantageous was the Scots propensity to operate in networks in smaller islands towards the end of Caribbean slavery, a period of perceived decline? Cameron's futile request for information, however, reflects the methodological challenges faced by historians of the British West Indies: what records exist – especially for non-elites – that allow the unravelling of profiteering in the slave economies?

---

[3] S. G. Checkland, 'Two Scottish West Indian liquidations after 1793', *Scottish Journal of Political Economy*, iv (1957), 127–43.

[4] D. Hamilton, 'Scottish trading in the Caribbean: the rise and fall of Houston & Co.', in *Nation and Province in the First British Empire: Scotland and the Americas, 1600–1800*, ed. N. C. Landsman (Lewisburg, 2001), pp. 94–126.

[5] M. Quintanilla, 'Mercantile communities in the ceded islands: the Alexander Bartlet and George Campbell Company', *International Social Science Review*, lxxix (2004), 14–26.

[6] M. Quintanilla, 'The world of Alexander Campbell: an eighteenth-century Grenadian planter', *Albion, A Quarterly Journal with British Studies*, xxxv (2003), 229–56.

[7] E. Rothschild, *The Inner Life of Empires: An Eighteenth-Century History* (Princeton, 2011), p. 166.

[8] D. Lambert, 'The Glasgow king of Billingsgate: James MacQueen and an Atlantic pro-slavery network', *Slavery and Abolition*, xxix (2008), 389–413.

While the Camerons of Glenloy were never to hear of Alexander again, other families as well as merchant firms received both correspondence and wealth from the many Scots resident in Grenada. Moreover, many had already repatriated profits to Scotland which were inventoried on their death. This type of evidence makes the task of the historian a little easier. This chapter unravels the connections between Glasgow-West India merchant firms and individuals in Grenada and the adjoining island of Carriacou, revealing how long-term commercial links contributed to the accumulation and repatriation of fortunes, some of which were dispersed across Scotland.

Grenada: an island in ferment

Previously a minor French colony, Grenada eventually became the second most important sugar producer in the British West Indies. Under the terms of the Treaty of Paris that ended the Seven Years War in 1763, France formally ceded Grenada to Great Britain. But unlike other ceded islands like Tobago, for example, around half of Grenada's acreage was already under cultivation by a resident French population.[9] With scope for development and expansion, the subsequent economic change was complemented by Anglicization of the island: ownership of many estates transferred from resident French to British owners, with associated names of landmarks changed.[10] With imperial restrictions removed after the Union of 1707, Scottish adventurers flooded into the region attracted by the prospect of wealth. According to Douglas Hamilton, up to 10,800 Scots travelled to the Windward Islands from 1750 to 1799.[11]

A British land grab followed in Grenada. In 1772, 334 estates – mainly sugar, but also coffee, indigo and cacao – were cultivated by over 26,000 enslaved people.[12] That year, fifty-four Scots (57 per cent of all British estate owners and 21 per cent of overall owners) possessed 40 per cent of land cultivated as sugar and coffee estates.[13] These Scots were resident in a thriving economy: Grenada was the wealthiest of the Leeward and

---

[9] D. L. Niddrie, 'Eighteenth-century settlement in the British Caribbean', *Transactions of the Institute of British Geographers*, xl (1966), 67–80, at p. 70.

[10] B. Steele, 'Grenada: an island state, its history and its people', *Caribbean Quarterly*, xx (1974), 5–43, at pp. 10–11.

[11] Hamilton, *Scotland, the Caribbean*, p. 23.

[12] R. Sheridan, *Sugar and Slavery: An Economic History of the British West Indies, 1623–1775* (Kingston, 2007 ed.), pp. 458–9.

[13] D. Hancock, 'Scots in the slave trade', in *Nation and Province in the First British Empire*, ed. N. C. Landsman (Lewisburg, 2001), p. 64.

Windward Islands – measured by exports to Great Britain – and second only to Jamaica in the British West Indies in 1774.[14]

The British takeover of Grenada, however, was delayed by a lack of credit and interrupted by invasion and revolt. With the collapse of many Scottish banks in 1772, 'the great want of money' almost brought cultivation in the ceded islands to a halt.[15] The French took the opportunity to recapture Grenada during the American War of Independence, although it was returned under the terms of the Treaty of Versailles in 1783. During the four-year occupation, the attitude of British residents and imperial policymakers hardened towards French residents. Initially, significant concessions were made after 1763: some French property holders were allowed into the House of Assembly despite their adherence to Catholicism and transubstantiation, which normally would have prohibited political office.[16] As Caitlin Anderson notes, French residents were defined as 'loyal subjects' in Grenada and granted privileges unprecedented among Catholics in any other part of the British empire. But after the French occupation, the Anglicization of Grenada intensified. There had been little interest in establishing an Anglican church in the island prior to the invasion, although afterwards the church's role in generating loyalty was acknowledged and actively encouraged.[17] At the same time, French Catholic churches were expropriated, and the resident population denied political rights.[18] Many French residents simply migrated to Trinidad after the Spanish government opened up the island via the *cédula* of 1782, which offered land grants to Catholics. But many stayed in Grenada, and up to 1795, island society was split by divisions based upon nationality, race, religion and rank.[19]

In the aftermath of the uprising on Saint Domingue in 1791, therefore, Grenada was an island in ferment. The British and French were at almost constant war, and with residents of the latter nationality denied property rights, the island was ripe for revolutionary activity. As noted in Chapter 2, between March 1795 and September 1796, the Franco-Grenadian free

---

[14] R. Sheridan, 'The condition of the slaves in the settlement and economic development of the British Windward Islands, 1763–1775', *The Journal of Caribbean History*, xxiv (1990), p. 125.

[15] P. J. Marshall, 'Empire and opportunity in Britain, 1763–1775', *Transactions of the Royal Historical Society*, vi (1995), 111–28, at p. 120.

[16] Steele, 'Grenada: an island state, its history and its people', pp. 10–11.

[17] C. Anderson, 'Old subjects, new subjects and non-subjects: silences and subjecthood in Fedon's rebellion, Grenada, 1795–96,' in *War, Empire and Slavery, 1770–1830*, ed. R. Bessell, N. Guyatt and J. Rendall (New York, 2010), pp. 201–17.

[18] R. P. Devas, *A History of the Island of Grenada, 1498–1796* (Carenage, 1974), pp. 120–1.

[19] K. Candlin, *The Last Caribbean Frontier, 1795–1815* (Basingstoke, 2012), pp. 11–12.

people of colour – led by Julien Fedon – joined forces with the enslaved to overthrow the British regime in favour of Revolutionary France. The island was decimated, with losses to the economy between 1795 and 1798 estimated at £2.5 million.[20] After the uprising, the British government supplied £1.5m to regenerate the system.[21] Nicholas Draper noted a total of £1.37m was paid out in over sixty loans to merchants and planters in both St Vincent and Grenada. Of this state aid, Scottish firms and individuals (including those of Scots descent) associated with Grenada were over-represented. The firm George Baillie & Co. claimed £250,000 (Baillie was born in Scotland and operated a merchant firm in London). The brother of William Johnstone Pulteney, Alexander Johnstone, borrowed £10,000 in order to rebuild the family estate, Westerhall.[22] Glasgow firms Alexander Houston & Co. and John Campbell senior & Co. collected £240,000 and £40,000 respectively from the fund.[23] Overall, it seems Scots collected as much as 40 per cent of the loan, with Glasgow firms taking approximately half of the Scottish total.

In 1795, several Glasgow-West India firms focused on Grenada. Alexander Houston & Co. increased their trade connections between 1778 and 1796 before their bankruptcy in the early 1800s.[24] By the nineteenth century, *Glasgow Herald* shipping advertisements suggest Grenada was the fifth most popular destination for the Clyde fleet, with around three or four voyages per year (see Table 4.1). Two merchant firms took over the Houston monopoly. During the period 1806–1834, John Campbell, senior, & Co. and Leitch & Smith controlled over 95 per cent of the advertised voyages between Glasgow and Grenada, and thus dominated the trade and the transportation of outward Scots. The capital St George's was the principal destination for Clyde ships, although landfall was usually made first on Carriacou, explaining the large Scottish presence on this small cotton

---

[20] E. Cox, 'Fedon's rebellion, 1795–96: causes and consequences', *Journal of Negro History*, lxvii (1982), 7–19, at p. 15.

[21] HCPP 1801 (98), *Report on the Petition of the Proprietors of Estates in the Island of Grenada*, p. 11.

[22] For details of the loans, see N. Draper, 'The British state and slavery: George Baillie, merchant of London and St Vincent, and the exchequer loans of the 1790s', Working Papers, *Economic History Society* (2015) <www.ehs.org.uk/dotAsset/de55e1a1-c7f6-450b-9a1a-831601ae46d9.docx> [accessed 29 Dec. 2018]. For rebuild, see Hamilton, *Scotland, the Caribbean*, p. 183.

[23] For the claims, see: The University of the West Indies – St Augustine, Alma Jordan Library, SC89 6/3, 'Minutes of the Board of Commissioners for the Issue of Exchequer Bills', fos. 29–30, 34, 40, 59–60. For context of the lobbying of Alexander Houston & Co., see Hamilton, *Scotland, the Caribbean*, pp. 183–5.

[24] Hamilton, 'Scottish trading in the Caribbean', p. 108.

island twenty miles north-east of Grenada (as discussed below). Based on estimated shipping voyages, it is very likely that no more than 1,000 Scottish adventurers embarked for Grenada and Carriacou from Clyde ports between 1806 and 1834. While these figures seem slight compared to Jamaica, this consolidated a powerful Caledonian presence on the smaller islands.

In the late eighteenth century, the white population in Grenada totalled around 1,000. By 1835 it had declined to around 600. By contrast, the enslaved population was over 21,000 in the same year.[25] St George's, the commercial trade hub, was the main residence of the white population. On reaching this port, Scots would have entered almost familiar surroundings. The warehouses at Carenage – some occupied by Glasgow merchants – were just a short walk from the adjoining town, which sat on a rocky peninsula. Fort St George, home to the island military, was situated on the isthmus that overlooked the natural harbour.[26] Indicative of the elevated status of Scots on the island, St Andrews Scots Kirk occupied a prominent spot next to the fort: the foundation stone was laid with full masonic honours in November 1831.[27] St Andrews Scots Kirk in St George's opened its doors on 14 July 1833 and catered for a significant Caledonian community on the island. According to its first chaplain, the Revd William Haig, the island's Presbyterian kirk – and two court houses which acted as places of worship – offered space for 440 persons by January 1835. The pews of St Andrews Scots Kirk held 300 people, and all were let. But the average attendance of Presbyterian worshippers across the island was between 250 and 300, the irregular attendance explained by the numbers of pewholders resident in out-parishes who could not always travel.[28] For comparison, in 1835 the white population of Grenada was around 600 (two-thirds of whom were male).[29]

Although not all Scots were Presbyterians, given a noted Scottish population specifically established a Presbyterian kirk on a small island, the above attendance figures likely provide relatively accurate estimates of the Caledonian contingent. It seems that Scots comprised around 30 to 50 per cent of the white population of Grenada towards the end of Caribbean slavery. As previously noted, Scots comprised around 14 per cent of the British population between 1801 and 1831.[30] Like Jamaica, therefore, Scots

[25] R. M. Martin, *History of the Colonies of the British Empire* (London, 1843), p. 44.

[26] J. E. Alexander, *Transatlantic Sketches* (Philadelphia, 1833), p. 139.

[27] 'Masonic ceremony', *Grenada Free Press and Public Gazette*, 30 Nov. 1831.

[28] TNA, CO101/79, Despatches, 1835, fos. 18–22.

[29] Martin, *Colonies of the British Empire*, p. 44.

[30] HCPP 1831 *Comparative Account of Population of Great Britain, 1801, 1811, 1821 and 1831*, p. 409.

were disproportionately over-represented in Grenada, although their absolute numbers on the island were much less. Except for Tobago, Grenada was the closest to a Scottish enclave in the British West Indies.[31]

Contemporary surveys also confirm a large Scottish presence on the neighbouring island of Carriacou. In the immediate aftermath of the return to British rule in 1783, Walter Fenner surveyed the island. This map suggests that while a significant French group were still present, Scots such as John Urquhart – who owned cotton estates Craigston and Meldrum – and William Todd owned four of the top five plantations on the island (including the largest single sugar and cotton estates).[32] Indeed, Scots dominated land-ownership and very likely production of both commodities, particularly the latter; just fifteen Scots (26 per cent of proprietors) controlled over 2,800 acres of cotton-producing land (c.42 per cent of the overall total on the island).[33] Although it seems very likely that Scots represented a relatively high proportion of Carriacou's population (c.25 per cent) from the eighteenth century onwards, in absolute terms this remained a small group up to emancipation in 1834. Yet, they must have had a major impact on their homeland: Carriacou exported as much as 14 per cent of all cotton produced in the British West Indies in the late eighteenth century.[34] A small number of Scottish planters on Carriacou sold cotton to Glasgow's merchants, underpinning Scotland's Industrial Revolution.

Legislation was in place to keep the numbers of white enslavers high, which had the effect of increasing Scottish migration to the Windward Islands. As the enslaved population increased with the development of the plantation system, colonial legislation encouraged Scottish arrivals. In 1790, an Act of the Grenada Assembly stipulated one white man must be present on each estate for every fifty slaves (known as deficiency laws).[35] As this decree made it 'absolutely necessary to have another white man upon the [Urquhart] Estate' in Carriacou in 1791, William Arbuthnot, a nephew of

---

[31] Hamilton, *Scotland, the Caribbean*, p. 63.

[32] For a study of these estates, see H. G. Slade, 'Craigston and Meldrum estates, Carriacou 1769–1841', *The Proceedings of the Society of Antiquaries of Scotland* (1984), 481–537.

[33] BL, W. Fenner, *A New and Accurate Map of the Island of Carriacou in the West Indies, 1784* (London, 1784). With thanks to John Angus Martin for this map and associated notes.

[34] David Beck Ryden concurs that Scots represented approximately a quarter of the Carriacou population in 1776 (c.12/46) and 1790 (13/52), which was around the same number of English on the island. See '"One of the finest and most fruitful spots in America": an analysis of eighteenth-century Carriacou', *Journal of Interdisciplinary History*, xliii (Spring 2013), 539–70, at pp. 545–6, 554. In 1829, there remained 50 white men on the island. See Martin, *Colonies of the British Empire*, p. 44.

[35] J. MacQueen, *The Colonial Controversy* (Glasgow, 1825), p. 187.

the family, requested Glasgow merchant firm John Campbell & Co. send out skilled Scottish labourers.[36] But it was difficult to retain white labourers on the island. In 1815, Adam Reid, manager on Dumfries estate, was paid £330 in local currency per annum (c.£214 stg.), per annum although this remuneration was lower than elsewhere: 'wages given on the small estates here are so little, that most of the young men are leaving them and going to the sugar islands'.[37] While the long-term trading connections between Glasgow merchants and Clyde ports meant Scots were widespread across Grenada and Carriacou, the opportunities and available wealth varied on each island. This chapter develops these themes through comparative case studies of a Scottish planter and merchant firm in Grenada up to Fedon's Rebellion in 1795.

Ninian Home: a Scottish planter in Grenada, 1763–95

Hailing from Berwickshire in Scotland, Ninian Home (1732–95) was of a middling background. His paternal grandfather, the Revd Ninian Home of Billie, began to acquire estates around 1711, mainly in lieu of debts owed. The Revd's son, Alexander Home of Jardinefield, married Isobel Home, and Ninian was one of three brothers. As the eldest, he travelled to Virginia (1749–51) to visit his uncle, George Hume of Culpeper County, and work in a store. He took up residence in the West Indies, first in St Kitts in 1759 and afterwards in Grenada in 1764, travelling back and forth to Scotland. He was appointed to several important civic positions on the island. In 1771, he was appointed judge of the Court of Common Pleas, in 1784 became a member of His Majesty's Council, and was ultimately made lieutenant governor in 1792. He was captured during Fedon's Rebellion in 1795 and was murdered on the island on 8 April of that year.[38] Political influence in the West Indies was, of course, based upon wealth and the ownership of estates and enslaved people. In 1764, Ninian Home acquired Waltham in St Mark and a third share of Paraclete in St Andrew, both in the north of the island. Stretching to 500 acres, Waltham's main crop was coffee and cocoa. Ninian Home was also involved with a Scottish commercial network

---

[36] NRAS, 2570/118, Letter from William Arbuthnot, 17 Nov. 1791.

[37] NRAS, 2570/96/2, 'Letter to John Urquhart from William Robertson, Carriacou', 2 June 1815. According to 1 contemporary source, 'the currency of Grenada, or rate of exchange, is commonly sixty-five per cent worse than sterling'. See W. Winterbottom, *Historical, Geographical, Commercial and Philosophical View of the American United States*, 2nd ed., vol. iv (London, 1795), p. 264.

[38] E. E. Hume, 'A colonial Scottish Jacobite family: establishment in Virginia of a branch of the Humes of Wedderburn, *The Virginia Magazine of History and Biography*, xxxviii (1930), 1–37.

in Grenada and with Alexander Campbell, also killed in 1795.[39] Home's correspondence – now held in the National Records of Scotland – survives from his early days as a planter until just before his death, and reveals the interconnections with Scottish planters and merchants in Great Britain.[40]

First, the correspondence reveals how young Scots were recruited for Grenada. Writing in January 1789 to Alexander Douglas – who owned land near Paraclete in St Andrew – Home illustrated how skilled Scottish labour was recruited for planters in the island economy:

> I have engaged a ploughman for you that I think will do, he is a good looking young man between 19 & 20 years of age, & has from his infancy been brought up to the business, he writes tolerably well & has learned rithmetic, and…has constantly been in a Smiths Shop attending the making and laying of Plough Irons…we may be the better able to Instruct your Smiths to do things.[41]

Home recommended Alexander Houston & Co.'s ships as the best route out from Glasgow. By mid February, the ploughman was settling into island life. Home thought him a 'good lad' but reminded him about his 'duty to behave well' and to promote the interest of Douglas. Home reckoned his wages were high (£25 sterling for the first year of the indenture, rising to £30 in years two and three), although this was considered a good investment. Within twelve months the ploughman would be 'just as good an overseer as you can get' and had already started teaching enslaved workers how to plough the fields.[42] Scottish planters recruited skilled tradesmen from Glasgow on relatively high wages, in the process improving the skills of tradesmen and transferring knowledge to the enslaved workforce.

The planter Ninian Home had an extensive transatlantic enterprise; he maintained an interest in America, on occasion shipping goods from Virginia to Simond & Hankey, and sugar from Grenada to Alexander Douglas, both London merchants. Home also had strong connections with Glasgow, shipping cotton to the Clyde via John Campbell, senior, & Co.[43] Ninian Home's correspondence with the latter firm in the 1780s reveals

---

[39] Hamilton, *Scotland, the Caribbean*, p. 68; Quintanilla, 'Alexander Campbell'.

[40] NRS, GD267/7/1–2, 'Out letter-books of Ninian Home' (available on microfilm NRS, RH4/64). See also GD267/7/3, 'Out letter-book of Ninian Home, Grenada and George Home'.

[41] NRS, GD267/7/1, 'Out letter-books of Ninian Home', 16 Jan. 1789.

[42] NRS, GD267/7/1, 'Out letter-books of Ninian Home', 15 Feb. 1789.

[43] NRS, GD267/7/1, 'Out letter-books of Ninian Home', 10 April 1787, 25 April 1787, 3 May 1787.

the unremarkable but essential financial operations that underpinned the connections between Glasgow and Grenada. On 3 May 1787, Home sent the firm ten bales of cotton which were insured by the Campbells, and at the same time he drew short-term credit on the firm's account on the island.[44] In return, the firm sent herrings to feed the enslaved workforce, although Ninian Home complained at times about both the price and quality.[45] The commercial relationship endured after Home's death in 1795, connecting the Berwickshire family's interests in Grenada with the Glasgow firm for over thirty years.[46] John Campbell senior & Co. maintained commercial relationships not only with resident Scottish planters in Grenada but also with absentees in Scotland, a commercial relationship which shall now be traced in more detail.

The great Glasgow firm of John Campbell, senior, & Co. and the Grenadines

John Campbell senior & Co. were one of the major Glasgow-West India firms of the slavery period. This short case study explores some aspects of their business as financiers and providers of credit in the Grenadines. Like Leitch & Smith, John Campbell senior & Co. were inextricably linked with Grenada from the 1780s up to abolition in 1834, as demonstrated by the interests of co-partners. The founder of the firm John Campbell senior (*c*.1735–1808) was the third son of Alexander Campbell of Kinloch. Other co-partners in 1790 included John's brother Colin Campbell of Park and their cousin, Alexander Campbell of Hallyards (1768–1817), also known as 'Business Sandy' due to his work ethic. Other co-partners included John Campbell's other brother Thomas, who was 'present in Grenada' in 1790 with their nephew, Alexander Campbell of Haylodge and Marran (d. 1835).[47] Although not a partner in the firm, another brother, Mungo Campbell of Hundleshope and Kailzie (d. 1793), owned a sugar estate, Marran, in the parish of St John. His son Alexander Campbell of Haylodge, who later became a partner in the firm, inherited the plantation on his death and took the nickname 'Marran' from the estate on the island.

John Campbell, senior & Co.'s operations and networks in Grenada and Carriacou can be traced through the papers of the Urquharts of Craigston and Meldrum, a landed family from the north-east of Scotland

---

[44] NRS, GD267/7/1, 'Out letter-books of Ninian Home', 3 May 1787.

[45] See, for example, NRS, GD267/7/1, 'Out letter-books of Ninian Home', 3 May 1787.

[46] See, for example, NRS, GD267/16/12, 'Letter to George Home from John Campbell senior & Co.', 28 Jan. 1819.

[47] GCA, TD1696, 'Contract of co-partnership', 1790, p. 1.

Figure 6.1 The buildings of Maran estate in the island of Grenada.
The property of Thomas Duncan Esqr. Nov. 1822. Courtesy
of the John Carter Brown Library. CC BY-SA 4.0.

who owned plantations in Carriacou.[48] Thomas Campbell, the brother of
John Campbell, was the main influence on the early development of the
merchant house across the Caribbean. Prior to the formal establishment
of the firm in 1791, he was an imperial careerist with interests in Grenada,
Bristol, London, Liverpool and Scotland.[49] Although Campbell eventually
viewed the West Indies as his home, he maintained a transient lifestyle
which allowed him to cultivate transatlantic networks:

> I must postpone my Northern jaunt till next summer…I promise myself,
> much pleasure in…a long summer among my friends in the west and north
> of Scotland, before I return to what I call my own country between the

[48] NRAS, 2570, 'Records of the Urquhart's of Craigston and Meldrum'.

[49] See D. Lambert and A. Lester (ed.), *Colonial Lives across the British Empire: Imperial
Careering in the Long Nineteenth Century* (Cambridge, 2006); NRAS, 2570/131, 'Thomas
Campbell to William Urquhart', 17 Oct. 1786.

tropics which after long use I find agrees best with me, and where also I find more employment than in this country. [50]

Thomas Campbell had connections in Scotland which created commercial opportunities in the Caribbean. In the summer of 1786, Campbell visited William Urquhart near Aberdeen with discussions evidently focused on the cotton market at Glasgow which was, by then, the epicentre of the Scottish Industrial Revolution. As Urquhart was looking for a merchant for the Glasgow market, Thomas recommended his brother John, who was working with their cousin Alexander at the counting house in Argyle Street.[51] In order to make a formal connection, Thomas Campbell organized a letter of introduction for Urquhart, who agreed: 'to establish a correspondence and to be connected with you for my Concerns in the West Indies...I believe your prices...were rather higher'.[52] Thus, economics – not simply a shared Scottish heritage – was the motivation for the long-term relationship between cotton plantations in Carriacou, the absentee estate owner based in Aberdeen and the merchant firm in Glasgow.

John Campbell's prompt reply outlined the terms of the commercial relationship. Campbell's ship was scheduled to depart for Grenada in September 1786 with 'Merchant Goods' as well as a November ship with 'Plantation Stores'. Essential goods destined for the Urquhart plantations were to be sent immediately by the first departure.[53] Campbell also initiated a discussion regarding credit with the absentee planter: 'Any accommodation in money matters that you may happen occasionally to want, will be at your service to the extent of my abilities.'[54] He also kept Urquhart updated on ship departures as well as the movements of Thomas Campbell, who was in London by September 1786 preparing for a return to the West Indies.[55] Their first account balance sheet demonstrates the practicalities of transatlantic commerce between the merchants in Glasgow and the planter in Carriacou. The firm's exports included herrings to feed the resident enslaved people on the cotton plantation.[56] It also charged Urquhart for goods sourced in Glasgow that were carted to the Broomielaw and then transported via

[50] NRAS, 2570/131, 'Thomas Campbell, Glasgow to William Urquhart', 18 Sept. 1790.

[51] N. Jones, *Reprint of Jones's Directory for the Year 1787* (Glasgow, 1868), p. 34.

[52] NRAS, 2570/120, 'Thomas Campbell to John Campbell', 7 July 1786.

[53] NRAS, 2570/120, 'John Campbell senior to William Urquhart', 17 July 1786.

[54] NRAS, 2570/120, 'John Campbell senior to William Urquhart', 17 July 1786.

[55] NRAS, 2570/120, 'John Campbell senior to William Urquhart', 2 Sept. 1786.

[56] NRAS, 2570/120, 'William Urquhart Esq. Acc Current', Aug. 1786.

lighter ships to large sea-going vessels docked at Port Glasgow.[57] In return, the insured cotton was shipped to the Clyde at six-monthly intervals.[58] On arrival, entry and landing charges were paid which allowed the unloading of the West India cargo. The cotton was subsequently carted to a nearby warehouse, which attracted further storage costs and delivery charges. At point of sale, the firm charged 2.5 per cent commission.

Thomas Campbell formally assumed co-partnership status in John Campbell, senior, & Co. around 1790 and requested the Urquhart trading account be officially transferred to his brothers' firm.[59] Thus, the informal arrangement among kinsmen that began with the Urquhart recommendation four years previously was ratified with a legal partnership. On 30 April 1791, William Urquhart was sent a printed letter stating the firm would hereafter be known as 'John Campbell, senior, and Co.' The letter further informed him the firm's partnership structure had altered and included signatures of each partner.[60] Thus, the firm went by its own social name and transacted on its terms in Scotland and the Caribbean.

After 1791, John Campbell, senior, & Co. embarked on an ambitious strategy of expansion across the West Indies which almost ended in bankruptcy. Much of their business at this point was based on financing plantations or individuals in the West Indies. Later correspondence from the firm suggested the level of finance could extend over long periods. In 1843, James Campbell described a fifty-year commercial relationship with the firm and one planter in St Vincent. According to Campbell, the firm acted in the 'capacity of Friends [rather] than merchants' and advanced over £50,000, which allowed the owners to reduce and work off debts with other merchants.[61] A series of letters from William Arbuthnot – a nephew of the Urquhart family based in Grenada from 1787 – offers a detailed account of how credit was obtained from the firm in the colonies. In this period, he received: 'every assurance of support, they [John Campbell, senior, & Co.] are well pleased with speculation'.[62] One example illustrates how this worked on a practical level. In early 1790, Arbuthnot pondered over the purchase of a cotton estate in Carriacou from Messrs Robertson of Glasgow. Arbuthnot wrote to his uncle William Urquhart to request a loan, although

[57] NRAS, 2570/120, 'Invoice of sundries Shippt.', Nov. 1789.

[58] NRAS, 2570/120, 'William Urquhart Esq. Acc Current', Aug. 1786.

[59] NRAS, 2570/131, 'Thomas Campbell to William Urquhart', 17 Feb. 1791.

[60] NRAS, 2570/122, 'John Campbell senior to William Urquhart', 14 May 1791.

[61] GCA, TD1696, 'John Campbell, senior, & Co., Letterbook', 1827–47, pp. 137–8.

[62] NRAS, 2570/130, 'William Arbuthnot to William Urquhart', 14 Nov. 1792.

he first consulted their preferred merchant whose firm were also prepared to finance the deal:

> I would go down to Grenada & consult Mr Thomas Campbell whose knowledge in business & Experience in the World, as well as personal friendships I have upon all occasions found to be very great, & with which you are indeed well acquainted...Should it be inconvenient for you to advance any money, Mr Campbell is so good, as say, that he will interest his brother Mr John Campbell in the business...I should think it proper to give him full powers to make the bargain.[63]

On the same day, Thomas Campbell also wrote to William Urquhart outlining a detailed plan of the location of the plantation in Carriacou, as well as the character of Arbuthnot's co-partner:

> I esteem them both so much & have so much reliance on the solid judgement and previous success of Dr Bell, who is much the elder planter of the two, that I did not hesitate to promise them any support in my Brothers power, provided their plan shall meet your approbation without which you may well believe your nephew will not engage in it, & of that I can scarsely doubt, knowing as I do, your great regard for him & how well he merits it...On all these considerations it seems only necessary for me to make you acquainted with the universal good character of Dr Bell for probity, sound judgement and experience as a cotton planter of all which the best test is his success from very small beginnings. I think a connection with so good & safe a man in so distant a country a very fortunate circumstance for Mr Arbuthnot & his friends.[64]

Thomas Campbell also wrote to his brother John in Glasgow informing him of the Bell-Arbuthnot partnership and requesting he enter negotiations with Robertson. Thus, interaction between Campbell and Arbuthnot over several years in Grenada had engendered trust, while Dr Bell's success in Grenada facilitated access to a commercial network. Campbell assessed the personal qualities of budding Scottish planters in Grenada and facilitated access to credit with merchant firms in Glasgow through personal recommendations. Although they were ultimately unsuccessful in the purchase (as Campbell expected), the correspondence illustrates how a transatlantic credit relationship was established through existing Scottish networks which could lead to the financing of Caribbean plantations.[65]

[63] NRAS, 2570/118, 'William Arbuthnot to William Urquhart', 3 March 1790.

[64] NRAS, 2570/131, 'Thomas Campbell to William Urquhart', 3 March 1790.

[65] NRAS, 2570/131, 'Thomas Campbell to William Urquhart', 18 Sept. 1790.

In the same period, Thomas Campbell established a foothold in the developing frontier colony of Demerara which was, at that stage, still under Dutch control. By late 1791, Campbell had made a 'considerable purchase…in the Country where a great many people have bought estates'.[66] He remained on the lookout for new opportunities and later compiled a dossier of commercial information on Cellsborough cotton plantation in Demerara, situated on the Windward seacoast. As well as information on soil fertility and the adjoining cotton house, he noted the existing credit agreements as well as the proposed payment plan, including the purchase price £10,500.[67] This information was sent to William Urquhart, although he eventually acquired the plantation himself.

The risky nature of transatlantic commerce and life in the colonies was illustrated by a series of events that struck the firm in this period. In June of 1793, John Campbell, senior, & Co. had to stop payments to creditors. As noted in Chapter 2, this occurred due to a run on Glasgow banks amid concerns over the war with Revolutionary France.[68] But this was simply an issue of short-term finance: William Urquhart, who owed several thousand pounds, was assured by the Campbells that all debts would be paid in full in the event of bankruptcy.[69] This event must have hit the firm's reputation in Glasgow, although they eventually recovered. While the firm avoided demise, their main colonial representative was not so lucky. By 1795, Thomas Campbell was part of the colonial council who took control of government at the outbreak of the Fedon Rebellion on 2 March that year. Thomas quickly fled but died in Demerara on 14 May 1795.[70] By this point, he was a large-scale plantation owner, having acquired shares in three estates in both Grenada and Demerara, including Cellsborough and Taymouth Park.

Fedon's Rebellion and Thomas Campbell's death marked a change in fortunes for the firm. A power of attorney lodged in Grenada Register Office in 1793 ensured Campbell's real and personal estate was divided among kinship networks in Scotland. His shares went to his brothers, John Campbell senior and Alexander Campbell, who afterwards appointed attorneys 'in our names to manage the foresaid plantations…to the best advantage in Concert with the other proprietors' in 1796.[71] In addition to taking control of his plantations in Demerara, Thomas Campbell's

---

[66] NRAS, 2570/118, 'William Arbuthnot to William Urquhart', 17 Sept. 1791.

[67] NRAS, 2570/120, 'Thomas Campbell to William Urquhart', 15 July 1792.

[68] C. Munn, *The Scottish Provincial Banking Companies, 1747–1864* (Edinburgh, 1981), p. 49.

[69] NRAS, 2570/130, 'William Arbuthnot to William Urquhart', 19 June 1793.

[70] *The Edinburgh Magazine or Literary Miscellany*, vol. vi (London, Aug. 1795), p. 160.

[71] Supreme Court Registry, St George's, Grenada, vol. Fii, 9 May 1796, pp. 178–80.

property was damaged during the uprising and his co-partners in Glasgow collected a loan of £40,000 on 24 July 1795, thus acquiring assets and injecting working capital into the firm.[72] The events of the mid-1790s initiated a change of mercantile strategy for John Campbell, senior, & Co. First, they expanded from Grenada into the frontier colony, Demerara, and the business passed to the next generation of merchants. Second, the firm not only advanced credit to individuals and planters but also purchased estates in Demerara directly. But Grenada remained a favoured location for the firm. The relationship with the Urquharts of Craigston and Meldrum endured at least to 1814.[73] Between 1806 and 1834, the firm sent out over forty voyages: these ships were scheduled to transport large groups of foremen and skilled tradesmen such as carpenters and brass-founders for their shipyards on the island.[74]

Tracing the Glasgow firm's dealings with the resident Ninian Home and absentee William Urquhart underlines the city of Glasgow's role as a commercial hub, connecting Grenada with Scotland over the long term. Home and Urquhart hailed from opposite ends of the country, Berwickshire and Aberdeen. Yet, both depended (albeit not exclusively) on the Glasgow firm for credit and goods and to sell their produce in Great Britain. In return, the Glasgow firm held their profits while sending out skilled young men to work their plantations. The increasing numbers of Scots in Grenada gradually reshaped island society, including the introduction of Presbyterianism to the island. Scotland received slave-grown cotton that powered the Industrial Revolution, alongside fortunes derived from Caribbean slavery that improved local societies.

Scots and their fortunes in Grenada and Carriacou

This section is based upon the inventories of twenty-eight individuals who had property in Scotland and were known to be in Grenada and Carriacou during the period 1775 to 1838. This group hailed from across Scotland, with around half from the central lowlands and others from the north.[75]

---

[72] The University of the West Indies, St Augustine, Trinidad and Tobago, the Alma Jordan Library, SC89 6/3, 'Minutes of the Board of Commissioners for the Issue of Exchequer Bills advanced to Persons connected to the Islands of Grenada and St. Vincent, June 1795–1 Sept. 1797', fos. 59–60.

[73] NRAS, 2570/145, 'Account current, John Campbell Senr & Co.', 30 April 1815.

[74] *Glasgow Herald*, 11 Nov. 1811, p. 4.

[75] Twenty-three family residences are known: Glasgow (4), Aberdeen (4), Dumbarton (2), Banff (2), Ayr (2), Wigtonshire, Stirling, Perth, Moray, Kirkcudbright, Kincardine, Inverness, Greenock and Edinburgh.

Table 6.1 Wealth on death of Scots in Grenada in the late slavery era (1775–1838) who died between 1784 and 1858.

Home Scottish region	Inventories	%Total inventories	Wealth	%Total wealth
Borders	2	7.1%	£2,360	1.1%
Western Lowlands	9	32.1%	£164,832	77.2%
Eastern Lowlands	4	14.3%	£1,407	0.7%
Highlands-Hebrides	1	3.6%	£10,000	4.7%
North-east	7	25.0%	£18,777	8.8%
Far north	0	N/A	N/A	N/A
Unknown	5	17.9%	£16,017	7.5%
Total	28		£213,393	

Source: National Records of Scotland: Wills, Testaments and Confirmation Inventories (see Bibliography).

Table 6.2 Range of wealth on death of Scots in Grenada in the late slavery era (1775–1838) who died between 1784 and 1858.

Decile	Range	Inventories	Average	%Total wealth
Top	£100,000–150,000	1	£124,604	58%
Second	£75,000–£99,999	0	N/A	N/A
Third	£50,000–£74,999	0	N/A	N/A
Fourth	£25,000–£49,999	0	N/A	N/A
Fifth	£10,000–£24,999	3	£13,818	19%
Sixth	£7,500–£9,999	2	£8,828	8%
Seventh	£5,000–£7,499	0	N/A	N/A
Eight	£2,500–£4,999	5	£3,222	4%
Ninth	£500–£2,499	10	£1,231	5%
Tenth	£20–£499	7	£178	5%
Total		28		

Source: National Records of Scotland: Wills, Testaments and Confirmation Inventories (see Bibliography).

The total wealth held in these inventories was £213,393, and averaged £7,621 (see Table 6.1). Overall, the pattern was identical to Jamaica; few individuals held most of the wealth, whilst the majority were relatively poorer. In the case of Grenada, the outstanding fortune was held by the merchant James Buchanan (£124,000), which represented over half of the overall wealth in the group (see Table 6.2). As in Jamaica, merchants and planters were the most common occupation, and although there are fewer examples for Grenada than Jamaica, the evidence also suggests those in the mercantile line acquired the most wealth.[76] Some of these fortunes improved Scotland. John Guthrie – the nephew of Archibald Smith of Jordanhill – was operating as a merchant in Grenada probably from 1792.[77] As revealed in Chapter 3, he operated a house of trade, Guthrie & Co., in the free port St George's as well as overseeing the Glasgow firm's operations in Grenada. It seems he accumulated a large fortune in under a decade (£8,977) and made a successful return to Scotland in 1800.[78] The impact of one exceptional mercantile fortune will be traced below.

While the fortunes acquired by planters in Grenada and nearby Carriacou were not as extensive as the wealth returned by their counterparts in Jamaica, some possessed substantial wealth.[79] Walter Macinnes was a resident of Carriacou in the early part of the nineteenth century. In 1824, he owned a one-third share in the 374-acre sugar estate Mount Rich in the parish of St Patricks in Grenada.[80] Back in Glasgow by 1826, he had accumulated a large fortune in long-term dealings with Glasgow firm John Campbell senior & Co., most likely from the proceeds of sugar imported to Glasgow. When he died in his landed estate in Dumbarton in January 1827, he was worth over £21,000, of which 80 per cent was held in accounts with the Glasgow firm.[81] Of the nine Scottish-Grenada planters on the island in this study, two-thirds held accounts with John Campbell senior & Co. and Leitch & Smith. Thus, the merchants of Glasgow held substantial capital for Grenada planters in account current, which they probably used to fund other investments in Scotland and the Caribbean. It was practically essential for Scottish planters in Grenada to have commercial dealings with the West India firms of Glasgow.

---

[76] Five merchants were worth a total of £144,449 – an average of £28,889.

[77] F. Armytage, *The Free Port System in the British West Indies* (London, 1953), p. 69.

[78] NRS, SC70/1/51, Inventory of John Guthrie, 15 Nov. 1834, pp. 513–23.

[79] Nine planters in Grenada were worth £54,373 – an average of £6,041.

[80] G. Smith, *Reference to the Plan of the Island of Grenada* (London, 1882), p. 7.

[81] NRS, SC65/34/1, 'Inventory of the personal estate of the late Walter MacInnes', 28 April 1827, pp. 258–75.

Not only elite merchants and planters acquired wealth and repatriated it to Scotland. Like all plantation economies, the estates required skilled tradesmen to establish the infrastructure. Scottish tradesmen's meagre fortunes were sometimes repatriated in person, a practically unquantifiable stream of capital that archival sources only sometimes reveal. Robert Fergusson, a mason who had 'resided some years in Grenada', died on the way home to Edinburgh in October 1793, possessing goods worth £57 sterling.[82] Representing around eighteen months' wages of a mason in Scotland in 1810, this would have been a considerable sum for his family in Edinburgh.[83] Tradesmen could earn relatively major sums that reshaped lives. John Chapman, a carpenter, died at sea on the way from Grenada to Scotland in August 1825. He left an inventory of over £1,100, most of which 'had been remitted home at different times' and 'directed to be applied…for the support of his mother' in Banff.[84] This vast sum represented over thirty-five years of wages of a carpenter in early nineteenth-century Glasgow.[85] Evidently, large fortunes were available to merchants and planters in the West Indies, while tradesmen repatriated wealth to family at home. These were exceptional by the standards of nineteenth-century Scotland.

This group of Grenada adventurers were just as likely to make it back to Great Britain as to die in the West Indies, a high level of absenteeism (36 per cent) which explains the high proportion of landed investments in Scotland.[86] Of the twenty-eight individuals, eight (35 per cent) owned urban property or landed estates in Scotland. Of the five who owned landed estates, at least one was very likely to have been a 'gentry capitalist' who already possessed landed property prior to departing for the West Indies.[87] Indeed, Patrick MacDougall of Woodlands, who died in St Georges in 1829, owned a landed estate in Scotland but seemingly possessed a meagre fortune on death, with several bad debts in Grenada.[88] Others were West India *nouveau riche* who used their spoils to transform their status back home. After around

---

[82] NRS, CC8/8/129, Inventory of Robert Fergusson, 10 Dec. 1793, pp. 933–6.

[83] The annual wage of masons in Glasgow was around £37 per annum. See J. Cleland, *Statistical Tables Relative to the City of Glasgow*, 3rd ed. (Glasgow, 1823), p. 132.

[84] NRS, SC70/1/34, 'Inventory of John Chapman', 3 May 1826, p. 787.

[85] The annual wage of joiners and house carpenters in Glasgow was around £24 per annum. See Cleland, *Statistical Tables Relative to the City of Glasgow*, p. 132.

[86] Locations of death were: Scotland (10), Grenada (10), Antigua, Carriacou, Martinique, England, Isle of Man, Jersey, 'at sea' and 1 unknown place of death.

[87] S. D. Smith, *Slavery, Family and Gentry Capitalism in the British Atlantic: The World of the Lascelles, 1648–1834* (Cambridge, 2006), p. 9.

[88] *Blackwood's Edinburgh Magazine*, vol. xxvi (Edinburgh, 1829), p. 842; see NRS, SC49/31/2, Settlement of Patrick MacDougall Esq. of Woodlands, 1841, pp. 77–125.

a decade in Grenada, John Guthrie returned to Scotland and purchased the 286-acre estate of Carbeth in the parish of Strathblane in Stirling around 1800. He immediately 'began to improve his new acquisition', building a grand mansion with ornamental gardens and pleasure grounds.[89] Between 1808 and 1817, Guthrie further improved the appearance and extended the acreage of the estate but also transformed local transport connections.[90] Newly rich adventurers from Grenada probably also purchased estates in Kincardine, Perth, Stirling and Dumbarton, including Walter Macinnes, the rich planter from Carriacou, who owned the estate of Auchenfroe on his death in January 1827. Some of the capital was invested in urban property too. James Buchanan – the second largest colonial fortune identified in this study – commissioned a house at Moray Place in Edinburgh's New Town which was designed by leading Scottish architect James Gillespie Graham.[91] In the same period, another Grenada returnee, James Stuart, lived at Hart Street, just one mile away.[92] But there is little doubt it was only the select few who made it home from the West Indies and even fewer with major fortunes to invest in land.

Individuals implemented contrasting strategies to property dispersal and transmission, and, on occasion, the wealth generated by Scottish planters remained in the West Indies. One example reveals the process. John Brander, the planter from Aberdeen, died in May 1806. He owned the 101-acre cocoa and coffee estate named Cottage (formerly known by the name of Morne Français) located in St John in the north-east of the island.[93] With wealth of over £3,000 sterling when he died in 1806 (most of which was held in 'negroes and cattle' on his estate), a large proportion had been remitted to Scotland and held in account current with John Campbell, senior, & Co.[94] His will and testament reveals something of his life and where he intended his fortune should go. He bequeathed Cottage estate to Rosette (described as a 'free cabresse', someone whose parents were mixed-race and African) and her four 'mulatto' children, Alexander, John, Ann and Peggy Brander, evidently his partner and children.[95] He also bequeathed to each

[89] J. G. Smith and J. O. Mitchell, *The Old Country Houses of the Old Glasgow Gentry* (Glasgow, 1878), 'Carbeth Guthrie'.

[90] J. G. Smith, *The Parish of Strathblane and Its Inhabitants from Early Times* (Glasgow, 1886), pp. 41–4.

[91] NRS, SC70/4/58, 'Trust deed and settlement of James Buchanan', 10 July 1858, p. 722.

[92] NRS, SC70/1/20, 'Inventory of James Stuart', 13 March 1820, pp. 667–76.

[93] Smith, *Reference to the Plan of the Island of Grenada*, p. 5.

[94] NRS, CC8/11/3, 'Testament testor of John Brander', 16 June 1807, pp. 291–302.

[95] NRS, CC8/11/3, 'Inventory and testament of John Brander', 4 June 1807, pp. 291–306.

of them enslaved people, thus securing his Grenadian family's economic future. Rosette had once been enslaved too, and at least one of her children remained so. Brander left instructions after his decease to manumit her eldest daughter May Louisa and her mulatto granddaughter Sarah. Under colonial law and practice, May Louisa would have been born into the enslaved status of her mother, although as Rosette and her subsequent children were not described as slaves, it is very likely John Brander manumitted his mistress before she gave birth to his own children.[96] This illustrated how the perverse dynamics of plantation society, as well as slavery and freedom, intersected across families. Rosette was manumitted due to her relationship with a Scottish planter, although her eldest daughter who was born into slavery passed the unfree status onto her own daughter. John Brander therefore owned both Rosette's daughter and granddaughter. As he approached the end of his life, he sought to free his children's eldest sister from slavery and secure their future as free people by gifting them property to become slave-owners themselves. As the Branders were still in ownership of Cottage estate in St John in the north-east of the island in 1824, it looks like he succeeded.[97] But much of his wealth was destined for his two sisters in Scotland and, through executors in Scotland and Grenada, it is most likely the planter's funds held in account current with the Glasgow merchant firm John Campbell senior & Co. were sent to his family in Aberdeen.[98] The Brander property and associated fortune would have reshaped families in Scotland and the West Indies, although within the confines of the direct family matrix. On rare occasions, West India fortunes were gifted to public institutions to be disseminated for the public good, which continued to transform lives many years after slavery was abolished.

West India philanthropy: James Buchanan's mortification

In January 1858, *The Spectator* reported on the 'most munificent bequests for charitable objects' by James Buchanan, formerly of Grenada (see Figure 8.1), and speculated as much as £200,000 was bequeathed to the city of Glasgow. While this figure was an exaggeration, the report accurately reported on Buchanan's substantial bequests to the city of Glasgow via the Merchants House, the Trades House, the Royal Infirmary and for the establishment of an industrial school.[99] Tracing Buchanan's rise, and examining his last will

---

[96] M. Craton, 'Slavery and slave society in the British Caribbean', in *The Slavery Reader*, ed. G. Heuman and J. Walvin (Eastbourne, 2007 ed.), p. 105.

[97] Smith, *Reference to the Plan of the Island of Grenada*, p. 5.

[98] NRS, CC8/11/3, 'Inventory and testament of John Brander', 4 June 1807, pp. 291–306.

[99] *The Spectator*, vol. mdxli, 9 Jan. 1858, p. 4.

and testament, reveals more about his social origins, as well as the extent, motives and dispersal of the largest single charitable bequest made by a returned West India adventurer in this study.

A hagiographical account of Buchanan's early years is recounted in *A Sketch of the Rise and Progress of the Trades' House of Glasgow*. He was the son of a farrier near the Trongate at Glasgow and often loitered around his father's yard in the late eighteenth century. Moses Steven and James Buchanan (no relation), both co-partners in the prominent West India firm Buchanan, Steven & Co. (later Dennistoun, Buchanan & Co.), had their horses shod at this blacksmith, thus introducing the farrier's younger son to the colonial elite of Glasgow. Aged around seventeen in 1800, James expressed a wish to travel to the West Indies and was fortunate enough to be provided with a letter of recommendation to George Wilson, partner of the firm in Grenada (as noted in Chapter 4).[100] After a seven-year training period under Wilson in Grenada, James Buchanan sought new opportunities and became the firm's managing partner in Kingston, Jamaica and Rio de Janeiro, Brazil. He was said to have retired aged thirty-three in 1816 and returned to Scotland and invested his fortune. Dennistoun, Buchanan & Co. accumulated a major portfolio of shares and investments in commerce and industry including Scottish and English railways and American banks and insurance companies. He also acquired urban property in Glasgow and a luxurious home in Moray Place in Edinburgh's New Town. On his death in December 1857, Buchanan had a personal fortune worth over £124,000 (and more in heritable property).[101] Based on Rubinstein's value of a nationally significant fortune in nineteenth-century Great Britain (£100,000), Buchanan was among the ranks of the super-wealthy of his time.[102] For comparison, Buchanan's £124,604 in 1858 is equivalent to £95.3m (relative to the worth of average earnings in 2020).[103]

James Buchanan and his bequest were, however, untypical in several aspects. First, he was a successful, returned adventurer and, of course, most

---

[100] G. Crawford, *A Sketch of the Rise and Progress of the Trades' House of Glasgow* (Glasgow, 1858), pp. 265–71.

[101] NRS, SC70/1/98, 'Inventory of James Buchanan', 10 July 1858, pp. 82–101. Buchanan had property valued at £31,553 in Scotland, £11,625 in England and $361,533 in America (*c*.£81,426, based on an exchange rate of £1 to $4.44). See M. A. Denzel, *Handbook of World Exchange Rates, 1590–1914* (Surrey, 2010), p. 405.

[102] W. D. Rubinstein, *Who Were the Rich? A Biographical Directory of British Wealth-Holders, Vol. I: 1809–1839* (London, 2009), p. 13.

[103] For modern values, see *Measuring Worth* <https://www.measuringworth.com/calculators/ukcompare/> [accessed 27 Oct. 2021.] Relative wage or income worth (average earnings), 2020 values have been used here.

died prematurely or failed to accumulate the wealth he did. In fact, he was the second wealthiest of all Scots known to have been in the West Indies identified for this study after John Shand of Jamaica. Moreover, this example complicates what can be considered a fortune derived from slavery. Buchanan spent sixteen years in the West Indies (seven in Grenada, nine in Jamaica), some time in Brazil (where slavery was not abolished until 1888) and around forty-one years in Edinburgh, investing in commerce and industry across Scotland, England and America. He was involved with the West India firm Dennistoun, Buchanan & Co. for at least twenty-five years, most of the time as a co-partner. The wealth, therefore, came from multiple Atlantic world sources. While it is impossible to quantify the exact sum derived from slavery, the West Indies provided the initial source of capital, which was probably boosted by residence in Brazil, which allowed him to diversify his investments in Scotland and ultimately to bequeath capital to the city of Glasgow.

James Buchanan's settlement (originally drawn up in 1852 and revised in 1857),[104] provided his wife with a substantial annuity of £2,000 but, unusually, restricted major sums to his family. For Buchanan, 'to give large sums of money to Relations is often times attended with mischievous results'.[105] By deliberately excluding family to the direct benefit of the city of Glasgow, the dispersal of Buchanan's West India fortune was unusual, even unique.[106] Buchanan prioritized charitable bequests to public institutions to benefit the common good. A bequest of £10,000 was made to both the Merchants House of Glasgow and the Trades' House of Glasgow – to be invested in Bank of England stock – for educational purposes, principally to educate sons of members who were not wealthy. The Royal Infirmary of Glasgow also received £10,000.[107] the city of Glasgow was bequeathed £30,000 (paid over ten years) to be invested in an 'Industrial Institution… for the maintenance and instruction of destitute children' on condition the city provided a building, and if a success after ten years, annual payments were to continue.[108] The extent of this bequest is on a par with that left by James Ewing (as described in the final chapter) and portions of these separate bequests were ultimately merged.

[104] NRS, SC70/4/58, 'Trust deed and settlement of James Buchanan', 10 July 1858, pp. 719–800.

[105] NRS, SC70/4/58, 'Trust deed and settlement of James Buchanan', 10 July 1858, pp. 774–5.

[106] Crawford, *Trades' House of Glasgow*, p. 265.

[107] For impact of Glasgow Royal Infirmary, see O. Checkland, *Philanthropy in Victorian Scotland: Social Welfare and the Voluntary Principle* (Edinburgh, 1980), pp. 155–8.

[108] NRS, SC70/4/58, 'Trust disposition and settlement of James Buchanan', 10 July 1858, pp. 775–8.

The impact of the Buchanan bequest is revealed by tracing two strands. As noted, James Buchanan bequeathed £10,000 to the Merchants House in trust 'to be exclusively appropriated and expended towards the Education of the sons of decayed members: and granting Bursaries to such of them as give evidence of future eminence in such a manner as the Directors of the Merchants House may deem best'.[109] However, by the early 1900s, fewer members were matriculating with the Merchants House, which meant that there were few candidates eligible for the bursary. In 1909, in legislation passed by the Secretary of State for Scotland, the Buchanan Bursary was merged with one of the three bequests made by James Ewing, an owner of a Jamaican estate. Titled the Merchants House of Glasgow (Buchanan and Ewing bequests) Order 1909, the order allowed for the repositioning of funds.[110] The value of these joint bequests in 1909 was around £22,000 (this was invested in, for example, English railway stock).[111] After an open application process, several institutions across Glasgow were awarded sums on an annual basis, mainly for student scholarships and staff costs. In 1914, the Royal Technical College (the main predecessor institution of the University of Strathclyde) received the highest proportion, followed by the Athenium Commercial College, the University of Glasgow, the Royal Infirmary, St Mungo's College, Glasgow School of Art, the Institution of Engineers and Shipbuilders, and Andersons College of Medicine.[112] The bequest is ongoing: in 2017, the Merchants House awarded £6,000 to educational institutions.[113] There are no existing estimates available for other institutions, although a recent study by the University of Glasgow suggested its historical income from the Ewing-Buchanan bequest, which was historically used to pay staff costs since 1909 could be as high as £8.4m (2016 values).[114]

Second, by providing a building for the Buchanan Institution that opened in 1859, the powers that be in Glasgow took advantage of the offer of £30,000 in

---

[109] NRS, SC70/4/58, 'Trust disposition and settlement of James Buchanan', 10 July 1858, pp. 775–6.

[110] GCA, T-MH, 56/6, 'Merchants House of Glasgow (Buchanan and Ewing Bequests)'.

[111] GCA, T-MH, 1/14, 'Merchants House: notanda by the collector for report on the future administration of the funds of the BUCHANAN and EWING EDUCATIONAL BEQUESTS', Nov. 1909.

[112] GCA, T-MH, 1/14, 'Minutes: 1909–1915', p. 438.

[113] 'The Merchants House of Glasgow: report and consolidated financial statements for the year ended 31 Dec. 2017' <https://www.merchantshouse.org.uk/desktop/web/ckfinder/userfiles/files/MH%20Financial%20statements%202017.pdf> [accessed 1 Jan. 2019], p. 32.

[114] S. Mullen and S. Newman, 'Slavery, abolition and the University of Glasgow' <https://www.gla.ac.uk/media/media_607547_en.pdf> [accessed 1 Jan. 2019], p. 23.

Buchanan's settlement of 1857. Olive Checkland has described the institution as a 'ragged school' on a hybrid model, based on philanthropic donations and public money.[115] As James Buchanan intended to extend 'the hand of charity to the helpless of every sect and denomination', religious instruction in the institution was unsectarian in nature.[116] Buchanan laid out a specific curriculum: pupils were to reside with parents (usually widowed mothers, although they could reside within the school if required) and were provided with breakfast, lunch and supper. They were instructed in reading, writing and arithmetic, navigation, gymnastics, tailoring, shoemaking and carpentry to make them fit for the navy, army and merchant marine or to emigrate to the colonies.[117] The school was specifically aimed at the urban poor. Children were only admitted if they were destitute (ie their father died or had deserted the family). On admission, the typical child was aged eight, and stayed for around four years. The average annual cost per boy was £5 10s, which would normally have excluded the local poor from attending. Buchanan's Institution proved a major success and over 1,600 boys were admitted in the establishment's first fourteen years.[118] By 1913, 6,000 were said to have been through its doors. Buchanan boys were reckoned to be 'heavier, healthier and stronger than the average Glasgow schoolboy'.[119] Buchanan's West India fortune, quite literally, fed the poor of the city into the twentieth century.

Buchanan's bequest to the Merchants House was intended to regenerate the mercantile ranks (the interest from which ultimately passed to the University of Glasgow) but provision was also made for the workers of the city: for tradesmen, the Royal Infirmary and Buchanan's Institution, which improved the health and educational standards of some of Glasgow's poorest children. It is no exaggeration this fortune derived from slavery in the West Indies improved the lives of many thousands of people. In a neo-Weberian class model, Buchanan's mortification, in theory and practice, enhanced the life chances of many, thus potentially lifting some from their economic order.[120] In this way, the labour of many enslaved people in the Caribbean created profits which fell into the hands of the select few

---

[115] Checkland, *Philanthropy in Victorian Scotland*, p. 250.

[116] NRS, SC70/4/58, 'Trust disposition and settlement of James Buchanan', 10 July 1858, p. 779.

[117] *Historical Sketch of The Buchanan Institution Glasgow* (Glasgow, 1913).

[118] *Reports from the Commissioners: Ecclesiastical Church Estates; Endowed Schools and Hospitals* (Scotland), vol. xvii (1874), pp. 192–210.

[119] *Historical Sketch of The Buchanan Institution Glasgow*, p. 35.

[120] For a discussion of neo-Weberian class theory, see S. Clegg (ed.), *Organization Theory and Class Analysis: New Approaches and New Issues* (New York, 1989), p. 115.

West India adventurers who, in rare philanthropic initiatives, ultimately improved the life chances of many thousands in Scotland.

Building on Douglas Hamilton's chapter on wealth repatriation, S. Karly Kehoe traced the investments of Scots in the West Indies – mainly residents of Grenada and Carriacou – in charitable enterprise in the Highlands, especially educational academies and hospitals. Thus, according to Kehoe, the impact of individual Scots in the Caribbean can be measured using different levels of analysis. First, historians should examine Caribbean adventurers of modest means who improved their own status and that of their families at home. Second, the more substantial fortunes of new elites might be traced, and their wealth often reshaped regional economies and societies.[121] Kehoe has noted educational establishments were favoured options for benefactors in Grenada and connected the wealth from Scots in the Caribbean to the opening of Fortrose Academy (1791), Inverness Royal Academy (1792) and Tain Royal Academy (1813). There were others too. In 1799, for example, the will of Mr James Wilson of Grenada bequeathed 'the whole stock…to be drawn from the funds and remitted to the magistrates of Banff, North Britain, to be by them laid out as a charitable fund [c.£8,000] in the best manner possible'. The town magistrates of Banff settled on an educational establishment which included an infant school, classrooms, a library and museum to benefit the 'most promising boys'.[122] In similar fashion, James Buchanan's bequest helped reshape Glasgow society from 1857 to the present day, yet it is distinctive in key aspects. The Buchanan Institution was a hybrid, part funded by the city of Glasgow to improve the conditions of destitute children. Schools come and go. However, the other Buchanan bequest (£10,000 to the Merchants House) was not intended to set up an institution; instead it educated learners in perpetuity. Capital derived from slavery underpinned the age of improvement, and this study shows that West India philanthropy improved the prospects and life chances of many across the lowlands, especially Glasgow, in a far more profound manner than it did for the Scottish Highlands.

[121] S. K. Kehoe, 'From the Caribbean to the Scottish Highlands: charitable enterprise in the age of improvement, c.1750–1820', *Rural History*, xxvii (2015), 1–23. See Hamilton, *Scotland, the Caribbean*, p. 195.

[122] *The New Statistical Account of Scotland*, vol. xiii (Edinburgh, 1845), p. 55; HCPP 1841 Session 1 (64) *Answers Made by Schoolmasters in Scotland to Queries Circulated in 1838, by Order of the Select Committee on Education in Scotland*, p. 153.

Conclusion

This chapter traces Scottish involvement in the British takeover in Grenada after the island was ceded to Great Britain in 1763. The percentages are startling. Scots were quick to move onto the island and by 1772 possessed 40 per cent of land cultivated for sugar and cotton. Scottish merchants and planters collected 40 per cent of the loan provided by the British government after Fedon's Rebellion in 1795. And by 1835, Scots probably comprised up to half the white population. The Scottish infiltration of nearby Carriacou was on a similar scale, forming one-fifth of the white population but owning 40 per cent of the land. The relatively high population of Scots on each island underpinned a self-perpetuating cycle of exploitation. Scottish planters and Glasgow merchants had a monopoly on Grenada, which attracted imports of sugar and cotton to the Clyde. In return, the monopoly promoted outward skilled migration via their shipping. Major profits were generated by the Glasgow merchants operating in Grenada (as revealed in the final chapter) but also by resident Scottish planters, merchants and tradesmen alike. Many skilled Scots were sent out, and a few fortunes came back in return. The mercantile networks were crucially important, therefore, to the advancement of Scots in the island, but also to the city of Glasgow and Scotland overall. The Camerons of Glenloy may not have benefited from their brother's fortune, if it ever existed, but other fortunes were built and repatriated, allowing many in Scotland to benefit directly from the Atlantic slavery economy despite never setting foot in the West Indies. The Buchanan Institution provides a compelling example of how Caribbean slavery improved life chances of Scots with no prior connection to slavery, in this case the industrial working poor in Glasgow.

7. Trinidad

In January 1833, James MacQueen, the chief propagandist of the British West India interest, arrived to a great welcome in Port of Spain, Trinidad. Hailing from Lanarkshire in west-central Scotland, the south-east Caribbean was familiar territory for him, as he had spent many years as an overseer in Grenada before returning to Glasgow around 1810 as editor of the pro-slavery *Glasgow Courier*. Given his transatlantic prominence, it was natural for the merchants and planters of Trinidad to honour MacQueen at a dinner that celebrated the British empire. An English-born artist resident in Trinidad, Richard Bridgens, produced decorations that included a wreath of intertwined banana and cocoa trees, sugar cane and coffee plant, thus symbolizing the slave-grown produce from which the planters' fortunes were derived. Bridgens also painted the lion rampant of Scotland adjoined to Ireland's harp and England's St George and the dragon. This shared commitment to empire, especially among Scots and English, cultivated a sense of Britishness in Trinidad.

At the dinner – attended by fellow Scots such as prominent merchant John Losh – the health of the king, queen and royal family was toasted amid loud celebration of MacQueen's homeland. Before his speech, in which he described Great Britain as the 'mistress of nations and arbitress of the world', the band played Robert Burns' radical anthem 'Scots wha hae wi' Wallace bled'. MacQueen's reaction was not recorded, but surely this educated propagandist would have understood the irony in Burns' stanzas that alluded to English subjugation of the Scots ('Who's sae base as be a slave? – let him turn, and flee'), while he defended his own compatriots' right to hold men, women and children as enslaved property.[1] MacQueen's visit to Trinidad is symbolic not only of an increasingly unified British-West

---

[1] 'Dinner to Mr. MacQueen', *Port of Spain Gazette*, 18 Jan. 1833, p. 2. For an account of MacQueen's life, see D. Lambert, 'The Glasgow king of Billingsgate: James MacQueen and an Atlantic pro-slavery network', *Slavery & Abolition*, xxix (2008), 389–413; see also R. Bridgens, *West India Scenery: With Illustrations of Negro Character, The Process of Making Sugar, etc.: From Sketches Taken During a Voyage to and Residence of Seven Years in the Island of Trinidad* (London, 1836).

India interest towards the end of the slavery period,[2] but also underlines just how much the Scots were fully integrated across frontier colonies in the British Caribbean. Nevertheless, historians have underestimated the Scottish involvement in a period of dramatic change on the island. Bridget Brereton's classic history of modern Trinidad suggests that Scottish merchants, planters and professionals only became part of the white ruling elite *after* 1838. Kit Candlin's more recent book on the free coloured population in the Caribbean's last frontier – Grenada, Trinidad and British Guyana – alludes to Scots in Trinidad but does not trace their standing in colonial society. Trinidad is also absent from seminal histories of Scotland and the Caribbean in the slavery period.[3] This chapter, therefore, seeks to understand more about Scottish involvement in the settlement and implementation of a plantation system in Trinidad, tracing connections with Glasgow via interconnected case studies of transatlantic Scots. This chapter has a simple premise: to identify Scots commercially associated with Trinidad and trace economic success, or lack thereof, towards the end of Caribbean slavery.

The settlement of British Trinidad: merchants and migration

Taken from the Spanish with ease in 1797, Trinidad was formally ceded to Great Britain under a secret clause of the Treaty of Amiens in March 1802. Alongside other third-phase colonies Demerara, Essequibo and Berbice, Trinidad represented, in Candlin's phrase, the 'last frontier' of the British West Indies.[4] According to the Scottish adjutant-general to the West Indies, General Sir George Murray, the island was of some commercial importance at this time:

> Its extent, the greatest proportion of land which is capable of Cultivation, the variety of its productions, the fertility of the soil, and…its favourable situation…entitle the colony of Trinidad to rank under Jamaica alone in all the British dependencies in the West Indies.[5]

---

[2] For a recent account, see M. Taylor, *The Interest: How the British Establishment Resisted the Abolition of Slavery* (London, 2020).

[3] B. Brereton, *A History of Modern Trinidad, 1783–1962* (London, 1981), p. 116, p. 119; K. Candlin, *The Last Caribbean Frontier, 1795–1815* (Basingstoke, 2012). Neither of the seminal works on Scotland and the Caribbean have 'Trinidad' in the index. See D. Hamilton, *Scotland, the Caribbean and the Atlantic World, 1750–1820* (Manchester, 2005); T. M. Devine (ed.), *Recovering Scotland's Slavery Past: The Caribbean Connection* (Edinburgh, 2015).

[4] Candlin, *The Last Caribbean Frontier*.

[5] NLS, Adv.MS. 46.11, Papers of General Sir George Murray, fo. 171.

In the late eighteenth and early nineteenth centuries, the British state continued to pursue expansionist policies in the Caribbean and on the South American mainland, although, according to Lowell Ragatz and others, the West Indian economy had already entered economic decline.[6] While it had considerable agricultural potential, the acquisition of Trinidad presented a unique series of challenges for the British imperial state. First, the island was underdeveloped, having been neglected by its previous imperial possessors, Spain. In October 1802, orders from Lord Hobart, secretary of state for the colonies, to the commissioners for the governing of the island noted that its resident population was limited and 'composed of various Nations', yet a considerable part of the island's fertile countryside was yet to be cultivated in a 'climate unfavourable to European industry'.[7] Second, the resident plantocracy, mainly Spanish and especially French, possessed a small enslaved labour force, although the British demanded higher numbers of enslaved people from Africa to facilitate large-scale cultivation. But Trinidad was subsumed into the British empire five years after the House of Commons committed to Henry Dundas' policy of 'gradual abolition' in April 1792.[8] A series of acts in the spirit of abolition after 1799 meant that Trinidad planters never acquired the extensive enslaved workforce of more mature slave economies before the abolition of the slave trade in 1807. As Gelien Matthews notes, the island subsequently became as a 'model colony in the grand scheme of British abolition' as reforms and regulations were introduced in the crown colony – by parliament, as the island did not have an assembly dominated by planters.[9] While Trinidad was subject to British slavery for only thirty-seven years, and was an idiosyncratic colony, studying the settlement of the island offers historians the opportunity to examine the activities of individuals on the island during the transition from Spanish to British control in the final decades of Caribbean slavery.

Trinidad is fifty-four miles long and, at its broadest, stretched to around forty-four miles, much of which was uncultivated. To remedy this situation, in the late eighteenth century various attempts were made to attract settlers. In November 1776, the Spanish Crown's *Cédula de población* offered land grants and trading concessions to Catholic foreigners – especially from

---

[6] L. Ragatz, *The Fall of the Planter Class in the British Caribbean, 1763–1833* (New York, 1928).

[7] TNA, CO 295/3, 'Commissioners for administering the government', fo. 4.

[8] R. Anstey, *The Atlantic Slave Trade and British Abolition, 1760–1810* (New Jersey, 1975), p. 314; S. Mullen, 'Henry Dundas: a "great delayer" of the abolition of the transatlantic slave trade', *The Scottish Historical Review*, c (2021), 218–48.

[9] G. Matthews, 'Trinidad: a model colony for British slave trade abolition', *Parliamentary History*, xxvi, S1 (2007), 84–96.

Grenada, Tobago, St Vincent and Dominica – in an attempt to attract settlers and boost the economy. Another *cédula* in November 1783 extended this concession to all settlers of the Roman Catholic faith. Migrants, including many free coloured people, arrived from French Caribbean islands, especially Grenada.[10] Records generated by the Spanish government following this edict suggest that it was unlikely that many Scots were prominent in Spanish Trinidad.[11] Land grants reveal a few names of Scottish origin, although some, such as William McNeill, took up land in Naparima (in the western-south of the island) to be used for sugar estates: he later operated as a merchant between Glasgow and Trinidad.[12] Since they hailed from a majority Presbyterian country, it seems unlikely that Scots infiltrated Spanish Trinidad immediately after both *cédulas*. However, this changed with British rule.

Trinidad was governed as a crown colony, which, according to Eric Williams, allowed the British government to retain complete control rather than devolve any power to a colonial legislature (which would likely have been dominated by slave-owning planters and free coloured people).[13] In December 1802, the secretary of state for the colonies advised the newly appointed commissioners of Trinidad that, alongside other incentives, employing ministers would encourage the settlement of Protestant dissenters from Scotland and Ireland. Indentures of five years included parcels of land as an inducement, with wages offered on an incremental scale dependent on skills.[14] In other words, developing the socio-religious environment on the island would encourage British settlers. In 1803, one such scheme was attempted by Alexander Macdonell, Chaplain to the Glengarry Fencibles, who tried to relocate 500 Highland military families to Trinidad, their loyalty to the British empire by then no longer in question after fighting in Ireland in 1798. Highland Scots were deemed particularly suitable as pioneering settlers. Families were to be provided with 100 acres of land in a specially constructed village, while plans were made to introduce a Gaelic-speaking chaplain of the Catholic Church and a Church of Scotland

---

[10] L. Newson, 'Foreign immigrants in Spanish America: Trinidad's colonisation experiment', *Caribbean Studies*, xix, (April–July 1979), 133–51.

[11] The University of the West Indies – St Augustine, Alma Jordan Library, SC100, 'Land granted by the Spanish government', sets 1–3.

[12] The University of the West Indies – St Augustine, Alma Jordan Library, SC100, 'Land granted by the Spanish government', sets 2 and 3. Mr Farquar Grant was listed as the actual proprietor of land in Pointa Piedra in 1783, while Messrs Lamont and Corrie were listed as proprietors of land in the same place in 1787.

[13] E. Williams, *History of the People of Trinidad and Tobago* (New York, 1962), p. 72.

[14] TNA, CO 295/3, 'Commissioners for administering the government', fos. 13–15.

minister to service the religious needs of the families.[15] Scots of any faith were envisioned as the ideal settlers for British Trinidad, and while this scheme was abandoned, many travelled there of their own accord.

In 1801, Scottish newspapers enticed young men to Trinidad by describing a colony of 'great extent, of uncommon fertility, the most healthy of West India islands, neither exposed to fevers or hurricane, capable of immense improvement in British hands, already adding considerably to our revenue'.[16] Trinidad certainly was a sugar planter's dream: the soil was rich and fertile, unlike that of older colonies such as Jamaica, and the land was offered at low cost to pioneering settlers.[17] Spanish under development presented imperial challenges and opportunities. With British rule came increased imports of enslaved people and commodity production. Trinidad and neighbouring Tobago are estimated to have received over 25,000 African enslaved people on British ships between 1797 and 1808, the third-highest number in the British West Indies after Jamaica and the colonies that became British Guiana.[18] In 1796, there were over 450 estates in Trinidad: coffee (130), cocoa (60), cotton (103) and especially sugar (159), increasing to 479 by 1802. While the numbers of coffee, cocoa and cotton estates remained broadly similar, the overall numbers of sugar estates increased by 20 per cent. Export statistics are even more impressive. Slight increases were noted in exports of cocoa and cotton between 1799 and 1803, coffee exports almost halved, while cotton outputs increased by a third and sugar exports almost doubled to 16 million lbs.[19] According to one contemporary commentator, there were over 210 sugar estates on Trinidad by 1807, and while several large plantations were increasingly productive, output was limited 'from want of hands'.[20] While sugar production quickly dominated in Trinidad, it never developed as a monocultural economy and the perennial shortage of labour prohibited larger-scale production.

Voyages from Clyde ports dramatically increased as the nineteenth century progressed, supporting the view of developing mercantile activity

---

[15] TNA, CO295/6, 'Commissioners for administering the government (Dec. 1803)', fos. 31–40.

[16] *Caledonian Mercury*, 10 Oct. 1801.

[17] Ragatz, *Fall of the Planter Class*, pp. 332–3.

[18] The transatlantic slave-trade database estimates that British ships carried 28,819 Africans to Trinidad and Tobago between 1797 and 1808. See *The Transatlantic Slave Trade Database* <http://www.slavevoyages.org/assessment/estimates> [accessed 10 Feb. 2020].

[19] L. M. Fraser, *History of Trinidad, 1781–1813*, vol. i (Port of Spain, 1891), pp. 149–51.

[20] J. F. Dauxion Lavaysse, *A Statistical, Commercial, and Political Description of Venezuela, Trinidad, Margarita and Tobago* (London, 1820), p. 335.

between Scotland and Trinidad. Ships departed from Glasgow ports for Trinidad in 1795 – even before it was subsumed into the British empire, which suggests that trade could have been well-established by the Treaty of Amiens in 1802.[21] In the years 1806 to 1834, shipping advertisements in the *Glasgow Herald* suggest just over 200 ships departed from Clyde ports for Trinidad. At the beginning of the nineteenth century, there was around one voyage every year, although this increased to an average of twelve a year by the 1830s (see Table 4.1). Thus, Trinidad became the third most important destination for ships departing from Clyde ports, after Jamaica and Demerara, up to the end of Caribbean slavery. The merchant firms of Glasgow such as Dennistoun, McGregor & Co., George Cole, Campbell, Rivers & Co., Wighton, Gray & Co., operated many of the ships, although the elite firm Robert Eccles & Co. was the most prolific of all. West India firms acted as shippers but also as recruiters offering assisted passage. The firm Campbell, Rivers & Co. advertised in the *Glasgow Herald* looking for 'A YOUNG MAN as an OVERSEER for an Estate in a healthy situation in Trinidad' who was offered 'freight and passage' from Port Glasgow.[22] Robert Eccles & Co. advertised in the *Glasgow Herald* in September 1828 looking for 'A HOUSE CARPENTER, to serve under Indenture for three years' on a healthy estate with 'good encouragement' on offer, if candidates came well-recommended.[23] The ships that arrived in Trinidad from Glasgow therefore not only serviced the planters' requirements but also brought many young Scotsmen as skilled tradesmen or labourers. Based on the over 200 *Glasgow Herald* advertisements of ships departing from Clyde ports for Trinidad (with between five and nine individuals per ship), it is possible between 1,000 and 1,900 Scots travelled on these ships between 1806 and 1834. Not all of these remained, and many likely went on to Tobago, twenty miles north-east, an island which was regarded as a 'Scotch colony' in this period.[24]

Contemporary newspapers referred to Scots as the most 'numerous of the natives of the British Islands residing in Trinidad' in 1838.[25] Even so, they were unlikely to have reached the sheer numbers of Jamaica, or the

[21] *Caledonian Mercury*, 3 Oct. 1795, p. 3.

[22] *GH*, 18 May 1812, p. 3.

[23] *GH*, 19 Sept. 1828, p. 3.

[24] Library of Congress, MS. 20353, J. McTear, 'Journal of a voyage to & residence in Tobago, 1825–6'. For description of Tobago, see the University of the West Indies, Mona, West Indies and Special Collections, 'Papers of Lachlan Campbell, Deputy Provost Marshall Tobago, 1772–1782'.

[25] *Port of Spain Gazette*, 23 Jan. 1838, quoted in C. B. Franklin, *After Many Days: A Memoir* (Port of Spain, 1910), p. 29.

Figure 7.1 Richard Bridgens, active 1838, British, Protector of Slaves Office
(Trinidad), *c.*1833, Graphite on medium, slightly textured, beige wove paper.
Yale Center for British Art, Paul Mellon Collection, B1981.25.2403. Public Domain.

relatively high proportion within Grenadian white society. A census in 1808 documented 31,478 persons in Trinidad, the vast majority black enslaved people (21,895) and Amerindians (1,635). Free people of colour numbered 5,450, double the white population. Of the white population of 2,476, the French and Spanish outnumbered the British, who comprised just under half.[26] The demographics shifted by 1825: the enslaved population slightly increased to 23,230, the free people of colour to 14,983, while indigenous Amerindians decreased to around 700. The white population of Trinidad was 3,310, yet those from the 'United Kingdom' almost halved to just over 600, of whom three-quarters were men.[27] This return suggests British men in Trinidad numbered 450 at most in 1825, no more than 14 per cent of the white population, and the Scottish proportion must have been lower, given the prevalence of English merchants on the island.

Many Scots were, however, prominent in island society. The ill-fated Robert McGregor Stirling – a Scot on the island who will be discussed below – described the partners of the Glasgow firm, Burnley, Gray & Co.

[26] Williams, *Trinidad and Tobago*, pp. 67–8.
[27] TNA, CO295/71, Trinidad dispatches, 1826, fo. 260.

– including John Losh – as the 'Bigwigs' of Trinidad.[28] By the 1830s, Scots were established enough to host regular events that publicly expressed patriotism, including St Andrew's Day dinners in Port of Spain and the event for James MacQueen described above.[29] Yet, Scots were part of a diverse Trinidadian society, initially outnumbered by the French, Spanish and free people of colour. Fewer in number than their counterparts in Jamaica and with nowhere near the relative importance of the Scots in Grenada, the Scots in Trinidadian society were a less pervasive presence in a colony in which chattel slavery was being brutally imposed. Nevertheless, as the overall British population of Trinidad declined between 1808 and 1825, many Scots rose to positions of some prominence, often expressing their national heritage in public spaces while extracting fortunes derived from slavery.

The 'Trinidad people' of Glasgow

The British settlement of Trinidad during Glasgow's sugar era ostensibly presented a prime opportunity for the city's mercantile speculators. However, the potential funders were less convinced. In February 1802, staff at the Glasgow branch of the Royal Bank of Scotland commented on the preliminary negotiations in the Treaty of Amiens (when it was assumed Trinidad would be returned to Spain) and speculated about the assumed negative impact on the fortunes of merchants described as the 'Trinidad people' in Glasgow.[30] The final cession of Trinidad in March 1802 attracted immediate speculative investment from the opportunistic West India merchants of Glasgow. Royal Bank correspondence in May that year suggested the mercantile community – to many of whom the bank provided short-term credit facilities – was investing in Trinidad, although Glasgow joint agent Robert Scott Moncrieff expressed concern at what were still regarded as high-risk ventures:

> I wish some of our young West Indians may not follow [in speculation] – A number of them I hear are buying Estates in Trinidad – I know not a more hazardous ruinous business – I would not take a complement of the best estate in the island.[31]

Although Royal Bank staff viewed this new generation as 'West India youths' whose ambition and desire for capital was limitless, some were

[28] UofGSPC, MS. Gen 1717/4/A/15/66, 1 Jan. 1831.
[29] *Port of Spain Gazette*, 25 Nov. 1834, p. 1.
[30] NWGA, RB/837/571, Simpson-Moncrieff Letters, 18 Feb. 1802.
[31] NWGA, RB/837/664, Simpson-Moncrieff Letters, 24 May 1802.

successful in applications for credit.[32] But this was a risky business even for well-known firms. Unlike other West India novices in the city, the Eccles were long-established, having been present in Spanish Trinidad since 1783, when they were listed as 'actual proprietors' of land used for the cultivation of sugar cane in Oropouche. The Eccles were based in Glasgow but, unusually for the time, were of Irish descent. It is likely that the patriarch of the family, William Eccles, became successful in Trinidad – his Roman Catholic faith providing access to land under *cédula* – and chose Glasgow as a metropolitan base for sugar imports. His son George Eccles died on the island in 1799, and his will, written in Spanish, revealed both his adherence to the Catholic faith and his connection to Glasgow. He nominated his three brothers, Robert, William and James, as executors.[33] The surviving brothers established an elite mercantile business, Robert Eccles & Co., located on Buchanan Street, around 1801.[34] The co-partners quickly mixed among the upper echelons of the city's elite West India interest. William Eccles and the firm were founding subscribers to the Glasgow West India Association in 1807. By 1820, a sister firm, William & James Eccles & Co., was established. The separate firms were established to manage discrete interests in separate colonies: Robert Eccles & Co. shipped mainly to Trinidad (indeed, they were the top shippers from the Clyde to the island between 1806 and 1834), whereas Wm. & Jas. Eccles & Co. shipped mainly to Demerara. By the 1820s, therefore, the Eccles were of considerable importance in mercantile Glasgow, with multiple firms importing sugar from third-phase colonies of the British West Indies.

Three generations of the Eccles were resident in Trinidad, and they had considerable standing in the island towards the end of the slavery era. In 1838, Rosina Eccles, daughter of James, married William Frederick Burnley, who moved to Glasgow to take up commercial pursuits. He was the son of William Hardin Burnley, owner of fourteen sugar estates and described by Trinidadian historian Selwyn Cudjoe as the 'wealthiest man and largest slave owner in Trinidad during the first half of the nineteenth century'.[35] Thus, the children of the most prominent mercantile and planting families on the island were paired, consolidating connections with Port of Spain and Glasgow. However, the high-status and prosperous business over the long term did not

---

[32] NWGA, RB/837/927, Simpson-Moncrieff Letters, 24 Dec. 1802.

[33] NRS, CC8/8/138, 'Inventory of George Eccles', 18 Dec. 1812, pp. 1126–32.

[34] *The Glasgow Directory* (Glasgow, 1801), p. 30.

[35] S. R. Cudjoe, 'Burnley, William Hardin (1780–1850)', *Oxford Dictionary of National Biography*, Sept. 2016 <http://www.oxforddnb.com/view/article/109518> [accessed 1 April 2018].

translate into large-scale mercantile fortunes. As noted by Selwyn Cudjoe, the Eccles and Burnley businesses were ultimately combined but were not efficiently managed.[36] The firm Eccles, Burnley & Co. was made bankrupt in 1847. On his death a year earlier, William Eccles' estate was initially valued at over £56,000, the majority of which was held in associated merchant firms in Glasgow, Trinidad and Demerara. With the bankruptcy of the firms, his holdings were deemed 'utterly worthless' three years later.[37] The family did maintain control of sugar estates in Trinidad through James's son, William Eccles junior, who was resident on the island for many years as proprietor of over ten estates. His death in 1859 was announced in Trinidad and Scotland as a 'public calamity…an irreparable loss to the whole colony'.[38] As will be shown, few Scottish adventurers generated major fortunes in Trinidad, although there were exceptional cases.

John Lamont of Cedar Grove

On the death of planter John Lamont on 21 November 1850, his obituary in the *San Fernando Gazette* was as follows:

> Mr Lamont had arrived at the age of 65 years, the greater part of his life which he passed in this Island [of Trinidad]: where he had accumulated a very large fortune, by care, perseverance, and intelligence, accompanied by the strictest integrity, and marked by honour in all his transactions. He was never married; and we believe it is not known who will become the possessors of his fine estates in Diego Martin and in Naparima. His body was attended from his residence to Cocorite by a numerous cortege of friends; and it was there placed on board the steamer, and brought to San Fernando – from thence it was conveyed (attended by his friends who are resident in Naparima) to the family burial ground at Canaan Estate, where it was finally deposited next to the grave of his late brother, Boyden Lamont Esq.[39]

Lamont hailed from Argyllshire in the Western Highlands of Scotland, and his trajectory makes him worthy of detailed study: the fortune he acquired was among the largest accumulated across the British West Indies towards the end of Caribbean slavery.

[36] S. R. Cudjoe, *The Slave Master of Trinidad: William Hardin Burnley and the Nineteenth-Century Atlantic World* (Amherst, 2018),

[37] NRS, SC36,48/33, 'Inventory of William Eccles', 18 June 1847, pp. 138–9; 'Amended inventory', 15 Oct. 1850, p. 326.

[38] 'Death of William Eccles Esq. of Trinidad', *Greenock Advertiser*, 17 Sept. 1859, p. 2.

[39] *San Fernando Gazette*, 23 Nov. 1850, reprinted in N. Lamont, *An Inventory of the Lamont Papers, 1231–1897* (Edinburgh, 1914), p. 440.

John Lamont was born in Argyllshire, Scotland, in 1782, the son of a local gentry laird and a woman of 'inferior station', whose lower social rank prohibited marriage between them.[40] Lamont was registered and baptised the same year as the 'natural son' (that is, a recognized child born out of wedlock) of James Lamont of Knockdow and Isabel Clerk, daughter of Duncan Clerk (or Clark).[41] While acknowledged illegitimacy was not unknown in the Western Highlands in the late eighteenth century, it was less common than in many urban centres of Scotland, perhaps due to the influence of Church discipline.[42] There were implications for John Lamont as he grew into manhood. As a shunned illegitimate without the appropriate respectability of descent, he had no legal claim to the family estate and would not have been accepted into the same social circles his paternal family frequented. Although the eldest son, there seems to have been no support from his father during childhood. Lamont's far-from-privileged start in life provided ample motivation to pursue fortune in the West Indies. Correspondence printed in a family history suggests this was an elective migration due to economic hardship. 'I had no other choice at the time circumstances favoured me. I only aimed at frugal independence', he later revealed.[43] Aged twenty in 1802, he departed from Scotland, most likely from Port Glasgow or Greenock, and was among the first influx of Scots in Trinidad after the Peace of Amiens.[44]

Lamont began as an overseer on the estates of Glasgow firm Eccles & Co. and within seven years became the owner of a 360-acre sugar plantation, Cedar Grove in South Naparima on the south-west coast of Trinidad.[45] According to William Hardin Burnley, the quarter in which it was situated was the most fertile on the island: 'there is no soil in any part of the world equal to the black sugar soil of South Naparima'.[46] The capital required to settle new plantations in Trinidad was immense. In 1799, the governor of Trinidad, Thomas Picton, estimated the smallest class of sugar plantation should consist of 200 acres of

[40] *Reports of Cases Decided in the Supreme Courts of Scotland, and in the House of Lords on Appeal from Scotland*, vol. xxviii (Edinburgh, 1856), p. 307.

[41] NRS, Old Parish Register Births, Inverchaolain, 8 Feb. 1782.

[42] R. Mitchison and L. Leneman, *Sexuality and Social Control: Scotland, 1660–1780* (Oxford, 1989), pp. 140–4.

[43] N. Lamont, 'Life of a West India planter one hundred years ago', *Public Lectures, Delivered under the Auspices of the Trinidad Historical Society during the Session, 1935–6* (Trinidad and Tobago, 1936), p. 15.

[44] *Reports of Cases Decided in the Supreme Courts of Scotland*, p. 307.

[45] Lamont, 'Life of a West India planter', p. 14.

[46] House of Commons Accounts and Papers, vol. xxix, Session 3 Feb.–12 Aug. 1842, 'Colonies: West Indies: Trinidad', p. 80.

fertile land, fifty acres for pasture and fifty acres for enslaved people. The cost was £8,000 sterling, over twice that of a small estate in Jamaica in the same period.[47] With John Corrie, Lamont was initially part-owner of Cedar Grove and resident enslaved people.[48] The Trinidad Land Register suggests that Corrie's part share was transferred to Lamont on 23 November 1819, reputedly for £28,750.[49] There is no record of how Lamont managed to raise such remarkable start-up capital, but it is likely he borrowed from the Eccles to finance the half-share, which became profitable enough to purchase the other.

Although he was the son of a laird, John Lamont's illegitimacy meant there was no privileged start in life, in contrast to William Hardin Burnley's schooling at Harrow.[50] The vastly differing starts in life perhaps help to explain why Burnley became a noted public commentator on slavery in Trinidad, while the latter seems to have been silent, at least in print, on these issues. Nevertheless, in March 1825 Lamont testified before a Committee of Council in Trinidad appointed 'for the purpose of obtaining a more correct knowledge of the Negro Character'. While he was not a learned man, Lamont recounted a spectacular rise in the planting business: first as overseer, then as manager (or attorney) and eventually as a plantation owner in his own right. By 1825, Lamont was proprietor of two sugar estates: Cedar Grove and the 320-acre estate Canaan, which he purchased in 1821. He later speculated in land and purchased the 120-acre La Grenade for £13,000 in 1829.[51] Lamont worked simultaneously as an attorney on sugar plantations, including Otaheite, located in Oropouche, southern Trinidad, which he managed for the Eccles firm.[52]

[47] Williams, *People of Trinidad and Tobago*, p. 74; R. Sheridan, *Sugar and Slavery: An Economic History of the British West Indies, 1623–1775* (Kingston, 1994 ed.), pp. 265; TNS CO 295/2, 'Colonial office and predecessors: Trinidad original correspondence', fos. 221–2.

[48] TNA, T71/501, 'Slave Registers, Trinidad: Plantation slaves', 1813, fo. 21. This data has been sourced from digitized slave registers on the Ancestry.com website: *Slave Registers of former British Colonial Dependencies, 1813–1834* [online database]. The original data is sourced from the National Archives of the UK, T71. As the digitized sources provide original references, this format will be adopted in all subsequent notes. In 1813, John Lamont was described as a 'part owner' of Cedar Grove sugar estate in South Naparima with John Corrie. Cedar Grove was known as Palmiste by 1938. See Hector McKechnie, *The Lamont Clan 1235–1935: Seven Centuries of Clan History from Record Evidence* (Edinburgh, 1938), p. 447.

[49] Lamont, *Inventory of the Lamont Papers*, pp. 4, 39; Lamont, 'Life of a West India planter', p. 16.

[50] Cudjoe, *The Slave Master of Trinidad*, p. 6.

[51] HCPP 1826–7 (479) *Trinidad Negroes. Return to an Address of the Honourable House of Commons, dated 12th June 1827*, pp. 44–7; Lamont, 'Life of a West India planter', p. 19.

[52] NA, T71/515, Slave Registration 1828, fo. 2024.

By 1825, Lamont was an experienced planter who had worked on sugar plantations for over twenty years. His testimony to the Committee of Council illustrates his prejudices towards enslaved people and his personal experiences of plantation management and general agricultural practices in Trinidad.[53] In terms of plantation management, Lamont operated a sugar monoculture system on his estates simply because 'no crops…pay so well as sugar, even in these times'. He employed Scots on his plantations, although not always in a mutually agreeable manner. As discussed below, the ill-fated Robert Stirling was appointed as an attorney on one of Lamont's smaller estates but left his employment 'inconsequence of the bad behaviour of that personage'.[54] He also employed free labourers such as peons – unfree labourers whom he described as 'very expert axemen' – to cut trees and clear land. Lamont divided his gangs of field-slaves into three classes which apportioned labour to the strength of individuals. He implemented a task system for fieldwork on his plantation, a practice typical of Trinidad, Demerara-Essequibo and Berbice in the 1820s and 1830s. According to Lamont, the task system meant the work was finished sooner as it afforded the 'industrious part of the gang more time to themselves', although it required more supervision than the alternative gang-work, as there was a natural tendency 'to hurry over the work as quickly as possible'. He also deployed gangs of enslaved people to cut sugar canes during harvest. The enslaved people's careful work ensured a second growth of canes after the first harvest, a process known as ratooning. In his testimony, he stated it was 'most advantageous' for a sugar planter to operate two cattle mills and two small sets of sugar works on different parts of the estate. The cane was carried from the fields by mule to the mill to be processed. Ideally, in his view, a distillery should have adjoined one of the sugar works as it saved labour in the transportation of cane refuse and distilled cane juice. Lamont retained the cattle mill, a traditional method he viewed as more efficient and cost-effective than the steam engine, which had been introduced to Trinidad in 1804. The older method, however, was more labour-intensive for cattle, as well as for free and enslaved labourers.[55]

While John Lamont's obituary attributed his fortune to his 'care, perseverance, and intelligence, accompanied by the strictest integrity, and marked by honour', the wealth was, of course, based on the exploitation of enslaved people. The conditions suffered by Lamont's labour force can

---

[53] HCPP 1826–7 (479) *Trinidad Negroes*, pp. 44–7.

[54] UofGSPC, MS. Gen 1717/4/A/15/68, Robt. Stirling to Duncan Macfarlan, 22 June 1832.

[55] HCPP 1826–7 (479) *Trinidad Negroes*, pp. 44–7.

be delineated from the slave registers which were first taken six years after the British parliament abolished the slave trade. Lives of the enslaved, and subsequent changes such as births, deaths and manumissions, were systematically documented. Abolitionists hoped to prevent the illegal importation and ill-treatment of enslaved people, yet planters and their allies were able to circumnavigate the system to increase the enslaved labour force.[56] In 1813, John Lamont's Cedar Grove estate held twenty-four enslaved people, of whom fourteen were male and ten were female. The eldest on the plantation was thirty-two, the youngest four months. Five children under the age of ten were held on the plantation. Fourteen enslaved people were African born, while another ten were described as Creoles, mainly from Trinidad, with some born in Grenada, Barbados or Guadeloupe. The register listed the enslaved by household and the remainder by sex. One family of prominence was the Taylor family. Assante Taylor was described as a thirty-year-old African Moco, likely hailing from modern-day Nigeria, who lived with his daughter. Assante's role as driver was a high-status position. A recent study of enslaved drivers in the nearby British colony of Berbice described them as the 'life and soul of the estate' with responsibility to keep production going and discipline other enslaved people.[57] The other members of the enslaved workforce were categorized based on their skills and the tasks on the estate. Most of the resident enslaved people on Cedar Grove worked in the fields, the duties split between eight males and eight females. Three children aged between six and thirteen, including Assante Taylor's daughter, worked in the small weeding gang into which they would have been forced from around the age of four.[58]

The work was both physically demanding and arduous, starting at 6am and often lasting until 11pm. Mothers of toddlers and those nursing infants were offered a little respite, starting later in the morning. During crop time, a half-hour was allowed for breakfast and an hour for dinner. Daily labour varied across the lifecycle of the sugar cane, and Lamont's preference for the task system meant he typically assigned tasks each morning, cutting wood for fuel, draining and lining the land, holing and embanking, planting the canes, weeding and when ripe cutting the cane, then stripping. If women were assigned weeding tasks, then Basil Dean, a seventeen-year-old Creole born in Trinidad, would have been expected to weed up to 300 holes per day with a hoe. A healthy adult male, such as François Clark, a thirty-two-year-old African Ibo, would have been expected to dig up to 300 holes per day, or plant

---

[56] Brereton, *Modern Trinidad*, pp. 52–4.

[57] R. Browne, *Surviving Slavery in the British Caribbean* (Philadelphia, 2017), p. 72.

[58] TNA T71/501, 'Slave registers, Trinidad: plantation slaves', 1813, fos. 21–22.

400 canes per day, or fill four to five cart loads of sugar cane on a daily basis. During harvest, mills and boilers worked twenty-four hours a day. It would not have been unusual for John Harris, a twenty-five-year-old Barbados-born boiler, to work thirty-hour shifts during this time. In terms of provisions, the enslaved were provided with three-and-a-half pounds of saltfish per week, although the head slave, Assante Taylor, received double. The task system supposedly offered some flexibility for those who had finished their tasks to undertake work on their own provision grounds. The provided clothing seems to have been wholly insufficient for arduous labour in such a climate. Males were provided with two shirts and trousers, a cloth jacket, a hat or cap and one blanket every two years. Females were provided with an Osnaburg petticoat, two shirts, a Kilmarnock cap and a blanket in the same period.[59]

Life was treacherous for the enslaved residents of Trinidad's plantations, and especially for those born on British-owned small sugar estates like John Lamont's Cedar Grove. In 1800, the British replaced the Spanish *Code Noir*, which had governed the lives of Trinidad's enslaved since 1798, with a slave code that led to a sharp deterioration of their conditions. Based on data from over 17,000 enslaved people in the 1813 and 1816 slave registries, historian J. A. Meredith estimated that the average life expectancy for an enslaved person born in Trinidad and working in a plantation in 1813 was seventeen years. The high incidence of disease and harsh working regimes in a colony under cultivation with limited labour led to a remarkably short life expectancy. One-third of the children born into plantation slavery in Trinidad died before their first birthday. Fewer than half reached the age of five, and few new-borns lived to be adults. Enslaved people working on smaller sugar estates with fewer than 200 enslaved people had a decreased chance of survival compared to those working on coffee plantations. The nationality of proprietors was a significant factor in deciding mortality rates of African male slaves. The (Catholic) French and Spanish planters treated enslaved people more humanely than the (Protestant) English and Scottish, who regarded enslaved people as chattel property, with cataclysmic results.[60] With good reason, the plight of Trinidad's plantation slaves has been described as possibly the 'most dismal known for any reliably reported population, save in time of natural disaster', although death rates of the

---

[59] Data from TNA T71/501, 'Slave registers, Trinidad: plantation slaves', 1813, fos. 21–22 has been complemented with information from N. Titus, *Amelioration and Abolition of Slavery in Trinidad, 1812–1834: Experiments and Protests in a New Slave Colony* (Indiana, 2009), pp. 143–4; and J. A. Meredith, 'Plantation slave mortality in Trinidad', *Population Studies*, xlii (1988), 161–82.

[60] Meredith, 'Plantation slave mortality in Trinidad', pp. 161–82.

enslaved in Jamaica and Grenada were not far behind.[61] This perpetual cycle of labour and death contributed to British economic development.

Fragmentary sources, albeit through second-hand accounts, provide the enslaved with a voice. The history of Maria Jones offers a rare perspective of the life and experience of an enslaved woman in Africa and the West Indies.[62] Maria was forcibly trafficked from Africa to St Vincent in the West Indies at the age of seven, before she was sold to a planter in Trinidad. She was subsequently put to work on Palmiste estate in South Naparima, which was supervised by a Scots attorney. According to Brinsley Samaroo, the attorney was none other than John Lamont, and evidence from slave registers seems to support this claim.[63] The register of slaves for John Lamont's Cedar Grove estate in 1813 lists a thirty-year-old African-born enslaved woman from the Gold Coast named Mary Jones, a labourer on the plantation with her infant son Robert, aged three, born in Trinidad. It is possible this was the same Maria Jones.[64] Maria recounted how this 'young Scotchman' was 'just commencing his career as a planter', having risen 'from the humblest beginning…to possess several valuable sugar plantations'. This attorney saw in Maria a 'noble independence of character not often found in oppressed slaves', and she felt he 'was not very cruel'. However, she contrasted her position in life with that of Lamont's: 'I am more rich than he for a' dat; he, poor, blind buckra sinner, while Father make me rich for ever'.[65]. Around 1816, Lamont was accused of 'violating the person of a young enslaved girl' on the Diamond estate. Thus, we catch a rare glimpse of the Scots planter's character: supposedly compassionate to one enslaved woman, the rapist of another. Although 'the evidence of a medical man proved the injury', the public authorities 'took no notice' of Lamont, who was by then deputy commandant of South Naparima.[66] After a complaint by the free people of colour on Trinidad, the governor Ralph J. Woodward refused to believe the 'contradictory statements' of the enslaved woman and exonerated Lamont, describing the episode as

[61] J. A. Meredith, *The Plantation Slaves of Trinidad, 1783–1816: A Mathematical and Demographic Enquiry* (Cambridge, 1988), p. xv; B. W. Higman, *Slave Populations of the British Caribbean, 1807–1834* (Baltimore, 1984), pp. 308–10.

[62] J. Law, *Maria Jones, Her History in Africa and in the West Indies* (Trinidad, 1851).

[63] B. Samaroo, 'Maria Jones of Africa, St. Vincent, and Trinidad', in *Gendering the African Diaspora: Women, Culture, and Historical Change in the Caribbean and Nigerian Hinterland*, ed. J. A. Byfield, L. Denzer and A. Morrison (Bloomington, 2010), p. 134.

[64] TNA, T71/501, Slave Registration, 1813, p. 21.

[65] Law, *Maria Jones, Her History*, p. 1.

[66] A Free Mulatto, *An Address to the Right Hon. Earl Bathurst, His Majesty's Principal Secretary of State for the Colonies Relative to the Claims which the Coloured Population of Trinidad* (London, 1824), p. 97.

a most 'improbable tale'.[67] As governor, Woodford implemented notorious policies that discriminated against Trinidad's free coloured population. However, Dr Jean Baptiste Philippe, son of a free coloured sugar planter in the Naparimas educated at the University of Edinburgh, later addressed the secretary of state for the colonies, Lord Bathurst, under the pseudonym 'a free mulatto'.[68] Philippe's searing critique perceptively described how 'every species of criminality is lost in the blaze and glare of whiteness', although there were reputational consequences for Lamont. His peers refused to serve with him in the local militia due to his crime, and he subsequently challenged one of the 'men in buckram suits' to a duel for supposedly slighting his honour.[69] In a public endorsement of British imperial rule, or perhaps as a simple thanks for disregarding due process, John Lamont provided the third largest donation in Trinidad to the subscription campaign to erect a monument to Governor Woodford after his death in 1828.[70] Trinidadian society was not one that was generally sympathetic to enslaved women's claims of physical and sexual abuse.[71]

By 1825, John Lamont was one of the most prominent planters on the island. When Dr James McTear arrived in the south-east Caribbean that year, he spent some time in Trinidad before his relocation to Tobago. In Port of Spain, McTear dined with Lamont, describing him as the 'upper class of company' on the island.[72] Lamont's success was based upon a strategy of acquiring enslaved people in the 1820s. This was set against the backdrop of legislation that prohibited the import of enslaved people from neighbouring colonies to Trinidad, exemplified by an 1824 act which became effective the next year.[73] In 1822, Lamont owned ten personal slaves (eight male, two female) not attached to any of his estates. He purchased them in Trinidad or imported from nearby islands such as Grenada.[74] The increase of his 'personal slaves, being his property' to ninety-one in the triennial return of 1825 suggests that he had embarked on a slave acquisition

---

[67] TNA, CO 295/63, Colonial Office Dispatches: Aug.–Dec. 1824, fos. 52–53.

[68] For an account of the free-coloured community of Trinidad and civil rights, see Brereton, *A History of Modern Trinidad*, pp. 63–9.

[69] A Free Mulatto, *An Address*, pp. 97–8, p. 101.

[70] *Port of Spain Gazette*, 22 July 1829, p. 2.

[71] J. Epstein, *Scandal of Colonial Rule: Power and Subversion in the British Atlantic during the Age of Revolution* (Cambridge, 2012).

[72] LOC, MS. 20353, James McTear, 'Journal of a voyage to & residence in Tobago, 1825–6', p. 40, p. 44, p. 53.

[73] Brereton, *A History of Modern Trinidad*, pp. 56–7.

[74] TNA, T71/501, fos. 2039–2040, Slave Registration, 1822.

policy in the preceding three years. Abuse of the inter-colonial slave trade offered one route for planters to increase their workforce; visitors from other islands arrived with 'domestic slaves' who were quickly sold into plantation slavery.[75] It is unclear what proportion of Trinidad's enslaved population Lamont owned in the mid-1820s, but it must have been substantial. For comparison, there were 23,230 enslaved people on Trinidad in 1825, of which 16,927 were on plantations. South Naparima held 1,319 plantation slaves, the highest concentration on Trinidad (approx. 8 per cent of island's total).[76] After abolition, John Lamont collected around £17,000 for almost 400 enslaved people.[77] This compares to William Hardin Burnley, the largest slave-owner on the island, who owned over 900 enslaved.[78] The average enslaver in Trinidad owned seven enslaved people in 1834, while only 1 per cent owned more than one hundred.[79] Lamont was therefore one of the most significant enslavers on Trinidad, perhaps second only to W. H. Burnley. Both were to remain on the island as residents post-Emancipation.

In 1841, John Lamont wrote to his half-brother Alexander, the laird of Knockdow in Argyll, Scotland:

> I think of making a short visit [to Scotland]…and returning [early to Trinidad], to endeavour to stem the downward tendency of things here. I find my absence very prejudicial, and that I am looked on as an absentee by all parties, from the Governor to the humblest labourer who works for us. This won't do, and I must act again as an every-day planter.[80]

Yet in late 1848 Lamont made plans to purchase the Highland estate of Benmore, near Dunoon, set in over 3,000 imperial acres of arable and grazing land.[81] The purchase for £13,000 was finally completed in January 1849, and although the existing house was said to be in good repair, Lamont began construction of a new mansion that befitted his wealth and status.[82] Despite

[75] TNA, Slave Registration, 1825, T71/512, 2220–3; Brereton, *A History of Modern Trinidad*, pp. 52–63.

[76] TNA, CO295/71, Trinidad Dispatches, 1826, fo. 260.

[77] 'John Lamont', *Legacies of British Slaveownership website* <https://www.ucl.ac.uk/lbs/person/view/28141> [accessed 24 Nov. 2015].

[78] 'William Hardin Burnley', *Legacies of British Slave-ownership* database <http://wwwdepts-live.ucl.ac.uk/lbs/person/view/28815> [accessed 13 July 2020].

[79] Brereton, *A History of Modern Trinidad*, p. 55.

[80] *Cases Decided in the Court of Session, Teind Court, Court of Exchequer and House of Lords*, vol. xix, 1856–57 (Edinburgh, 1857), pp. 779–85.

[81] 'Highland estate for sale', *GH*, 25 Sept. 1848, p. 3.

[82] *Cases Decided in the Court of Session*, p. 784.

the purchase, Lamont revealed he had no intention of retirement in Scotland, writing that 'you will never make me a Scotch laird' and it was instead bequeathed to a nephew.[83] The almost sixty-year-old Highland migrant had no desire to become an absentee in Scotland. Lamont's correspondence reveals he was unusual in one other important way: unlike many other Scots in Jamaica and Grenada, he chose to remain as a resident planter after he acquired a fortune. He died on the island in 1850, and while typical of British settlers in Trinidad, he was an exception to the sojourning mentality said to be a defining feature of the Scots *mentalité* in the West Indies.

John Lamont remained on Trinidad post-emancipation and managed the transition by importing indentured labourers to work on his estates. With his friend William Hardin Burnley, an active promoter of immigrant labour, he imported African labourers from Sierra Leone, which had been established as a British settlement for free black people and former enslaved people in 1787. In a letter to his brother in 1841, Lamont described these African labourers as 'the most valuable lot of immigrants…yet received'. After 1845, Lamont also took advantage of 'coolie' labour imported from India. In November that year, he described his workers on Cedar Grove estates as 'steady', although he was unimpressed with such labour in general as they wandered about 'neglecting their work'.[84] Thus, the Lamont fortune that arrived in Scotland, as discussed below, was built on successive eras of exploitation of labour from across the globe: African, Creole and Indian. Other Scots operated in Trinidad, including workers on elite planter John Lamont's estates, but were unable to exploit the island's resources and people in quite the same manner.

Robert Stirling: from Old College to Naparima

Robert McGregor Stirling was of a middling background. He was the son of William McGregor Stirling, a minister in Port of Menteith, and nephew of Duncan Macfarlan, the principal of Old College (now the University of Glasgow) from 1823 until 1857. Robert enjoyed a good education at Old College, taking an MA in 1820 and afterwards studying theology in 1823–4.[85] After a period of idleness, a military career was suggested, or a position as a clerk in Register House in Edinburgh. But 'conscious of

---

[83] McKechnie, *The Lamont Clan 1235–1935*, p. 441.

[84] Lamont, 'Life of a West India planter', p. 22, p. 26; Cudjoe, 'Burnley, William Hardin (1780–1850)', *ODNB*.

[85] W. I. Addison, *The Matriculation Albums of the University of Glasgow, From 1728 to 1858* (Glasgow, 1913), p. 281.

being a deadweight', he decided that his future lay in the West Indies.[86] Through family, he had impeccable connections. In late 1828, word arrived from General David Stewart of Garth, a Scottish military commander and governor of St Lucia, that he had secured Robert a position in St Lucia.[87] Stirling departed soon after in January 1829.[88]

By early 1830, Robert McGregor Stirling was in Trinidad under the patronage of General Stewart's brother, John Stewart, who owned Garth estate in Savanna Grande in the south-west of the island. Indeed, he provided Stirling with 'the greatest attention' and an assurance he would better his circumstances.[89] Unfortunately for Stirling, John Stewart died on 28 March 1830.[90] Lacking kinship connections to open the door with the resident Scottish plantocracy, Stirling afterwards worked on several estates in what became an increasingly desperate quest for advancement on the island. First, Stirling was recommended as an overseer to a Mr Bell of Camden estate in Couva, which was owned by Alexander Fraser of Inchcoulter in Rosshire. Stirling hoped 'to be comfortable, learn wonders and get promoted', although he left within three months, due to Bell's 'impertinence'. Within two days of leaving Camden, Stirling was recommended to Archibald Colquhoun, and although he felt he was ready to manage an estate, he accepted an overseer's position on Vista Bella estate in North Naparima, formerly the property of Alexander MacMillan.[91]

In October 1830, Vista Bella was sold to French owners and Stirling was unemployed. Although his health was good, having recovered from serious illness, former employers delayed paying wages, which obviously exacerbated his financial troubles. He lived with another Scot, Daniel McAlpine, and travelled around Trinidad chasing payment. Waiting desperately on £10 from the owners of Vista Bella, Stirling resided in a tavern, in the process incurring costs equal to two-thirds of the wages. He bemoaned his lot as a struggling overseer:

> Had Garth been alive this would not have been but such a miserably poor place. You can form little conception of and before accepting of a situation:

---

[86] UofGSPC, MS. Gen 1717/4/A/15/63, Letter from Robt. M. Stirling, 26 Oct. 1826.

[87] UofGSPC, MS. Gen 1717/4/A/15/50, Letter from William MacGregor Stirling, 28 Nov. 1828.

[88] UofGSPC, MS. Gen 1717/4/A/15/52, Letter from William MacGregor Stirling, 10 April 1829.

[89] UofGSPC, MS. Gen 1717/4/A/15/65, Letter from Robt. M. Stirling, 18 July 1830.

[90] *Blackwood's Edinburgh Magazine*, xxviii (Edinburgh, 1830), p. 571.

[91] UofGSPC, MS. Gen 1717/4/A/15/65, Letter from Robt. M. Stirling, 18 July 1830.

one in my place would do well to calculate whether years becoming a slave for his victuals or for any chance of getting a farthing.[92]

Diasporic networks were crucial but were dependent upon the personal recommendations that provided opportunities. After two months of unemployment, he begged his uncle in Glasgow, Duncan Macfarlan, to enquire if 'anything could be done for my advancement' by speaking to representatives of Eccles and Co., the prominent Glasgow merchant firm. Stirling was also strategic in his employment choices, refusing several offers while unemployed as they offered too few prospects of progression. It was at this stage that he considered departing for Demerara.[93]

On 10 January 1831, Stirling was appointed overseer on one of the three estates managed by Duncan McAlpine. In May that year, he was subsequently promoted to attorney of John Lamont's cattle pen (simply titled '25'). In charge of sickly mules and some enslaved people, he felt he had secured a position that offered 'prospects of advancement…feasible enough to prevent my immediate departure from the island'. In his mind, he weighed up his prospects on Trinidad against travelling to Demerara, where his brother Archibald was a medical doctor. As attorney for Lamont, Robert Stirling was on a generous wage of $500 Trinidad Dollars (c.£104 stg.) and some perquisites. After five failed overseer's positions on Trinidad, however, he was not keen on a similar trajectory in Demerara. While wages were smaller in Trinidad, Stirling decided to stay put, as he did not fancy a 'subordinate situation in Demerara with a much larger income'.[94]

As it turned out, Robert Stirling was under the employment of John Lamont for just six months. He left Lamont in January 1832 'inconsequence of the bad behaviour of that personage' and his prospects remained 'sufficiently gloomy' until the summer. There was little recruitment during the crop-season (generally January–June) and the few jobs on offer paid little or were deemed to be reputationally damaging. By June, just as vacancies were becoming available, Stirling was forced to borrow £30 from his father, which he notified his uncle of in case of 'sudden or unforeseen accidents'.[95] Sometime after the summer, Stirling was appointed attorney of Santa Margarita estate in North Naparima. However, his charge was to be short-lived. On 5 October 1832, after five days of a putrid fever, he died in the residence of Campbell Colquhoun,

[92] UofGSPC MS. Gen 1717/4/A/15/66, Letter from Robt. M. Stirling, 1 Jan. 1831.
[93] UofGSPC MS. Gen 1717/4/A/15/66, Letter from Robt. M. Stirling, 1 Jan. 1831.
[94] UofGSPC MS. Gen 1717/4/A/15/67, Letter from Robt. M. Stirling, 9 Aug. 1831.
[95] UofGSPC, MS. Gen 1717/4/A/15/68, Letter from Robt. M. Stirling, 22 June 1832.

although in 'very little pain and...sensible almost to the last'.[96] His father in Scotland took his son's death very badly and was said to be exhibiting symptoms of mental illness soon afterwards.[97]

The Stirling letters are unusual: they reveal the *mentalité* of a white Scottish overseer before and during his time in the West Indies, the impact of his stay in Trinidad upon his financial, physical and mental health, and on that of family in Scotland after his decease. This was a rare glimpse into the human condition during a failed economic sojourn to the British West Indies. Like many other Scots searching a fortune derived from slavery, Robert Stirling was highly mobile across the Atlantic world, travelling first to St Lucia, then Trinidad, and he afterwards considered Demerara. But Stirling was not a typical Scottish adventurer. As a privileged son of the manse, he enjoyed an excellent standard of education in Glasgow, and although highly literate, there is no indication he had the appropriate commercial skills suitable for work as a budding planter in the south-eastern Caribbean. He had impeccable connections in Glasgow and the West Indies, enjoying the patronage of David Stewart, governor of St Lucia, although the death of John Stewart of Garth left him somewhat isolated. His increasingly desperate correspondence reveals the mindset of a troubled young man worried about failure in life: settling on a lowly overseer's position in the West Indies but always imagining he was worth more. Even in the abolition era, this well-connected alumnus of Old College seemed to have no issues about the immorality of work in slavery economies.

Stirling operated within a tight group of Scots on Trinidad, and while he was not short of offers, the smaller community of planters did not provide well-remunerated positions. He benefited from access to jobs, but these positions did not confer automatic economic advancement and diasporic networks did not always generate positive outcomes. Overseers clearly lived on the edge in the Trinidad of the 1830s, dependent on the appropriate seasonal employment becoming available and employers paying wages on time. Stirling seemed happiest when in charge of John Lamont's small cattle pen with enslaved people, but had issues with authority, twice removing himself from employment, allegedly because of the behaviour of others, which left him in near poverty. This example underlines that acquiring a fortune in the West Indies was far from certain. With his privileged start in life, Stirling had more chances than most. But he was very typical in one important way: after seven positions in less than two years on Trinidad,

[96] UofGSPC MS. Gen 1717/4/A/15/53, Letter from William MacGregor Stirling, 14 Dec. 1832.

[97] UofGSPC MS. Gen 1717/4/A/12/11, Letter from George C. Scott, 5 Jan. 1833.

and indebted to his father for £30, his story ended with premature death via disease aged just thirty. After 1775, most Scots in the West Indies met their end in a similar fashion: penniless and dying among near strangers in slavery societies that were increasingly viewed by many in British society as evil anachronisms.

Scots and their Trinidad fortunes

In 1838, the *Trinidad Standard* newspaper surveyed the success of adventurers in the West Indies, painting a gloomy picture of penniless Scots dying abroad with no prospects of a return:

> The fate of the English or Scotch agricultural adventurer, emigrating to distant shores…in a strange and distant land, has to struggle with a climate different from his own, and a mode of agriculture to which he is a stranger – and separated by thousands of miles from the land he emigrated from, if he fails as alas! Too many have done, altho' prudent and industrious he has only to lay down and die [as] return to his native home is impossible.[98]

Although this commentary was part of a wider effort to attract free black labour in the post-emancipation period by suggesting their conditions would be better than they were for white workers, this chapter queries this claim by surveying the fortunes and trajectories of Scots fortunes on the island. This is undertaken by examining the inventories of a group of twenty Scots known to have been in Trinidad between 1800 and 1838 with inventoried property in Scotland. Although this is a small group, some of the findings are startling when compared to other islands.

Major slavery fortunes were rare on Trinidad and were mainly restricted to planters. Planting was the most popular occupation for this group of Scots, followed by the mercantile line.[99] Overall, the average fortunes (£6,481) were on a par with those in Jamaica and Grenada, although the Lamont planting wealth (see below) skews these conclusions. Of the overall wealth of £129,639, around 80 per cent was held by elite sibling planters, John and Boyden Lamont (see Table 7.1 and Table 7.2). If these two fortunes were removed, the average falls to £1,472 per person. Overall, however, planters were the wealthiest, on average, with £17,103 per person, followed by a surgeon (£1,752), a physician (£1,230), merchants (average of £744), an attorney (£705) and a millwright (£32). Some were able to accumulate modest capital, although not sums that would have made them

---

[98] *The Trinidad Standard and West India Journal*, lxxxiv, 9 Oct. 1838.

[99] Known occupations (16) confirm they varied across Trinidad. Planters (7), merchants (5), physician/surgeon (2), millwright (1), attorney (1) were identified.

Table 7.1 Wealth on death of Scots in Trinidad in the late
slavery era (1797–1838) who died between 1799 and 1850.

Home Scottish region	Inventories	%Total inventories	Wealth	%Total wealth
Borders	0	0.0%	£0	0.0%
Western Lowlands	8	40.0%	£9,578	7.4%
Eastern Lowlands	3	15.0%	£11,696	9.0%
Highlands-Hebrides	3	15.0%	£103,834	80.1%
North-east	0	0.0%	£0	0.0%
Far north	1	5.0%	£391	0.3%
Unknown	5	25.0%	£4,140	3.2%
Total	20		£129,639	

Source: National Records of Scotland: Wills, Testaments
and Confirmation Inventories (see Bibliography).

Table 7.2 Range of wealth on death of Scots in Trinidad in the late
slavery era (1797–1838) who died between 1799 and 1850.

Decile	Range	Inventories	Average	%Total wealth
Top	£100,000–150,000	0	N/A	N/A
Second	£75,000–£99,999	1	£76,291	58.8%
Third	£50,000–£74,999	0	N/A	N/A
Fourth	£25,000–£49,999	1	£26,838	20.7%
Fifth	£10,000–£24,999	1	£10,293	7.9%
Sixth	£7,500–£9,999	0	N/A	N/A
Seventh	£5,000–£7,499	0	N/A	N/A
Eight	£2,500–£4,999	2	£2,931	4.5%
Ninth	£500–£2,499	7	£1,296	7.0%
Tenth	£20–£499	8	£160	1.0%
Total		20		

Source: National Records of Scotland: Wills, Testaments
and Confirmation inventories (see Bibliography).

independently wealthy. Dougald Dawson, attorney of Jordanhill estate (owned by William Smith, son of Archibald Smith senior, as described in Chapter 3) was worth over £700 in 1841. Having lodged over 95 per cent of his earnings with the Glasgow firm Smith & Browns, he died on the way home to Scotland.[100] Thus, planters represented the real financial power on Trinidad, at least among propertied Scots on the island, in contrast to Jamaica and Grenada, where merchants reigned supreme.

Trinidad, moreover, was not a sojourning island for Scots in the manner of Jamaica and Grenada. Based on the compensation awards at the emancipation of slavery in 1834, Nicholas Draper has noted the percentage of absentee claimants was lower in Trinidad than it was in other British West India colonies, particularly British Guiana and Jamaica, in 1834. In other words, planters were more likely to remain residents on Trinidad than they were elsewhere.[101] Places of death of inventoried Scots underline that this was not just restricted to enslavers. Around two-thirds of this group of Scots died in Trinidad (65 per cent),[102] compared to the proportions of the same groups who died in Jamaica (46 per cent) and the Scots who died on Grenada (36 per cent). Remarkably, Scots with assets in Scotland were almost twice as likely to die in Trinidad compared to nearby Grenada. The explanation is three-fold; first, it took more time and capital to establish as planters in Trinidad, especially with the shortage of enslaved labour. Second, the Scottish community was not as well-established on Trinidad, which meant fewer supervisory and managerial positions on the island. Third, the wage levels for these positions in Trinidad seem to have been lesser than, for example, Demerara. In short, the common trajectory for Scots to progress from overseer, to attorney, to planter was disrupted in Trinidad, and they had to remain longer hoping to develop large planting fortunes. A select few, like John Lamont, enjoyed the status afforded to white planters in the island's nefarious slavery society.

This era was reminiscent of the earlier settler-colonization period in the first-phase colonies of the British West Indies, albeit with lower profits, which had implications for wealth repatriation strategies. Except from the Lamonts' major planting fortunes (see below), the wealth tended to be held in merchant firms in Trinidad with branches in Scotland (five holdings worth a total of £5,585). One merchant, John Campbell, a partner in Glasgow firm Campbell Rivers & Co., had £2,000 held in the merchant house on

[100] NRS, SC70/1/62, Inventory of Dougald Dawson, 24 Aug. 1842, pp. 675–6.

[101] N. Draper, 'The rise of a new planter class? Some countercurrents from British Guiana and Trinidad, 1807–33', *Atlantic Studies*, ix (2012), 65–83, at p. 70.

[102] Places of death: Trinidad (13), Scotland (6) and unknown (1).

his death in Trinidad in 1817.[103] The holdings in Scottish banks tended to be small-scale and below £500. George Mackay, a planter of Savanna Grande, died on 3 September 1837 with just over £300 in the British Linen Bank.[104] There was no identifiable large-scale transfer of slavery wealth from Trinidad into the Scottish countryside. Although John Munro owned urban property in Edinburgh, and James Coulter Graham and Alexander Duncanson in Glasgow, John Lamont is the only known Scot in Trinidad to purchase a landed estate.[105] And, as will be explained below, John Lamont was the solitary owner of a country estate, yet never intended to return home. There were no identified investments in industry in Scotland. And, although last testaments do not exist for all of this group, it seems few had philanthropic concerns in mind. John Campbell did bequeath £50 to the poor of Port Glasgow.[106] Why should Trinidad Scots invest in their homeland if they had no intention to return, at least not in the short term?, Scots tended to stick around longer in Trinidad compared to other islands, hoping to acquire enough wealth to lodge in Scottish merchant firms and banks. Those with modest property in Scotland were more likely to remain on the island rather than return home. This model, however, fails to explain why two individuals did not depart for Scotland, despite possessing huge fortunes that should have allowed them to live in style there.

Repatriating planting wealth

Examining the Lamont planting fortunes in comparative context is important for two reasons. First, the fortunes of the brothers represented 80 per cent of the total wealth in this group of Scots in Trinidad. Second, the brothers were long-term residents on Trinidad, in contrast to the sojourning lifestyle favoured by many Scots across the West Indies. As noted above, this was not unusual for Scots in Trinidad, although it is unknown how many considered themselves permanent like John Lamont. It can only be presumed that the illegitimate son enjoyed the lifestyle, social rank and status in Trinidad more than he did in Scotland. The case of Boyden Lamont's residence is harder to explain, since he could have returned and lived an independent lifestyle in Scotland. Perhaps he did not consider the

---

[103] NRS, CC8/8/145 and NRS, SC70/1/19, Inventory of John Campbell, 14 June 1819 and 25 June 1819.

[104] NRS, SC70/1/57, Inventory of George Mackay, 21 Aug. 1838.

[105] NRS, SC36/48/24, Inventory of Alexander Duncanson, 10 June 1834; NRS, SC70/1/47, Inventory of John Munro, 15 Nov. 1832; NRS, SC36/48/29, Inventory of James Coulter Graham, 17 Feb. 1842.

[106] NRS, SC70/1/19, Inventory of John Campbell, 14 June 1819, p. 395.

fortune to be enough. Crucially, even for those who were long-term and even permanent residents of Trinidad, the importance of kinship ties meant the slavery fortunes returned to Scotland. This section, therefore, offers fresh insights into elite strategies of wealth repatriation during the era of decline among the sugar islands.

John Lamont, as noted above, was an illegitimate son of the Lamonts of Knockdow. This gentry family took notice of his planting success, reaching out after fourteen years, and he subsequently promoted their interests on Trinidad. In 1816, John Lamont offered to provide his sibling born legitimately in the family, Boyden Lamont, with a start in the process, revealing the privileged route enjoyed by Scots with the appropriate connections on the island:

> If [our brother] Boyden is inclined to try his fortune here, I can be of service to him by placing him in one of the most respectable [merchant] houses here, and where I could obtain for him a share of an extensive and lucrative concern after twelve months, which is necessary to understand things here.[107]

Boyden Lamont travelled to Trinidad around 1817, and rather than choosing the mercantile route he took up planting. His brother John purchased the 320-acre Canaan estate on 1821 and, no doubt after his younger brother had completed an apprenticeship, transferred legal ownership to Boyden on 1 March 1823.[108] Boyden Lamont also collected compensation, but his planting career was cut short. On 21 March 1836, he was awarded almost £4,000 for seventy-eight enslaved people on Canaan estate, although he died soon afterwards in August 1837 on Trinidad.[109] Boyden Lamont's last will – lodged in Scotland – reveals a sophisticated risk management strategy implemented by elite Scots in the Caribbean, while his confirmation inventory outlines the extent and nature of his wealth.

The Lamont examples demonstrate how wealthy planters crossed the Atlantic in order to settle their affairs to ensure the smooth transition of property in Scotland. In late 1832, having been in Trinidad for around fifteen years, Boyden Lamont returned to Scotland to lodge his will in order to settle his affairs and 'to prevent misunderstandings' on the event of his decease. His will prioritized certain family members and allocated landed property and wealth. First, he ensured that the Canaan estate would be transferred back to John Lamont.

---

[107] Lamont, 'Life of a West India planter', p. 15.

[108] Lamont, *Inventory of the Lamont Papers*, p. 439; 'Life of a West India planter', p. 18.

[109] 'Boyden Lamont', *Legacies of British Slaveownership website* <https://www.ucl.ac.uk/lbs/person/view/28929> [accessed 24 Nov. 2015].

Second, as executors, he named his brothers John Lamont, Alexander Lamont, Writer to the Signet in Edinburgh, James Lamont of the Royal Navy, and George Cole (although the latter eventually refused the role). Executors in the colonies were notoriously dishonest, and by choosing executors from the direct family matrix based in Scotland and Trinidad, Boyden increased the chances of a smooth post-mortem transmission of property across the Atlantic.[110] John Lamont stood to inherit or dispose of his brother's colonial property, including land, enslaved people and ships. In Glasgow, Lamont's preferred West India merchant, George Cole, would disperse funds held in the merchant house. His other brother, Alexander Lamont, a prominent lawyer, would supervise all of this in Edinburgh. Thus, by lodging the will in Scotland (instead of dying intestate abroad) Boyden Lamont ensured the fortune and executors came under the jurisdiction of the Scottish legal system. As succession and legacy was governed by the 'law of the domicile', by settling his affairs in Scotland Boyden Lamont seemingly affirmed his status as a temporary economic migrant to the Caribbean (although his brother's case – which will be examined in turn – led to a legal challenge).[111] In practical terms, this meant court proceedings could be lodged in Scotland against executors (in the event of dishonesty, for example), and the crown was also entitled to legacy duty from the deceased's estate. Boyden Lamont left a personal fortune of over £26,000 in Great Britain, including almost £20,000 in the Ship Bank of Glasgow.[112] As sugar planting had been his principal source of income since 1817, this allows a tentative estimate of the level of profits acquired by an elite Scottish planter in twenty years in the plantation economy of Trinidad: it was possible to accumulate c.£1,000 per annum from sugar planting and compensation. John Lamont's fortune was much greater.

In life, John Lamont made 'constant and large remittances' from Trinidad to agents in Glasgow, probably via bills of exchange to be lodged in the Western and Union Banks in Scotland.[113] This practice contrasted with methods employed by Scots in the East Indies, who remitted capital via the London-based English East India Company and through the exportation of valuables such as jewels to Scotland.[114] Thus, banks in Glasgow were

---

[110] NRS, SC70/1/57, Inventory of Boyden Lamont, 12 Oct. 1838, pp. 294–7.

[111] J. McLaren, *The Law of Scotland in Relation to Wills and Succession*, vol. i (Edinburgh, 1868), p. 73.

[112] NRS, SC70/1/57, Inventory of Boyden Lamont, 12 Oct. 1838, pp. 294–7.

[113] *Cases Decided in the Court of Session*, p. 781.

[114] G. McGilvary, 'Return of the Scottish nabob, 1725–1833', in *Back to Caledonia: Scottish Homecomings from the Seventeenth Century to the Present*, ed. M. Varricchio (Edinburgh, 2012), pp. 94–5.

recipients of large personal sums accrued from slavery, which could be used as interest-bearing capital in loans to manufacturers and merchants across the West of Scotland. Lamont prepared a post-mortem transmission strategy designed to bequeath and dispose of his heritable and moveable property on either side of the Atlantic. While in Glasgow on 10 October 1849, John Lamont had a will written up which appointed his brother Alexander Lamont, Writer to the Signet, his nephew James Lamont and the agent James Newton as trustees and executors in Scotland. He appointed Alexander Stewart and William Eccles in Trinidad.[115] These trustees also had special power:

> To appoint an attorney or attornies in the Island of Trinidad for realizing and managing such parts of my Estates and effects as may be situated in that island…to sue for uplift and receive the principal sums of the debts…[and] also to sell…any part of the said Estates and Effects and that by Private Sale or Public Auction or Bargain upon Advertisements and such way and manner as may appear to them most advantageous.[116]

Lamont evidently maintained a close relationship with Alexander Stewart and William Eccles in life, which meant he entrusted them to undertake the dispersal of his estate in Trinidad after his death. Despite his residence in Trinidad, the family retained his interests afterwards.

John Lamont died aged sixty-nine in his home at Casa de Diego Martin on 21 November 1850, thus fulfilling his wish to 'die in harness' in Trinidad.[117] He was buried next to his brother Boyden at Canaan estate, San Fernando. Although there is some debate about the true extent of his fortune, by all accounts it was substantial, and this is remembered in modern Trinidad.[118] In a recent work, Father Anthony de Verteuil memorably described Lamont as a 'billionaire bastard'.[119] Lamont's confirmation inventory on death suggests his moveable property (that is, his wealth less the value of land in Scotland and Trinidad) was worth just over £76,000.[120] This sum was on a par with moderate Glasgow-West India mercantile fortunes of the same period (see Chapter 8) and other great West India planting fortunes in this study, such as those of John Shand and William Rae in Jamaica. For

---

[115] NRS, SC70/4/14, Inventory of John Lamont, 5 May 1851, pp. 901–2.

[116] NRS, SC70/4/14, Inventory of John Lamont, 5 May 1851, pp. 896–7.

[117] *Cases Decided in the Court of Session*, pp. 781–4.

[118] McKechnie, *The Lamont Clan*, p. 441.

[119] A. de Verteuil, *The Black Earth of South Naparima* (Port of Spain, 2009), p. 159.

[120] NRS, SC70/1/72, Inventory of John Lamont, 5 May 1861, pp. 655–8

comparison, Lamont's £76,291 in 1850 is equivalent to £64m (relative to the worth of average earnings in 2020).[121]

While the extent of the fortune was exceptional, Lamont's personal holdings were also distinctive. His confirmation inventory of 1851 outlined most of the fortune (£71,000 or over 90 per cent) was held in bank accounts, Exchequer bills and shares in banks.[122] Unlike many Glaswegian merchants, he held no industrial investments in Scotland. In other words, Lamont had extricated vast profits solely from one source: the sugar plantations of Trinidad via his occupation, in his own words, as an every-day planter. Thus, while it is conceivable some of the fortune came from other sources, the majority came directly from the expropriation of enslaved labour.

Following John Lamont's death, the crown raised a court case against the executors of his estate, as they disputed that Lamont's permanent place of domicile was Trinidad, which had implications for the level of legacy duty to be paid. Succession duty was paid at the rate of 7 per cent to the Treasury of Trinidad, while the Imperial Exchequer could demand 10 per cent.[123] The resulting court case found in favour of the family and decided that Lamont had willingly cut ties with Scotland, not least because he was an 'illegitimate son [and] the domicile of origin was not marked by those family ties and associations which tend to give it so much weight and importance'.[124] The irony, then, is that the Lamonts of Knockdow – who likely shunned the eldest son born out of wedlock – received the bulk of the West India fortune as well as his landed estates in Scotland and the Caribbean, which allowed them to improve their own status at home. John Lamont's moveable and heritable property passed directly to family members. He had previously supported his mother's family in Argyll and after death bequeathed to relatives 'of the name of Clark…the sums for which they have credit on my Guarantee in the Western Bank'.[125] Thus, Caribbean wealth allowed a lower-order family to maintain an existence in the Highlands, although he prioritized his father's family and they received most of the fortune, particularly his brother Alexander and nephew James Lamont. Father and son were also named residuary legatees of John Lamont's fortune and inherited two-thirds of the fortune after all bequests and bills had been paid. The Caribbean's legacy to

---

[121] For modern values, see *Measuring Worth* <https://www.measuringworth.com/calculators/ukcompare/> [accessed 27 Oct. 2021]. Relative wage or income worth (average earnings, 2020 values) has been used here.

[122] NRS, SC70/1/72, Inventory of John Lamont, 5 May 1861, pp. 655–8.

[123] Lamont, 'Life of a West India Planter One Hundred Years Ago', p. 30.

[124] *Cases Decided in the Court of Session*, p. 790.

[125] NRS, SC70/4/14, Inventory of John Lamont, 5 May 1851, p. 895.

the Scottish Highlands did not end with emancipation in 1834. As late as 1861, sales of sugar, rum and molasses from the family estates in Trinidad attracted annual profits of almost £5,000, which passed to Alexander Lamont.[126]

The trajectory of both John and Boyden Lamont can be contrasted with Robert McGregor Stirling's experience on the island. After his arrival in 1802, John Lamont had some connection with the prominent Glasgow firm Robert, William & James Eccles and worked irregularly with them as an attorney. In turn, John Lamont integrated his brother Boyden into the plantation economy by providing capital and opportunities for experience. Boyden Lamont subsequently became part of the plantocracy when John Lamont transferred legal ownership of Canaan estate on 1 March 1823. By contrast, Robert Stirling was without capital or connections, instead relying on *ad hoc* opportunities with strangers within the Scottish diasporic community. The rise of the Lamont brothers can ultimately be measured in respective property-ownership and wealth levels, while the economic failure of Stirling is exemplified by the debts owed to his father at his time of death. The figures suggest that planters in Trinidad – in a period of perceived decline – were able to accumulate fortunes during a planting career commensurate with those made by elite adventurers and merchants in the metropolis in the same period. However, the Lamonts were especially unrepresentative of the sample identified here. Most Scots, if they survived at all, earned relatively meagre fortunes in thirty-seven years of British slavery in Trinidad. The early demise of the penniless Robert McGregor Stirling was more representative of the Scottish experience than was the prosperous lifestyle of John Lamont. Even so, the minority who did return wealth from the British West Indies had a significant impact on personal fortunes in Scotland.

The influx of West India fortunes to Scotland: a regional approach

This section summarizes the influx of West India fortunes to Scotland in a regional framework.[127] There are contrasting positions about the impact of

---

[126] Argyll and Bute Council Archives, DR8/8/8 Accounts and inventories of sugar from Trinidad, 1861–1920.

[127] The Scottish population, and counties from 1801, are developed from HCPP (1841) *Accounts of Population and Number of Houses According to Census, 1841, of Each County in Great Britain*, p. 6. The regions are as follows: the Western Lowlands are defined as Ayr, Dunbarton, Renfrew and Lanark; Eastern Lowlands: Clackmannan, Edinburgh, Fife, Forfar, Haddington, Kincardine, Kinross, Linlithgow, Perth and Stirling. North-east is Aberdeen, Banff, Elgin (Moray), Nairn. Highland-Hebrides is Argyll, Bute, Inverness, Orkney and Shetland, Ross and Cromarty and Sutherland. Borders are Berwick, Dumfries, Kirkcudbright, Peebles, Roxburgh, Selkirk, Wigtown. The far north is Caithness.

Scottish-West India fortunes. R. H. Campbell envisioned a 'few Scots' profiting from the colonial trades and sojourns. In this view, repatriated capital increased the influence of a few gentry families but did little for the wider economy, since the impact was confined to great estates.[128] On the other hand, Andrew Mackillop claimed Scots in the West Indies secured one of the greatest per capita returns and that slavery wealth 'percolated widely through Scottish society'.[129]

This study explores the fortunes of the 138 Scots known to be in the British West Indies between 1775 and 1838, identified through confirmation inventories in Scottish courts (hereafter known as 'Scottish inventories').[130] This group died between 1784 and 1858; for all intents and purposes this was a nineteenth-century cohort, with the vast majority of wealth inventoried post-1800. These legal sources provide information about wealth at the end of life. Scots in the West Indies also made investments throughout their lifetimes, a figure that cannot be gauged from Scottish inventories. And many did not leave wills and testaments at all, making any estimation of how they transmitted such wealth in death more difficult. However, some conclusions can be reached. First, this group left property valued at £1.044m in Scotland on death, an average of £7,569 per person (see Table 7.3). Second, this means that Scots-West India fortunes were worth less than half of the wealth held by Scottish returnees from the East Indies. Andrew Mackillop's most recent work confirms the highest per capita returns were, in fact, made by Scots in the East Indies.[131] Third, compared to modern equivalents, however, the influx of Scottish-West India fortunes was enormous over a half-century. The average of £7,569 in 1821 – a mid-point of all dates of death – is equivalent to £6.76m (relative to the worth of average earnings in 2020).[132] The £1.044m repatriated to Scotland between

---

[128] R. H. Campbell, *Scotland Since 1707: The Rise of an Industrial Society*, 2nd ed. (Edinburgh, 1992 ed.), pp. 39–43.

[129] A. Mackillop, '"As hewers of wood, and drawers of water": Scotland as an emigrant nation, *c.*1600 to *c.*1800', in *Global Migrations: The Scottish Diaspora since 1600*, ed. A. McCarthy and J. M. MacKenzie (Edinburgh, 2016), p. 36.

[130] Confirmation inventories in the National Records of Scotland (NRS) were identified via *Scotland's People* website via searches of 'Jamaica', 'Grenada' and 'Trinidad' as key words. Individuals with property over £20 were included in the sample. There were 90 Scottish inventories associated with Scots in Jamaica, 28 associated with Grenada and 20 associated with Trinidad.

[131] A. Mackillop identified 347 East India fortunes in Scotland between 1730 and 1820 (total of £5,567,521, average £16,044). See *Human Capital and Empire: Scotland, Ireland, Wales and British Imperialism in Asia, c.1690–c.1820* (Manchester, 2021), p. 231. I am grateful to Dr Mackillop for sharing data in advance of publication.

[132] For modern values, see *Measuring Worth* <https://www.measuringworth.com/calculators/ukcompare/> [accessed 27 Oct. 2021]. Relative wage or income worth (average

1784 and 1858 is equivalent to £894.93m in modern values (relative to the worth of average earnings in 2020).[133] As Scotland rapidly industrialized, Scots in the West Indies repatriated the equivalent of hundreds of millions of pounds homewards, especially in the 1820s and 1830s.

But there was great inequality in the wealth holding. As Table 7.4 shows, just two individuals acquired the nationally significant fortune of £100,000. And just four individuals (c.3 per cent of sample) held £410,425 (c.40 per cent of the assets). Only twenty-three people left estates worth £10,000 and over, a figure generally regarded as allowing an independent, elite lifestyle in Scotland. Thus, in the British West Indies after 1780, nationally significant fortunes were a rarity. Moreover, although there were remarkably high levels of absenteeism among this group (47 per cent), the reality is that for even successful Scots in the West Indies, the majority died there.[134] The dream of many young men returning to Scotland to live out their days in salubrious estates purchased with West India fortunes remained just that.

Scottish-West India fortunes tended to be held in merchant firms, banks, shares and government consols.[135] The large sums provided merchant firms with large sums to loan to other planters, while the monies in Scottish banks added an external injection of capital to a system that was the most developed in Europe in 1772. The banks helped satisfy the demands of industrialization.[136] At first glance, the sojourning mindset seems to have had a profound influence on Scottish economic development, especially agriculture.[137] Indeed, T. M. Devine suggested returned West India capital was a 'prime source' for Scotland's eighteenth-century agricultural improvement.[138] While this study here relates

---

earnings, 2020 values) has been used here.

[133] See *Measuring Worth* <https://www.measuringworth.com/calculators/ukcompare/> [accessed 27 Oct. 2021]. For estimates of modern equivalent value, each of the 138 inventoried totals was entered into *Measuring Worth* alongside year of death. The total provided an estimate of the relative worth of all inventories in modern values. The relative wage or income worth (average earnings, 2020 values) is used here. In modern values, Jamaica adventurers left the most (£608m stg.), followed by Grenada (£175m) and Trinidad (£110m). In terms of levels of wealth inventoried by decade, 1780s (£2.86m); 1790s (£2.2m); 1800s (£31.9m); 1810s (£141.9m); 1820s (£270.9m); 1830s (£205.9m); 1840s (£24.9m); 1850s (£214.1m).

[134] Of this group of 138 Scots, 67 died in the West Indies, 60 in Scotland, 5 in England, 3 at sea and 3 unknown.

[135] Of the £1.044m, £172,744 was held in merchant firms, £154,783 was held in banks. Scots in Jamaica held £183,760 in shares in firms and government consols.

[136] S. G. Checkland, *Scottish Banking: A History, 1695–1973* (Glasgow, 1975), p. 92.

[137] Hamilton, *Scotland, the Caribbean*, pp. 195–216.

[138] T. M. Devine, 'Did slavery make Scotia great? A question revisited', in *Recovering Scotland's Slavery Past: The Caribbean Connection*, ed. T. M. Devine (Edinburgh, 2015), p. 238 and p. 244 note 56.

Table 7.3 Scottish West India fortunes, by region (Scots in West Indies who died between 1784 and 1858).

Scottish region	Inventories	%Total inventories	Wealth	%Total wealth	Average wealth
Borders	9	6.5%	£94,607	9.1%	£10,512
West Lowlands	50	36.2%	£384,873	36.8%	£7,697
East Lowlands	28	20.3%	£279,946	26.8%	£9,998
Highlands-Hebrides	7	5.1%	£150,140	14.4%	£21,449
North-east	17	12.3%	£45,624	4.4%	£2,684
Far north	1	0.7%	£391	0.0%	£391
Unknown	26	18.8%	£88,957	8.5%	£3,421
Total	138		£1,044,538		£7,569

Source: National Records of Scotland: Wills, Testaments and Confirmation Inventories (see Bibliography).

Table 7.4 Range of Scottish West India fortunes (Scots in the West Indies who died between 1784 and 1858).

Decile	Range	Inventories	%Inventories	Wealth	%Total wealth
Top	£100,000–150,000	2	1.4%	£257,965	25%
Second	£75,000–£99,999	2	1.4%	£152,460	15%
Third	£50,000–£74,999	0	0.0%	£0	0%
Fourth	£25,000–£49,999	8	5.8%	£266,205	25%
Fifth	£10,000–£24,999	11	8.0%	£157,556	15%
Sixth	£7,500–£9,999	7	5.1%	£62,076	6%
Seventh	£5,000–£7,499	5	3.6%	£28,715	3%
Eight	£2,500–£4,999	17	12.3%	£58,707	6%
Ninth	£500–£2,499	40	29.0%	£52,010	5%
Tenth	£20–£499	46	33.3%	£8,844	1%
Total		138		£1,044,538	

Source: National Records of Scotland: Wills, Testaments and Confirmation Inventories (see Bibliography).

mostly to the period at the end of, and after, the classic phase of the agricultural revolution (1760–1800), the evidence suggests that the impact was a little less dramatic. Based on the 138 Scottish inventories in this study, it was common for successfully returned adventurers (around a quarter) to be involved in the ownership of some form of heritable property. Some individuals possessed urban properties and smaller rural farms (17 in Jamaica, 3 from Grenada, 3 from Trinidad). In terms of achieving the dream – purchasing and returning to large estates in Scotland – nineteen individuals owned, resided in or purchased landed estates (13 from Jamaica, 5 in Grenada, 1 in Trinidad). Of this group, around a third (6) died before they got home. Yet, some super-successful returnees owned both urban property and estate. John Miller, a merchant in Kingston, Jamaica, purchased the Muirshiel estate on his return to Scotland, as well as a property in St Vincent Street, Glasgow, where he died on 20 December 1854.[139] But at least two others were renting, and another had property that was already in his possession prior to departure. Thus, only around 10 per cent of the group of Scots were successful enough to purchase outright. If this figure is extrapolated to the estimates of Scots travelling to the Caribbean after 1750, this movement of capital from the minority who survived could have had a significant effect on Scottish agricultural development, although this requires further research. While the vision of Scots returning with enough Caribbean wealth to invest in idyllic country estates was wishful thinking for even the most successful of returnees, ownership of smaller properties, often in urban areas, was more realistic.

Wider investments to improve Scottish economic development and social provision were even rarer. No Scots in Grenada or Trinidad seem to have invested in industrial enterprise in Scotland, although nearly ten individuals resident in Jamaica did, investing a total of c.£43,000. The available evidence also suggests that the transfer of post-mortem capital from the West Indies for social provision in Scotland was slight. As noted in the Grenada chapter, few invested in philanthropic enterprise, although James Buchanan's bequest was invested in the city of Glasgow. Just one Scot in Trinidad, John Campbell, sent a paltry sum home to the poor of Port Glasgow, and a handful in Jamaica bequeathed wealth to improve Scotland. Only a few Scots wealthy from Caribbean sojourns invested in industrial enterprise and philanthropic provision, although these investments were sometimes large enough to reshape lives in rural and urban communities. Instead, Caribbean slavery's greatest legacy to Scotland was the capital disbursed among families across the country, mainly to the non-landed ranks. As noted by Douglas Hamilton, many Scots in the West Indies were

---

[139] NRS, SC36/48/41, Inventory of John Miller, 16 July 1855, p. 685.

'scions of noble or gentry families, or drawn from the aspiring middling sort', inferring that the profits were contained within these social ranks.[140] However, in 1770, there were just over 8,100 landowning families in Scotland, a group which had decreased by around 5 per cent by 1814.[141] There is no question that such a sizeable, privileged community in Scotland sent many sons to the West Indies, but they were only a small proportion of the population. The previous chapters illustrate that those of lower rank, including many tradesmen, were desired in the plantation economy and some acquired and repatriated fortunes. And the landed ranks are but a small proportion of this group examined here.

Ascertaining the regional flow of labour and capital is made possible by comparing outward shipping lists with the wealth in these inventories, facilitating comparison from whence the Scots left and the influx of West India fortunes in return. The only available shipping lists concern two ports, Port Glasgow and Greenock, and two destinations, Jamaica and Antigua, in late 1774 and the summer of 1775. There are issues with extrapolating from such a small group. While not all Scottish migrants destined for the West Indies left from Clyde ports, official records suggest as many as three-quarters did (with smaller numbers departing from Aberdeen and Leith).[142] The lists here, therefore, likely underestimate the proportions of those who departed from the north of Scotland and the Highlands. Moreover, while Scots were spread further than these two islands, as noted in Chapter 4, Jamaica was the premier destination for most Scots travelling to the West Indies: the social characteristics and backgrounds of those on board these ships were likely to be a good indicator of the average Scot who departed.

In September 1774, the ship *Jamaica* departed from Port Glasgow destined for the island of the same name, with ten clerks aboard hoping for 'better encouragement'. In July 1775, twenty-seven people in the *Isabella* cleared Greenock for Jamaica. Another ship, the *Chance*, cleared Greenock for Antigua, with some on board intent on pursuing mercantile careers. It cannot be understood exactly how the outward bound felt as they left the firth of Clyde, but we do know where the majority resided prior to departure (Table 4.4). Of the forty-one individuals on these ships, residences were provided for thirty-four Scots (a small minority on these

---

[140] Hamilton, *Scotland, the Caribbean*, p. 196.

[141] L. Timperley, 'A pattern of landholding in eighteenth-century Scotland', in *The Making of the Scottish Countryside*, ed. M. L. Parry and T. R. Slater (London, 1980), p. 150.

[142] *Accounts and Papers of the House of Commons: Revenue, Population, Commerce*, vol. lvi (1843), p. 315.

ships were English and some Irish).[143] Forty per cent of this group hailed from the Western Lowlands, which was much more than expected, given that the region was home to a small proportion of the Scottish population. In 1801, the overall Scottish population was 1,599,000, with the Western Lowlands home to some 329,000 people (20 per cent).[144] By contrast, just under 10 per cent of the outward bound hailed from the Eastern Lowlands and 5 per cent hailed from the Borders. This compares with over a third of the Scottish population who resided in the Eastern Lowlands (584,777), and over 10 per cent in the Borders (184,834). In other words, both regions were under-represented in the outward bound relative to their population size. Almost half of the outward bound departed from the Highlands (20 per cent), the north-east of Scotland (20 per cent), and Caithness (2 per cent) in the far north of Scotland combined. This compares favourably to actual population sizes in those areas: Highlands-Hebrides (17.7 per cent of Scottish population), north-east (12 per cent) and far north (1 per cent). In other words, while the Western Lowlands provided more of the outward bound than any other single region, disproportionately large numbers of Scots are likely to have departed for the West Indies from the Highlands, the north-east and northern Scotland.

Families in the Western Lowlands were the main beneficiaries of wealth returning to Scotland from the West Indies. The over-representation of departees from this region among the outward bound is also reflected in the Scottish inventories: over a third (£384,873) of the overall West India fortunes in this study were repatriated to family residences in the Western Lowlands (see Table 7.3). Mothers and fathers living around Glasgow and its hinterlands were well accustomed to their sons leaving for the West Indies and, less often, to the return of wealth. The dynamics of sojourning shaped everyday life in west-central Scotland more than any other region, in terms of the outward bound and return of capital.

The Eastern Lowlands, holding a larger population, shipped out around 10 per cent of the outward bound but took around a quarter of the wealth in return (£279,946). The north-east and far north were especially under-represented in terms of a return of wealth, shipping almost a quarter of the outward bound, but took less than 5 per cent of the wealth (£46,015) in total. Combined, the north-east and Caithness seem to have shipped out five times more men than fortunes returned. The Borders shipped out

---

[143] V. R. Cameron, *Emigrants from Scotland to America, 1774–1775* (Baltimore, 1990), pp. 45–6, p. 80, p. 87.

[144] HCPP (1841) *Accounts of Population and Number of Houses according to Census, 1841, of Each County in Great Britain*, p. 6.

around 5 per cent of the outward bound yet received nearly 10 per cent of the wealth (£94,607). According to the rare emigration lists, Highlanders likely comprised one-fifth (20 per cent) of departing Scots to the West Indies, when the Highlands held 18 per cent of the Scottish population in 1801. The repatriation of wealth in the Scottish inventories was less than might be expected, with around 14 per cent of the wealth being taken in return (£150,140). Further explanation is required.

The Scottish Highlands had a unique relationship with British imperialism, outlined in Iain Mackinnon's analysis of the Highlands as colonized, or its people, the *Gàidhealtachd*, as colonizers.[145] The Caribbean was a major arena in which these shared histories (which are not mutually exclusive narratives) played out, with some Highlanders who were banished from Scotland going on to become enslavers. Allan Macinnes has described the post-1745 period as the 'first phase of clearance' for the Highlands of Scotland, arguing that Scottish Gaeldom exported raw materials and manpower, thus becoming an 'internal colony [of Britain], rather than a beneficiary of Empire like the industrialized Lowlands'.[146] Yet, Macinnes' study of the lucrative activities of the Malcolms of Poltalloch established the view of Highland landlords as 'active members of the imperial exploiting classes as planters, slave traders, colonial officials, military commanders and merchant adventurers'.[147] The work of the *Legacies of British Slave-ownership* project reveals many more enslavers of Highland descent.[148] Subsequent studies have assumed absentee slave-ownership had a powerful effect on the economic development of the Highlands, yet without the qualification that absentees did not develop local economies to the same extent as colonial merchants.[149]

Questions of representativeness also remain, and it may be that the typical Highland absentee was Lord Seaforth, whose estates in Berbice were economic failures, rather than the London-based merchant-

---

[145] I. Mackinnon, 'Colonialism and the Highland clearances', *Northern Scotland*, viii (2017), 22–48.

[146] A. I. Macinnes, 'Scottish Gaeldom: the first phase of clearance', in *People and Society in Scotland, Vol I: 1760–1830*, ed. T. M. Devine and R. Mitchison (Edinburgh, 1988), p .85.

[147] A. I. Macinnes, 'Scottish Gaeldom from clanship to commercial landlordism, *c.*1600–*c.*1850', in *Scottish Power Centres from the Early Middle Ages to the Twentieth Century*, ed. S. M. Foster, A. I. Macinnes and R. K. MacInnes (Glasgow, 1998), pp. 172–3.

[148] *Legacies of British Slavery* <https://www.ucl.ac.uk/lbs/> [accessed 20 June 2022].

[149] S. K. Kehoe, 'Jacobites, Jamaica and the establishment of a Highland Catholic community in the Canadian maritimes', *The Scottish Historical Review*, c (2021), 199–217, at p. 202; K. Morgan, *Slavery, Atlantic Trade and the British Economy, 1660–1800* (Cambridge, 2000), pp. 53–4.

proprietors Malcolms of Poltalloch.[150] Moreover, even successful Highland absentee planters may have had a detrimental effect on local economies. Beneficiaries of slavery purchased over sixty estates in the west Highlands and Islands of Scotland between 1726 and 1939, totalling over a million acres. As the wealth created a new slavery elite, some contributed to a period of rural transformation that has become known as the 'Highland Clearances' (during which landowners cleared tenants from land, often to introduce sheep farming). New slavery elites often had little or no ancestral connection to traditional, communal forms of micro-economy, and these were quickly abandoned, which destroyed local ways of life and resilience. While many Highlanders were complicit in Caribbean slavery, 'the wealth it generated also impacted upon the region in ways that worked against many of its already vulnerable communities'.[151] It is, therefore, now being contested that Atlantic slavery and its commerce were uniformly beneficial to the development of the Scottish Highlands or permeated equally throughout its society.

David Alston recently advanced the view that slavery and the Atlantic trades were significant contributors to the economic development of the Scottish Highlands. In *Slaves and Highlanders* (2021), Alston provided a regional analysis supporting the view that slavery was central to the regional economy, with major trickle-down effects throughout society (thus, ostensibly adding support to Eric Williams' claims in *Capitalism and Slavery*). However, there was no evidence provided that mercantile commerce – or its multiplier effects via merchant capital or manufacturing processes – was of much importance. Moreover, Alston's descriptive case studies of slavery-derived investments rarely quantified scale and significance. The lack of analytical context means it remains unclear if the Atlantic slavery economy was a significant factor in the *overall* development of the Scottish Highlands, that slavery-profits were widespread or decisive in developing enterprise or that ancillary manufacturing employed large sectors of society.[152]

[150] F. McKichan, *Lord Seaforth: Highland Landowner, Caribbean Governor* (Edinburgh, 2018).

[151] I. MacKinnon and A. Mackillop, 'Plantation slavery and landownership in the west Highlands and islands: legacies and lessons' <https://www.communitylandscotland.org.uk/wp-content/uploads/2020/11/Plantation-slavery-and-landownership-in-the-west-Highlands-and-Islands-legacies-and-lessons.pdf> [accessed 10 Nov. 2020]; E. Richards, *The Highland Clearances* (Edinburgh, 2005).

[152] D. Alston, *Slaves and Highlanders: Silenced Histories of Scotland and the Caribbean* (Edinburgh, 2021), pp. 89, 223. For example, the merchant firm Sandbach, Tinne & Co. was cited as evidence of relevant mercantile connections, but the effects on the Highlands were negligible (since the firm or its partners were never based in the Highlands). And there

Recent historiography centred around Highlanders in South America addressed the question of slavery fortunes after 1790. David Alston retains a sceptical approach to the widespread accumulation of large fortunes by Highlanders in Guyana.[153] However, the same historian's earlier study, which questioned the possibility of 'very rapid and splendid fortunes', noted one speculator in Berbice was reputed to have made an astounding £40,000 in one trip, and returned adventurers were often characterized 'as rich as a Demerary man'.[154] Particularly in the absence of evidence about levels of West India fortunes, the grain of truth behind such stereotypes can be viewed as representative, but this wealth was not typical of the average Highland experience.

The evidence here suggests historians must be cautious when assessing the significance of the repatriation of sojourning wealth to the Scottish Highlands. John Lamont's fortune, recounted above, infers 'splendid fortunes' were also available in the third-phase sugar islands, yet the return of that level of post-mortem wealth from the British West Indies to the Scottish Highlands was a rare occurrence indeed. Among those who travelled from Scotland to the West Indies with the aim of repatriating wealth, Highlanders likely comprised 20 per cent of Scots departing for the West Indies (Table 4.4). While around 14 per cent of the sojourning wealth (£150,140) in this study returned to the Highlands, this does not tell the full story. Only seven of 138 Scottish inventories (5 per cent) could be connected to Scots with family residences in the Highlands, yet, like John Lamont's fortune, these were, on average, large-scale (Table 7.3). In fact, Highlanders acquired the highest average sojourning fortunes in this study, almost double the second wealthiest (individuals in the Borders region). In other words, disproportionately high numbers of young men (compared to population size) likely departed from the Highlands, yet very few post-mortem fortunes returned, although those that did were large-scale. While this evidence ostensibly adds to the 'Highlanders as colonizers' thesis, it should not be assumed this individual pursuit of colonialism represented a net gain for the Highland economy.

---

is no evidence provided of large-scale employment in ancillary industries connected to the Atlantic trades.

[153] D. Alston, '"You have only seen the fortunate few and draw conclusions accordingly"': behavioural economics and the paradox of Scottish emigration', in *Global Migrations: The Scottish Diaspora since 1600*, ed. A. McCarthy and J. M. MacKenzie (Edinburgh, 2016), pp. 46–63.

[154] D. Alston, '"Very rapid and splendid fortunes"? Highland Scots in Berbice (Guyana) in the early nineteenth century', *Transactions of the Gaelic Society of Inverness*, lxiii (2002–2004), 208–36.

Most Highland families waiting for West India fortunes would have been disappointed. In addition to the high death rates, a key question remains to be answered: why would Highland sojourners wish to return when large swathes of their homelands, and their families, were being cleared? Between 1763 and 1815, many Highlanders migrated to western Canada instead. Others joined them, some already cash rich from Jamaica sojourns, and repatriated limited wealth to Scotland.[155] S. Karly Kehoe, however, pointed to the wider impact of slavery fortunes on the Scottish Highlands via charitable enterprise, especially educational institutions and hospitals. In this view, fortunes accrued by adventurers from Caribbean slavery improved the status of those concerned and that of their families at home. On a broader scale, more substantial fortunes often reshaped regional economies and societies through social provision.[156] However, it is problematic to assume unrepresentative examples of success were typical, while failing to contextualize the returns relative to the loss of skilled labour. Indeed, outward migration sometimes cleared local societies of adult male workers. When surveying Kiltarlity in Inverness in 1793, the Revd John Fraser noted the 'decrease of adult males' was not due to premature death but 'owing to their leaving the parish', including a 'few' to the West Indies.[157] The loss of skilled young men contributed to the decline of local societies (as argued in Chapter 4), while the limited return of sojourning wealth went into few hands, which had a minimal effect on the development of local economies. Caribbean sojourning improved the living conditions of some families in the Scottish Highlands, but simultaneously contributed to the under development of the region.

Scotland's national story of sojourning was defined by the loss of thousands of young men, and the repatriation of fortunes by a select few. For those that survived, the West India wealth they repatriated to Scotland was huge over a half-century – especially after 1800 – and this made Scottish families cash rich, especially in the central region. But this influx requires contextualization alongside the loss of labour. Young men departed from Scotland after 1775 in the hope of mainly unrealizable West India fortunes, and most never returned. Based on mortality estimates for

[155] J. M. Bumsted, 'The Scottish diaspora: emigration to British North America, 1763–1815', in *Nation and Province in the First British Empire: Scotland and the Americas, 1600–1800*, ed. N. C. Landsman (Lewisburg, 2001), p. 128; Kehoe, 'Jacobites, Jamaica'.

[156] S. K. Kehoe, 'From the Caribbean to the Scottish Highlands: charitable enterprise in the age of improvement, c.1750–1820', *Rural History*, xxvii (2015), 1–23. See Hamilton, *Scotland, the Caribbean*, p. 195.

[157] J. Sinclair, *The Statistical Account of Scotland*, Kiltarlity, Inverness, vol. xiii (Edinburgh, 1794), p. 517.

Demerara, Jamaica and Tobago, it seems likely most would have been dead before they managed to repatriate wealth of any significance. The wealth holding was also unequal. The typical pattern was one of low-to-medium returns, and less than one-fifth of the minority – that is, those who actually lived – managed to accumulate fortunes that allowed them to live out independent lifestyles in Scotland. Instead, most Scots who travelled to the West Indies died among strangers, like Robert McGregor Stirling, in debt, having failed in their quest for riches based on the exploitation of enslaved labour. This group deserve no sympathy, but the likelihood is that Caribbean sojourning – and the departure of educated and skilled labour – contributed to the development of some Scottish regions and the under-development of others.

Conclusion

The opening of Trinidad during Glasgow's sugar era ostensibly cleared the way for the city's mercantile elite to accumulate great wealth from the British West Indies. With a well-established financial infrastructure and mercantile community, the city's role as a metropolis should have facilitated large-scale involvement. However, Scottish banks were reluctant to support new entrants operating in a high-risk environment, a decision which was less to do with morals than with economics. The city's economy was by then geared towards manufacturing and less reliant upon Atlantic commerce and slavery. Nevertheless, despite coming in the era of gradual abolition and West Indian economic decline, prominent merchant firms ensured a dramatic surge in commercial activity in the sugar islands. Yet, from the economic perspective, the banks were proven right: even the most successful firms did not generate major fortunes. The rise and fall of the Eccles mercantile dynasty is emblematic of the relative failure of the Glasgow-Trinidadian metropolitan elite. As noted above, this major mercantile fortune was built on weak foundations and folded in 1847. More broadly, based upon average wealth on death, this group was far less successful than merchants whose principal interests focused on Jamaica, Grenada or Demerara. As will be described in the next chapter, the 'Trinidad People' were the poor relations as far as Glasgow's 'sugar aristocracy' were concerned. The paucity of finance and the relatively few Glasgow firms focused on Trinidad had implications for the success of Scots in the island. For every John Lamont, there were many more like Robert McGregor Stirling. In the era of decline, Scotland's sugar and slavery boom was over.

8. Glasgow-West India 'spheres of influence': embedding the profits of Caribbean slavery

At the height of Glasgow's sugar era, James Morrison published a treatise on bookkeeping that included a *Dissertation on the Business of the Counting House* (1820). Originally written in a Glasgow mercantile academy in 1808, the work opened with a triple-dedication encapsulating the city's legal-commercial connections – to Gilbert Hamilton, agent for the Bank of Scotland, John More, agent for the Royal Bank, and Walter Ewing MacLae, an accountant specializing in West India bankruptcies. The section on the Glasgow-West India trades contained some remarkable claims:

> Of all the various employments calculated to promote public, as well as private prosperity, there is none upon which industry, foresight, and economy, have a more striking influence than that of the Merchant. An imprudent step may not only ruin his fortune and family, but, perhaps, the fortune of hundreds connected with him in Business, and likewise have a tendency to injure the Trade of his Country in general; while, on the other hand, a plan properly digested, and well executed, may not only establish him, but add to the prosperity of all those who are within the sphere of his influence.[1]

In doing so, the educator publicly acknowledged that the merchants in his midst were fabulously wealthy, but also that Glasgow, Scotland and Great Britain's economic development was dependent on their continued success. And Morrison had a point, at least in a Scottish context. In 1820, the leading sectors of Scotland's export-oriented textile economy remained strategically dependent upon Atlantic commerce. In 1820, Europe was Scotland's principal import and export market. However, of £3.28m imports (by official value), 19 per cent arrived from the British West Indies, compared to 20.4 per cent from Africa, Asia, British North America and the United States combined! Of £5.89m exports from Scotland (by official value), 24 per cent was exported to the British West Indies, with 15 per cent sent to Africa, Asia, British North America and the United States combined. The export goods to the West Indies (mainly textiles) were the mainstay of the Scottish

---

[1] J. Morrison, *A Complete Treatise on Practical Book-Keeping*, 3rd ed. (London, 1820), p. xiii.

economy.[2] West India commerce, and accumulation of mercantile capital, promoted wider public prosperity through the transferral of colonial profits into agricultural, commercial, industrial and philanthropic initiatives. The challenge for historians, then, is to define how deep and how broad the West India spheres of influence really were. This chapter examines the investments in life and wealth at death of Glasgow's sugar aristocracy, in the process revealing how the profits of slavery influenced the development of local economies and societies up to the present day.

Demographics

Glasgow's West India merchants lived extraordinarily long lives. In the 1790s, the average life expectancy in Scotland varied between regions: thirty-six in the Western Lowlands and forty-eight in the north-east.[3] Adult death rates in Scotland only showed a significant decline from 1870 onwards and by 1912, the average male was only expected to live to fifty.[4] Years of birth and death are known in eighty-eight cases of the Glasgow-West India elite, and they lived, on average, to seventy, almost double the expected age in their region at the end of the eighteenth century. These mercantile lives therefore spanned three separate centuries. One of the last born of this group, William Frederick Burnley (1810–1903), died in early twentieth-century Edinburgh. The presence of British Caribbean enslavers in Scotland is just outside living memory.

Their places of death suggest the majority lived, worked and died in the west of Scotland in general and Glasgow in particular.[5] James Ewing (1775–1853), for example, was a classic absentee who seemingly never visited his properties in Jamaica. Some died in the Highlands and Dumbarton, while others retired to Helensburgh, such as Archibald Smith (1795–1883), who passed away in a smaller home on the banks of the Clyde. Around 10 per cent of the group died in England. The Malcolms of Poltalloch, for example, were based in London from 1771 but successive generations

---

[2] National Archives of the U.K. [TNA], CUST 14/32, 'Ledgers of Imports and Exports, Scotland (1820)', fols. 206-7.

[3] M. Flinn (ed.), *Scottish Population History from the 17th Century to the 1930s* (Cambridge, 1977), p. 270.

[4] G. Morton, 'Identity out of place', in *A History of Everyday Life in Scotland, 1800–1900*, ed. G. Morton and T. Griffiths (Edinburgh, 2010); M. Anderson and D. J. Morse, 'The people', in *People and Society in Scotland, Vol. II: 1830–1914*, ed. W. H. Fraser and R. J. Morris (Edinburgh, 1990), p. 30.

[5] Of 93 known places of death, 51 died in Glasgow (54 per cent), 8 in Edinburgh (9 per cent), 6 in Dumbarton (6 per cent), 5 in Ayrshire (5 per cent) and abroad: 9 in England (10 per cent), America (1) and the West Indies (1).

Figure 8.1 Marble busts of James Ewing of Strathleven (1775–1853) and James Buchanan (1785–1857). Photograph: the author. © Merchants House of Glasgow.

retained the family estates in Argyll and co-partnership shares in the Glasgow firm Stirling, Gordon & Co. Just two died across the Atlantic: George Parker in New York and Aeneas MacBean in St Thomas in the West Indies. The demographics reveal a mercantile elite that mostly remained domiciled around the west of Scotland for most of their long lives.

Glasgow-West India fortunes

This chapter assesses the nature and extent of West India fortunes by examining wills, testaments and confirmation inventories in Scottish courts associated with members of the Glasgow-West India elite who died between 1800 and 1903. Of the initial group of 150 West India merchants in this study, 105 were known to have left confirmation inventories (with seventy-seven associated wills and testaments). This sample of inventories is around 40 per cent greater than that compiled for the most recent study.[6] Sampling confirmation inventories – analogous to probate inventories in England – as indicators of personal wealth is an imperfect methodology as there

---

[6] A. Cooke, 'An elite revisited: Glasgow West India merchants, 1783–1877', *Journal of Scottish Historical Studies*, xxxii (2012), 127–65, at p. 143.

are issues with interpreting a 'snapshot' of wealth on death. The sources can underestimate each individual's holdings in life and might not always accurately represent peak wealth. Moreover, inventories only list moveable goods, such as cash, stock and shares, while heritable property, such as land in Scotland or the West Indies, is not included by value.[7] Nevertheless, large samples of personal inventories do offer insights into the distribution of wealth and investments.[8] In this case, the inventories suggest the high personal incomes and wealthy lifestyles of West India merchants, in the process revealing major investments across the nineteenth century.

Transatlantic commerce in general and the West India trades in particular did carry a high degree of inherent risk. Natural disasters in the Caribbean such as hurricanes, as well as warfare and the loss of shipping, interrupted trade. And, of course, the enslaved themselves rebelled against their condition, which ultimately expedited emancipation.[9] The volatility of the sugar market, and economic and political conditions in Great Britain, all affected business. Chapter 1 illustrated a notably high pattern of bankruptcy among the city's early West India community. Across Great Britain more broadly, many mercantile proprietors became bankrupt due to the economic decline exacerbated by the abolition in 1807 and emancipation in 1834.[10] Overall, around 10 per cent of Glasgow-West India merchants in this study are known to have been bankrupted in the course of a commercial career, although this is most likely to be an underestimate, since just under a third left no inventory at all.[11] Nevertheless, over 100 Glasgow-West India merchants retained substantial wealth on death, suggesting most thrived to acquire often immense fortunes which remained with them throughout their lives.

The Glasgow-West India merchants and planters who died between 1800 and 1903 possessed combined wealth valued at £4,806,712 (105 individuals, an average of £45,788). The average wealth was enormous. The sum of £45,788 in 1851 (a midpoint of dates of death) is equivalent to £38.9m in

---

[7] W. Alexander, *The Practice of the Commissary Courts in Scotland* (Edinburgh, 1859), pp. 8–27.

[8] N. Morgan and R. H. Trainor, 'The dominant classes', in *People and Society in Scotland, Vol. II: 1830–1914*, ed. W. H. Fraser and R. J. Morris (Edinburgh, 1990), p. 113.

[9] M. Craton, *Testing the Chains: Resistance to Slavery in the British West Indies* (Ithaca, 1982).

[10] N. Draper, 'Helping to make Britain great: the commercial legacies of slave-ownership in Britain', in *Legacies of British Slave-Ownership*, ed. C. Hall, N. Draper et al. (Cambridge, 2014), p. 83.

[11] Since 45 of the wider group of 150 West India merchants did not leave inventories on death, the 10 per cent figure is almost certainly an underestimate of the actual number of bankruptcies.

modern values (relative to the worth of average earnings in 2020).[12] The rise and decline of average wealth is as would be expected: rising inexorably from 1800 onwards, peaking after 1845 before a steady downward trajectory into the twentieth century (see Table 8.1). Between 1800 and 1839, average fortunes of the West India merchants were higher than those of other

Table 8.1 Holdings on death of 105 Glasgow-West India elites who died between 1800 and 1905.

Year death	Inventories no.	Total value of holdings	Assets in WI merchant firms	Shares in banks (British)	Shares in manufactories (textiles, extractive)
1800–14	10	£196,412	£100,319 (7)	£1,800 (1)	£3,887 (1)
		ave. £19,641	ave. £14,331	ave. £1,800	ave. £3,887
1815–29	25	£1,159,732	£617,530 (17)	£12,193 (2)	£115,584 (6)
		ave. £46,389	ave. £36,325	ave. £6,097	ave. £19,264
1830–44	28	£1,475,781	£146,188 (11)	£232,739 (11)	£32,366 (7)
		ave. £52,706	ave. £13,289	ave. £21,158	ave. £4,624
1845–59	20	£1,101,235	£161,241 (6)	£211,258 (11)	£33,326 (2)
		ave. £55,061	ave. £26,873	ave. £23,473	ave. £16,663
1860–74	17	£731,752	£28,689 (2)	£88,544 (5)	
		ave. £43,044	ave. £14,345	ave. £17,709	
1875–89	4	£133,892		£50,473 (3)	
		ave. £33,473		ave. £16,824	
1890–1905	1	£7,908		£3,807 (1)	
		ave. £7,908		ave. £3,807	
Total	**105**	**£4,806,712**	**£1,053,967 (43)**	**£600,814 (32)**	**£185,163 (16)**
		ave. £45,778	**ave. £24,511**	**ave. £18,775**	**ave. £11,573**

Source: National Records of Scotland: Wills, Testaments and Confirmation Inventories (see Bibliography).

[12] For modern values, see *Measuring Worth* <https://www.measuringworth.com/calculators/ukcompare/> [accessed 27 Oct. 2021]. Relative wage or income worth (average earnings, 2020 values) has been used here.

Glasgow elites, the cotton masters.[13] From 1845 onwards, however, and consistent with Eric Williams' view that manufacturing replaced the West India commerce that helped create it, the cotton masters left higher average fortunes compared to their formerly wealthier counterparts.

But what exactly was a West India fortune? Not all the above wealth was derived from slavery, as some individuals held substantial interests elsewhere. James Ewing of Strathleven was at once a West India merchant in Glasgow, an absentee owner of Jamaican plantations, an East India merchant, a shipping agent and invested in industrial concerns in Scotland. His vast estate thus came from multiple sources.[14] While it is impossible to ascertain which was the most profitable stream, West India profits were a mainstay among various other concerns. Others hailed from previously landed, wealthy families. Colin Campbell of Jura was a scion of the Lochnell branch of the House of Argyll who inherited landed interests and most likely a substantial personal fortune on the death of his father in 1835.[15] While some of his fortune was based upon the West India trades, inheritance and agricultural enterprise would also have contributed. Nevertheless, the social background of those who left inventories suggests only a small minority hailed from 'gentry capitalist' families (like Campbell of Jura) who increased their already significant wealth and status through long-term connections with the Caribbean.[16] Instead, it seems most hailed from middling families, especially colonial backgrounds.[17]

Slavery and its commerce certainly propelled some Glasgow-West India merchants and planters into the ranks of the British financial elite. William D. Rubinstein defined those individuals leaving personal assets of £100,000 or more in nineteenth-century Great Britain as the 'wealthiest of their time'.[18] In Glasgow, a super-wealthy group of twelve left £100,000 or more (see Table 8.2),

---

[13] A. Cooke, 'The Scottish cotton masters, 1780–1914', *Textile History*, xl (2009), 29–50, at p. 39.

[14] NRS, SC65/34/7/183–207, 'Inventory of James Ewing', 24 Feb. 1854.

[15] J. Burke, *A Genealogical and Heraldic Dictionary of the Landed Gentry of Great Britain and Ireland*, vol. i (London, 1847), p. 179.

[16] S. D. Smith, *Slavery, Family and Gentry Capitalism in the British Atlantic: The World of the Lascelles, 1648–1834* (Cambridge, 2006), p. 9.

[17] The social backgrounds of 89 of 105 individuals with inventories are known: 53 hailed from colonial backgrounds (West India commerce 38, American merchants 15). Nine individuals hailed from gentry families with no previous connections to colonial commerce. The remainder hailed from middling backgrounds such as general merchants (12), agriculture (5) and the Church of Scotland (4).

[18] W. D. Rubinstein, *Who Were the Rich? A Biographical Directory of British Wealth-Holders, Vol. I: 1809–1839* (London, 2009), p. 13, p. 17.

most hailing from families already established in colonial business, supporting the view it took two generations to accumulate great wealth. The highest fortunes were left by Neil Malcolm of Poltalloch (1769–1837), who was worth £549,955 on death, and his son, Neil Malcolm of Poltalloch (1797–1857), who was worth £399,666 on death (they died in London and Brighton respectively). The wealthiest of all Scottish-based merchants, James Ewing of Strathleven (1775–1857), was worth £281,296 on death.[19] Of the approximately 900 individuals who died leaving over £100,000 in Great Britain between 1809 and 1839, Nicholas Draper noted around 150 (one-sixth) derived some or all of their fortunes from transatlantic slavery, of which just thirty-five were merchants (c.4 per cent).[20] Five of the super-wealthy Glasgow-West India elite died between 1800 and 1839, and since just ten individuals died in Scotland leaving personal property that exceeded £100,000 in that period, half of the nation's richest men derived at least some of their wealth from West India commerce conducted in Glasgow.[21] While Draper suggests that Caribbean slavery was not especially important to great British fortunes between 1809 and 1839, it was a different story in Scotland.

Participation in West India commerce created great Scottish fortunes, but there were no guarantees of success. The bulk of the overall wealth (over half of the assets) was held by the super-wealthy group of twelve (c.11 per cent of the group). On the other hand, the less wealthy (45 per cent) were in possession of just 8 per cent of assets (see Table 8.2). Nineteen left £5,000 or less, personal wealth that would barely have placed them among the middle ranks in Glasgow and Edinburgh (whose average fortunes were estimated to be c.£5,800 in 1822–4).[22] Overall, however, almost a third of Glasgow-West India merchants were worth £30,000 and over on death, which meant they left greater fortunes than late eighteenth-century slave-traffickers in Liverpool (of whom just 10 per cent left fortunes exceeding this sum).[23] West India commerce was more profitable than trafficking in enslaved people, on average. While comparative evidence of Liverpool's West India fortunes is

---

[19] NRS, SC65/34/7, 'Inventory of James Ewing', 24 Feb. 1854, p. 185.

[20] N. Draper, 'Possessing people: absentee slave-owners within British society', in *Legacies of British Slave-ownership*, ed. C. Hall, Nicholas Draper et al. (Cambridge, 2014), p. 47.

[21] Rubinstein, *Who Were the Rich?*, p. 17. Rubinstein included James McInroy, Charles Stuart Parker and John Gordon but omitted John Stirling of Kippendavie and James Dennistoun of Golfhill.

[22] A. McCrum, 'Inheritance and the family: the Scottish urban experience in the 1820s', in *Urban Fortunes: Property and Inheritance in the Town*, ed. J. Stobart and A. Owens (Aldershot, 2000), pp. 156–7.

[23] D. Pope, 'The wealth and aspirations of Liverpool's slave merchants', in *Liverpool and Transatlantic Slavery*, ed. D. Richardson et al. (Liverpool, 2007), p. 169.

Table 8.2 Range of wealth on death of the Glasgow-West
India elites who died between 1800 and 1905.

Decile	Range	Inventories	% Total inv.	Wealth	% Total wealth
Top	£300,000+	2	1.9%	£949,621	19.8%
Second	£200,000–£299,000	3	2.9%	£727,600	15.1%
Third	£100,000–£199,000	7	6.7%	£961,010	20.0%
Fourth	£75,000–£99,000	3	2.9%	£232,716	4.8%
Fifth	£50,000–£74,999	6	5.7%	£381,038	7.9%
Sixth	£30,000–£49,999	18	17.1%	£681,551	14.2%
Seventh	£20,000–£29,999	19	18.1%	£481,752	10.0%
Eight	£10,000–£19,999	17	16.2%	£268,448	5.6%
Ninth	£5,000–£9,999	11	10.5%	£85,298	1.8%
Tenth	£250–£4,999	19	18.1%	£37,678	0.8%
		105			

Source: National Records of Scotland: 'Wills, testaments
and confirmation inventories' (see Bibliography).

scarce, S. G. Checkland argued that the city's 'West India men were really in decline, enjoying the last great flush of prosperity' from the 1790s, while the American traders [in Liverpool] afterwards took the lead.[24] Similarly, comparison with Kenneth Morgan's study of Bristol's West India merchants suggests that Glasgow-West India fortunes were of higher value and more diversified than those made by Bristolian counterparts.[25] Glasgow-West India trades made some fabulously successful. Others became independently rich, while a large minority acquired middling wealth.

The Glasgow-West India elite's assets were held mainly in Great Britain, with a scattering of investments across the Atlantic world. Of known holdings, 70 per cent were held in Scotland (£3,351,487), over a quarter held in England (£1,313,937) with small holdings in the West Indies (£37,006, or under 1 per cent). Twenty-nine individuals held property in England including two of the individuals classed as wealthiest of their time. As the only individuals whose English holdings were worth more than their respective values in Scotland, however, the Malcolms of Poltalloch – who

[24] S. G. Checkland, 'American versus West Indian traders in Liverpool, 1793–1815', *The Journal of Economic History*, xvii (1958), 141–60, at p. 142.

[25] K. Morgan, 'Bristol West India merchants in the eighteenth century', *Transactions of the Royal Historical Society*, 6th series, iii (London, 1993), p. 186, pp. 200–1.

permanently relocated to England – and Thomas Dunlop Douglas were unusual. Other merchants branched out into international ventures. Merchants such as Archibald Smith of Jordanhill diversified their wealth into the New Zealand and Australia Land Company. While some were involved with East India lobbying in Glasgow before 1830, it seems unlikely there was widespread commercial involvement in the Indian subcontinent.[26] The wealth on death of the Glasgow-West India elite does not reveal any sustained investment in East India firms, suggesting that unlike enslavers in post-emancipation England, there was no large-scale 'swing to the east'.[27] The Campbells of Colgrain seem to have been unique: shifting from the West to East India sugar trade in the later nineteenth century, dramatically improving the family wealth.[28] At least one merchant firm, Dennistoun, Buchanan & Co., diversified into Argentina and Brazil, where slavery was not abolished until 1861 and 1888 respectively. Thus, the major fortunes of partners such as James Buchanan of Dowanhill were probably derived from multiple slavery economies.[29] Overall, however it seems that international investments were of negligible importance to the Glasgow-West India elite.

West India merchant firms

Merchant firms were the main facilitators of Glasgow-West India fortunes. Forty per cent of this group (forty-three of 105 confirmation inventories) held shares and stock in merchant firms in Glasgow at time of decease (see Table 8.1). Almost one-third – the bulk of the wealth in Scotland – was held in such firms. The average holding was £24,500.[30] Of the merchants known to have died between 1800 and 1840, almost half held shares in Glasgow-West India firms, while of those who died after 1840, just a fifth held shares in firms. This significant decrease is explained by merchants removing themselves from business through retirement or bankruptcies after the abolition of plantation slavery in 1834. This process of removal was elucidated in the correspondence of John Campbell, senior, & Co.:

---

[26] Y. Kumagai, *Breaking into the Monopoly: Provincial Merchants and Manufacturers' Campaigns for Access to the Asian Market, 1790–1833* (Leiden, 2013), pp. 43–4, p. 82.

[27] Draper, 'Helping to make Britain great', pp. 93–8.

[28] S. Mullen, 'The great Glasgow-West India house of John Campbell senior & Co.', in *Recovering Scotland's Slavery Past: The Caribbean Connection*, ed. T. M. Devine (Edinburgh, 2015), p. 140.

[29] University of Glasgow, Special Collections, MS. Murray 605, 'Minute book of Dennistoun, Buchanan, & Co. Glasgow, 1806–42', p. 17.

[30] Forty-three individuals had interests in Glasgow merchant firms on death valued at £1,053,967 (31% of the overall wealth in Scotland of £3,351,487).

That the West India outstandings, consisting of debts and property in Estates, being greatly diminished in amount by Government Compensation money and other causes, the same extent of capital [£180,000] as formerly *is not required* [my italics] to hold the property and carry on the business of the concern and the capital shall be accordingly reduced.[31]

This allowed the partners to pare back their personal investment, and by 1858, the firm was dissolved. Overall, holdings in Glasgow-West India merchant firms fluctuated throughout the early nineteenth century (see Table 8.1). There was a dramatic decline in the 1830s and 1840s. The seemingly large investments in the 1840s and 1850s are explained by the anomalously high holdings of James Ewing (£115,000), who retained an interest in Jamaica estates for life. In general, the holdings of Glasgow-West India firms examined here faded after 1834, in contrast to Anthony Cooke's vision of increasing holdings in Glasgow-West India merchant houses into the Victorian period. Cooke's estimates of mercantile holdings increased due to the substantial estates of Thomas and James Richardson, whose firm traded in Mauritius in the East Indies between 1839 and 1872. By including the significant estates of East India merchants with principal interests in Mauritius, Cooke's estimates of holdings in Glasgow-West India firms were over-stated and a 'swing to the east' was cited as evidence of continued investment in the Caribbean.[32] In actuality, Glasgow's West India merchants reduced their personal wealth in associated merchant firms in the aftermath of emancipation, which freed up large reserves of surplus capital for investment in Scotland.

The Glasgow-West India elite and their firms often owned estates in the British West Indies. Over ten inventories referred to shares in plantations or mortgages held over them. On his death in 1853, James Ewing bequeathed Taylor Caymanas plantation and all other lands he owned in Jamaica to a family trust in Scotland.[33] However, the possession of enslaved people and the securities over them was far more extensive than these figures suggest.

---

[31] GCA, TD1696, 'John Campbell, senior, & Co., Minute book', 1803–42, n.p., letters 11–12.

[32] Anthony Cooke included the substantial estates of father and son, James Richardson (d. 1860) and Thomas Richardson (d. 1872). Both were partners in a Glasgow merchant house that traded with Mauritius. The former held £201,424 in the merchant firm on his death in 1860. The latter held £19,262 in the Mauritius-based merchant firm on his death in 1872. See Cooke, 'An elite revisited', pp. 142–3, p. 163; NRS, SC58/42/26, 'Inventory of James Richardson', 4 April 1860, p. 416; NRS, SC58/42/39, 'Inventory of Thomas Richardson', 30 July 1872, p. 969. For further discussion of the mercantile 'swing to the east', including Mauritius, see E. Williams, *Capitalism and Slavery* (London, 1981 ed.), pp. 150–1; Draper, 'Helping to make Britain great', pp. 93–8.

[33] NRS, SC65/34/7, 'Inventory of James Ewing', 24 Feb. 1854, p. 190.

The *Legacies of British Slave-Ownership* project allows the untangling of the Gordian knot of compensation claims by the Glasgow-West India elite when slavery was abolished in the British West Indies on 1 August 1834.[34] The Glasgow claims were made for enslaved people resident in British Guiana, Grenada, Jamaica, St Kitts, St Vincent and Trinidad. The major sums were collected for British Guiana.[35] A significant proportion of these claims were made in the frontier territories annexed in the second and third phases of colonization in the British Caribbean. Less than half of the surviving Glasgow-West India elite claimed compensation. Of the 150 known individuals, at least fifty-eight died before 1834. Of the remainder, thirty-nine individuals claimed £436,996. Although large-scale, the figures pale in comparison with the £2m collected by members of the London-based Society of West India Planters and Merchants.[36] While the Atlantic trades were crucial to the development of Glasgow-West India fortunes, slave-ownership and the compensation awards were not, although the latter provided liquid capital for investment in domestic enterprise.

Landed estates and urban property

From 1760, Scottish 'improvers' introduced revolutionary agricultural methods that transformed the countryside, which occurred alongside what T. C. Smout described as a 'revolution in manners' (high-consumption lifestyles, especially in foodstuffs, clothing and education).[37] New demands put financial pressures on the traditional landed elites, and as a result, estates regularly came to the market. The American War of Independence (1775–83) also lowered land prices, which brought land to auction. Some merchants were bankrupted, while the availability of cheap credit when peace arrived provided others with the opportunity to scoop up estates.[38]

---

[34] *Legacies of British Slave-ownership* <http://www.ucl.ac.uk/lbs/> [accessed 9 Sept. 2014].

[35] Merchants from the same firm often had multiple claims on the same award, so double counting has been avoided. Analysis suggests at least 39 of the Glasgow West India elite claimed compensation valued at £436,996. Claims for slaves in British Guiana were valued at £223,714; Jamaica, £106,788; Trinidad, £69,586; Grenada, £30,253; St Vincent, £2,727; and St Kitts, £3,928.

[36] D. B. Ryden, 'The society of West India planters and merchants in the age of emancipation, *c.*1816–35', Economic History Society Annual Conference, 27–9 March 2015 <http://www.ehs.org.uk/dotAsset/e389027d-9708-42cb-a13d-85106e90e947.pdf> [accessed Oct. 2016].

[37] T. C. Smout, *A History of the Scottish People, 1560–1830* (Glasgow, 1972; 1987 ed.), pp. 265–81.

[38] T. M. Devine, 'Glasgow colonial merchants and land, 1770–1815', in *Land and Industry: The Landed Estate and the Industrial Revolution*, ed. J. T. Ward and R. G. Wilson (Newton Abbot, 1971), p. 217.

The rapid accumulation of West India fortunes after 1775, therefore, underpinned a challenge to the hegemony of landed elites in the west of Scotland, both established gentry and colonial.

Existing historiography suggests that Glasgow-West India mercantile landownership was small-scale in a localized area. T. M. Devine's study of landownership and colonial elites reveals thirty-six West India merchants owned seventy-one properties at some point in their lives.[39] Anthony Cooke's study of the same elites into the Victorian period suggested a decline in patterns of ownership towards death, with forty-one individuals owning forty-three estates across Scotland.[40] This study here reveals the West India influx into the Scottish countryside was more extensive than has previously been understood. Cross-referencing records of land transfers in Scotland ('sasines'), confirmation inventories and contemporary sources, this study identifies seventy-five West India proprietors as owners of 133 landed estates (see Table 2.2).[41] Thus, half of the mercantile grouping in this study owned an estate at some point in their lives, and many owned more than one estate across different counties. Some estates, such as Jordanhill in Renfrew, detailed in Chapter 3, were owned multiple times by different owners, often passing hands through bankruptcies or inheritance. The 1780s was the peak decade for acquisition, although peak West India investment came after 1800 (as will be explained below).[42] The estates were located mainly in west-central Scotland. Stirling, Renfrew, Ayr and Dunbarton were popular locations, but Lanarkshire was the most favoured location in general and the Barony of Glasgow in particular.[43] The West India elite tended to reside

[39] Devine, 'Glasgow colonial merchants and land, 1770–1815', pp. 248–62.

[40] Cooke, 'An elite revisited', p. 147.

[41] This is principally based upon a survey of Abridgements of Sasines held in Glasgow City Archives, T-SA 1/1 Argyll (vol. i, 1781–1820; vol. ii, 1821–50); GCA, T-SA 2/1 Ayr (vol. i, 1781–1806; vol. ii, 1806–20; vol. iii, 1821–30; vol. iv, 1831–40); GCA, T-SA 4/1 Dunbartonshire (vol. i, 1781–1820; vol. ii, 1821–30; vol. iii, 1831–40); GCA, T-SA 5/1 Glasgow (Barony and Regality) (vol. i, 1781–1808; vol. ii, 1809–20; vol. iii, 1821–30; vol. iv, 1831–40); GCA, T-SA 6/1 Lanarkshire (vol. i, 1781–1820; vol. ii, 1821–30; vol. iii, 1831–40); GCA, T-SA 7/1 Renfrewshire (vol. i, 1781–1807; vol. ii, 1807–1820; vol. iii, 1821–30; vol. iv, 1831–40). It has been supplemented with data from probate inventories, Devine 'Glasgow colonial merchants and land, 1770–1815', pp. 248–62, and J. G. Smith and J. O. Mitchell, *The Old Country Houses of the Old Glasgow Gentry* (Glasgow, 1878).

[42] Year of acquisition is known in 122 cases. By decade: 1750s (3); 1770s (4); 1780s (25); 1790s (22); 1800s (21), 1810s (20); 1820s (13); 1830s (11); 1840s (3). Of known cases, 55% came after 1800.

[43] Of 133 cases of estate ownership, locations are known for: Barony of Glasgow (30), Lanark (21), Dunbarton (20), Stirling (18), Renfrew (14), Ayr (12), Argyll (8), Peebles (5), Perth (3), Wigtown (1).

in estates around a concentrated area in the west of Scotland, their presence influencing the development of the local economy in different ways.

Not all West India merchants owned landed estates. For lesser merchants, urban townhouses became a primary place of residence, although the most successful maintained both. Ownership of the landed estate, however, was the real marker of success. Of 129 known methods of acquisition, forty-one estates passed through inheritance, often consolidating colonial dynasties over several generations. Some were inherited from fathers involved with tobacco commerce, and over ten individuals inherited estates from fathers involved in the West India trades, and, on occasion, from other family members. William Smith inherited Carbeth on the death of his unmarried cousin John Guthrie in 1834.[44] The transfer of land via strategic marriages was rare, with just one recorded example during Glasgow's sugar era, compared to seven in the tobacco heyday.[45] That pairing, however, consolidated a major family inheritance. Around 1783, Moses Steven (1749–1831) was a partner in the Glasgow-West India firm Buchanan, Steven & Co., and successor firm Dennistoun, Buchanan & Co. Wealth secured, he purchased Polmadie on the south side of Glasgow. He married Janet Rowan, the laird's daughter on neighbouring Bellahouston, an estate he eventually purchased parts of. The entire estate passed into the hands of the Steven children, which, as will be discussed later, had important implications for the city of Glasgow.[46]

While inheritance was an important means of acquisition for West India merchants and marriage less so, most estates were purchased directly (fifty-five merchants, eighty-seven estates). Most were procured between 1780 and 1819, with the early nineteenth century an important period. West India purchases tailed off at the end of the Napoleonic wars in 1815 and declined in the later decades.[47] Slavery compensation probably funded some land acquisition, albeit on a small scale. Of the eight known estates purchased after 1834, six were acquired by holders of compensation from the British government, such as Colin Campbell of Colgrain.[48] The accumulation of

---

[44] J. Burke, *A Genealogical and Heraldic History of the Commoners of Great Britain*, vol. iv (London, 1838), p. 62.

[45] T. M. Devine, *The Tobacco Lords: A Study of the Tobacco Merchants of Glasgow and Their Trading Activities, c. 1740–90* (Edinburgh, 1975), p. 19.

[46] J. G. Smith, *Strathendrick and Its Inhabitants from Early Times* (Glasgow, 1896), p. 217, p. 344.

[47] Year of purchase is known in 82 cases. By decade: 1750s (3); 1770s (3); 1780s (17); 1790s (15); 1800s (17); 1810s (11); 1820s (7); 1830s (7); 1840s (3). Of known cases, 54% came after 1800.

[48] GCA, T-SA 4/1/3, Dunbartonshire, 1831–140, 920.

West India fortunes thus had important consequences, underpinning the purchase of new estates across the west of Scotland, especially after 1800.

The influx of West India capital from the 1790s onwards is explained by the length of time it took for merchants to acquire wealth. In 1781, after some twenty years' experience as a mercantile landowner, James Hopkirk reasoned senior merchants were best suited to this dual role. Becoming a country gentleman at a young age was 'perfectly wrong' as early mercantile lives should be 'wholly devoted to business'.[49] Whether by accident or design, many of his peers followed the same maxim. Merchants who inherited estates among this long-lived group did so around the age of thirty-six, while those who purchased tended to procure them almost a decade later in their lives.[50] In 1801, for instance, Archibald Smith purchased the estate of Jordanhill, aged 52, twenty-two years after taking up a partnership in Leitch & Smith.[51] Not all West India merchants withdrew immediately from commerce and took up a landed lifestyle: a high proportion (twenty-six out of seventy-five West India proprietors, or 35 per cent) retained shares in Glasgow firms on death, transferring colonial wealth to the Scottish countryside throughout their long lives.

Motivations behind mercantile land-purchases varied. The possession of land retained considerable significance in Scotland between 1760 and 1830. An estate of the right size brought social prestige, political influence and a solid income through agricultural rents. These factors partially explain why *arriviste* merchants were so attracted to the land.[52] The social background of West India purchasers provided further insights into the influx. Of the fifty-five Glasgow-West India merchants who purchased directly, twenty-two hailed from the landed ranks, the majority of whom were younger sons.[53] A higher proportion were *parvenus* who reached the landed ranks via West India commerce and new colonial wealth. Within this influx, merchants with interests in Trinidad, Grenada and Demerara were prominent, though the Jamaica interest were the most conspicuous of all.[54]

---

[49] RB 837/165, 'Letter from James Hopkirk to William Simpson', 18 April 1801.

[50] The age of West India merchants on acquisition of estates was known in 105 cases. The average age on acquisition was 42. For those who purchased (72 known cases), the average age was 45, compared to 36 for those who inherited (33 known cases).

[51] GCA, T-SA 7/1/1, Renfrewshire, 1781–1807, 6456.

[52] R. H. Campbell, 'The landed classes', in *People and Society in Scotland, Vol. I: 1760–1830*, ed. T. M. Devine and R. Mitchison (Edinburgh, 1994), pp. 91–109.

[53] Twenty-two merchant-purchasers (who purchased 38 estates) hailed from landed families, and rank of birth is known in 19 cases. Of these, 11 were second sons or younger.

[54] Of estates purchased by *parvenu* merchants, location of their firm's principal trading focus is known in 33 cases. Jamaica merchants were the most important land purchasers (14), followed by Grenada (7), Trinidad (4), Demerara (4), Antigua (2), St Thomas (1).

John Gordon (1753–1828) exemplifies the Glasgow-Jamaica *nouveau riche*. The son of a bailie, he took up a partnership in Stirling, Gordon & Co. in 1790, the firm that took his name. In 1808, Gordon acquired Aikenhead for £22,000 (seemingly borrowing from the University of Glasgow to facilitate the purchase).[55] However, despite the prominence of those who came to land via West India commerce, individuals who hailed from the landed ranks – both inheritors of estates and those who purchased in their own right – held most of the land overall (forty-one merchants, seventy-eight estates). In other words, the accumulation of Glasgow-West India fortunes helped create a new colonial landed elite, but the major effects were to perpetuate and expand the landed portfolios of established families, many of them already involved with the colonial trades.

Whether established gentry or *arriviste* mercantile-landowners, the effects of such a rapid transfer of colonial wealth into west-central Scotland's countryside were spectacular. At the peak of Glasgow's sugar era in 1814, the noted improver Sir John Sinclair extolled the positive effects of mercantile investment and practices on Scottish agricultural development:

> The effects of commerce and manufactures on agriculture ought not to be here omitted. They furnish an advantageous market for the productions of the soil; and thus tend to raise the value of the estates, and the rent of lands. Nay, the opulent merchant is often found a most enterprising improver. And though his experience in agriculture is not commensurate to his capital, yet he often becomes a great benefactor to his country; and in a few years, by his accuracy in accounts, he learns where to spare, and where to lay out his money.[56]

In addition to debates about the extent of ownership noted above, historians have disputed the importance of West India capital on Scottish agriculture. R. H. Campbell was pessimistic about the importance of colonial capital in general, arguing the wealth was in few hands and while it increased the influence of some families and great estates, other sectors of the economy were only indirectly affected.[57] On the other hand, T. M. Devine argued colonial merchants were a significant factor in Scottish agrarian transformation, as they tended to purchase small estates around urban centres, channelling high incomes into agricultural re-organization. In short, there was 'little doubt' this colonial flow made a 'contribution of the first order' to the Scottish

---

[55] NRS, GD1/1209/9, 'Journal of John Gordon', p. 21, p. 25.

[56] J. Sinclair, *General Report of the Agricultural State, and Political Circumstances, of Scotland*, vol. iii (Edinburgh, 1814), p. 326.

[57] R. H. Campbell, *Scotland Since 1707: The Rise of an Industrial Society*, 2nd ed. (Edinburgh, 1992 ed.), pp. 39–43; 'The landed classes', p. 99.

'agricultural revolution'.[58] Previous conclusions have been based upon both Chesapeake and West India merchants, although this section focuses on the latter in isolation. While the West Indian influence on Scottish agriculture was more extensive than has been commonly understood, the greater effects came after 1800.

In 1814, Sir John Sinclair defined the great Scottish landowners as those who owned estates – of which there were 400 – that attracted rents of at least £2,000 Scots. That same year, just over 1,000 'middling properties' attracted rents between £500 and £2,000. However, the most extensive estates in Scotland – over 6,100 – were regarded as 'small properties' with rents under £500 Scots (£12 Scots was equivalent to £1 stg.). It is important to note that great landowners were judged by the extent of the agricultural wealth their estates generated, rather than the size of the properties.[59] For comparison, in 1771 there were 785 'small' proprietors in Lanarkshire, including Glasgow, (which was around 90 per cent of all landowners), rising to almost 1,100 in 1814.[60] Land tax records for 1771 suggest West India merchants tended to come into possession of small properties.[61] Since that was typical in the counties of west-central Scotland they tended to congregate in, this is an unsurprising conclusion.[62] However, confirmation inventories of West India merchants on death indicate rental income tended to be large-scale. Indeed, based upon a sample of twenty-five known estate rents, Sinclair would have classified almost 90 per cent of this group as great landlords.[63] Though there are issues with using land tax rolls as a baseline (as they may not reflect the actual rental income at that point), this analysis tentatively suggests West India merchants generally came into small properties (as defined by rental

---

[58] Devine, 'Glasgow colonial merchants and land, 1770–1815', p. 206; *The Rural Transformation of Scotland: Social Change and the Agrarian Economy, 1660–1815* (Edinburgh, 1994), p. 94.

[59] Sinclair, *General Report of the Agricultural State*, p. 89.

[60] Campbell, 'The landed classes', p. 92.

[61] Annual rents in 1770 are known in 48 cases, ranging from Ballimore (£2,665 Scots) to Glengaber (£40 Scots). Thirty-seven estates (77 per cent) had rents of under £500 Scots. This data was culled from Loretta Timperley's, *A Directory of Land Ownership in Scotland, c.1770* (Edinburgh, 1976). Of the 133 estates in this study, T. M. Devine identified that 71 of them were at least 500 acres. It seems probable many estates were large in acreage, yet small in rental income before West India acquisition. See Devine, 'Glasgow colonial merchants and land, 1770–1815', pp. 248–62.

[62] Campbell, 'The landed classes', p. 92.

[63] Twenty-two of 25 known estate rental incomes at death were above Sir John Sinclair's threshold of £2,000 Scots valued rent (or £153 stg.). They range from Neil Malcolm III, who collected rents of £7,994 sterling on his death in 1857, to Thomas Campbell Hagart, who collected £50 rents from Bantaskine on his death in 1868.

income), yet many, even most, subsequently enjoyed the rentier-incomes of great landowners – very likely after ambitious improvement schemes attracted new tenants to the land.

Glasgow-West India improvement programmes were sometimes ambitious and long-term. After purchasing Jordanhill in 1800 at a cost of £16,500, Archibald Smith sunk almost the same amount into improvements.[64] While the subsequent value of the estate did not rise with this level of investment, the rewards came via increased rental income. Soon after acquiring his estate, Smith discussed plans for improvement with a nearby estate owner, George Oswald of Scotstoun, and how to increase rents beyond what husbandry alone would bring. The effects were seemingly dramatic. A late eighteenth-century valuation roll listed Jordanhill's rental income at £266 Scots: a 'small property' in Sinclair's classification. On Smith's death in 1821, the rental income was £397 sterling (£4,764 Scots): apparently a seventeen-fold increase since 1783.[65] The influx of the Glasgow-West Indians stimulated agricultural and urban development in the west of Scotland. However, the effects of West India improvement, and by extension Caribbean slavery, should not be viewed as especially influential in the classic era of Scottish agricultural change. Just over fifty estates were acquired during the 'agricultural revolution' (1760–1800). As noted above, most estates acquired by the sugar aristocracy came after 1800 (sixty-eight of 122 known acquisition dates). Even so, especially from the 1780s onwards, West India landownership embedded the profits of Caribbean slavery in the Scottish countryside in a variety of different ways.

Improvement of estates almost always began with the house.[66] Confirmation inventories generated on the death of West India merchants provide a record of valuable household effects. Over ninety held goods valued at £131,326, around 4 per cent of the overall wealth held in Scotland. Sixty-one inventories listed holdings in landed estates valued at £96,597 (average £1,583), while thirty-two inventories listed holdings in townhouses valued at £22,142 (average £691). Given that most middling ranks in Glasgow possessed overall wealth of less than £1,000 on death at the time, we begin to understand the grand opulence the West India elites enjoyed.[67] Some merchants probably

[64] GCA, TD1/1095, 'Daybook extracts', 1800–17.

[65] GCA, TD1/27, 'Proposals from George Oswald to Archibald Smith', Dec. 1800; NRS, E106/27/4, 'Renfrewshire valuation rolls' (1784), fo. 9; NRS, CC10/7/4, 'Inventory of Archibald Smith of Jordanhill', 31 Oct. 1821, p. 245.

[66] T. R. Slater, 'The mansion and policy' in *The Making of the Scottish Countryside*, ed. M. L. Parry and T. R. Slater (London, 1980), p. 224.

[67] S. Nenadic, 'The middle-ranks and modernisation', in *Glasgow, Vol. 1: Beginnings to 1830*, ed. T. M. Devine and G. Jackson (Manchester, 1995), pp. 305–7.

stockpiled aesthetically pleasing goods as investments. After his death in 1846, Robert Douglas Alston's 'furniture, pictures, plate and other plenishings' in Auchinraith estate sold for a remarkable £8,824 at auction.[68]

The improvement of Scottish rural estates also had important effects on local economies. The everyday work required for building of new mansions and upkeep of estates provided local tradesmen with employment. On his father's death in 1786, John Smith inherited Craigend castle and immediately rearranged farms and constructed roads. By 1800, 'the laird having by this time become a West India proprietor, had more money to spend and built a very comfortable suitable house'. After John Smith's death in 1816, his son James, also a West India merchant, pulled down the barely two-decades-old edifice. He erected a castle and tower that became known as 'Smith's Folly'.[69] Whether conspicuous extravagance or not, these constructions ensured West India profits seeped into local economies over several years.

Charles Stirling of Kenmure and Cadder (1771–1830), a partner in Stirling, Gordon & Co., was regarded as 'no less active as an agriculturist than as a merchant' perhaps due to his famous rebuilding of Cadder House and improvement of grounds.[70] In 1813, Stirling commissioned Allan & James Scott, timber merchants at Clyde Street in Glasgow, to provide timber, for which they were paid almost £1,000. These employers probably sourced many dozens of skilled tradesmen and manual labourers from the local area for the work. Over the course of thirty individual months of refurbishment between March 1813 and December 1815, Charles Stirling laid out over £5,000 in wages in less than two years. Masons and carpenters were employed throughout, undertaking the vast bulk of the work, as well as skilled woodworkers and plasterers.[71] For comparison, this was equivalent to £4 million in modern wages (relative to worth of average earnings in 2020).[72] This level of investment over the thirty-month period of refurbishment would have provided many thousands of hours of employment for around

[68] NRS, SC36/48/32, Inventory of Robert Douglas Alston, 22 Feb. 1847, p. 549; NRS, SC36/48/35, Additional Inventory of Robert Douglas Alston, 31 Jan. 1849, p. 149.

[69] J. G. Smith, *The Parish of Strathblane and Its Inhabitants from Early Times* (Glasgow, 1886), p. 55.

[70] W. H. Fraser, *The Stirlings of Keir, and Their Family Papers* (Edinburgh, 1858), p. 78.

[71] GCA, T-SK/18/24/1, 'Receipts by tradesmen for wages and other payments during the rebuilding of Cadder House', March 1813–Oct. 1815; *The Glasgow Directory, Containing a List of Merchants, Manufacturers and Traders, From July 1815 until February 1817* (Glasgow, 1815), p. 108, p. 136.

[72] For modern values, see *Measuring Worth* <https://www.measuringworth.com/calculators/ukcompare/> [accessed 21 June 2022]. Relative wage or income worth (average earnings, 2020 values) has been used here.

thirty-five masons and carpenters, or many more of less well-remunerated labourers.[73] This chapter supports Richard Pares' claim that 'West India millionaires [built]…more Fonthills [ie mansions] than factories among them' yet challenges the view that mercantile investment in land was unproductive.[74] While the traditional landed ranks struggled to maintain salubrious lifestyles in late eighteenth-century Scotland, the West India elite that replaced them injected slavery-derived fortunes into improvement and construction schemes in the countryside, facilitating a higher standard of living which served to stimulate developing urban economies.

Commerce: banking, insurance and mercantile credit

Scotland's eighteenth-century financial networks were structured around public and provincial banks. Mercantile involvement with these institutions – such as the eighteenth-century harnessing of the Glasgow banking system for the tobacco trade – is well-known.[75] As noted in Chapter 2, the Glasgow-West India elite had support from Scottish banks and this chapter outlines the quid pro quo of the relationship, assessing capital held in banks as well as wider financial networks. Fifty-nine of the Glasgow-West India elite held c.£870,000 in British banks in shares and account current (13 per cent of all holdings in Britain). Thirty-two individuals held shares in British banks valued at £600,000 (see Table 8.1). A few held shares in English banks, but the vast majority kept their fortunes in Scottish banks, in stock and shares (£553,000) and deposit and current accounts (£273,000). James Ewing of Strathleven was the exceptional case, possessing stock valued at £10,000 in the Bank of England, and investing over £110,000 in Glasgow Union Bank shares on his death in 1853.[76] For comparison, investments in commercial institutions in Scotland were lesser in scale. Inventories reveal that thirty-two West India merchants held stock, shares and policies in insurance firms such as North British Life Insurance and Scottish Widows Insurance –

---

[73] In 1813, the day rate for masons in Glasgow was 3 shillings for a 9-hour day. House carpenters were paid 3 shillings for a 10-hour day. Labourers employed in buildings were paid 1s 10d for a 9-hour day. If employing 35 masons and carpenter a day cost £5 5s, £5,092 allowed for 969 days of work or 33,946 individual paid shifts of employment. See J. Cleland, *Enumeration of the Inhabitants of the City of Glasgow*, 2nd ed. (Glasgow, 1831), p. 231.

[74] R. Pares, 'The economic factors in the history of empire', *The Economic History Review*, vii (May 1937), 119–44, at p. 132.

[75] C. H. Lee, 'The establishment of the financial network', in *The Transformation of Scotland: The Economy Since 1700*, ed. T. M. Devine, C. H. Lee and G. C. Peden (Edinburgh, 2005), p. 106.

[76] NRS, SC65/34/7, 'Inventory of James Ewing', 24 Feb. 1854, pp. 186–7.

worth over £76,000.[77] And just eight individuals held around £100,000 in 3 per cent government consols, underlining that the overall wealth was based upon the Atlantic trades and associated commercial, industrial and agricultural investments across Great Britain rather than rentier income from government stock.

Joint-stock banks in Glasgow, in the view of S. G. Checkland, spearheaded the city's transition to the second 'money centre' of Scotland after 1830.[78] In the period after slavery was abolished in the British West Indies, there was enthusiastic West India support for such institutions. Indeed, in terms of banking assets in Scotland, there were noticeably contrasting investment strategies. Of the wealth held in account current, one-third was in banks in the west of Scotland, especially Glasgow, while two-thirds were held in Edinburgh public banks (with Glasgow branches): the Royal Bank of Scotland (£100,000), the Bank of Scotland (£60,000) and the British Linen Company (£16,000). In terms of stock investment (£556,000), the opposite is true: a small proportion was held in Edinburgh banks (13 per cent), with the remainder sunk into Glasgow banks, especially in two joint-stocks: the Union (£297,000) and the Western (£84,000). James Buchanan (of Dowanhill), James Ewing and Colin Campbell possessed almost £220,000 worth of shares in the Union Bank when they died between 1844 and 1863. Given the nominal capital of the Glasgow Union Banking Company was £2m when it was established as the city's first joint bank in 1830 (of which just £287,000 was paid up within four years), the West India influx must have been substantial.

Timing was important too. Of the shares held in British banks by the Glasgow-West India merchants who died between 1830 and 1859 (valued at £444,000), 77 per cent were in the city's banks. As Glasgow developed into a commercial centre, West India elites provided a substantial influx of capital. This contrasts with the patterns of industrial investments, such as cotton, which tended to be invested in mills outside Glasgow. To summarize, the Glasgow-West India merchants held large reserves of capital in Edinburgh's secure private enterprise banks, yet speculated larger sums in riskier investments in embryonic companies in Glasgow at a critical period.

West India merchants in Glasgow also provided credit that stimulated domestic ventures across Scotland. As discussed in Chapter 2, analysis of confirmation inventories revealed a web of mercantile credit. Almost half of all West India inventories on death contained over 240 references to outlying

---

[77] See, for example, NRS, SC65/34/11, 'Inventory of Colin Campbell', 26 March 1863, p. 463.

[78] S. G. Checkland, *Scottish Banking: A History, 1695–1973* (Glasgow, 1975), pp. 325–42.

credit – bills, bonds, promissory notes – totalling £415,123 (see Table 2.1). For comparison, the average paid capital of provincial banking companies in Scotland in 1810 was £31,000.[79] The nature and extent of the loans are significant: this represented around 12 per cent of their overall assets held in Scotland. The vast majority was owed by debtors resident in Scotland, especially Glasgow, Renfrewshire, Inverness-shire and Lanarkshire. A minority were resident in England and Jamaica. In laying out the capital of around thirteen provincial banks, the Glasgow-West India elite took on the role of a major financial network in the west of Scotland.

The credit was laid out almost exclusively after 1800. Almost half the overall loans had known dates of agreement and the average period of loan (between agreement and death of creditor) was just over five years.[80] The chronology of outlying credit is important. There were financial crises in Scotland in 1793, 1803, 1809–12, 1815, 1818–19, 1825–6 and 1836–7, which, as will be explained below, created a credit shortage as banks refused to discount bills.[81] Since around a third of West India credit with known dates was disbursed in these years, the Glasgow-West India merchants intervened in times of financial crisis. After the abolition of slavery in 1834, large reserves of West India capital stimulated the economy. West India loans disbursed after 1834 tended to be higher value (almost two-thirds of the total value was disbursed after this year). In the peak years of 1834–6 alone, over £76,000 of West India credit flooded onto the domestic market. After slavery was abolished, therefore, Glasgow's merchants increasingly provided large volumes of short-to-medium-term credit to domestic lenders, a practice which extended into the later Victorian period.

A cross-section of Scottish society borrowed from the West India elite of Glasgow (see Table 2.1). As noted in Chapter 2, loans among the West India community of Glasgow themselves were the most common type of debt, totalling £112,748. At just over a quarter of total outlying credit, the West India elite's premier debtors were mercantile peers. This type of relationship boosted the reserves of merchants at different times and furthered their overall enterprise. Others loaned capital to individuals outside the merchant

---

[79] C. Munn, *The Scottish Provincial Banking Companies, 1747–1864* (Edinburgh, 1981), p. 105.

[80] Dates have been identified for a subset of 110 loans totalling £190,203. Approximately two-thirds of loans with known dates (68) were agreed up to 1833, the remainder between 1834 and 1871. However, the smaller sample agreed from 1834 onwards (42) disbursed most of the capital (£121,550).

[81] J. Butt, 'The Scottish cotton industry during the Industrial Revolution, 1780–1840', in *Comparative Aspects of Scottish and Irish Economic and Social history, 1600–1900*, ed. L. M. Cullen and T. C. Smout (Edinburgh, 1977) p. 124; Checkland, *Scottish Banking*, p. 769.

fraternity, and it was common to loan among the family. Often serving as an advance on patrimonial inheritance, relatives not involved with the West India trades were promoted into elite lifestyles. Other types of commercial debtors included the general mercantile community and industrialists. As will be described below, most loans to industrialists were made to those involved with the textile industries. The Scottish aristocracy, gentry and minor landowners were also significant borrowers. John Blackburn was a prominent example of a West India supplier of credit to the elites. On his death in 1840, landed elites, including by the Duke of Hamilton and two sons of Baron MacDonald of the island of Skye, owed interest-bearing debts of over £30,000.[82] In this way, West India merchants propped up the landed elites with colonial credit. With the decline of the provincial banks and the rise of the joint-stock companies in Glasgow after 1810,[83] West India merchants took up some of the slack by offering substantial sums of credit, including in financial crises. In the post-emancipation period, the dissemination of West India capital increased. While the direct investments of Glasgow's West India merchant capital stimulated local industry, especially textiles, their financial networks had a much broader effect. Glasgow's 'sugar aristocracy' should be principally regarded as a commercial interest, meaning a broad range of their activities – investments of merchant capital, credit and Atlantic operations – contributed to the development of Scottish industry.

Industrialization

Although the exact take-off year of the Scottish Industrial Revolution is a matter of some debate (as early as 1760, or as late as 1778), key aspects are not in dispute: the process began later than the English version, and ultimately progressed more quickly. In its first phase, the leading sectors were based upon the manufacture and export of textiles.[84] Whatever starting point is chosen, Scottish economic development was already dependent upon trade with the Americas. From the mid eighteenth century, textile manufacturing – silk, linen and cotton – was the 'secret spring' of the Scottish Industrial Revolution.[85] Linen – made from flax – was the precursor to the cotton industry, establishing an important transatlantic relationship. According to historian Alastair Durie, the European markets were of 'negligible

---

[82] NRS, SC70/1/59, Inventory of John Blackburn, 24 Aug. 1840, pp. 635–49.

[83] Munn, *Scottish Provincial Banking Companies*, p. 80.

[84] C. A. Whatley, *The Industrial Revolution in Scotland* (Cambridge, 1997), pp. 6–7, p .24.

[85] A. Cooke, *The Rise and Fall of the Scottish Cotton Industry, 1778–1914* (Manchester, 2010), p. 1.

importance' to the Scottish linen trade, while North America and the West Indies were the main export markets after 1750. By 1796, as much as 90 per cent of all exports of Scottish linen went to these two regions. Jamaica was the premier market for linen produced in Scotland.[86] Between 1778 and 1785, cotton replaced flax as the raw material powering Scottish industry and added another dimension to the transatlantic relationship.[87] Unlike flax that could be cultivated in Europe, including Scotland, cotton was grown by enslaved people in the Americas and imported to Scotland in large volumes, thus providing employment for handloom weavers and in mills, with finished goods re-exported across the Atlantic. Printed textiles – linen and cotton cloth, handkerchiefs and gowns – were shipped out to the colonies, thus stimulating associated industries such as alum mining, bleaching and dyeing.[88]

Historians are divided on the significance of West India merchant capital to the textile industries. Noting that only a handful of the Glasgow-West India elite held shares in cotton manufactories – alongside the prevalence of capital from other domestic sources – T. M. Devine argued they were unlikely to be a 'decisive influence' on the cotton industry.[89] Anthony Cooke agreed the number of West India merchants who held investments on death were few, just eight, but they generally made large-scale investments (totalling £142,698). Yet, Cooke remained cautious, noting that direct investments were small compared to the fixed capital of Glasgow cotton mills, which were valued at £1m in 1819.[90]

Merchant capital contributed to the development of the linen industry, with Virginia merchants prominent in the eighteenth century.[91] West India merchants certainly diversified into cottage industries and larger-scale textile enterprise. Archibald Smith employed handloom weavers and in 1799 also established Smith, Hutchison and Co., one of the great Glasgow linen houses.[92] The West India elite had a greater impact on the expansion of the

[86] A. Durie, *The Scottish Linen Industry in the Eighteenth Century* (Edinburgh, 1979), p. 152.

[87] I. Donnachie and G. Hewitt, *Historic New Lanark: The Dale and Owen Industrial Community since 1785* (Edinburgh, 2015 ed.), pp. 1–16.

[88] Cooke, *Rise and Fall*, p. 22.

[89] Devine, 'An eighteenth-century business elite', p. 46. See also Devine, 'The colonial trades and industrial investment in Scotland, c.1700–1815', *The Economic History Review*, new series, xxix (1976), 1–13.

[90] Cooke, 'An elite revisited', pp. 144–5.

[91] A. Durie, 'The Scottish linen industry in the eighteenth century: some aspects of expansion', in *Comparative Aspects of Scottish and Irish Economic and Social History, 1600–1900*, ed. L. M. Cullen and T. C. Smout (Edinburgh, 1977), pp. 94–7.

[92] GCA, TD1/107, Day book.

cotton industry, investing in several prominent works after 1778. William McDowall provided capital for the establishment of Houston, Burns & Co., a cotton-works established on the rivers Calder and Cart in 1788.[93] Robert Dennistoun, Alexander Campbell of Hallyards and Colin Campbell entered into a partnership with Robert Owen in the New Lanark Company in 1810–12, putting up £70,000 (38 per cent) of the £182,000 capital.[94] According to Owen, his partners were 'commercial men carrying on business for profit' who opposed his plans for 'increased comforts of villagers' as well as generous wage levels and education provision.[95] After the death of Dennistoun in 1815 and Hallyards in 1817, their shares in Robert Humphrey & Company, a cotton-spinning work in Glasgow, was valued at £21,000.[96] As described by Cooke, the Glasgow-West India merchant firm Dennistoun, Buchanan & Co. invested £160,000 in Stanley Mills in Perth after 1823.[97] James Finlay and Co. was the largest producer of textiles in early nineteenth-century Scotland, with three cotton mills at Ballindalloch, Catrine and Deanston. In 1792, 60 per cent of Finlay and Co.'s capital stock of £22,000 was held by West India merchants (which was decisive). With capital stock rising to £65,000 in 1800, the West India share (£28,000) was by then around 40 per cent.[98]

Confirmation inventories reveal that just nine (who died between 1808 and 1847) held shares in cotton enterprises on death: a total of £136,058, averaging c.£15,100 each. On his death in 1828, the largest holder, John Gordon, possessed stock and shares in James Finlay & Co. valued at £68,725: a four-fold increase on his investments in the firm since 1800.[99] On his death in 1815, Adam Bogle, partner in Robert Bogle & Co., held over £28,000 in Monteith, Bogle & Co. (equivalent to a third of the firm's stock of £86,000 in 1810).[100] The firm co-owned by Henry Monteith operated Blantyre Mill and diversified into Turkey red (dyeing) works in Barrowfield in 1805.

[93] The capital stock for the new works in 1788 was set at £18,000, with William McDowall liable for a third of that. GCA, TD263/194, Contract of Co-Partnery, 1788; HCPP Eighteenth Parliament of Great Britain: fourth session (24 Sept. 1799–29 July 1800), 'Report on Mr. McDowall's petition, &c. &c', p. 181.

[94] NRS, GD64/1/274/13, Contract of Copartnership, 5 Oct. 1810, p. 3.

[95] R. Owen, *The Life of Robert Owen Written by Himself: With Selections from His Writings and Correspondence*, vol. i (London, 1857).

[96] GCA, TD 1696/Box 1, Campbell of Hallyards Papers.

[97] Cooke, *Rise and Fall*, p. 113.

[98] GUA, UGD91/1/4/1/3/1, Ledger of James Finlay and Co., 1792–1800, p. 27, pp. 105–6.

[99] GUA, UGD91/1/4/1/3/1, Ledger, 1792–1800, p. 153; NRS, SC36/48/21, Inventory of John Gordon, 11 Aug. 1828, p. 618.

[100] NRS, SC36/48/13, Inventory of Adam Bogle, 16 July 1818, p. 530; NRS, GD113/5/19e, State of the Affairs of H. Monteith, Bogle & Co., 12 July 1810.

On his death in 1847, Alexander Garden – married to Henry Monteith's daughter – still held £19,952 in Henry Monteith & Co.[101] However, as noted above, financial crises in nineteenth-century Scotland affected medium-size cotton firms, as banks refused to discount bills.[102] West India merchants also provided large-scale credit to major works. For example, Archibald Smith loaned £5,000 on bond to Houston, Burns & Co. in December 1800.[103] Confirmation inventories reveal the Glasgow-West India elite also financed textile and finishing industries in the west of Scotland. Almost £40,000 was loaned to firms and individuals in Lanarkshire, the majority of which went to linen houses, cotton mills and calico printers in Glasgow. West India lenders stepped into the breach, providing loans in crisis years – especially in the 1830s – which probably limited the harmful effects on the industry.

West India commerce provided large-scale employment opportunities in Scotland. In 1831, Sir John Sinclair noted that the cotton industry was 'by far the most important in the kingdom in regard to both the number of persons employed and to the value of their labour'. Textile manufacturers were the largest employers in Scotland, comprising 257,900 workers, of which 154,000 were employed in cotton (60 per cent), with the remainder working in linen (30 per cent) and wool (10 per cent).[104] Approximately 78,000 handloom weavers, working from home or in small manufactories in rural and semi-urban west-central Scotland, were generally dependent upon the Atlantic trades.[105] The majority of Scotland's labouring population were not culpable in the business of chattel slavery, but by working in industries dependent upon the perpetuation and expansion of the system in the British West Indies, they were complicit in, and benefited from, the integrated Atlantic slavery economy. Glasgow-West India merchant capital was sunk into large manufactories and enterprises that helped sustain employment, in contrast to Bristol's eighteenth-century West India merchants, who invested in small-scale industries.[106] The industries chosen by the Glasgow-West India elites had significant multiplier effects and brought large swathes of the Scottish population into the West India spheres of influence.

---

[101] NRS, SC65/34/5, Inventory of Alexander Garden, 23 Dec. 1847, p. 153.

[102] Butt, 'The Scottish cotton industry', p. 769.

[103] GCA, T-SA 7/1/1, Renfrewshire, 1781–1807, 6170.

[104] J. Sinclair, *Analysis of the Statistical Account of Scotland* (Edinburgh, 1831), p. 333; Cooke, *Rise and Fall*, p. 57.

[105] N. Murray, *The Scottish Handloom Weavers, 1790–1850: A Social History* (Edinburgh, 1978), pp. 17–23.

[106] Morgan, 'Bristol West India merchants', p. 186, pp. 200–1.

The extractive industries were also a major component of Scotland's Industrial Revolution. However, the Glasgow-West India elite did not have the same enthusiasm for investing in these as they did for textiles. The much smaller investments are probably explained by the low potential for vertical integration: cotton and finished textiles were obvious investments for West India merchants involved with transatlantic commerce, while coal and iron were of less value as an export commodity. West India investments in Scottish coal firms were negligible, with just one merchant, James Martin, holding just over £2,000 in Stevenson coal company on his death in 1842.[107] Nevertheless, merchants often promoted the exploitation of mineral resources on their estates. Robert Houston Rae's estate, Little Govan, was valued at a remarkable £83,000 in 1800, no doubt due to the large reserves of coal seams underneath the land. This attracted lease income of £30,000, accruing to Houston Rae and Andrew Houston.[108] The mining of coal seams across Glasgow's estates continued throughout the nineteenth century. In 1863, James Smith of Jordanhill leased the mineral rights on the Houstons' land to the Monkland Coal and Iron Company, although the income was only a tenth of the Houston enterprise.[109]

Iron and alum companies attracted only marginally more interest. The Bogle merchant dynasty held investments in the Shotts Iron Company, a prominent producer of pig-iron. The firm was established in 1801 but floated on the Scottish market in 1824 (capital of £100,000 was fully subscribed within a year).[110] On his death in 1821, Robert Bogle junior of Gilmorehill held over £7,700 in the firm.[111] Probably inheriting and extending his father's shares, Archibald Bogle retained investments in the firm valued at over £25,000 on his death in 1858.[112] The alum mining industry was closely associated with the development of textile manufacturing, providing natural dyestuffs for printed linens such as handkerchiefs. Two works near Glasgow were of major importance: George Macintosh's Cudbear Works (established in 1777) and Hurlet & Campsie Alum Company (established

---

[107] NRS, SC36/48/29, Inventory of James Martin, 26 May 1842, p. 185.

[108] HCPP Eighteenth Parliament of Great Britain: fourth session (24 Sept. 1799–29 July 1800) 'Report on Mr. McDowall's petition, &c. &c', p. 181.

[109] GCA, TD1/1100, Lease with Monkland Iron and Steel Company, 1863, p. 2.

[110] R. C. Michie, *Money, Mania and Markets: Investment, Company Formation and the Stock Exchange in Nineteenth-Century Scotland* (Edinburgh, 1981), p. 34.

[111] NRS, CC10/7/4, Inventory of Robert Bogle, 29 Nov. 1821, p. 260.

[112] NRS, SC70/1/98, Inventory of Archibald Bogle, pp. 945–6; NRS, SC70/1/122, Inventory of Archibald Bogle, 14 Sept. 1864, p. 825.

c.1805).[113] There was West India involvement with both. Hugh Hamilton loaned £3,000 to George Macintosh & Company in 1828.[114] There was more significant West India investment in the latter firm. On his death in 1830, West India merchant Charles Stirling of Cadder held shares and stock valued at £24,000 in the Hurlet & Campsie Alum Co., which was the first enterprise of its type in the world.[115] While substantial, these investments do not seem to have been decisive.

Overall, West India merchants invested (in life and death) up to *c*.£500,000 in textile and extractive concerns and provided £45,000 in loans to associated firms and individuals. Textiles were of the greatest interest. Archibald Smith is known to have established a great linen house, while a maximum of around twenty merchants invested in cotton firms. These merchants were usually high ranking, with large investments in cotton enterprise, although disposal before death was not uncommon. The diversification of West India merchant capital was instrumental to the development of some of the great Scottish cotton mills and greatly boosted the personal fortunes of the merchants concerned. While West India merchant capital was not decisive in the establishment of the Scottish cotton industry overall, these merchants were integral at each stage of the process: sourcing and importing cotton, investing fixed capital, providing short- and long-term credit in crisis years and exporting finished goods to the West Indies. The evidence regarding extractive industries, while far from comprehensive, reveals West India investment in only a handful of concerns. While Glasgow-West India merchant capital was important, but not decisive, to the textile-based first phase of Scottish industrialization (*c*.1770s–1830), the merchants' Atlantic and financial operations *were* critically important. Scotland's Industrial Revolution would have accelerated at a much slower pace, and perhaps begun even later, if Glasgow-West India merchants had not supplied the raw materials, facilitated access to markets and provided investment capital and credit in times of financial crisis. By the second phase of industrialization after 1830, the West India contribution to the development of the iron, steel and engineering industries was of negligible importance.

Shipping, canals and railways

West India commerce and capital boosted the development of Scotland's transport infrastructure. The Clyde's rise to a globally renowned centre for

---

[113] B. S. Skillen, 'Aspects of the alum mining industry about Glasgow', *British Mining*, xxxix (1989), 53–60.

[114] NRS, SC6/44/4, Inventory of Hugh Hamilton, 12 Nov. 1829, p. 331.

[115] NRS, SC36/48/22, Inventory of Charles Stirling, 14 July 1830, p. 137.

the construction of steamships poses questions for the early nineteenth century, although Anthony Slaven argued the skills from traditional shipbuilding before 1840 provided little impetus for the later period. Before 1840, the Clyde was a 'very minor' river in terms of the construction of wooden ships. Traditional shipbuilding was an eighteenth-century, innovation, originating with the establishment of the Scotts shipyard of Greenock in 1711. The American War of Independence (1775–83) provided a boost, as it ended the supply of ships and timber from across the Atlantic.[116]

West India firms in Glasgow certainly commissioned new vessels from shipbuilders along the Clyde in Greenock. In December 1806, John Campbell, senior, & Co. hosted a 'great entertainment' in honour of the builders – John Scott and Sons of Greenock – to celebrate the launch of the *Grenada*, which had been put to sea 'amid the loud huzzas of a great concourse of spectators' earlier that day. [117] However, the few investments in ships and shipping companies held by West India merchants on death suggests the ships were held by firms (rather than individuals) as assets.[118] It was more common for individuals to invest in the embryonic steamship enterprise.[119] Nevertheless, the Glasgow-West India fleet assessed in Chapter 4 appears to have included around 340 individual ships between 1806 and 1834. While the exact proportion of the West India contribution to locally built ships awaits detailed examination, the shipping requirements of Glasgow-West India merchants generated a significant trade with multiplier effects elsewhere. A committee of the Royal Bank in Edinburgh examined 'Bonds, Debts and Bills lying over at Glasgow' in 1818 and were of the opinion, due to the extent of bills they received, that West India merchants had a significant impact on local shipping which served to stimulate the local economy:

> The West Indian Merchant builds up a ship for that trade, and purchases goods for that Market; he makes Insurances in both, he grants Bills to the Ship Builder and to the Manufacturer who Endorse them to the Wood Merchant, and the Importer of Cotton, & they discount them to raise Money & purchase fresh Cargoes of Timber and Cotton. In this way an extensive West India Trade must require a great deal of money to carry it on and Banks seem to be safe in furnishing it to them. They get the Security in this case of the General Merchant, of the Wood Merchant, and of the

---

[116] A. Slaven, *The Development of the West of Scotland 1750–1960* (London, 1975), p. 125.

[117] *Caledonian Mercury*, 18 Dec. 1806, p. 3.

[118] The inventories outlined that 4 individuals owned shares in ships valued at £11,609.

[119] Nine individuals held a total of £16,510 shares in firms such as Clyde Steam Navigation Company (£15,200) and Clyde Shipping Co. (6 merchants, shares of £1,278).

ship Builder; in the other case, the security of the General Merchant, of the Manufacturer and of the Cotton Merchant; at least three respectable persons for each advance…It is difficult [for the Bank] to employ money for a short period more profitably & securely than in such discounts. When the ship returns from the West Indies, the Merchant, to enable him to take up the bills granted for her outfit must sell the cotton, the Sugar, the Rum, the Coffee, the Mahogany & other India produce imported, each of these articles probably to one or more different persons or copartneries, from each of whom he obtains Bills. These bills or part of them are offered for discount, if it is thought they are entitled to credit at the Bank, if the situation of the Cash there admits of discount at the time for here, as in the former case, there is reason to expect both profit and safety, the Bills being fairly onerous transactions in the way of trade.[120]

Joseph Inikori has described how 'backward linkages' of shipping and shipbuilding stimulated iron, copper, ropes and wood production, which were important multiplier effects in the British economy in the mercantilist period.[121] While there is no evidence that West India merchant capital was a significant influence on the growth of shipbuilding in the west of Scotland before 1840, this banking intelligence suggests the systemic influence of West India commerce upon the wider economy was profound.

West India merchant capital did improve the regional transport infrastructure, especially canals. The Forth and Clyde Canal, which traversed Scotland, resulted from 'enlightened commercial thinking', as it facilitated the shipment of produce by Glasgow merchants to Europe and the transportation of agricultural products to larger markets in the west. Perhaps unsurprisingly, 'tobacco lords' John Glassford and John Ritchie were involved at the outset, although the outbreak of the American War of Independence stalled its progress. Building began in 1768 and it took twenty-two years to build the canal at a cost of nearly £394,000. The Monkland Canal allowed deeper exploitation of rich Lanarkshire coalfields and took twelve years to construct, opening in 1793 at a cost of £120,000.[122] Naturally, West India merchants invested in both canal systems. The Forth and Clyde Canal allowed the re-export of produce to Europe, while merchants hoped the construction of the Monkland Canal would break the monopoly of coal-masters over transportation. Twenty West India merchants who died between 1805 and 1869 (almost a fifth of all confirmation inventories) held

[120] RB12/17, 'Directors minutes', 1817–20, fos. 135–145.

[121] J. Inikori, *Africans and the Industrial Revolution in England: A Study in International Trade and Economic Development* (Cambridge, 2002), pp. 265–6.

[122] T. J. Dowds, *The Forth and Clyde Canal: A History* (East Linton, 2003), pp. 9–10; Slaven, *Development of the West of Scotland*, pp. 32–4.

a total of £139,444 in Scottish canals and navigation companies. These included the Forth and Clyde Canal (£86,864), the Union Canal (£26,500), the Monkland Canal (£14,520) and the Edinburgh and Glasgow Union Canal (£1,200). The extraordinary investment held in the Forth and Clyde Canal reveals West India merchants such as Thomas Dunlop Douglas had an integral role in what one historian described as a 'Glasgow takeover' of the highly profitable enterprise after 1815.[123]

The advance of railways gradually made the canal system obsolete. Glasgow's West India merchants invested in both – a pattern consistent with other British enslavers in the 1830s. The impact of West India capital has been underestimated in previous studies of railway funding; while the contribution of 'merchants' has been noted, specific sources of mercantile capital remained undefined due to the ambiguous nature of the occupational description.[124] Anthony Cooke noted that colonial merchants and returnees invested in railways after 1834. Thus, for Cooke, merchant capital had an impact in Scotland beyond 'manufacturing, mining and agriculture', as laid out in T. M. Devine's 'Did slavery make Scotia great?'[125] Cooke claimed that West India merchants were 'actively involved in the "second phase" of Scotland's economic transformation through substantial railway investment in the 1840s and 1860s'.[126] However, the investments by these West India merchants were small-scale in the context of overall Scottish railway investments, which totalled £28 million by 1860.[127] This assertion is further reinforced if examined over the longer period, as nearly £47 million had been invested by 1870.[128]

Glasgow-West India investment was of overall negligible importance to the development of Scottish railways in the Victorian period. In fact, this group invested more in Scottish canals and English railways. Of the fifty-seven Glasgow-West India merchants who died after 1839, approximately one-third (19) held

---

[123] D. A. R. Forrester, 'Early canal company accounts: financial and accounting aspects of the Forth and Clyde navigation, 1768–1816', *Accounting and Business Research*, x (1980), 109–23, at p. 119; NRS, SC6/44/34, Inventory of Thomas Dunlop Douglas, 26 March 1869, p. 679.

[124] W. Vamplew, 'Sources of Scottish Railway share capital before 1860', *Scottish Journal of Political Economy*, xvii (1970), 425–40, at p. 437; T. R. Gourvish and M. C. Reed, 'The financing of Scottish railways before 1860 – a comment', *Scottish Journal of Political Economy*, xviii (1971), 209–20, at p. 215.

[125] T. M. Devine, 'Did slavery make Scotia great?', *Britain and the World*, iv (2011), 40–64, at p. 57.

[126] Cooke, 'An elite revisited', pp. 144–6.

[127] Vamplew, 'Scottish Railway share capital', p. 425.

[128] Devine, 'Industrialisation', pp. 61–2.

investments valued at £298,498 in British railways. Of this, seventeen held £118,989 in Scottish companies, with five holding investments worth £179,509 in English companies. Thomas Dunlop Douglas was the leading investor in British railways.[129] Archibald Smith (1795–1883) was the top investor in Scottish railways, speculating widely in the mid nineteenth century – although it is unlikely the subscriptions were ever paid up in full. The investments he retained on death (c.£19,000) represented a small proportion of the subscriptions he made by 1846 (c.£460,000).[130] Large investments of West India capital undoubtedly contributed to the 'railway mania' in mid nineteenth-century Britain, although this represented a tiny proportion of the capital raised in Scotland. Speculation by the West India elite stimulated a boom that increased local interest and the value of their own shares, although, in general, this group invested more in Scotland's canal infrastructure.

Charity and philanthropy

In 1834, the radical weekly *The Reformers Gazette* represented Glasgow's 'sugar lords' as reluctant contributors to the maintenance of the poor: 'What a heartless narrow-minded set! – wallowing in wealth, yet grudging a miserable pittance to support their poor helpless fellow-creatures!'[131] This section assesses that claim through an examination of testamentary bequests in the wills of the Glasgow-West India elite – with the caveat that testamentary bequests may not actually have reached intended recipients if, for example, the post-mortem evaluation of assets did not cover all bequests. Nevertheless, as will be explained, many such bequests evidently did reach their intended donations, and some are still dispersed today.[132]

Charity was an essential feature of many religious faiths: donations to the less fortunate were viewed as 'thank offerings' for the elevated lives of givers which salved the conscience of the wealthy. By contrast, philanthropy was less rooted in judgement of beneficiaries and intended to improve conditions within existing societal structures. In pre-Victorian Scotland, these two concepts – traditional charity and philanthropy – centred around the parish poor law, education provision, orphaned children, the elderly, the sick and

---

[129] NRS, SC 6/44/34, Inventory of Thomas Dunlop Douglas, 20 March 1869, pp. 677–92.

[130] *GH*, 14 Aug. 1846, p. 1; NRS, SC65/34/26, Inventory of Archibald Smith, 16 April 1883, pp. 295–310; S. Mullen, 'A Glasgow-West India merchant house and the imperial dividend, 1779–1867', *Journal of Scottish Historical Studies*, xxxiii (2013), 196–233.

[131] *The Reformers' Gazette*, 1 Feb. 1834, pp. 2–4.

[132] This is based on a sample of 77 last wills and testaments showing 21 Glasgow West India merchants and planters left philanthropic and charitable bequests between 1811 and 1869 valued at £79,855 (of overall wealth £3,351,487 held in Scotland).

benevolent institutions.[133] The donations examined here are consistent with these key functions: only orphanages seem not to have received West India money. Thus, some gifts were intended for the improvement of society overall, while others were designated for a specific purpose based on social rank, sex and age.

The Glasgow-West India elite donated substantial sums in life and death that contributed to improving lives in Scotland, especially Glasgow. One prominent merchant, Charles Stirling of Cadder, donated almost £200 to charity in a twelve-month period.[134] In death, twenty-one West India merchants (a fifth of the inventoried group) made philanthropic and charitable bequests valued at £79,000 between 1811 and 1869, the vast majority (by value) in the Victorian period. This was c.2 per cent of their overall wealth held in Scotland. None of the West India merchants bequeathed more than 5 per cent of their personal wealth to charities – most left under 1 per cent – except James Ewing of Strathleven. Among Glasgow's sugar aristocracy, Ewing's various bequests (totalling c.£68,000) were truly exceptional: around a quarter of his West India fortune was bequeathed to charitable and philanthropic causes on his death in 1853. From 1819, Ewing was an acolyte of the Revd Thomas Chalmers, whose belief in social bond philosophy in St John's Parish in Glasgow compelled his followers to assist those less fortunate than themselves.[135] Consistent with this, Ewing made substantial donations to the Free Church of Scotland (£18,100) and the Royal Infirmary (£10,000). The largest legacy was £31,000 to the Merchants House.[136] For comparison, Ewing's gifts seem to be slightly more than the Buchanan bequest described in Chapter 6, but just over half of the bequest left by returned Jamaica sojourner James Dick, which was among the largest of its kind in nineteenth-century Scotland.[137] In terms of contemporary value and long-term legacy, James Ewing's donation of £100 to the University of Glasgow in 1828 is equivalent to £433,000 (2016 values). It is estimated to have generated income of around £1.6 million for

[133] O. Checkland, *Philanthropy in Victorian Scotland: Social Welfare and the Voluntary Principle* (Edinburgh, 1980), p. 2, p. 12.

[134] GCA, T-SK 18/26/5/22, Charles Stirling's Books, 30 June 1829.

[135] I. Maver, 'Power and politics in the Scottish city: town council in the nineteenth century', in *Scottish Elites*, ed. T. M. Devine (Edinburgh, 1994), p. 105; Checkland, *Philanthropy in Victorian Scotland*, p. 3.

[136] NRS, SC65/34/7, 'Inventory of James Ewing', 24 Feb. 1854, p. 193.

[137] M. Cruickshank, 'The Dick Bequest: the effect of a famous nineteenth-century endowment on parish schools of north east Scotland', *History of Education Quarterly*, v (1965), 153–65.

student scholarships between 1828 and 2017.[138] Seemingly minor donations had major implications.

The West India elite sought, albeit rarely, to give something back to the source of their wealth. These gestures often came with the proviso of Christianizing enslaved people and their descendants. Citing his belief in the Established Church of Scotland in 1829, Charles Stewart Parker begged for 'the forgiveness of God and even of my fellow man and Christians...at many periods of my life I know I have said and done many things which I ought not'. Whether Parker was referring to his status as an owner of enslaved people in Demerara is unknown, but it is possible his bequests to the Auxiliary Moravian Society in the West Indies were intended as atonement.[139] But Glasgow-West India merchants mainly donated to institutions across Scotland with the majority (80 per cent of total value) bequeathed to institutions in Glasgow. From the nineteenth century onwards, the ways in which Glasgow's middling ranks dealt with social problems and the poor dramatically shifted. Throughout the previous century, charitable donations tended to be administered to beneficiaries known to the donors or through the Church, trade guilds and town council. This model endured alongside the establishment of new charitable bodies in the early nineteenth century, which immediately attracted West India donations.[140] The Merchants House received the highest sums in the city (£31,325). Some of this was for the maintenance of the institution, such as James Ewing's £1,000 to the dean of guild 'for behoof of that Incorporation', but three separate bequests of £10,000 were intended for dispersal among failing merchants and their families (the latter bequest, Ewing No. 2, was merged in 1909 with the Buchanan bequest as described in Chapter 6). Thus, Ewing's nepotistic bequests regenerated the mercantile ranks fallen on hard times.[141] While the Merchants House received the most capital for dispersal in wider society, the Royal Infirmary of Glasgow was the institution favoured most by West India philanthropists.

An early nineteenth-century shift in the nature of charitable donations (from the giving of personal alms to institutional dispersal) explains why Glasgow-West India merchants were more philanthropic in death than their eighteenth-century predecessors, the 'tobacco lords', although it does not explain why they donated more than their successors, the 'cotton

---

[138] S. Mullen and S. Newman, 'Slavery, abolition and the University of Glasgow' <https://www.gla.ac.uk/media/media_607547_en.pdf> [accessed 1 Jan. 2019].

[139] NRS, SC36/51/7, Will of Charles Stewart Parker, 5 Jan. 1829, p. 475, p. 485.

[140] Nenadic, 'The middle ranks', pp. 296–9.

[141] NRS, SC65/34/7, Inventory of James Ewing, 24 Feb. 1854, pp. 199–200.

masters'.[142] The more extensive West India philanthropy can be explained as an attempt to shape post-mortem reputations. As Katie Donington has noted, philanthropy's 'silent power' allowed many slave-owning donors to reshape their reputations and obtain 'terrestrial fame' in perpetuity.[143] Consistent with the functions of traditional charity and philanthropy in pre-Victorian Scotland, West India fortunes were bequeathed to kirk parishes for the poor, to institutions for educational provision, the sick and elderly, including through a range of benevolent institutions.[144] Gifts were often connected to religious beliefs. Prior to 1845, the Church of Scotland had a crucial role administering relief. Kirk sessions and ministers in locations such as Mouline in Perthshire, Ayr, Alloway and Girvan in Ayrshire as well as Moy and Dallaross near Nairn received ten bequests, especially for the use of the poor. And donations were not restricted to a single sect. James Ewing was a major influence on the advance of the Free Church and evangelical Protestantism across Scotland and abroad. Thus, philanthropic bequests often reflected the religious affiliations of Glasgow merchants which directed where slavery wealth rested in home parishes across Scotland.

There was a rich tradition of voluntary donations to Scottish education; indeed most education provision before 1872 depended on endowments.[145] West India merchants bequeathed donations totalling £11,520 that named education or educational institutions in Glasgow and a couple in Ayrshire. James Ewing set aside £10,000 to the Merchants House – Ewing's Bequest No.2 – to be used for 'the purpose of educating, training and settling in business the sons of decayed Glasgow merchants' (and the interest that accrued from this was ultimately gifted to educational institutions across the west of Scotland). Eight other West India merchants left donations totalling c.£1,500. These bequests went to schools, with some bequests designated based upon sex. In 1815 James Smith left £100 to Archibald Millar's charity school on 151 George Street.[146] Founded in 1790, the school was for 'female children…[and] daughters of reputable parents or who live

---

[142] Devine's *Tobacco Lords* does not reveal any substantial philanthropy. Anthony Cooke shows just 5 'cotton masters' bequeathed a total of £87,000, though the majority of this was from slave-owner James Ewing, who sunk West India capital into manufacturing interests (Ewing's charity donations were listed at £49,000, an underestimation of his philanthropic donations by around a quarter). Cooke, 'Scottish cotton masters', Appendix.

[143] K. Donington, *The Bonds of Family: Slavery, Commerce and Culture in the British Atlantic World* (Manchester, 2019), p. 256.

[144] Checkland, *Philanthropy in Victorian Scotland*, p. 2, p .12.

[145] Checkland, *Philanthropy in Victorian Scotland*, p. 15.

[146] NRS, SC36/48/9, Inventory of James Smith, 9 June 1815, p. 695, p. 704.

with reputable people' who were eligible to attend for three years if they were free from infectious disease and not in receipt of parochial aid (that is, not the poor underclass).[147] West India capital thus provided an education for daughters of 'deserving' people of Glasgow, an education they could not have afforded otherwise. Less often, gifts to educational institutions were intended to improve life chances of the poor. In 1829, for example, Hugh Hamilton donated £60 to Ayr Academy, some of which was intended for the 'poor scholar natives of Ayr and Alloway'.[148] Other bequests were targeted at specific groups. Charles Stuart Parker's £500 to the Gaelic school of Glasgow catered for the Highland community of the city. Parker was not a Highlander by birth but frequented the Gaelic Club of Glasgow and married into a prominent Highland-West India family.[149]

Attitudes to the care of the sick shifted in early nineteenth-century Scotland, explaining why most of the individual bequests (43, or 35 per cent) were left to institutions to improve public health. The Royal Infirmary of Glasgow – founded in 1792 – was the single most popular institution, attracting fifteen separate bequests totalling over £12,000 (over 80 per cent was donated by James Ewing). Given the annual subscriptions in 1842 totalled c.£2,500, this was a considerable sum, yet the contributions were probably not given for entirely altruistic purposes.[150] In 1837, West India merchant Patrick Playfair left post-mortem instructions for his bequest of £150: 'the Barony Parish shall…have right to recommend annually six patients'.[151] While most bequests were seemingly intended to improve the premier hospital in the city, these bequests probably catered for the nominees made by the institution's hierarchy or local parishes rather than the poor.

West India donations also catered for the less able, the dispossessed and the elderly. The Glasgow Blind Asylum was established in 1804, with its first building erected in 1828. West India merchant John Leitch bequeathed £5,000 in the early years.[152] In death, others bequeathed six gifts totalling £1,550 to the Blind Asylum between 1834 and 1869. The Glasgow Lunatic Asylum was founded in 1814 and received nine donations from West India merchants between 1815 and 1854 (£2,650).[153] The Glasgow Deaf and Dumb Asylum, established in 1819, received £580 in six donations between 1823

---

[147] *Post Office Glasgow Directory, 1865–6* (Glasgow, 1865), p. 762.

[148] NRS, SC6/44/4, Settlement of Hugh Hamilton, 12 Nov. 1829, p. 338.

[149] NRS, SC36/51/7, Last Will of Charles Stewart Parker, 5 Jan. 1829, p. 475, p. 485.

[150] Checkland, *Philanthropy in Victorian Scotland*, p. 162.

[151] NRS, SC36/51/14, Settlement of Patrick Playfair, 24 March 1837, p. 77.

[152] J. Christie, *The Medical Institutions of Glasgow* (Glasgow, 1888), p. 170.

[153] Christie, *The Medical Institutions of Glasgow*, p. 123.

and 1869. Around 20 per cent of children from the 'respectable poor' were admitted free, no doubt assisted by West India wealth.[154] The Glasgow Eye Infirmary was established in 1824 and received three donations totalling £600 between 1845 and 1852.[155] The House of Refuge in Glasgow received £2,200 between 1852 and 1853. From 1838, a House of Refuge for women and another for boys were under the same management, catering for criminals, prostitutes and delinquents.[156] In 1854, the Night Asylum received £300 from James Ewing 'for the houseless'.[157] The Old Man's Society received £650 between 1845 and 1869. Gifts from West India merchants to such institutions underline that wealth derived from Caribbean slavery had a wider social impact, improving the lives of a broad group of individuals comprising the most vulnerable of Glasgow society with no direct connections to the Atlantic trades.

This chapter now turns to one of the greatest philanthropic gifts in the history of Glasgow. The Ewing bequests to the city of Glasgow were described by a biographer in 1857 as 'almost unparalleled', yet were superseded later in the nineteenth century.[158] The Bellahouston bequest was established in March 1892 after the death of Miss Elizabeth Steven. Her brother Moses Steven and her sister Grace had accumulated property valued between £400,000 and £500,000, which was held in trust to be administered by trustees for the benefit of 'charitable, educational and benevolent institutions' of the city.[159] The initial source of the family wealth was their father, Moses Steven of Polmadie, who, as noted above, was a landed West India merchant in Glasgow. Moses Steven (1749–1831) was in partnership with his first cousin, James Buchanan of Dowanhill, and others in two prominent West India merchant firms in Glasgow: Buchanan, Steven & Co., and its successor firm Dennistoun, Buchanan & Co.[160] A West India fortune secured, he purchased a country estate, Polmadie, just south of Glasgow, and married the daughter of neighbouring laird, William Rowan of Bellahouston.[161] Steven died in 1833, leaving personal wealth of

---

[154] Christie, *The Medical Institutions of Glasgow*, pp. 173–4.

[155] Christie, *The Medical Institutions of Glasgow*, p. 112.

[156] Checkland, *Philanthropy in Victorian Scotland*, p. 236.

[157] NRS, SC65/34/7, 'Inventory of James Ewing', 24 Feb. 1854, p. 201.

[158] G. Blair, *Biographic and Descriptive Sketches of Glasgow Necropolis* (Glasgow, 1857), p. 182.

[159] *GH*, 17 March 1892, p. 6.

[160] Smith, *Strathendrick*, p. 217.

[161] GCA, T-SA 7/1/2, 'Renfrewshire, 1809–1820', 8428.

over £31,000: a mid-ranking fortune below the average of other West India merchants in this study.[162]

Yet, much of his wealth was in land. In addition to Polmadie, he purchased some plots on the Bellahouston estate, and in 1824 the full estate was bequeathed to his son. His daughters were left £10,000 each with his son as heir (although it is very likely the daughters received slightly less). Moses Steven junior died in 1871, leaving a fortune of £36,872.[163] Before his death, he expressed 'a wish that his fortune, which had come from Glasgow, should go back to Glasgow', and his sisters carried out this wish. A joint deed of 25 August 1871 executed what was effectively a joint will.[164] By 1892, Miss Elizabeth Steven left between £400,000 and £500,000 in trust to be administered for 'charitable, educational and benevolent institutions' of the city.[165] The bequest established bursaries at the University of Glasgow, with other grants to various institutions within the city boundaries. These included Glasgow Royal Infirmary, Glasgow Western Infirmary, Glasgow Society for the Education of the Deaf and Dumb, Glasgow Blind Asylum, West of Scotland Convalescent Seaside Homes, Glasgow City Mission or the Society for Promoting the Religious Interests of the Poor of Glasgow and its Vicinity, Glasgow Royal Asylum for Lunatics, Society for Relief of Indigent Gentlewomen of Scotland, Glasgow Night Asylum and the Kirk session of Govan and Bellahouston 'for the relief of poor persons not receiving parochial aid'.[166] When the Glasgow School of Art commissioned a new building – which ultimately became the Mackintosh building – in 1897, almost half by value (£10,000) of the initial estimated costs of £21,000 came from the Bellahouston bequest. A further £2,500 was granted for an extension scheme in 1926.[167] For comparison, these donations are equivalent to £4.91m, relative to worth of average earnings in modern values.[168]

The Bellahouston bequest continues to be dispersed across the city on an annual basis. In 2019, the Bellahouston Fund was worth just over £5.5m

---

[162] NRS, SC58/42/6, Inventory of Moses Steven, 10 July 1833, pp. 389–96.

[163] NRS, SC36/48/67, Inventory of Moses Steven junior, 27 Oct. 1871, p. 198.

[164] *GH*, 28 March 1892, p. 13.

[165] *GH*, 17 March 1892, p. 6.

[166] *GH*, 8 April 1892, p. 4.

[167] *The Scotsman*, 2 Feb. 1897, p. 8; 27 Oct. 1926, p. 10.

[168] For modern values, see *Measuring Worth* <https://www.measuringworth.com/calculators/ukcompare/> [accessed 21 June 2021]. Relative wage or income worth (average earnings, 2020 values) has been used here.

sterling.[169] Charitable donations of c.£1.2m were disbursed to organizations 'within the parliamentary boundaries of the City of Glasgow' in a four-year period up to 2019, with around sixty-five funded each year.[170] Among other recipients, the Scottish Opera, Bellahouston Academy, the National Theatre of Scotland and the Prince and Princess of Wales Hospice received grants in 2016.[171] West India spheres of influence remain a quotidian, if unacknowledged, feature of life in Glasgow today.

Assessing the proportion of slavery wealth that made up the Bellahouston bequest is impossible. The trust was established via a second-generation mercantile fortune, inherited from a father whose personal wealth derived from multiple sources: West India commerce and landed estates in Glasgow. Slavery-based Atlantic trades provided the principal accumulation of capital which facilitated diversification into landed property, although marriage increased the portfolio. In this case, land was probably of more value than West India commerce, yet the estates would not have been acquired in the first place without colonial profits. Slavery and its associated commerce were principal factors in the accumulation of the Bellahouston fortune and remain an important part of the fabric of Glasgow today.

This chapter has unravelled a broad mosaic of institutions into which capital derived from slavery has historically seeped: religious institutions, women's and Gaelic schools, universities, hospitals, infirmaries, homeless shelters, asylums. Ascertaining the exact proportions of who benefited most is no easy task. The *Reformers Gazette*'s representation of a miserly West India elite was not entirely accurate. However, while gifts specifically intended for the poor were common, they tended to be low value. Only around 20 per cent of all testamentary gifts – a total of c.£4,000 – made explicit references to the poor in Scotland. Some gifts, like Wilson's charity, actively discriminated against those who had been in receipt of parochial aid – the 'undeserving poor' – a prejudice not uncommon in pre-Victorian Scotland.[172] The irresistible conclusion is that while *all* ranks of society benefited from the West India elite's charitable and philanthropic donations, Victorian Glasgow's middle class, especially those who had fallen on hard times, gained the most.

[169] The Bellahouston Bequest Fund, Report and Statement of Financial Activities, for the year ended 30 June 2019.

[170] Bellahouston Bequest Fund <https://www.oscr.org.uk/about-charities/search-the-register/charity-details?number=SC011781> [accessed 5 Oct. 2020].

[171] The Bellahouston Bequest Fund, Report and Statement of Financial Activities, for the year ended 30 June 2016, p. 5, pp. 9–10.

[172] Checkland, *Philanthropy in Victorian Scotland*, p. 15.

Conclusion

In a *Dissertation on the Business of the Counting House* (1820), commercial educator James Morrison noted the successful accumulation of merchant capital created 'spheres of influence' in which the prosperity extended outwards: to family and friends and influencing Scottish trade and commerce more broadly.[173] Important arenas in which Glasgow-West India merchant capital rested have been assessed here: agriculture, commerce, industry, infrastructure development, charitable and philanthropic causes. West India capital also had a profound effect on Scottish agricultural development, bringing new tenants to the land and employing dozens of tradesmen in construction enterprises. Previous studies have characterized the Glasgow-West India elite as principally transferring capital from Atlantic trades to agricultural and industrial enterprise, especially influencing the development of the Scottish textile industry and railways.[174] While the significance of West India merchant capital to the development of railways was negligible, it was of some importance to the Scottish cotton industry. And this study reveals a wider relationship which not only involved the investment of the fixed capital and the facilitation of imports and exports, but also the provision of credit at crisis points. The first phase of Scotland's Industrial Revolution, principally centred around textiles, would not have progressed in the same timescale, or provided the same employment opportunities, in the absence of an established West India mercantile community in Glasgow. Given West India commerce was so fundamental to wider economic development in the take-off period of Scotland's Industrial Revolution, it seems these men were proportionately more important to the development of local economies than their respective counterparts in Bristol or Liverpool. West India 'spheres' of industrial influence, overall, extended to hundreds of thousands of textile workers but became less important with the rise of heavy industry in the Victorian period.

While West India merchant capital, and its wider processes, had a significant influence on Scottish industrialization, this study suggests a rethink is required. The Glasgow 'sugar aristocracy' were a commercial interest first, and an industrial interest second. Indeed, in terms of extent of holdings, the greater investments lay in commerce; wealth held in banking and insurance; and the laying out of large-scale loans across the west of Scotland. The true effects on the development of Scottish banking can only be surmised, but large reserves of West India merchant capital were held in account current, and in stocks and shares, all of which stimulated

---

[173] Morrison, *Complete Treatise on Practical Book-Keeping*, p. xiii.

[174] Devine, 'An eighteenth-century business elite'; Cooke, 'An elite revisited', p. 146.

wider development. The effects of the major loans both taken and loaned by the 'sugar aristocracy' are even harder to gauge, but a large cross-section of Scottish society, including many involved with developing industries, were both indebted to them and accrued annual interest from outlying (and often large-scale) loans.

Finally, the greatest effects of Glasgow-West India merchant capital might have come from only a small proportion of their overall wealth: charitable and philanthropic initiatives. In terms of providing employment through the industries they invested in, as well as charity and philanthropy, the West India elites took the profits of slavery to the masses in a way that their predecessors, the 'tobacco lords', did not. The legacies of slavery were, and remain, an everyday feature of the west of Scotland, though on a much less significant scale today than in the era discussed here. Nevertheless, institutions and trust funds with antecedents in the colonial period are conduits of slavery wealth and continue to disburse the profits today in Glasgow and across Scotland more broadly. If capital is managed properly – as is the case in many institutions – by only expending income from the principal on an annual basis, these funds remain in perpetuity. The challenge is to identify these pots of West India merchant capital and to ascertain slavery's collective impact from inception to the modern period. While the effects of Glasgow-West India mercantile 'spheres of influence' were profound in the sugar heyday, their reach has gradually contracted as the centuries have passed. Nevertheless, Caribbean slavery and its capital influenced various aspects of eighteenth- and nineteenth-century society, and remains a quotidian, if unseen, fact of life in the city of Glasgow today.

Conclusion

By the late eighteenth century, Glasgow was a great commercial metropolis. The city's eighteenth-century 'tobacco lords' had established a system of global commerce centred around the Atlantic trades, utilizing local capital and credit, and making numerically limited but strategically significant investments in industry. While laying the foundations, however, their heyday was all but over by the onset of the Scottish Industrial Revolution in 1778. After the American War of Independence (1775–1783) ended Glasgow's monopoly of the Virginia tobacco trade, Atlantic traders in the city shifted commercial focus to sugar and the Caribbean, taking advantage of long-term Scottish diasporic networks (which counterparts in Liverpool and Bristol could not do). The West India trades underpinned Scotland's rapid industrial growth post-1783.

This marked the dawn of a new social order as the Glasgow 'sugar aristocracy' rose to prominence as the city's wealthiest and most influential commercial grouping. Yet this was not an entirely new cohort; some were sons of 'tobacco lords', while others married into tobacco families, taking advantage of capital via tochers. The West India trades were largely financed from domestic sources (especially via the wealth of fathers and fathers-in-law already involved with the colonial trades), quickly generating profits that ensured the rise of multi-generational dynasties as younger male relatives, especially sons, became involved. West India commerce often generated considerable personal wealth: some went on to become the richest men in Scotland, with diverse portfolios of personal investments in land, industry and commerce. Many of the men involved became citizens of considerable social distinction with significant political influence, in possession of landed estates, who socialized in exclusive social clubs and married women from elite families. In death, many left substantial philanthropic commitments that improved wider society. But questions remain. How important was Glasgow-West India merchant capital to the commercial and industrial development of the city? To what extent did the West India trades drive regional and national development? What were the effects upon Scottish society? And how important was slavery-derived capital to Scotland more broadly?

R. H. Campbell noted three interpretive positions on the importance of trade to industry during the transformation of Glasgow from a commercial to an industrial city.[1] This study adds support to the third: namely that the West India trades were fundamental to industrial expansion after the 1770s, with important continuities after the American Revolution. Major industries in and around Glasgow were dependent upon West India commerce, although this was not the only factor driving change. Nevertheless, the commercial system, and by extension Caribbean slavery, was fundamental to industrial growth from the 1770s up to 1830. At the same time, it must be recognized that West India merchant capital had greater significance in industry (especially cotton) *outside* Glasgow's boundaries. As the evidence here underlines, the Glasgow-West India elite invested across successive phases of Scotland's Industrial Revolution, in cotton and, to a much lesser extent, iron and coal. They also invested in the infrastructure that made the transportation of goods more efficient: canals and, to a lesser extent, the railway system after 1840. Personal investments were rarely a decisive factor, but they were substantial. As Campbell perceptively noted, the merchants' greatest contribution to the development of Glasgow industry was not in turning into large-scale industrialists, but instead in continuing to work as merchants.[2] The linen phase of Scottish proto-industrialization (not exclusively a Glasgow industry) was dependent upon export markets. In the 1790s, over 60 per cent of Scottish linen was exported to North America and especially the West Indies. The cotton phase of Scotland's Industrial Revolution (*c.*1778–1800) was reliant upon both imports and exports from the West Indies in particular. In the 1820s, 86 per cent of the cotton workforce in Scotland produced goods for foreign export compared to the 14 per cent involved in production for the Scottish and English market.[3] The West India merchants were instrumental to these processes in Glasgow and its hinterlands, which had important multiplier effects for large swathes of the Scottish population, especially in the west-central region.

The greatest effects of the Glasgow 'sugar aristocracy' have been characterized in terms of direct industrial investments and wider processes that influenced the development of the Scottish textile industry.[4] These

[1] R. H. Campbell, 'The making of the industrial city', in *Glasgow, Vol 1: Beginnings to 1830*, ed. T. M. Devine and G. Jackson (Manchester, 1995), pp. 190–2.

[2] Campbell, 'The making of the industrial city', p. 191.

[3] A. Durie, *The Scottish Linen Industry in the Eighteenth Century* (Edinburgh, 1979), p. 152; A. Cooke, *The Rise and Fall of the Scottish Cotton Industry, 1778–1914* (Manchester, 2010), p. 58.

[4] T. M. Devine, 'An eighteenth-century business elite: Glasgow West India merchants, 1740–1815', *The Scottish Historical Review*, lvii (1978), 40–67; A. Cooke, 'An elite revisited: Glasgow West India merchants, 1783–1877', *Journal of Scottish Historical Studies*, xxxii (2012), 127–65.

effects were indeed substantial, but this study underlines their importance as a commercial, financial and philanthropic interest. The extension of the national banking system to Glasgow (the Royal Bank opened its first branch in 1783, the Bank of Scotland in 1802) was a necessary precondition for the progression of the city's capital-hungry West India commerce. Merchants held large sums of capital in account current and often invested directly in stock and shares in banks. Assets held by the West India elite on death in British banks, in Glasgow in particular, were more than three times the investments in cotton manufactories, and more than all investments in the transport infrastructure. As Glasgow developed into a commercial centre after 1830, West India merchants sunk over half-a-million pounds into the developing financial infrastructure; this contrasts with the patterns of industrial investments, such as cotton, which tended to be invested in mills outside the city. Glasgow-West India merchants also provided credit to others that stimulated domestic ventures across Scotland. They loaned to their peers, stimulating Atlantic commerce, which retained the profits within the community. Crucially, they intervened in times of financial crisis, providing loans to industrialists and particularly after the abolition of slavery in 1834.

As such, a revision about the significance and nature of West India merchant capital and credit is required: this holistic approach here reveals they invested directly in fixed capital of industrial concerns, but also provided credit for working capital when required. On death, they were owed wealth (including from family sources) equivalent to the capital of around thirteen provincial banks. West India assets in banking and their outlying own credit – a combined value of over £1m – vastly exceeded industrial investments: they must be viewed first as a commercial interest in nineteenth-century Scotland, and second as industrialists. Nevertheless, it is harder to assess the positive effects of loaning credit than to estimate how many people worked in ancillary industries connected to the Atlantic trades.

The wider effects of the West India trades on the Scottish economy and society were five-fold. First, West India merchant capital was invested in commercial and industrial enterprise, which, in the case of the latter, tended to take the form of vertically integrated enterprise (such as cotton firms). In this study, the effects were mainly localized to the west of Scotland. Second, imports and exports facilitated the growth of associated industries (and backward linkages into, for example, shipping) which provided wider employment, especially in cotton manufactories. Third, this study underlines the inextricable connections between West India commerce and banking across the period under scrutiny, initially in Edinburgh but increasingly in Glasgow, which meant banks shared in the profits of slavery via credit dealings, investments and deposits. Further case study research of institutions should elucidate the scale and significance. Fourth, slavery-derived wealth – accumulated by both merchants and planters – was often invested in local economies, sometimes with the explicit aim of improving conditions of local societies through philanthropic initiatives in hospitals and education institutions, or indirectly via landed estates, including the wider effects of improvements and consumption. Many absentee planters across Scotland dealt exclusively with Glasgow merchants and were also dependent on mercantile operations. Fifth, the return of sojourning wealth had the potential to reshape local societies and improve the standard of living of kin and often complete strangers via philanthropy, although some regions received more returns than others.

Glasgow-West India merchants acted as both shipping and recruitment agents, transporting many thousands of Scots to the West Indies. Every decent-sized Caribbean plantation and all of the islands' mercantile houses employed a bookkeeper, and sometimes more than one, and many of these men arrived with skills and trades acquired in Scotland. This study estimates that up to 16,000 individuals could have travelled from Clyde ports to the West Indies during the period 1806 to 1834, which facilitates a new estimate of between 37,000 and 46,000 Scots travelling to the West Indies between 1750 and 1834. Third-phase colonies in the British West Indies, such as Demerara, became increasingly important destinations into the nineteenth century, thus providing new, lucrative opportunities, although Jamaica remained the principal Scottish outpost. Evidence of the Scots who lived, worked and in many cases died on Jamaica, Grenada, Carriacou and Trinidad illustrates earning capacity and career trajectory. Many profited from the slave economy, and some became owners of enslaved people.

This study set out to understand more about the movement of capital between Scotland and the West Indies. The young men who temporarily emigrated to the colonies were initially intent on the repatriation of capital and a return to the homeland. This crucial difference between emigration patterns to the transient colonies of the Indies and the settler colonies of North America has implications for studies of the economic development of Scotland based on imperial connections. The legal opinion of Lord Corehouse that few sought to remain in the West Indies once they had acquired fortunes is consistent with both contemporary sources and modern historiography. However, this monograph adds nuance to the contemporary and historiographical orthodoxy of the sojourning Scot. Many chose to remain in situ, very likely in the never-ending quest to accumulate more capital, but others chose to remain, especially in Trinidad. In reality, the Scots who went to the West Indies were commercial adventurers, the majority of whom died on the other side of the Atlantic. During their lives, Scottish adventurers in the West Indies conveyed profits via Glasgow merchant houses, particularly through bills of exchange and plantation produce. Many selected the same merchant houses as executors to ensure that wealth was dispersed among beneficiaries at home, often via banks. Scots not only depended on diasporic networks for credit and jobs in the colonies, but they also used Glasgow merchant firms and Scottish banks to repatriate the capital and disperse the profits at home. Scots were agents of ecclesiastical change in the colonies, introducing Scottish Presbyterianism once they were wealthy and influential enough to do so. In turn, Scotland received capital: these men did make fortunes *and* repatriate them to nineteenth-century Scotland.

The study, therefore, makes several key claims. First, West India merchants were central to the process of industrial and commercial change in Glasgow and the surrounding region in a manner that was unparalleled in other British-Atlantic outports. While the impact of their merchant capital was not decisive for any single enterprise, it influenced several initiatives across successive eras of change. If the city and its West India entrepreneurs are placed in comparative outport context, this group had the most profound impact of all British outports during the Industrial Revolution era. S. G. Checkland argued that Liverpool's West India elites were in decline in the 1790s, while the American traders afterwards took the lead. For Kenneth Morgan, the narrow specialization of Bristol's West India elite, allied with entrepreneurial failure, hindered eighteenth-century regional economic development. By the early nineteenth century, there was no local industry of national scale.[5] Nicholas Draper has also concluded that, due to the diversified nature of the economy, Caribbean slavery was not instrumental to the development of London.[6] By contrast, the Glasgow 'sugar aristocracy' underpinned – via direct investments and the Atlantic trade – the development of the city and the west of Scotland for the entirety of the Scottish Industrial Revolution (1778–1830), contributing to Glasgow's rise to be a commercial centre afterwards. Glasgow-West India commerce, and by extension Caribbean slavery, had a more decisive role, in relative terms, in the industrial and commercial development of the city and wider region than any other Atlantic port in Great Britain.

[5] S. G. Checkland, 'American versus West Indian traders in Liverpool, 1793–1815', *The Journal of Economic History*, xviii (June 1958), 141–60, p. 142; K. Morgan, *Bristol and the Atlantic Trade in the Eighteenth Century* (Cambridge, 2002), pp. 219–25.

[6] N. Draper, 'The City of London and slavery: evidence from the first dock companies, 1795–1800', *The Economic History Review*, lxi (2008), 432–66.

Second, Glasgow and its hinterlands benefited from a triple influx of West India merchant capital, returned adventuring wealth and the wider commercial processes associated with the Caribbean trades. This was not the case for all Scottish regions. The contemporary view expressed by Thomas Somerville, minister of Jedburgh, that Jamaica was 'the grave of Scotland' is confirmed by this study. Even those who had successfully repatriated capital from the West Indies were more likely to die before they returned. On the other hand, Somerville's position that 'few added to the stock of national wealth' is undermined by the excess of £1m identified in Scottish legal records (equivalent to £894.93m in modern values) that can be connected with Caribbean slavery.[7] Indeed, this study provides the largest-ever survey of returned fortunes of British adventurers who travelled to the West Indies in the colonial period. While Alan Karras claimed there was little repatriation of Jamaica property to eighteenth-century Scotland, the opposite was true for the next century.[8] In fact, as a commercial infrastructure developed and Scots repatriated more and more slavery profits, Jamaica was the premier source of West India wealth for a rapidly industrializing nineteenth-century Scotland. Caution is required. A Caribbean sojourn was high-risk, with only low-to-medium returns generally available. Only 1 per cent of the group of Scots in the West Indies surveyed here left what were regarded as nationally significant fortunes.[9] And the three major West India fortunes in this study (Rae in Jamaica, Buchanan in Grenada, Lamont in Trinidad) all had the same thing in common: a longer than average life. Scots were more likely to die young from disease in penury in the West Indies – like Robert McGregor Stirling – than to repatriate wealth to Scotland. Small fortunes of less than £500 were the typical return. In modern terms, however, this was still substantial capital.

Did slavery really make Scotia great?[10] 'Greatness' is, of course, a subjective term, but the Atlantic trades in general and West India commerce in particular contributed to the industrial and commercial development of central Scotland. But not all regions received the same imperial riches or underwent the same developmental processes. A regional comparison suggests the drain of manpower to the West Indies could be more damaging to local economies than the rare flows of repatriated post-mortem wealth was beneficial for wider development. Scottish adventurers were less likely

---

[7] T. Somerville, *My Own Life and Times, 1741–1814* (Edinburgh, 1861), p. 359.

[8] A. Karras, *Sojourners in the Sun* (Ithaca, 1992), p. 60.

[9] W. D. Rubinstein, *Who Were the Rich? A Biographical Directory of British Wealth-holders, Vol. I: 1809–1839* (London, 2009), p. 13.

[10] T. M. Devine, 'Did slavery make Scotia great?', *Britain and the World*, iv (2011), 40–64.

to return with wealth to the Highlands, for example, than to west-central Scotland. The profits and processes associated with slavery made some, but not all, parts of Scotland economically 'great' and may have contributed to the underdevelopment of others. This work offers a model to assess both merchant and sojourning capital in one analytical frame, which can be developed for other regional studies. This should be complemented with research on the effects on local commerce and industry, as well as individual institutions. Historians of other British cities – especially Atlantic outports – are now presented with the challenge of addressing similar questions in a comparative framework.

Third, rather than an abolitionist hub, Scotland was a pro-slavery nation, with large swathes of the population complicit in the Atlantic slavery economy. In an era in which, as Eric Williams claims, the West India economy was in decline, Scotland's connections with Caribbean slavery dramatically increased, which provided the foundation for the economic transformation of the nation.[11] As the abolition movement gathered pace from 1787, many thousands of Scottish people were directly *culpable* in West India commerce and slavery, while the profits and wider industrial and commercial processes created opportunities for hundreds of thousands of people who became *complicit* in Scotland's Atlantic slavery economy. As noted at the outset of this study, when Peter Borthwick, the paid agent of the West India interest, spoke in Edinburgh Assembly Rooms in March 1833, he argued that Caribbean slavery underpinned the economies of British-Atlantic ports:

> Then what is your Bristol, your Liverpool, your Manchester, your Glasgow, your Paisley, your Dundee, your eastern end of the great metropolis, even London itself – if you take from them the West India Colonies? Nothing – worse than nothing; one universal scene of beggary and starvation.[12]

Borthwick's claims were exaggerated with the intention of gathering public support for the continuation of chattel slavery, although the economy of Glasgow and hinterlands *was* dependent upon the Atlantic trades up to the end of Caribbean slavery. West India commerce was not the only factor driving change, but it was a transformative force and the most significant in early nineteenth-century Scotland. This mode of commerce underpinned the rise of new textile industries in the late eighteenth and early nineteenth centuries. As a result, large swathes of the early nineteenth-century Scottish

[11] E. Williams, *Capitalism and Slavery* (London, 1981 ed.), p. 120.
[12] P. Borthwick, *A Lecture on Colonial Slavery and Gradual Emancipation, Delivered in the Assembly Rooms on Friday 1 March 1833* (Edinburgh, 1833), pp. 4–5.

working population were dependent upon the Atlantic trades in general and West India commerce in particular. The multiplier effects of cotton were truly staggering. Estimates for the 1820s suggest that over 230,000 people in Scotland worked in textile employment (two-thirds of whom were in cotton production).[13] Of this, approximately 78,000 were handloom weavers working in homes across Scotland.[14] Given the Scottish population was just over 1.5 million in 1801, this suggests that at least 15 per cent (and probably much more) were directly complicit in, and benefited from, the wider Atlantic slavery economy.[15] Around Glasgow and its hinterlands in 1819, there were fifty-two cotton mills, sixteen weaving works and eighteen calico printing works in addition to 32,000 handlooms in employment of Glasgow manufacturers. By 1834, it is possible that this group of weavers increased to as many as 50,000.[16] This compares to the quarter of Glasgow's population (39,000 residents) who signed an abolitionist petition in the 1820s.[17]

West India commerce was not exclusively an elite enterprise, and rank and class were not accurate indicators of participation in the Atlantic slavery economy. Those connected to manufacturing dependent upon the Atlantic trades, for example, may not have understood they benefited from West India commerce, and they did not vocalize support for the cause. However, their employment was dependent upon the continuation of Atlantic slavery. David Livingstone (1813–73), the missionary-explorer, is a famous example of a textile 'lad of pairts' who began life in humble origins in the west of Scotland but went on to gain a medical qualification and afterwards became a 'hero' of the British empire. Yet, his trajectory was made possible due to employment as an adult cotton spinner just outside Glasgow in Blantyre Mill works – owned by Henry Monteith, who was part-financed by West India merchant capital – an employer that paid relatively high wages.[18] While few experienced such a remarkable trajectory as Livingstone, many across the west of Scotland were dependent upon industries powered by Caribbean slavery for sustenance. Not all individuals benefited *equally*

---

[13] J. Sinclair, *Analysis of the Statistical Account of Scotland* (Edinburgh, 1831), p. 333; Cooke, *Rise and Fall*, pp. 57–8.

[14] N. Murray, *The Scottish Handloom Weavers, 1790–1850: A Social History* (Edinburgh, 1978), p. 23.

[15] H. Hamilton, *An Economic History of Scotland in the Eighteenth Century* (Oxford, 1963), Appendix 1.

[16] Sinclair, *Analysis of the Statistical Account of Scotland*, Appendix, p. 62; Murray, *Scottish Handloom Weavers*, p. 18.

[17] I. Whyte, *Scotland and the Abolition of Black Slavery, 1756–1838* (Edinburgh, 2006), p. 187.

[18] S. Mullen, 'One of Scotia's sons of toil: David Livingstone and Blantyre Mill', in *David Livingstone: Man, Myth, Legacy*, ed. S. Worden (Edinburgh, 2012), pp. 15–33.

from the profits of slavery, even in Glasgow and its hinterlands. And the Victorian city later had appalling poverty and housing conditions. Yet it is indisputable that individuals within *all* sectors of society benefited from the opportunities provided by profits of Caribbean slavery.

Finally, the profits of Caribbean slavery were embedded across late eighteenth- and early nineteenth-century Scotland, and the Atlantic slavery economy was a quotidian feature of everyday life. Many thousands of mothers and fathers would have been accustomed to losing sons to the West Indies, and many others enjoyed improved standards of living due to repatriated wealth. Glasgow offers the best case study of change, as the economy and society were reshaped by slavery and its commerce, providing employment opportunities, disrupting patterns of traditional landownership, transforming the nature of banking, improving the provision and quality of education, revamping the transport and communication systems. In terms of trickle-down, Glasgow-West India philanthropic commitments were smaller in scale than the commercial or industrial investments but had important consequences at the time and now. The poor young lads who attended Buchanan's Institution – founded on a returned West India fortune – were reckoned to be 'heavier, healthier and stronger than the average Glasgow schoolboy'.[19] Caribbean philanthropy left a verifiable legacy. In this sense, the West India 'spheres of influence' remain in Glasgow today: the industrial and commercial investments declined in importance from 1875, but those philanthropic commitments still have influence in the modern period, albeit on a much smaller scale. The University of Glasgow is a case in point. It has disbursed the equivalent of up to £91m, accrued from donations by those associated with Atlantic slavery.[20] Some, such as the Ewing prizes (based on the £100 donated in 1828 by Jamaica planter James Ewing of Strathleven) are still awarded annually to postgraduates; these specific awards rotate annually between students in Medieval and Modern History. It is almost certain the income from slavery from the eighteenth century onwards benefited almost exclusively staff and students racialized as white British.[21] Other philanthropic funds, such as the Dick Bequest, continue to disburse slavery-derived wealth

[19] *Historical Sketch of The Buchanan Institution Glasgow* (Glasgow, 1913), p. 35.

[20] S. Mullen and S. Newman, 'Slavery, abolition and the University of Glasgow' <https://www.gla.ac.uk/media/media_607547_en.pdf> [accessed 20 Nov. 2020].

[21] Exactly 1% of the student population of the University of Glasgow in 2017–18 identified as African, Caribbean or Black. Data taken from correspondence with Ms Mhairi Taylor, Head of Equality, Diversity and Inclusion at the University of Glasgow, 30 Sept. 2019. The author is grateful to Ms Taylor for permission to quote.

into Scottish society.[22] The West India 'spheres of influence' established then set in place inequalities that continue today, although the relative significance of the effects on society has gradually decreased.

This study of Glasgow's 'sugar aristocracy', and Scots across the British West Indies, substantiates and significantly expands upon Eric Williams' main thesis in *Capitalism and Slavery* in a Scottish context.[23] Glasgow-West India merchant capital, and its Atlantic operations, were central to the origins and progress of the Scottish Industrial Revolution, helping establish and accelerating the process. Indeed, in the absence of West India merchants, this cataclysmic event that transformed the nation would have begun later and progressed at a much slower pace. In a counter-factual analysis, cotton would have likely been supplied via East India merchants in London in any case, but such an irregular supply could hardly have sustained large-scale manufacturing processes before the end of the East India monopoly in 1813. In actuality, Caribbean slavery underpinned textile manufacturing from 1778, a system which employed many thousands of Scots who often had no knowledge of their complicity.

Ironically, Peter Borthwick's public observations in Edinburgh Assembly Rooms are almost identical to the second of Eric Williams' claims made around a century later (ie that the slave trade and commerce with the slave economies powered the British Industrial Revolution). Borthwick's arguments were made in support of the British empire and slavery, while Williams attacked the ideological foundation on which it rested. Borthwick warned of catastrophe on emancipation, while Williams viewed the landmark event as ushering in a new era of British *laissez-faire* trade dominance. Both pro-slavery propagandist and anti-imperialist historian, however, agreed that the industrial and commercial development of Great Britain and its manufacturing towns and port cities was powered by trade with the West Indies and Caribbean slavery. Not even Borthwick or Williams could have appreciated the true importance of Caribbean slavery to Scottish economic development, at least in some regions. West India commerce shaped Glasgow and west central Scotland in a way unparalleled along Britain's Atlantic seaboard, with large sections of the population dependent on the continuation of the trades and, by extension, Caribbean slavery. Even today, Glasgow-West India merchant capital, and returned Scottish-Caribbean wealth, improves lives in British society.

---

[22] D. Alston and D. Morrison, 'James Dick and the Dick Bequest' <https://www.davidalston.info/documents/james-dick-bequest/james-dick-and-the-dick-bequest-a-legacy-of-slavery-v5.pdf> [accessed 23 Sept. 2021].

[23] E. Williams, *Capitalism and Slavery* (Chapel Hill, 1944).

Appendix

One hundred and fifty Glasgow-West India merchants, planters or merchant-proprietors involved with the West India Club or Glasgow West India Association as personal attendees/subscribers or associated firms, 1775–1838, including details of wealth on death, and principal landed estate (archival references to wills, testaments and confirmation inventories, are provided).

NRS: National Records of Scotland
W: Wealth on Death

Adamson, Frederick (d. 1848). W: £25,134. NRS, Glasgow Sheriff Court Inventories, SC36/48/34, 17/8/1848; SC36/48/37, 20/1/1851.

Alexander, Robert Fulton of Thornbank (d. 1843). W: £1,108. NRS, Glasgow Sheriff Court Inventories, SC36/48/30, 21/12/1843. Glasgow Sheriff Court Wills, SC36/51/19, 21/12/1843.

Alston, George of Muirburn (d. 1850). W: £8,825. NRS, Glasgow Sheriff Court Inventories, SC36/48/37, 30/10/1850.

Alston, John of Westertown (d. 1835). W: £979. NRS, Dumbarton Sheriff Court, SC65/34/3, 30/9/1836.

Alston, Robert Douglas of Whistleberry/Auchinraith (d. 1846). W: £62,637. NRS, Glasgow Sheriff Court Inventories, SC36/48/32, 22/2/1847; SC36/48/35, 31/1/1849. Glasgow Sheriff Court Wills, SC36/51/23, 2/2/1847.

Anderson, George (d. 1846).

Bannatyne, John (d. 1878). W: £77,206. NRS, Forfar Sheriff Court, SC47/40/45, 5/10/1878.

Blackburn, John of Killearn (d. 1846). W: £107,109. NRS, Edinburgh Sheriff Court Inventories, SC70/1/59, 24/8/1840.

Bogle, Adam (d. 1817). W: £28,875. NRS, Glasgow Sheriff Court Inventories, SC36/48/13, 16/7/1818.

Bogle, Archibald of Donaldshill/Gilmorehill (d. 1858). W: £31,213. NRS, Edinburgh Sheriff Court Inventories, SC70/1/98, 12/10/1858; SC70/1/122, 14/9/1864. Edinburgh Sheriff Court Wills, SC70/4/60, 12/10/1858.

Bogle, George (d. 1808). W: £9,524. NRS, Glasgow Sheriff Court Inventories, SC36/48/4, 11/1/1809; SC36/48/5, 26/4/1810.

Bogle, George of Rosemount (d. 1854). W: £8,436. NRS, Edinburgh Sheriff Court Inventories, SC70/1/100, 8/4/1859. Edinburgh Sheriff Court Wills, SC70/4/63, 9/4/1859.

Bogle, Hugh of Calderbank (d. 1834). W: £24,606. NRS, Glasgow Sheriff Court Inventories, SC36/48/24, 15/10/1834. Glasgow Sheriff Court Wills, SC36/51/11, 15/10/1834.

Bogle, James (d. 1832). W: £6,916. NRS, Glasgow Sheriff Court Inventories, SC36/48/23, 16/5/1833. Glasgow Sheriff Court Wills, SC36/51/10, 16/5/1833.

Bogle, Robert of Daldowie (d. 1808). W: £2,579. NRS, Hamilton & Campsie Commissary Court, CC10/7/1, 26/1/1809.

Bogle (junior), Robert of Donaldshill/Gilmorehill (d. 1821). W: £63,127. NRS, Hamilton & Campsie Commissary Court, CC10/7/4, 29/11/1821; CC10/7/4, 29/3/1822. Glasgow Sheriff Court Inventories, SC36/48/19, 21/9/1824.

Brown, Robert (d. 1873). W: £18,901. NRS, Ayr Sheriff Court, SC6/44/37, 27/10/1873. Ayr Sheriff Court Wills, SC6/46/9, 27/10/1873.

Brown, William of Kilmardinny (d. 1884). W: £6,188. NRS, Glasgow Sheriff Court Inventories, SC36/48/107, 15/10/1884. Glasgow Sheriff Court Wills, SC36/51/89, 15/10/1884.

Buchanan, Andrew of Ardenconnell (d. 1835). W: £9,948. NRS, Dumbarton Sheriff Court, SC65/34/3, 10/9/1835.

Buchanan, James of Ardenconnell (d. 1860). W: £1,342. NRS, Stirling Sheriff Court, SC67/36/43, 1/6/1861.

Buchanan, James of Dowanhill (d. 1844). W: £129,464. NRS, Glasgow Sheriff Court Inventories, SC36/48/30, 11/7/1844; SC36/48/30, 5/10/1844. Glasgow Sheriff Court Wills, SC36/51/2, 11/7/1844.

Burnley, William Frederick (d. 1903). W: £7,908. NRS, Edinburgh Sheriff Court Inventories, SC70/1/420, 3/2/1903. Edinburgh Sheriff Court Wills, SC70/1/345, 4/2/1903.

Campbell, Alexander of Hallyards (d. 1817). W: £34,432. NRS, Glasgow Sheriff Court Inventories, SC36/48/17, 16/4/1822. Glasgow Commissary Court, CC9/7/84, 3/10/1823.

Campbell, Alexander of Haylodge (d. 1835). W: £17,374. NRS, Peebles Sheriff Court, SC42/20/3, 19/12/1835.

Campbell, Colin of Colgrain (d. 1863). W: £169,350. NRS, Dumbarton Sheriff Court SC65/34/11, 26/3/1863.

Campbell, Colin of Hagtonhill (The Lynn) (d. ?).

Campbell, Colin of Jura (d. 1848). W: £49,609. NRS, Dunoon Sheriff Court, SC51/32/6, 15/3/1849.

Campbell (senior), John of Morriston (d. 1807). W: £59,801. NRS, Glasgow Sheriff Court Inventories, SC36/48/3, 3/10/1808; SC36/48/3, 5/7/1809.

Campbell (junior), Mungo (d. 1866). W: £44,689. NRS, Edinburgh Sheriff Court Inventories, SC70/1/134, 9/5/1867.

Campbell, Mungo (d. 1859). W: £6,830. NRS, Glasgow Sheriff Court Inventories, SC36/48/46, 1/9/1860. Glasgow Sheriff Court Wills, SC36/51/41, 1/9/1860.

Campbell, Mungo Nutter of Ballimore/Belvidere (d. 1862). W: £23,274. NRS, Dunoon Sheriff Court, SC51/32/12, 16/3/1863.

Campbell, Thomas (d. 1866). W: £31,494. NRS, Edinburgh Sheriff Court Inventories, SC70/1/129, 24/4/1866. Edinburgh Sheriff Court Wills, SC70/4/103, 24/4/1866.

Coats, William (d. 1800). W: £15,702. NRS, Glasgow Commissary Court, CC9/7/78, 14/6/1804.

Cole, George (d. 1853). W: £34,766. NRS, Edinburgh Sheriff Court Inventories, SC70/1/81, 29/10/1853. Edinburgh Sheriff Court Wills, SC70/4/29, 29/10/1853.

Colquhoun, Patrick of Berridyke/Woodcroft (later Kelvingrove) (d. 1820).

Connell, Arthur (d. 1864). W: £2,791. NRS, Glasgow Sheriff Court Inventories, SC36/48/52, 2/1/1865. Glasgow Sheriff Court Wills, SC36/51/47, 2/1/1865.

Connell, David (d. 1819). W: £29,979. NRS, Glasgow Sheriff Court Inventories, SC36/48/15, 16/9/1819; SC36/48/20, 20/11/1826. Glasgow Commissary Court, CC9/7/83, 18/1/1820.

Connell, James (d. 1819). W: £29,813. NRS, Glasgow Commissary Court, CC9/7/83, 24/1/1820; SC36/48/18, 29/12/1823. Glasgow Sheriff Court Wills, SC36/51/1, 14/8/1821.

Craigie, Laurence (d. 1853).

Crooks, Adam (d. 1823). W: £34,024. NRS, Glasgow Sheriff Court Inventories, SC36/51/4, 16/5/1823; SC36/48/19, 18/10/1824.

Cross, William of Auchintoshan (d. 1813). W: £14,469. NRS, Glasgow Sheriff Court Inventories, SC36/48/8, 26/3/1814. Glasgow Commissary Court, CC9/7/81, 26/3/1814.

Cunningham, William of Lainshaw (d. 1849). W: £33,118. NRS, Ayr Sheriff Court, SC6/44/18, 3/5/1850.

Cunninghame, Alex of Craigends (d. 1790).

Dennistoun, James of Colgrain (d. 1834). W: £3,207. NRS, Dumbarton Sheriff Court, SC65/34/3, 5/10/1835.

Dennistoun, James of Golfhill (d. 1835). W: £204,786. NRS, Glasgow Sheriff Court Inventories, SC36/48/25, 15/4/1836. Glasgow Sheriff Court Wills, SC36/51/13, 15/4/1836.

Dennistoun, James Robert (d. 1851). W: £766. NRS, Glasgow Sheriff Court Inventories, SC36/48/38, 15/9/1851; SC36/48/39, 6/4/1853.

Dennistoun, Richard of Kelvingrove (d. 1834). W: £1,468. NRS, Glasgow Sheriff Court Inventories, SC36/48/24, 16/12/1833. Glasgow Sheriff Court Wills, SC36/51/11, SC36/48/24.

Dennistoun, Robert (d. 1815). W: £47,294. NRS, Glasgow Sheriff Court Inventories, SC36/48/10, 24/2/1816.

Dennistoun, Robert of Dunnerboak (d. 1833).

Dewar, Robert (d. 1829). W: £32,456. NRS, Glasgow Sheriff Court Inventories, SC36/48/21, 1/4/1829. Glasgow Sheriff Court Wills, SC36/51/7, 1/4/1829.

Douglas, Archibald of Glenfinart (d. 1860). W: £28,096. NRS, Dunoon Sheriff Court, SC51/32/11, 22/1/1861; SC51/32/11, 8/7/1861.

Douglas, James (d. 1852). W: £37,151. NRS, Glasgow Sheriff Court Inventories, SC36/48/39, 11/1/1853. Glasgow Sheriff Court Wills, SC36/51/31, 11/1/1852.

Douglas, John (d. 1840). W: £71,497. NRS, Edinburgh Sheriff Court Inventories, SC70/1/60, 16/4/1841.

Douglas, Thomas Dunlop of Dunlop (d. 1869). W: £241,518. NRS, Ayr Sheriff Court, SC6/44/34, 26/3/1869. Ayr Sheriff Court Wills, SC6/44/6, 26/3/1869.

Dunlop, James (d. 1815).

Dunmore, Robert of Kelvinside (d. 1799).

Eccles, James (d. 1833). W: £27,639. NRS, Glasgow Sheriff Court Inventories, SC36/48/24, 30/10/1834.

Eccles, Robert (d. 1848). W: £38,658. NRS, Edinburgh Sheriff Court Inventories, SC70/1/68, 15/5/1848. Edinburgh Sheriff Court Wills, SC70/4/5, 13/5/1848.

Eccles, William (d. 1846). W: £1,058. NRS, Glasgow Sheriff Court Inventories, SC36/48/33, 18/6/1847; SC36/48/37, 15/10/1850. Glasgow Sheriff Court Wills, SC36/51/23, 18/6/1847.

Edgar, James (d. 1841).

Edgar, Thomas (d. 1831).

Ewing, James of Levenside (later Strathleven) (d. 1853). W: £281,296. NRS, Dumbarton Sheriff Court, SC65/34/7, 24/2/1854.

Ewing, William Leckie of Arngomery (was Broich) (d. 1866). W: £23,292. NRS, Stirling Sheriff Court, SC67/36/52, 9/10/1866.

Ferguson, John (d. 1831).

Findlay, Robert of Easter Dalbeth/Easterhill (d. 1802).

Findlay (junior), Robert of Easterhill (d. 1862). W: £23,292. NRS, Dumbarton Sheriff Court, SC65/34/11, 8/11/1862.

Fyffe, James of Smithfield (d. 1831). W: £17,469. NRS, Glasgow Sheriff Court Inventories, SC36/48/22, 6/7/1831. Glasgow Sheriff Court Wills, SC36/51/9, 6/7/1831.

Garden, Alexander of Croy (d. 1847). W: £20,469. NRS, Dumbarton Sheriff Court, SC65/34/5, 23/12/1847.

Garden, Francis (d. 1831). W: £1,989. NRS, Glasgow Sheriff Court Inventories, SC36/48/28, 1/7/1841. Glasgow Sheriff Court Wills, SC36/51/17, 1/7/1841.

Gordon, Alexander (d. 1828).

Gordon, John of Aikenhead (d. 1828). W: £118,543. NRS, Glasgow Sheriff Court Inventories, SC36/48/21, 11/8/1828. Glasgow Sheriff Court Wills, SC36/51/7, 11/8/1829.

Graham, David (d. 1827). W: £754. NRS, Glasgow Sheriff Court Inventories, SC36/48/20, 22/1/1828. Glasgow Sheriff Court Wills, SC36/51/6, 22/1/1828.

Gray, William (d. 1853).

Greig, Benjamin (d. ?). NRS, Glasgow Sheriff Court Wills, SC36/51/18, 21/1/1842.

Guthrie, John of Carbeth (d. 1834). W: £8,977. NRS, Edinburgh Sheriff Court Inventories, SC70/1/51, 15/11/1834.

Haddow, Robert (d. 1826). W: £1,977. NRS, Glasgow Sheriff Court Inventories, SC36/48/20, 18/4/1827.

Hagart, Charles of Bantaskine/Dumbreck (d. 1813). W: £41,342. NRS, Stirling Sheriff Court, SC67/36/2, 10/1/1814.

Hagart, Robert (d. 1850). W: £10,726. NRS, Edinburgh Sheriff Court Inventories, SC70/1/72, 18/2/1851. Edinburgh Sheriff Court Wills, SC70/4/13, 18/2/1851.

Hagart, Thomas Campbell of Bantaskine/Dumbreck (d. 1868). W: £73,142. NRS, Stirling Sheriff Court, SC67/36/56, 23/11/1868.

Hamilton, Alexander West of Pinmore/Belleisle (d. 1837). W: £11,680. NRS, Ayr Sheriff Court, SC6/44/9, 6/6/1838; SC6/44/10, 31/10/1840.

Hamilton, Hugh of Pinmore (d. 1829). W: £15,059. NRS, Ayr Sheriff Court, SC6/44/4, 12/11/1829.

Hamilton, John of Northpark (d. 1829). W: £26,067. NRS, Glasgow Sheriff Court Inventories, SC36/48/21, 6/11/1829. Glasgow Sheriff Court Will, SC36/51/8, 6/11/1829.

Hamilton, William of Plantation (later Mavisbank) (d. 1866). W: £831. NRS, Glasgow Sheriff Court Inventories, SC36/48/56, 5/9/1866. Glasgow Sheriff Court Wills, SC36/51/50, 5/9/1866.

Hopkirk, James of Dalbeth (d. 1835). W: £6,752. NRS, Glasgow Sheriff Court Inventories, SC36/48/25, 6/1/1836. Glasgow Sheriff Court Wills, SC36/51/12, 6/1/1836.

Hopkirk, Thomas (d. 1811). W: £2,333. NRS, Glasgow Sheriff Court Inventories, SC36/48/6, 28/12/1811. Glasgow Commissary Court, CC9/7/80, 11/1/1812.

Houston, Alexander of Jordanhill (d. 1822).

Houston, Andrew of Jordanhill (d. 1800).

Houston-Rae, Robert of Little Govan/Shawfield-Polmadie (d. 1828).

Kinnier, Robert (d. 1838). W: £23,369. NRS, Glasgow Sheriff Court Inventories, SC36/48/27, 12/4/1839.

Kirkland, William Scott (d. 1852). W: £5,557. NRS, Glasgow Sheriff Court Inventories, SC36/48/39, 7/2/1853.

Laird, David (d. 1828).

Lamb, James (d. 1828).

Lang, Archibald Graham (d. 1875).

Leitch, John of Kilmardinny (d. 1805).

Lightbody, Adam (d. ?).

Lyon, Jasper (d. 1828).

MacBean, Æneas (d. 1810). W: £27,614. NRS, Edinburgh Sheriff Court Inventories, SC70/1/4, 11/9/1811.

Mackay, Robert (d. 1802). W: £489. NRS, Glasgow Commissary Court, CC9/7/79, 12/7/1805.

Malcolm, Neill of Poltalloch (d. 1837). W: £549,955. NRS, Edinburgh Sheriff Court Inventories, SC70/1/55, 29/5/1837.

Malcolm, Neill of Poltalloch (d. 1837). W: £399,666. NRS, Dunoon Sheriff Court, SC51/32/9, 27/5/1858.

Malcolm, David Orme Cuthbert (d. 1832). W: £15,535. NRS, Glasgow Sheriff Court Inventories, SC36/48/23, 14/3/1833.

Martin, James (d. 1842). W: £17,053. NRS, Glasgow Sheriff Court Inventories, SC36/48/29, 26/5/1842; SC36/48/29, 2/10/1843; SC36/48/32, 26/12/1846. Glasgow Sheriff Court Wills, SC36/51/18, 26/5/1842.

Mathieson, William (d. 1846). W: £24,101. NRS, Glasgow Sheriff Court Inventories, SC36/48/32, 29/3/1847.

McCaul, John (d. 1846). W: £15,270. NRS, Glasgow Sheriff Court Inventories, SC36/48/15, 14/8/1819.

McCunn, Robert (d. ?).

McDowall, James (d. ?).

McDowall, William (d. 1784).

McDowall, William (d. 1810).

McInroy, James of Lude (d. 1825). W: £172,912. NRS, Perth Sheriff Court, SC49/31/15, 8/7/1826.

McInroy, James Patrick of Lude (d. 1878). W: £16,827. NRS, Perth Sheriff Court, SC49/31/109, 25/2/1879.

McLachlan (also MacLachlan), Colin of Ardmore (d. 1822). W: £8,262. NRS, Glasgow Sheriff Court Inventories, SC36/48/19, 13/12/1824; SC36/48/21, 30/6/1828; SC36/48/21, 30/6/1829.

MacQueen, James (d. 1870).

Muirhead, Alexander (d. ?).

Muirhead, Michael (d. ?).

Munro, John Spens of Garthwat (d. 1798).

Parker, Charles Stewart of Fairlie (d. 1828). W: £117,589. NRS, Glasgow Sheriff Court Inventories, SC36/48/21, 5/1/1829; SC36/48/25, 2/5/1836; SC36/48/25, 25/7/1836. Glasgow Sheriff Court Wills, SC36/51/7, 5/1/1829.

Parker, George (d. 1860). W: £3,198. NRS, Edinburgh Sheriff Court Inventories, SC70/1/129, 27/3/1866.

Playfair, Patrick of Dalmarnock (d. 1836). W: £16,150. NRS, Glasgow Sheriff Court Inventories, SC36/48/26, 24/3/1837. Glasgow Sheriff Court Wills, SC36/51/14, 24/3/1837.

Ranken, Andrew of Ashburn (d. 1851).

Riddell, John (d. 1803).

Robertson, John of Plantation (d. ?).

Ronald, John (d. ?).

Rowan, Stephen of Bellahouston (d. 1818). W: £14,248. NRS, Glasgow Sheriff Court Inventories, SC36/48/15, 21/1/1819. Glasgow Commissary Court, CC9/7/84, 21/1/1819.

Russell, David of Woodside/Hamilton Farm/part Torwoodhead (d. 1808).

Ryburn, John (d. 1844). W: £82,368. NRS, Glasgow Sheriff Court Inventories, SC36/48/31, 28/1/1845. Glasgow Sheriff Court Wills, SC36/51/20, 28/1/1845.

Scheviz, George (d. ?).

Smith, Archibald (d. 1823). W: £20,682. NRS, Glasgow Sheriff Court Inventories, SC36/48/19, 10/8/1824. Glasgow Sheriff Court Wills, SC36/51/4, 20/9/1821.

Smith, Archibald of Jordanhill (d. 1821). W: £47,107. NRS, Hamilton & Campsie Commissary Court, CC10/7/4, 31/10/1821; CC10/7/4, 11/10/1822.

Smith, Archibald of Jordanhill (d. 1883). W: £33,726. NRS, Dumbarton Sheriff Court, SC65/34/26, 16/4/1883. Dumbarton Sheriff Court, SC65/34/26, 31/8/1883.

Smith, James of Craigend (d. 1836). W: £19,591. NRS, Glasgow Sheriff Court Inventories, SC36/48/25, 15/12/1836. Glasgow Sheriff Court Wills, SC36/51/13, 15/12/1836.

Smith, John of Craigend (d. 1816). W: £46,168. NRS, Glasgow Sheriff Court Inventories, SC36/48/11, 24/6/1816.

Smith, James of Craighead (d. 1815). W: £71,027. NRS, Glasgow Sheriff Court Inventories, SC36/48/9, 9/6/1815.

Smith, James of Jordanhill (d. 1867). W: £17,727. NRS, Paisley Sheriff Court, 7/10/1867, SC58/42/34, 3/10/1867. Paisley Sheriff Court, SC58/42/52, 29/1/1886.

Smith, William of Carbeth Guthrie (d. 1871). W: £4,639. NRS, Edinburgh Sheriff Court Inventories, SC70/1/153, 12/6/1871. Edinburgh Sheriff Court Wills, SC70/4/133, 12/6/1871.

Somervell, James of Hamilton Farm/part Scotstoun (d. 1791).

Steven, Moses of Polmadie/parts Bellahouston (d. 1831). W: £31,176. NRS, Paisley Sheriff Court, SC58/42/6, 10/7/1833.

Stirling, Charles of Cadder/Kenmure (d. 1830). W: £52,949. NRS, Glasgow Sheriff Court Inventories, SC36/48/22, 15/7/1830; SC36/48/24, 18/9/1834. Glasgow Sheriff Court Wills, SC36/51/8, 15/7/1830.

Stirling, Charles of Gargunnock (d. 1839). W: £14,467. NRS, Glasgow Sheriff Court Inventories, SC36/48/27, 29/4/1840.

Stirling, John of Kippendavie/Kippenross (d. 1816). W: £146,043. NRS, Dunblane Commissary Court, CC6/5/33, 14/9/1818; CC6/5/34, 14/9/1818; CC6/5/34, 30/4/1823.

Stirling, William (d. 1862). W: £20,427. NRS, Edinburgh Sheriff Court Inventories, SC70/1/113, 1/9/1862. Edinburgh Sheriff Court Wills, SC70/4/8, 21/9/1862.

Tasker, James (d. ?).

Thomson, Colin (d. 1818). W: £33,273. NRS, Glasgow Sheriff Court Inventories, SC36/48/22, 5/3/1831. Glasgow Sheriff Court Wills, SC36/51/9, 5/3/1831.

Ure, James (d. ?).

Ure (junior), John (d. ?).

Wallace, John of Cessnock/Kelly (d. 1805). W: £22,449. NRS, Glasgow Sheriff Court Inventories, SC36/48/1, 13/4/1805. Glasgow Commissary Court, CC9/7/80, 28/4/1809.

Wallace, Robert of Kelly (d. 1855). W: £1,219. NRS, Paisley Sheriff Court, SC58/42/22, 14/8/1855.

Wardrop, David (d. 1854).

Whytlaw, Thomas (d. 1805).

Wighton, Alexander (d. 1824). W: £4,841. NRS, Glasgow Sheriff Court Inventories, SC36/48/20, 1/3/1826.

Bibliography and manuscript sources

Manuscript sources

United States of America

Library of Congress
James McTear, 'Journal of a voyage to & residence in Tobago, 1825–6', MS. 20353

Princeton University Library, Department of Rare Books and Special Collections
Rae Family Estate Collection, 1800–57, C1222

University of Michigan, William L. Clements Library
Tailyour Family Papers

England

Bristol Record Office
Records of the Society of Merchant Venturers, SMV/8

British Library, London
Walter Fenner, *A New and Accurate Map of the Island of Carriacou in the West Indies, 1784* (London, 1784), Maps Collection

The National Archives of the UK
Colonial Office: Jamaica, Original Correspondence, 1788–1817, CO137/88–144
Colonial Office: Grenada, Original Correspondence, 1786–1835, CO101/26–79
Colonial Office: Trinidad, Original Correspondence, 1783–1836, CO295/1–110
Despatches: Offices and Individuals, CO101
Ledgers of Imports and Exports, Scotland (1755–1827), CUST 14
Records of the Board of Trade, BT/18

Grenada

Grenada Supreme Court Land Registry, St George's
Deed Books, 1785 vol. i (F1) – 1840 (A3)

Jamaica

Island Record Office, Twickenham Park
Wills, vol. lvi (1792) – vol. cxiv (1833)
Jamaica Deeds, years 1829–30

National Library of Jamaica, Kingston
Correspondence of Andrew Taylor, MS. 706
Letterbooks of Georgia Estate, MS. 132
Letter from Leitch & Smith, 28 September 1820, MS. 707/2
Questionnaire proposed to Mr. R. Hamilton, MS. 708

The National Archive of Jamaica, Spanishtown
Records of St Andrews Scots Kirk, 5/20/1–2
Probate inventories, vol. lxxvii (1791–2) – vol. cl (1833), 1B/11/3

The University of the West Indies, Mona, West Indies and Special Collections
Journal of Spencer Mackay, MS.1798–1800
Papers of Lachlan Campbell, Deputy Provost Marshall Tobago, 1772–82

Scotland

Argyll and Bute Council Archives
DR8/8/8 Accounts and inventories of sugar from Trinidad, 1861–1920

Glasgow City Archives
Abridgements of Sasines, T-SA 1/1 Argyll (vol. i, 1781–1820; vol. ii,
    1821–50); GCA, T-SA 2/1 Ayr (vol. i, 1781–1806; vol. ii, 1806–20; vol.
    iii, 1821–30; vol. iv, 1831–40); GCA, T-SA 4/1 Dunbartonshire (vol. i,
    1781–1820; vol. ii, 1821–30; vol. iii, 1831–40); GCA, T-SA 5/1 Glasgow
    (Barony and Regality) (vol. i, 1781–1808; vol. ii, 1809–20; vol. iii, 1821–
    30; vol. iv, 1831–40); GCA, T-SA 6/1 Lanarkshire (vol. i, 1781–1820;
    vol. ii, 1821–30; vol. iii, 1831–40); GCA, T-SA 7/1 Renfrewshire (vol. i,
    1781–1807; vol. ii, 1807–20; vol. iii, 1821–30; vol. iv, 1831–40)

Campbell of Hallyards papers, TD1696

Dobbie family of Glasgow papers, TD440

Documents relating to the Barr and Smith families, TD1710

Glasgow Town Council Minutes 1779–81, C1/1/36

MacNeill & Stewart, Brokerage books, B1/18

Minutes of the Glasgow West India Association 1807–53, TD1683

Minute book of the Glasgow Gaelic Club, vol. i, TD746/1–2

Opinions of counsel for creditors of Mackay & Co, 1808, TD569/1

Records of the Chamber of Commerce of Glasgow, TD1/1671

Records of St Andrew's by the Green Episcopal Church, TD423

Records of St George's (West Parish) Kirk, CH2/818

Smiths of Jordanhill collection, TD1

Stirling of Keir collection, T-SK

The Merchants House, T-MH

National Library of Scotland

Alexander Houston & Co., Merchants, Glasgow, MS. 8793–800 and 8895–8

Journal of [unknown] of Banffshire, MS. 17956

Papers of General Sir George Murray, Adv.MS. 46.1.1

National Records of Scotland

Condescendence for Messrs Leitch & Smith, 1822, CS44/38/29

Daniel Ross and Company, Sederunt book, 1837–8, CS96/4291

Decreet discharging Richard Dennistoun of all debts contracted prior to 3 April 1826, CS44/178/56

Gilbert Douglas of Douglas Park, Ledgers 1801–12, CS96/4901

Hugh Milliken and Company, mercantile agents, Port Glasgow. Rum import and delivery book, CS96/4361

James McNair, merchant and sugar refiner, Glasgow. Raw sugar book, CS96/4260

Journal of John Gordon of Aikenhead, 1806–19, GD1/1209/9

Letter book of George Oliphant Kinloch, 1772–5, GD1/8/36

Letters from the Kirk family in Grenada, West Indies and Kilmarnock, GD1/632

Minutes, memoranda, letters, lists and statements relating to the financial business of the Royal Bank of Scotland, 1809–10, GD113/5/19c

Papers of the Home-Robertson Family of Paxton, Berwickshire (Home of Wedderburn), GD267

Papers relating to estate and debts of Richard Dennistoun of Kelvingrove, GD64/1/261

Sederunt books of Richard Dennistoun sequestration, vols. 1 and 2, CS96/4808–9

William MacNeill of Hayfield, Cash registers and letter books, 1806–8, CS96/966

Wills, Testaments and Confirmation Inventories (Scotland) –

Aberdeen Commissary Court, 1657–1823, CC1

Ayr Sheriff Court Inventories, 1824–1925, SC6

Banff Sheriff Court, 1824–1925, SC2

Brechin Commissary Court, 1577–1823, CC3

Cupar Sheriff Court, 1824–1925, SC20

Dumbarton Sheriff Court Inventories and Wills, 1824–1925, SC65

Dunblane Commissary Court, 1539–1825, CC6

Dunoon Sheriff Court, 1815–1925, SC51

Edinburgh Commissary Court, 1514–1829, CC8

Edinburgh Sheriff Court Inventories, 1808–1925, SC70

Edinburgh Sheriff Court Wills, 1844–1925, SC70

Elgin Sheriff Court Inventories, 1824–1925, SC26

Elgin Sheriff Court Wills, 1823–1925, SC26

Forfar Sheriff Court, 1824–1925, SC47

Glasgow Commissary Court, 1547–1823, CC9

Glasgow Sheriff Court Inventories, 1804–1925, SC36

Glasgow Sheriff Court Wills, 1817–1925, SC36

Hamilton and Campsie Commissary Court, 1564–1823, CC10

Kirkcudbright Sheriff Court, 1824–1925, SC16

Moray Commissary Court, 1684–1827, CC16

Paisley Sheriff Court, 1824–1925, SC58

Peebles Commissary Court, 1681–1827, CC18

Peebles Sheriff Court, 1814–1925, SC42

Perth Sheriff Court, SC49

Ross Commissary Court Registers of Testaments, 1802–24, CC19
St Andrews Commissary Court, 1549–1823, CC20
Stirling Sheriff Court, 1809–1925, SC67
Stonehaven Sheriff Court, 1824–1925, SC5
Wigtown Sheriff Court, 1826–1925, SC19

National Register of Archives Scotland
Records of Urquharts of Meldrum and Carriacou, NRAS 2570

NatWest Group Archives, Edinburgh
Letters from George King regarding Adelphi Estate, 13 October 1802–4 January 1803, RB/1378.
Royal Bank, Directors Minutes 1780–1833, RB/12/vols. 13–21
Simpson-Moncrieff Letters, RB/837

Private ownership
John Kennedy correspondence, Jamaica 1833

University of Glasgow Archives
Records of James Finlay and Co., UGD91
Records of Glasgow Fire Insurance Society, UGD71

University of Glasgow Special Collections
Letter to James Ewing Esq. LLD of Dunoon Castle from a Reformer, 19 July 1832, Bh11–c.15
Minute book of Dennistoun, Buchanan, & Co. Glasgow, 1806–42, MS. Murray 605
Samuel Rose Papers, MS. Gen, 520/58
Papers of Duncan Macfarlan, MS. Gen 1717
Appraisement of Invera Estate, Tobago, 1829 MS. Gen 946/4

University of Strathclyde Archives and Special Collections
Records of Andersons Institution, GB 249

Trinidad

**The University of the West Indies, St Augustine,
Special Collections and West India Collection**
London West India Committee records, special collections, SC89

Land granted by the Spanish government, SC100/1–3

Greyfriars Church of Scotland (Trinidad) original records (Microfilm), West Indiana Collection, BX9033.T7 G74

Newspapers and journals

Blackwood's Edinburgh Magazine
Caledonian Mercury
Edinburgh Gazette
Glasgow Courier
Glasgow Herald
Greenock Advertiser
Grenada Free Press and Public Gazette
Jamaica Mercury
London Gazette
Morning Chronicle
Morning Post
Port of Spain Gazette
The Anti-Slavery Reporter
The Edinburgh Annual Register
The Edinburgh Magazine or Literary Miscellany
The Edinburgh Monthly Magazine and Review
The Essequibo and Demerary Royal Gazette
The Glasgow Advertiser
The Lancaster Gazette and General Advertiser
The Law Advertiser
The Liverpool Mercury
The Loyal Reformers Gazette
The Reformers Gazette
The Royal Gazette (Kingston, Jamaica)
The Scots Times
The Scotsman
The Times
The Trinidad Standard and West India Journal

Parliamentary papers

HCPP 1787 *An Account of The Quantities of Sugar, Rum, Cotton, Coffee, Cocoa, Indigo, Ginger, Aloes, and Other Goods, Imported into the Several Ports of Great Britain, from the British Sugar Colonies, from Christmas 1786 to Christmas 1787 Inclusive.*

HCPP 1801 (98) *Report on the Petition of the Proprietors of Estates in the Island of Grenada.*

HCPP 1801–2 (43) *An Account of the Loans Advanced, in Exchequer Bills and Cash, to the Planters and Merchants Interested in the Islands of Grenada and St. Vincent's.*

HCPP 1808 (178) *Report from the Committee on the Distillation of Sugar and Molasses.*

HCPP 1821 *House of Commons Papers*, 14.

HCPP 1826–7 (479) *Trinidad Negroes. Return to an Address of the Honourable House of Commons, dated 12th June 1827.*

HCPP 1830 (63) *Twentieth Report of the Commissioners of Inquiry into Post-Office Revenue, Vol. III, Scotland.*

HCPP 1831 *Comparative Account of Population of Great Britain, 1801, 1811, 1821 and 1831.*

HCPP 1831–2 (721) *xx Select Committee on the Extinction of Slavery throughout the British Dominions.*

HCPP 1837–8 (215) 48 *Slavery Abolition Act: An Account of All Sums of Money Awarded by the Commissioners of Slavery Compensation.*

HCPP (1841) *Accounts of Population and Number of Houses According to Census, 1841, of Each County in Great Britain.*

HCPP 1841 (64) *Answers Made by Schoolmasters in Scotland to Queries Circulated in 1838, by Order of the Select Committee on Education in Scotland.*

HCPP *Accounts and Papers of the House of Commons: Revenue, Population, Commerce*, vol. lvi (1843).

Published contemporary sources

A Free Mulatto, *An Address to the Right Hon. Earl Bathurst, His Majesty's Principal Secretary of State for the Colonies Relative to the Claims which the Coloured Population of Trinidad* (London, 1824).

Alexander, J. E., *Transatlantic Sketches* (Philadelphia, 1833).

Alexander, W., *The Practice of the Commissary Courts in Scotland* (Edinburgh: Adam & Charles Black, 1859).

Alison, A., *Some Account of My Life and Writings: An Autobiography*, vol. i (Edinburgh, 1883).

Archer, J. H. L., *Monumental Inscriptions of the British West Indies from the Earliest Date* (London, 1875).

Bartlett, W. H., Harding, J. D. and Creswick, T., *The Ports, Harbours, Watering-Places and Picturesque Scenery of Great Britain*, vol. i (London, 1840).

Bell, G. J., *Commentaries on the Laws of Scotland and on the Principles of Mercantile Jurisprudence*, 5th ed., vol. ii (Edinburgh, 1826).

Borthwick, B., *A Lecture on Colonial Slavery and Gradual Emancipation, Delivered in the Assembly Rooms on Friday 1 March 1833* (Edinburgh, 1833).

Bridgens, R., *West India Scenery: With Illustrations of Negro Character, the Process of Making Sugar, etc.: From Sketches Taken during a Voyage to and Residence of Seven Years in the Island of Trinidad* (London, 1836).

Burke, J., *A Genealogical and Heraldic History of the Commoners of Great Britain*, various (London).

Christie, J., *The Medical Institutions of Glasgow* (Glasgow, 1888).

Cleland, J., *Abridgement of the Annals of Glasgow* (Glasgow, 1817).

——, *The Rise and Progress of the City of Glasgow* (Glasgow, 1820).

——, *Statistical Tables Relative to the City of Glasgow*, 3rd ed. (Glasgow, 1823).

——, *Enumeration of the Inhabitants of the City of Glasgow and County of Lanark for the Government census of 1831*, 2nd ed. (Glasgow, 1832).

Craik, J., Eadie, J. and Galbraith, J. *Memoirs and Portraits of One Hundred Glasgow Men Who Have Died During the Last Thirty Years, and in Their Lives did Much to Make the City What It Now Is* (Glasgow, 1886).

Crawford, G., *A Sketch of the Rise and Progress of the Trades' House of Glasgow* (Glasgow, 1858).

Dauxion Lavaysse, J. F., *A Statistical, Commercial and Political Description of Venezuela, Trinidad, Margarita and Tobago* (London, 1820).

Dennistoun, J. W., *Some Account of the Family of Dennistoun of Dennistoun and Colgrain* (Glasgow, 1906).

Ewing, J., *View of the History, Constitution, & Funds of the Guildry and Merchants House of Glasgow* (Glasgow, 1817).

Fraser, L. M., *History of Trinidad, 1781–1813*, vol. i (Port of Spain, 1891).

Fraser, W., *The Stirlings of Keir, and Their Family Papers* (Edinburgh, 1858).

Gordon, J. (ed.), *The New Statistical Account of Scotland* (Edinburgh, 1845).

Gordon, W. H., *The General Counting House, and Man of Business* (Edinburgh, 1766).

——, *The Universal Accountant and Complete Merchant*, 3rd ed., vol. i (Edinburgh, 1770).

Hutcheson, J., *Notes on the Sugar Industry* (Glasgow, 1901).

Hyde, J. W., *A Hundred Years by Post: A Jubilee Retrospect* (London, 1891).

Law, J., *Maria Jones, Her History in Africa and in the West Indies* (Trinidad, 1851).

Leslie, C., *A New History of Jamaica* (London, 1740).

Long, E., *A History of Jamaica*, vol. ii (London, 1774).

Mackay, M., *Memoir of James Ewing Esq., of Strathleven* (Glasgow, 1866).

Mackenzie, P., *Old Reminisces of Glasgow*, vol. ii (Glasgow, 1890).

MacQueen, J., *The Colonial Controversy* (Glasgow, 1825).

Martin, R. M., *History of the Colonies of the British Empire* (London, 1843).

Marx, K., *Capital*, vol. i (England, 1990 ed.).

McMahon, B., *Jamaica Plantership* (London, 1839).

McLaren, J., *The Law of Scotland in Relation to Wills and Succession*, vol. i (Edinburgh, 1868).

Moreton, J. B., *West India Customs and Manners: Containing Strictures on the Soil, Cultivation, Produce, Trade, Officers, and Inhabitants, with the Method of Establishing and Conducting a Sugar Plantation to Which Is Added the Practice of Training New Slaves* (London, 1793).

Morrison, J., *The Elements of Book Keeping, by Single and Double Entry* (London, 1813).

——, *A Complete Treatise on Practical Book-Keeping*, 3rd ed. (London, 1820).

Oldmixon, J., *The British Empire in America, Containing the History of Discovery, Settlement, Progress and Present State of all the British Colonies on the Continent and Islands of America*, 2 vols. (London, 1708).

Owen, R., *The Life of Robert Owen Written by Himself: With Selections from His Writings and Correspondence*, vol. i (London, 1857).

Potter, B. (transcribed by Leslie Linder), *The Journal of Beatrix Potter from 1881 to 1897* (Harmondsworth, 2012).

Paterson, J., *History of the Counties of Ayr and Wigtown, Vol. 1: Kyle* (Edinburgh, 1863).

Reid, R. (Senex), *Old Glasgow and its Environs* (Glasgow, 1864).

Senex, *Glasgow: Past and Present*, vol. iii (Glasgow, 1884).

Sinclair, J., *The Statistical Accounts of Scotland*, various (Edinburgh, 1794).

——, *Analysis of the Statistical Account of Scotland* (Edinburgh, 1831).

——, *General Report of the Agricultural State, and Political Circumstances, of Scotland*, vol. iii (Edinburgh, 1814).

Smith, A., *Wealth of Nations* (Oxford, 1998 ed.).

Smith, G., *Reference to the Plan of the Island of Grenada* (London, 1882).

Smith, J. G., *The Parish of Strathblane and Its Inhabitants from Early Times* (Glasgow, 1886).

——, *Strathendrick and Its Inhabitants from Early Times* (Glasgow, 1896).

——, and Mitchell, J. O., *The Old Country Houses of the Old Glasgow Gentry* (Glasgow, 1878).

Snagg, W. (ed.), *The Laws of Grenada and the Grenadines* (Grenada, 1852).

Somerville, T., *My Own Life and Times, 1741–1814* (Edinburgh, 1861).

Stewart, G., *Curiosities of Glasgow Citizenship, as Exhibited Chiefly in the Business Career of its Old Commercial Aristocracy* (Glasgow, 1881).

Strang, J., *Glasgow and Its Clubs or Glimpses of the Condition, Manners, Characters and Oddities of the City during the Past and Present Centuries* (London and Glasgow, 1857).

Thom, W., *The Works of the Rev. William Thom, Late Minister of Govan, Consisting of Sermons, Tracts, Letters* (Glasgow, 1799).

Votes of the Honourable House of Assembly of Jamaica in a Session, 3 November 1829–20 February 1830 (Kingston, Jamaica, 1830).

Winterbottom, W., *Historical, Geographical, Commercial and Philosophical View of the American United States*, 2nd edn, vol. iv (London, 1795).

Published primary sources

A List of Matriculated Members of the Merchant's House, from 3rd October 1768, to 5th October 1857 (Glasgow, 1858).

Blair, G., *Biographic and Descriptive Sketches of Glasgow Necropolis* (Glasgow, 1857).

Cameron, V. R., *Emigrants from Scotland to America, 1774–1775* (Baltimore, 1990).

Cases Decided in the Court of Session 1826–1827, vol. v (Edinburgh, 1827).

Cases Decided in the Court of Session, Teind Court & c., and House of Lords, 1863–1864, 3s., vol. ii (Edinburgh, 1864).

Cases Decided in the Court of Session, Teind Court, Court of Exchequer and House of Lords, vol. xix, 1856–7 (Edinburgh, 1857).

Chalmers, T., *Fifth Report of the Committee of the General Assembly of the Church of Scotland in Church Extension* (Edinburgh, 1839).

——, *Seventh Report of the Committee of the General Assembly of the Church of Scotland on Church Extension* (Edinburgh, 1841).

Decisions of the First and Second Divisions of the Court of Session, November 1812–1814 (Edinburgh, 1815).

Decisions of the Court Session from 12 November 1837 to 12 July 1838 (Edinburgh, 1839).

Donald, C. D., *Minute Book of the Board of Green Cloth, 1809–1820* (Glasgow, 1891).

Donald, T. F., *The Hodge Podge Club 1752–1900: Compiled from the Records of the Club* (Glasgow, 1900).

John Tait's Directory for the City of Glasgow (Glasgow, 1783).

Jones's Directory (various).

Jones, N., *Reprint of Jones's Directory for the Year 1787* (Glasgow, 1868).

Renwick, R. (ed.), *Extracts from the Records of the Burgh of Glasgow, 1796–1808*, vol. ix (Glasgow, 1914).

Reports of Cases Decided in the Supreme Courts of Scotland, and in the House of Lords on Appeal from Scotland, vol. xxviii (Edinburgh, 1856).

Reports from the Commissioners: Ecclesiastical Church Estates; Endowed Schools and Hospitals (Scotland), vol. xvii (1874).

The Glasgow Directory.

The Post Office Annual Directory.

The Scottish Jurist, vol. i–vol. xvii (Edinburgh, 1829–40).

Secondary sources

Addison, W. I., *The Matriculation Albums of the University of Glasgow, From 1728 to 1858* (Glasgow, 1913).

Alston, D., '"Very rapid and splendid fortunes"? – Highland Scots in Berbice (Guyana) in the early nineteenth century', *Transactions of the Gaelic Society of Inverness*, lxiii (2002–4), 208–326.

——, '"You have only seen the fortunate few and draw conclusions accordingly": behavioural economics and the paradox of Scottish emigration', in *Global Migrations: The Scottish Diaspora since 1600*, ed. A. McCarthy and J. M. Mackenzie, (Edinburgh, 2016), pp. 46–63.

——, *Slaves and Highlanders: Silenced Histories of Scotland and the Caribbean* (Edinburgh, 2021).

Anderson, C., 'Old subjects, new subjects and non-subjects: silences and subjecthood in Fedon's rebellion, Grenada, 1795–96', in *War, Empire and Slavery, 1770–1830*, ed. R. Bessell, N. Guyatt and Jane Rendall (New York, 2010), pp. 201–17.

Anderson, J., *The Burgesses and Guild Brethren of Glasgow, 1751–1846* (Edinburgh, 1935).

Anderson, M., 'Guesses, estimates and adjustments: Webster's 1755 "census" of Scotland revisited again', *Journal of Scottish Historical Studies*, xxxi (2011), 26–45.

——, and Morse, D .J. '"The people", in *People and Society in Scotland, Vol. II: 1830–1914*, ed. W. H. Fraser and R. J Morris (Edinburgh, 1990), pp. 8–46.

Anon., 'The rise of Glasgow's West Indian trade, 1793–1818', *Three Banks Review*, li (1961), 34–44.

Anon., 'An early Glasgow-West Indian miscellany', *Three Banks Review*, liv (1962), 29–43.

Armytage, F., *The Free Port System in the British West Indies* (London, 1953).

Anstey, R., *The Atlantic Slave Trade and British Abolition, 1760–1810* (New Jersey, 1975).

Barclay, K., *Love, Intimacy and Power: Marriage and Patriarchy in Scotland, 1650–1850* (Manchester, 2011).

Bailyn, B., *Voyagers to the West: A Passage in the Peopling of America on the Eve of the Revolution* (New York, 1986).

Behrendt, S. D., and Graham, E. J., 'African merchants, notables and the slave trade at old calabar, 1720: evidence from the National Archives of Scotland', *History in Africa*, xxx (2003), 37–61.

Berg, M. and Hudson, P., 'Slavery, Atlantic trade and skills: a response to Mokyr's "holy land of industrialism"', *Journal of the British Academy*, ix (2021), 259–81.

Blackburn, R., *The Making of New World Slavery* (London, 1998; new ed. 2010).

Brereton, B., *A History of Modern Trinidad, 1783–1962* (London, 1981).

Brogan, C., *James Finlay & Company Limited: Manufacturers and East India Merchants, 1750–1950* (Glasgow, 1951).

Brown, C. G., *Religion and Society in Scotland since 1707* (Edinburgh, 1997).

Brown, J., 'Duncan Kennedy: from Gaelic poet to Glasgow accountant', *Scottish Local History*, lxxxviii (2014).

Brown, V., *The Reaper's Garden: Death and Power in the World of Atlantic Slavery* (Cambridge, Mass., 2008).

Browne, R., *Surviving Slavery in the British Caribbean* (Philadelphia, 2017).

Bumsted, J. M., 'The Scottish diaspora: emigration to British North America, 1763–1815', in *Nation and Province in the First British Empire: Scotland and the Americas, 1600–1800*, ed. N. C. Landsman (Lewisburg, PA, 2001), pp. 127–51.

Burnard, T., 'Inheritance and independence: women's status in early colonial Jamaica', *The William and Mary Quarterly*, 3rd series, xlviii (January 1991), 93–114.

——, 'European migration to Jamaica, 1655 to 1780', *The William and Mary Quarterly*, 3rd series, liii (1996), 769–96.

——, '"The countrie continues sicklie": white mortality in Jamaica, 1655–1780', *Social History of Medicine*, xii (1999), 45–72.

——, 'Prodigious riches: the wealth of Jamaica before the American Revolution', *The Economic History Review*, liv (2001), 506–24.

——, '"The great mart of the island": the economic function of Kingston, Jamaica in the mid-eighteenth century', in *Jamaica in Slavery and Freedom*, ed. K. Monteith and G. Richards (Kingston, 2002), pp. 225–41.

——, 'Passengers only', *Atlantic Studies*, i (2004), 178–95.

——, 'Et in Arcadia ego: West Indian planters in glory, 1674–1784', *Atlantic Studies*, ix (2012), 19–40.

——, *Planters, Merchants, and Slaves: Plantation Societies in British America, 1650–1820* (Chicago, 2015).

——, *Jamaica in the Age of Revolution* (Philadelphia, 2020).

Butler, K. M., *The Economics of Emancipation: Jamaica and Barbados, 1823–1843* (Chapel Hill, 1995).

Butt, J., 'The Scottish cotton industry during the Industrial Revolution, 1780–1840', in *Comparative Aspects of Scottish and Irish Economic and Social History, 1600–1900*, ed. L. M. Cullen and T. C. Smout (Edinburgh, 1977), pp. 116–29.

Cain, P. J., and Hopkins, A. J., *British Imperialism, 1688–2000*, 2nd ed. (Singapore, 2002).

Campbell, R. H., 'Scotland', in *The Scots Abroad: Labour, Capital, Enterprise, 1750–1914*, ed. R. A. Cage (London, 1985), pp. 1–28.

——, *Scotland since 1707: The Rise of an Industrial Society*, 2nd ed. (Edinburgh, 1992 ed.).

——, 'The landed classes', in *People and Society in Scotland, Vol. 1: 1760–1830*, ed. T. M. Devine and R. Mitchison (Edinburgh, 1994), pp. 91–109.

——, 'The making of the industrial city', in *Glasgow, Vol. 1: Beginnings to 1830*, ed. T. M. Devine and G. Jackson (Manchester, 1995), pp. 184–214.

Candlin, K., *The Last Caribbean Frontier, 1795–1815* (Basingstoke, 2012).

Carr, R., *Gender and Enlightenment Culture in Eighteenth-Century Scotland* (Edinburgh, 2014).

Carrington, S. H. H., *The Sugar Industry and the Abolition of the Slave Trade, 1775–1810* (Gainesville, 2002).

Chapman, S., *Merchant Enterprise in Britain: From the Industrial Revolution to World War 1* (Cambridge, 1992).

Checkland, S. G., 'John Gladstone as trader and planter', *The Economic History Review*, new series, vii (1954), 216–29.

——, 'Two Scottish West Indian liquidations after 1793', *Scottish Journal of Political Economy*, iv (1957), 127–43.

——, 'Finance for the West Indies, 1780–1815', *The Economic History Review*, new series, x (1958), 461–9.

——, 'American versus West Indian traders in Liverpool, 1793–1815', *The Journal of Economic History*, xviii (1958), 141–60.

——, *The Gladstones: A Family Biography 1764–1851* (Cambridge, 1971).

——, *Scottish Banking: A History, 1695–1973* (Glasgow, 1975).

Checkland, O., *Philanthropy in Victorian Scotland: Social Welfare and the Voluntary Principle* (Edinburgh, 1980).

Clegg, S. (ed.), *Organization Theory and Class Analysis: New Approaches and New Issues* (New York, 1989).

Clemens, P. G. E., 'The rise of Liverpool, 1665–1750', *The Economic History Review*, xxix (May 1976), 211–25.

Clark, P., *British Clubs and Societies, 1580–1800: The Origins of an Associational World* (Oxford, 2000).

Coelho, P., 'The profitability of imperialism: the British experience in the West Indies, 1768–1772', *Explorations in Economic History*, x (1973), 253–80.

Cooke, A. 'The Scottish cotton masters, 1780–1914', *Textile History*, xl (2009), 29–50.

——, *The Rise and Fall of the Scottish Cotton Industry, 1778–1914* (Manchester, 2010).

——, 'An elite revisited: Glasgow West India merchants, 1783–1877', *Journal of Scottish Historical Studies*, xxxii (2012), 127–65.

Cox, E., 'Fedon's rebellion, 1795–96: causes and consequences', *Journal of Negro History*, lxvii (1982), 7–19.

Craton, M., 'Slavery and slave society in the British Caribbean', in *The Slavery Reader*, ed. J. Walvin and G. Heuman (London, 2003), 103–12.

Crispin, B., 'Clyde shipping and the American war', *The Scottish Historical Review*, xli, part 2 (1962), 124–34.

Cruickshank, M., 'The Dick Bequest: the effect of a famous nineteenth-century endowment on parish schools of north east Scotland', *History of Education Quarterly*, v (1965), 153–65.

Cudjoe, S. R., 'Burnley, William Hardin (1780–1850)', *Oxford Dictionary of National Biography* (Oxford University Press, 2016 <http://www.oxforddnb.com.ezproxy.lib.gla.ac.uk/view/article/109518> [accessed 11 Dec. 2016].

——, *The Slave Master of Trinidad: William Hardin Burnley and the Nineteenth-Century Atlantic World* (Amherst, 2018).

Davies, K. G., 'The origins of the commission system in the West India trade', *Transactions of the Royal Historical Society*, v (1952), 89–107.

Davis, R., *A Commercial Revolution: English Overseas Trade in the Seventeenth and Eighteenth Centuries* (London, 1967).

——, *The Industrial Revolution and British Overseas Trade* (Bath, 1979).

De Verteuil, A., *The Black Earth of South Naparima* (Port of Spain, 2009).

Denzel, M. A., *Handbook of World Exchange Rates, 1590–1914* (Surrey, 2010).

Devas, R. P., *A History of the Island of Grenada, 1498–1796* (Carenage, 1974).

Devine, T. M., 'Glasgow colonial merchants and land, 1770–1815', in *Land and Industry: The Landed Estate and the Industrial Revolution*, ed. J. T. Ward and R. G. Wilson (Newton Abbot, 1971), pp. 205–45.

——, 'Transport problems of Glasgow West India merchants during the American War of Independence, 1775–83', *Transport History*, iv (1971), 266–304.

——, 'Glasgow merchants and the collapse of the tobacco trade 1775–1783', *The Scottish Historical Review*, lii (1973), 50–74.

——, 'Sources of capital for the Glasgow tobacco trade, *c*.1740–1780', *Business History*, xvi (1974), 113–29.

——, *The Tobacco Lords: A Study of the Tobacco Merchants of Glasgow and Their Trading Activities, c. 1740–90* (Edinburgh, 1975).

——, 'The American War of Independence and Scottish economic history', in *Scotland, Europe and the American Revolution*, ed. O. Dudley Edwards and G. Shepperson (Edinburgh, 1976), pp. 61–6.

——, 'The colonial trades and industrial investment in Scotland, *c*.1700–1815', *The Economic History Review*, xxix (1976), 1–13.

——, 'Colonial commerce and the Scottish economy, *c*.1730–1815', in *Comparative Aspects of Scottish and Irish Economic and Social History, 1600–1900*, ed. L. M. Cullen and T. C. Smout (Edinburgh, 1977), pp. 176–92.

——, 'An eighteenth-century business elite: Glasgow–West India merchants, c. 1750–1815', *The Scottish Historical Review*, lvii (1978), 40–67.

——, 'The paradox of Scottish emigration', in *Scottish Emigration and Scottish Society*, ed. T. M. Devine (Edinburgh, 1992), pp. 1–15.

——, *The Rural Transformation of Scotland: Social Change and the Agrarian Economy, 1660–1815* (Edinburgh, 1994).

——, 'The development of Glasgow to 1830: medieval burgh to industrial city', in *Glasgow, Vol. 1: Beginnings to 1830*, ed. T. M. Devine and G. Jackson (Manchester, 1995), pp. 1–17.

——, 'The golden age of tobacco', in *Glasgow, Vol. 1: Beginnings to 1830*, ed. T. M. Devine and G. Jackson (Manchester, 1995), pp. 139–84.

——, *Scotland's Empire 1680–1815* (London, 2004).

——, 'Industrialisation', in *The Transformation of Scotland: The Economy since 1700*, ed. T. M. Devine, C. H. Lee and G. C. Peden (Edinburgh, 2005), pp. 34–70.

——, 'The transformation of agriculture: cultivation and clearance', in *The Transformation of Scotland: The Economy Since 1700*, ed. T. M. Devine et al. (Edinburgh, 2005), pp. 71–99.

——, 'Did slavery make Scotia great?', *Britain and the World*, iv (2011), 40–64.

——, 'Did slavery make Scotia great? A question revisited', in *Recovering Scotland's Slavery Past: The Caribbean Connection*, ed. T. M. Devine (Edinburgh, 2015), pp. 225–45.

——, *To the Ends of the Earth: Scotland's Global Diaspora* (London, 2011).

——, and Rössner, P. R., 'Scots in the Atlantic economy, 1600–1800', in *Scotland and the British Empire*, ed. by J. M. MacKenzie and T. M. Devine (Oxford, 2011), pp. 30–53.

Dobson, D., *Scottish Emigration to Colonial America, 1607–1785* (Athens, Ga., 1994).

——, *Scots in the West Indies, 1707–1857*, vol. i (Baltimore, 1998).

——, *Scots in the West Indies, 1707–1857*, vol. ii (Baltimore, 2006).

Donington, K., *The Bonds of Family: Slavery, Commerce and Culture in the British Atlantic World* (Manchester, 2019).

Donnachie, I., and Hewitt, G., *Historic New Lanark: The Dale and Owen Industrial Community since 1785* (Edinburgh, 2015 ed.).

Dowds, T. J. *The Forth and Clyde Canal: A History* (East Linton, 2003).

Draper, N., 'The City of London and slavery: evidence from the first dock companies, 1795–1800', *The Economic History Review*, lxi (2008), 432–66.

——, *The Price of Emancipation: Slave Ownership, Compensation and British Society at the End of Slavery* (Cambridge, 2010).

——, 'The rise of a new planter class? Some countercurrents from British Guiana and Trinidad, 1807–33', *Atlantic Studies*, ix (March 2012), 65–83.

——, '"Dependent on precarious subsistences": Ireland's slave-owners at the time of emancipation', *Britain and the World*, vi (2013), 220–42.

——, 'Helping to make Britain great: the commercial legacies of slave-ownership in Britain', in *Legacies of British Slave-Ownership*, ed. C. Hall, N. Draper et al. (Cambridge, 2014), pp. 78–126.

——, 'Possessing people: absentee slave-owners within British society', in *Legacies of British Slave-ownership*, ed. C. Hall, N. Draper et al. (Cambridge, 2014), pp. 34–77.

——, 'The British state and slavery: George Baillie, merchant of London and St Vincent, and the exchequer loans of the 1790s', working papers, *Economic History Society* (2015) <www.ehs.org.uk/dotAsset/de55e1a1-c7f6-450b-9a1a-831601ae46d9.docx> [accessed 29 Dec. 2018].

——, 'Scotland and colonial slave-ownership: the evidence of the slave compensation records', in *Recovering Scotland's Slavery Past: The Caribbean Connection* (Edinburgh, 2015), pp. 166–87.

Drescher, S., *Econocide: British Slavery in the Era of Abolition*, 2nd ed. (Chapel Hill, 2010).

Dresser, M., *Slavery Obscured: The Social History of the Slave Trade in an English Provincial Port* (London and New York, 2001).

——, and Hann, A. (ed.), *Slavery and the British Country House* (Swindon, 2013).

Duffill, M., 'The Africa trade from the ports of Scotland, 1706–66', *Slavery & Abolition*, xxv (2004), 102–22.

Dunn, R. S., *Sugar and Slaves: The Rise of the Planter Class in the English West Indies, 1624–1713* (Chapel Hill, N.C., 1972).

Durie, A., 'The Scottish linen industry in the eighteenth century: some aspects of expansion', in *Comparative Aspects of Scottish and Irish Economic and Social History, 1600–1900*, ed. L. M. Cullen and T. C. Smout (Edinburgh, 1977), pp. 88–100.

——, *The Scottish Linen Industry in the Eighteenth Century* (Edinburgh, 1979).

Eltis, D., and Engerman, S. L., 'The importance of slavery and the slave trade to industrializing Britain', *Journal of Economic History*, lx (2000), 123–44.

Engerman, S. L., 'The slave trade and British capital formation in the eighteenth century: a comment on the Williams thesis', *The Business History Review*, xlvi (1972), 430–43.

Epstein, J., *Scandal of Colonial Rule: Power and Subversion in the British Atlantic during the Age of Revolution* (Cambridge, 2012).

Evans, C., *Slave Wales: The Welsh and Atlantic Slavery, 1660–1850* (Cardiff, 2010).

Flinn, M. (ed.), *Scottish Population History from the 17th Century to the 1930s* (Cambridge, 1977).

Forte, A. D. M., 'Some aspects of the law in Scotland: 1500–1700', in *Marriage and Property*, ed. E. Craik (Aberdeen, 1984), 104–18.

Forrester, D. A. R., 'Early canal company accounts: financial and accounting aspects of the Forth and Clyde navigation, 1768–1816', *Accounting and Business Research*, x (1980), 109–23.

Frank, A. G., *World Accumulation, 1492–1789* (New York and London, 1978).

——, *Dependent Accumulation and Underdevelopment* (New York and London, 1979).

French, C. J., '"Crowded with traders and a great commerce": London's domination of English overseas trade, 1700–1775', *The London Journal*, xvii (1992), 27–35.

Gauci, P., *Emporium of the World: The Merchants of London, 1660–1800* (London, 2007).

Genovese, E. F., and Eugene D., *The Fruits of Merchant Capital: Slavery and Bourgeois Property in the Rise and Expansion of Capitalism* (New York, 1983).

Gourvish, T. R., and Reed, M. C., 'The financing of Scottish railways before 1860 – a comment', *Scottish Journal of Political Economy*, xviii (1971), 209–20.

Graham, E., *Burns and the Sugar Plantocracy of Ayrshire* (Ayr, 2009).

——, 'The Scots penetration of the Jamaican plantation business', in *Recovering Scotland's Slavery Past: The Caribbean Connection*, ed. T. M. Devine (Edinburgh, 2015), pp. 82–99.

Guasco, M., 'Indentured servitude', 'Atlantic History', in *Oxford Bibliographies*, ed. T. Burnard (New York, 2011).

Haggerty, S., 'Liverpool, the slave trade and the British-Atlantic empire, 1750–1775', in *The Empire in One City? Liverpool's Inconvenient Imperial Past*, ed. S. Haggerty, A. Webster and N. J. White (Manchester, 2008), pp. 17–34.

——, *'Merely for Money'? Business Culture in the British Atlantic, 1750–1815* (Liverpool, 2012).

Hall, C., '"The most unbending Conservative in Britain": Archibald Alison and pro-slavery discourse', in *Recovering Scotland's Slavery Past: The Caribbean Connection*, ed. by T. M. Devine (Edinburgh, 2015), pp. 206–25.

——, Draper, N. and McClelland, K., 'Introduction', in *Legacies of British Slave-ownership: Colonial Slavery and the Formation of Victorian Britain*, ed. C. Hall, N. Draper et al. (Cambridge, 2014), pp. 1–33.

Hall, D., 'Absentee-proprietorship in the British West Indies to about 1850', *Jamaican Historical Review* (1964), 15–35.

Hamilton, D., 'Scottish trading in the Caribbean: the rise and fall of Houston & Co.', in *Nation and Province in the First British Empire: Scotland and the Americas, 1600–1800*, ed. N. C. Landsman (Lewisburg, Pa., 2001), pp. 94–126.

——, *Scotland, the Caribbean and the Atlantic World, 1750–1820* (Manchester, 2005).

——, 'Transatlantic ties: Scottish migration networks in the Caribbean, 1750–1800', in *A Global Clan, Scottish Migrant Networks and Identities since the Eighteenth Century*, ed. A. McCarthy (London, 2006), pp. 48–66.

Hamilton, H., *An Economic History of Scotland in the Eighteenth Century* (Oxford, 1963).

——, *The Industrial Revolution in Scotland* (London, 1966).

Hancock, D., *Citizens of the World: London Merchants and the Integration of the British Atlantic Community, 1735–1785* (Cambridge, 1997).

——, 'Scots in the slave trade', in *Nation and Province in the First British Empire: Scotland and the Americas, 1600–1800*, ed. N. C. Landsman (Lewisburg, 2001), pp. 60–94.

Harley, K., 'Slavery, the British Atlantic economy, and the industrial revolution', in *The Caribbean and the Atlantic World Economy: Circuits of Trade, Money and Knowledge, 1650–1914*, ed. A. B. Leonard et al. (Basingstoke, 2015), pp. 161–83.

Harper, M., *Emigration from North-east Scotland: Willing exiles*, vol. i (Aberdeen, 1988).

Higman, B. W., *Slave Population and Economy in Jamaica, 1807–1834* (Cambridge, 1976).

——, *Slave Populations of the British Caribbean, 1807–1834* (Baltimore, 1984).

——, *Plantation Jamaica, 1750–1850: Capital and Control in a Colonial Economy* (Kingston, 2008).

Hill, S., 'The Liverpool economy during the War of American Independence, 1775–83', *The Journal of Imperial and Commonwealth History*, xliv (2016), 835–56.

Historical Sketch of The Buchanan Institution Glasgow (Glasgow, 1913).

Hook, A., and Sher, R., 'Introduction: Glasgow and the Enlightenment', in *The Glasgow Enlightenment*, ed. A. Hook and R. Sher (Edinburgh, 1995), pp. 1–17.

Hudson, P., *The Industrial Revolution* (London, 1992).

——, 'Slavery, the slave trade and economic growth: a contribution to the debate', in *Emancipation and the Remaking of the British Imperial World*, ed. C. Hall, N. Draper and K. McClelland (Manchester, 2014), pp. 40–9.

Hume, E. E., 'A colonial Scottish Jacobite family: establishment in Virginia of a branch of the Humes of Wedderburn, *The Virginia Magazine of History and Biography*, xxxviii (1930), 1–37.

Hyde, F. E., *Liverpool and the Mersey: The Development of a Port, 1700–1970* (Newton Abbot, 1971).

Ingram, K. E., *Manuscript Sources for the History of the West Indies* (Kingston, 2000).

Inikori, J., 'Capitalism and slavery, fifty years after: Eric Williams and the changing explanations of the industrial revolution', in *Capitalism and Slavery Fifty Years Later: Eric Eustace Williams – A Reassessment of the Man and His Work*, ed. H. Cateau and S. H. H. Carrington (New York, 2000), pp. 79–103.

——, *Africans and the Industrial Revolution in England: A Study in International Trade and Economic Development* (Cambridge, 2002).

——, and Behrendt, S. et al, 'Roundtable', *International Journal of Maritime History*, xv (2003), 279–361.

Jackson, G., 'New horizons', in *Glasgow, Vol. 1: Beginnings to 1830*, ed. T. M. Devine and G. Jackson (Manchester, 1995), pp. 214–39.

——, and Munn, C., and, 'Trade, commerce and finance', in *Glasgow, Vol. II: 1830–1912*, ed. W. H. Fraser and I. Maver (Manchester, 1996), pp. 52–95.

Jones, A. M., 'Race, religion, and the Scottish empire: St. Andrew's Kirk, Nassau, ca. 1810–1852', *International Journal of Bahamian Studies*, xxvi (2020), 1–12.

Karras, A., *Sojourners in the Sun* (Ithaca, 1992).

Kehoe, S. K., 'From the Caribbean to the Scottish Highlands: charitable enterprise in the age of improvement, *c.*1750–1820', *Rural History*, xxvii (2015), 1–23.

——, 'Jacobites, Jamaica and the establishment of a Highland Catholic Community in the Canadian Maritimes', *The Scottish Historical Review*, c (2021), 199–217.

Kidd, S., 'Gaelic books as cultural icons: the maintenance of cultural links between the Highlands and the West Indies', in *Within and Without Empire: Scotland Across the (Post)colonial Borderline*, ed. C. Sassi and T. van Heijnsbergen (Newcastle, 2013), pp. 46–60.

Kinsey, J., 'The economic impact of the port of Liverpool on the economy of Merseyside – using a multiplier approach', *Geoforum*, xii (1981), 331–47.

Kumagai, Y., *Breaking into the Monopoly: Provincial Merchants and Manufacturers' Campaigns for Access to the Asian Market, 1790–1833* (Leiden, 2013).

Lambert, D., 'The Glasgow king of Billingsgate: James MacQueen and an Atlantic pro–slavery network', *Slavery and Abolition*, xxix (2008), 389–413.

——, *Mastering the Niger: James MacQueen's African Geography and the Struggle over Atlantic Slavery* (Chicago and London, 2013).

——, and Lester, A. ed. *Colonial Lives across the British Empire: Imperial Careering in the Long Nineteenth Century* (Cambridge, 2006).

Lamont, N., *An Inventory of the Lamont Papers, 1231–1897* (Edinburgh, 1914).

——, 'Life of a West India planter one hundred years ago', *Public Lectures, Delivered under the Auspices of the Trinidad Historical Society during the Session, 1935–6* (Trinidad and Tobago, 1936).

Landsman, N. C., *Scotland, and Its First American Colony, 1683–1765* (Princeton, 1985).

Lawton, R., 'The population of Liverpool in the mid-nineteenth century', *Transactions of the Historical Society of Lancaster and Cheshire* (1955), 89–120.

Leask, N., *Robert Burns and Pastoral: Poetry and Improvement in Late Eighteenth-Century Scotland* (Oxford, 2010).

Lee, C. H., 'The establishment of the financial network', in *The Transformation of Scotland: The Economy Since 1700*, ed. T. M. Devine, C. H. Lee and G. C. Peden (Edinburgh, 2005), pp. 100–28.

Lenman, B., *Economic History of Modern Scotland* (London, 1977).

——, 'Review: Michael Morris, Scotland and the Caribbean, c.1740–1833', *Eighteenth-Century Scottish Studies Society Newsletter*, xxxi (2017), 24.

Livesay, D., *Children of Uncertain Fortune: Mixed-Race Jamaicans in Britain and the Atlantic Family, 1733–1833* (Chapel Hill, 2018).

Longmore, J., '"Cemented by the blood of a negro"? The impact of the slave trade on eighteenth-century Liverpool', in *Liverpool and Transatlantic Slavery* ed., D. Richardson, S. Schwarz and A. Tibbles (Liverpool, 2007), pp. 227–251.

——, 'Rural retreats: Liverpool slave traders and their country houses', in *Slavery and the British Country House*, ed. M. Dresser and A. Hann (Swindon, 2013), pp. 43–54.

Macinnes, A. I., 'Scottish Gaeldom: the first phase of clearance', in *People and Society in Scotland, Vol. 1: 1760–1830*, ed. T. M. Devine and R. Mitchison (Edinburgh, 1988), pp. 70–91.

——, 'Scottish Gaeldom from clanship to commercial landlordism, c.1600–c.1850', in *Scottish Power Centres from the Early Middle Ages to the Twentieth Century*, ed. S. M. Foster, A. I. Macinnes and R. K. MacInnes (Glasgow, 1998), pp. 162–90.

——, 'Commercial landlordism and clearance in the Scottish Highlands: The case of Arichonan', in *Communities in European History: Representations, Jurisdictions, Conflicts*, ed. J. Pan-Montojo and F. Pedersen (Pisa, 2007), pp. 47–64.

——, *Union and Empire: The Making of the United Kingdom in 1707* (Cambridge, 2007).

——, 'Scottish circumvention of the English Navigation Acts in the American colonies 1660–1707', in *Making, Using and Resisting the Law in European History*, ed. Gunther Lottes, E. Medijainen and J. V. Sigurðsson (Pisa, 2008), pp. 109–30.

——, 'The treaty of union: made in England', in *Scotland and the Union, 1707–2007*, ed. T. M. Devine (Edinburgh, 2008), pp. 54–77.

——, and Fryer, L. G., *Scotland and the Americas, c.1650–c.1939: A Documentary Source Book* (Edinburgh, 2008).

Mackillop, A., 'The Highlands and the returning nabob: Sir Hector Munro of Novar, 1760–1807', in *Emigrant Homecomings: The Return Movement of Emigrants, 1600–2000*, ed. M. Harper (Manchester, 2005), pp. 233–62.

——, 'A union for empire? Scotland, the English East India Company and the British Union', *The Scottish Historical Review*, lxxxvii (supplement) (2008), 116–34.

——, '"As hewers of wood, and drawers of water": Scotland as an emigrant nation, *c.*1600 to *c.*1800', in *Global Migrations: The Scottish Diaspora since 1600*, ed. A. McCarthy and J. M. MacKenzie (Edinburgh, 2016), pp. 23–45.

——, *Human Capital and Empire: Scotland, Ireland, Wales and British Imperialism in Asia, c.1690–c.1820* (Manchester, 2021).

MacKinnon, I., 'Colonialism and the Highland clearances', *Northern Scotland*, viii (2017), 22–48.

——, and Mackillop, A. 'Plantation slavery and landownership in the west Highlands and Islands: legacies and lessons' <https://www.communitylandscotland.org.uk/wp-content/uploads/2020/11/Plantation-slavery-and-landownership-in-the-west-Highlands-and-Islands-legacies-and-lessons.pdf> [accessed 10 Nov. 2020].

Marshall, P. J., 'Empire and opportunity in Britain, 1763–1775', *Transactions of the Royal Historical Society*, vi (1995), 111–28.

Mathew, W. M., 'The origins and occupations of Glasgow students 1740–1839', *Past and Present*, xxxiii (1966), 74–94.

Matthews, G., 'Trinidad: a model colony for British slave trade abolition', *Parliamentary History*, xxvi, S1 (2007), 84–96.

Mathias, P., 'Risk, credit and kinship in early modern enterprise', in *The Early Modern Atlantic Economy*, ed. J. McCusker and K. Morgan (Cambridge, 2000), pp. 15–35.

Maver, I., 'Power and politics in the Scottish city: town council in the nineteenth century', in *Scottish Elites*, ed. T. M. Devine (Edinburgh, 1994), pp. 98–130.

McCrum, A., 'Inheritance and the family: the Scottish urban experience in the 1820s', in *Urban Fortunes: Property and Inheritance in the Town, 1700–1900*, ed. J. Stobart and A. Owens (Aldershot, 2000), pp. 149–71.

McCusker, J. J., 'The current value of English exports, 1697 to 1800', *The William and Mary Quarterly*, xxviii (1971), 607–28.

McGilvary, G., 'Return of the Scottish nabob, 1725–1833', in *Back to Caledonia: Scottish Homecomings from the Seventeenth Century to the Present*, ed. M. Varricchio (Edinburgh, 2012), pp. 90–109.

McGinn, C., 'The Scotch bard and "the planting line": new documents on Burns and Jamaica', *Studies in Scottish Literature*, xliii (2017), 255–66.

McKechnie, H., *The Lamont Clan 1235–1935: Seven Centuries of Clan History from Record Evidence* (Edinburgh, 1938).

McKichan, F., 'Lord Seaforth: Highland proprietor, Caribbean governor and slave owner', *The Scottish Historical Review*, xc (2011), 204–35.

——, *Lord Seaforth: Highland Landowner, Caribbean Governor* (Edinburgh, 2018).

Meredith, J. A., *The Plantation Slaves of Trinidad, 1783–1816: A Mathematical and Demographic Enquiry* (Cambridge, 1988).

——, 'Plantation slave mortality in Trinidad', *Population Studies*, xlii (1988), 161–82.

Michie, R. C., *Money, Mania and Markets: Investment, Company Formation, and the Stock Exchange in Nineteenth-Century Scotland* (Edinburgh, 1981).

Mitchell, B. R., with the collaboration of P. Deane, *Abstract of British Historical Statistics* (London, 1962).

Mitchison, R., and Leneman, L., *Sexuality and Social Control: Scotland, 1660–1780* (Oxford, 1989).

Montgomery, F., 'Glasgow and the struggle for Parliamentary Reform, 1830–1832', *The Scottish Historical Review*, lxi (October 1982), 130–45.

Morgan, K., 'Bristol West India merchants in the eighteenth century', *Transactions of the Royal Historical Society*, 6th series, iii (1993), 185–208.

——, 'Atlantic trade and British economic growth in the eighteenth century', in *International Trade and British Economic Growth: From the Eighteenth Century to Present Day, Vol. 5: The Nature of Industrialization*, ed. P. Mathias, J. A. Davis (Oxford, 1996), pp. 14–33.

——, *Slavery, Atlantic Trade and the British Economy, 1660–1800* (Cambridge, 2000).

——, *Bristol and the Atlantic Trade in the Eighteenth Century* (Cambridge, 2002 ed.).

Morgan, N., and Trainor, R. H., 'The dominant classes', in *People and Society in Scotland, Vol. II: 1830–1914*, ed. W. H. Fraser and R. J. Morris (Edinburgh, 1990), pp. 103–37.

Morris, M., *Scotland and the Caribbean, c.1740–1833: Atlantic Archipelagos* (New York and London, 2015).

Morris, R. J. 'The middle class and the property cycle during the Industrial Revolution', in *The Search for Wealth and Stability*, ed. T. C. Smout (London, 1979), pp. 91–114.

Morton, G., 'Identity out of place', in *A History of Everyday Life in Scotland, 1800–1900*, ed. G. Morton and T. Griffiths (Edinburgh, 2010), pp. 256–88.

Mullen, S., 'One of Scotia's sons of toil: David Livingstone and Blantyre Mill', in *David Livingstone: Man, Myth, Legacy*, ed. S. Worden (Edinburgh, 2012), pp. 15–33.

——, 'A Glasgow-West India merchant house and the imperial dividend, 1779–1867', *Journal of Scottish Historical Studies*, xxxiii (2013), 196–233.

——, 'The Great Glasgow–West India house of John Campbell Senior & Co.', in *Recovering Scotland's Slavery Past: The Caribbean Connection*, ed. T. M. Devine (Edinburgh, 2015), pp. 124–44.

——, 'The Scots kirk of colonial Kingston, Jamaica', *Records of the Scottish Church History Society*, xlv (2016), 99–117.

——, 'Glasgow', in *Oxford Bibliographies 'Atlantic History'*, ed. T. Burnard (New York, 2018).

——, 'British universities and transatlantic slavery: the University of Glasgow case', *History Workshop Journal*, xci (Spring 2021), 210–33.

——, 'Henry Dundas: a "great delayer" of the abolition of the transatlantic slave trade', *The Scottish Historical Review*, c (2021), 218–48.

——, 'Centring transatlantic slavery in Scottish historiography', *History Compass*, xx (2022), 1–14.

Munn, C., *The Scottish Provincial Banking Companies, 1747–1864* (Edinburgh, 1981).

Munro, N., *The History of the Royal Bank of Scotland* (Edinburgh, 1928).

Murdoch, A., 'Hector McAllister in North Carolina, Argyll and Arran: family and memory in return migration to Scotland in the eighteenth century', *Journal of Scottish Historical Studies*, xxxiii (2013), 1–19.

Murdoch, S., 'The repatriation of capital to Scotland: a case study of seventeenth-century Dutch testaments and miscellaneous notarial instruments', in *Back to Caledonia: Scottish Homecomings from the Seventeenth Century to the Present*, ed. Mario Varricchio (Edinburgh, 2012), pp. 34–54.

Murray, N., *The Scottish Handloom Weavers, 1790–1850: A Social History* (Edinburgh, 1978).

Nenadic, S., 'The rise of the urban middle class', in *People and Society in Scotland, Vol. I: 1760–1830*, ed. T. M. Devine and R. Mitchison (Edinburgh, 1994), pp. 109–26.

——, 'The middle-ranks and modernisation', in *Glasgow, Vol. 1: Beginnings to 1830*, ed. T. M. Devine and G. Jackson (Manchester, 1995), pp. 278–312.

Nenadic, S., 'The Victorian middle classes', in *Glasgow, Vol. II: 1830–1912*, ed. W. H. Fraser and I. Maver (Manchester, 1996), pp. 265–99.

Newson, L., 'Foreign immigrants in Spanish America: Trinidad's colonisation experiment', *Caribbean Studies*, xix (1979), 133–51.

Niddrie, D. L., 'Eighteenth-century settlement in the British Caribbean', *Transactions of the Institute of British Geographers*, xl (1966), 67–80.

Nisbet, S., 'That nefarious commerce – St Kitts slavery and the West of Scotland', *Proceedings of Caribbean Studies Conference* (2008), 1–14.

O'Brien, P., 'Economic development: the contribution of the periphery', *The Economic History Review*, new series, xxxv (1982), 1–18.

Olegario, R., *A Culture of Credit: Embedding Trust and Transparency in American Business* (Cambridge and London, 2006).

O'Shaughnessy, A., *An Empire Divided: An American Revolution and the British Caribbean* (Philadelphia, 2000).

Pares, R., 'The economic factors in the history of empire', *The Economic History Review*, vii (1937), 119–44.

——, *A West India Fortune* (Bristol, 1950).

——, *Merchants and Planters*. Economic History Review Supplement, No. 4 (Cambridge, 1960).

Petley, C., *Slaveholders in Jamaica: Colonial Society and Culture during the Era of Abolition* (London, 2009).

——, 'Plantations and homes: the material culture of the early nineteenth-century Jamaican elite', *Slavery & Abolition*, xxxv (2014), 437–57.

Pettigrew, W. A., *Freedom's Debt: The Royal African Company and the Politics of the Atlantic Slave Trade, 1672–1752* (Chapel Hill, 2013).

Phillips, K., *Bought and Sold: Scotland, Jamaica and Slavery* (Edinburgh, 2022).

Plackett, R. L., 'The old statistical account', *Journal of the Royal Statistical Society*, series A, cxlix (1986), 247–51.

Pope, D., 'The wealth and aspirations of Liverpool's slave merchants', in *Liverpool and Transatlantic Slavery*, ed. D. Richardson, S. Schwarz and A. Tibbles (Liverpool, 2007), pp. 164–227.

Porter, A., '"Gentlemanly capitalism" and empire: the British experience since 1750?', *The Journal of Imperial and Commonwealth History*, xviii (1990), 265–95.

Price, J., 'The rise of Glasgow in the Chesapeake Tobacco Trade, 1707–1775', *The William and Mary Quarterly, Third Series*, xi (1954), 179–99.

——, 'New time series for Scotland's and Britain's trade with the thirteen colonies and states, 1740 to 1791', *The William and Mary Quarterly*, xxxii (1975), 307–25.

——, *Capital and Credit in British Overseas Trade: The View from the Chesapeake, 1700–1776* (Cambridge and London, 1980).

——, 'What did merchants do? Reflections on British overseas trade 1660–1790', *Journal of Economic History*, xlix (1989), 267–84.

——, and Clemens, P. G. E., 'A revolution of scale in overseas trade: British firms in the Chesapeake trade, 1675–1775', *Journal of Economic History*, xlvii (1987), 1–43.

——, 'Credit in the slave trade and plantation economies', in *Slavery and the Rise of the Atlantic System*, ed. B. L. Solow (Cambridge, 1993), pp. 293–340.

Quintanilla, M., 'The world of Alexander Campbell: an eighteenth-century Grenadian planter', *Albion, A Quarterly Journal with British Studies*, xxxv (2003), 229–56.

——, 'Mercantile communities in the ceded Islands: the Alexander Bartlet and George Campbell Company', *International Social Science Review*, lxxix (2004), 14–26.

Radburn, N., 'Guinea factors, slave sales, and the profits of the transatlantic slave trade in late eighteenth-century Jamaica: the case of John Tailyour', *The William and Mary Quarterly*, lxxxii (2015), 243–86.

——, and Roberts, J., 'Gold versus life: jobbing gangs and British Caribbean slavery', *The William and Mary Quarterly*, lxxvi (2019), 223–56.

Ragatz, L., *The Fall of the Planter Class in the British Caribbean, 1763–1833* (New York, 1928).

Reid, A., 'Sugar, slavery and productivity in Jamaica, 1750–1807', *Slavery & Abolition*, xxxvii (2016), 159–82.

Richards, E., *The Highland Clearances* (Edinburgh, 2005).

Rice, C. D., *The Scots Abolitionists* (Baton Rouge and London, 1981).

Robertson, J., *Gone is the Ancient Glory: Spanish Town, Jamaica, 1534–2000* (Kingston, 2005).

Robertson, M. L., 'Scottish commerce and the American War of Independence', *The Economic History Review*, new series, ix (1956), 123–31.

Rodger, R., and Newman, J., 'Property transfers and the register of Sasines: urban development in Scotland since 1617', *Urban History Yearbook*, xv (1988), 49–57.

Rönnbäck, K., 'On the economic importance of the slave plantation complex to the British economy during the eighteenth century: a value-added approach', *Journal of Global History*, xii (2018), 309–27.

Rössner, P. R., *Scottish Trade in the Wake of Union (1700–1760): The Rise of a Warehouse Economy* (Stuttgart, 2008).

Rothschild, E., *The Inner Life of Empires: An Eighteenth-Century History* (Princeton, 2011).

Richardson, D., 'Slavery and Bristol's "golden age"', *Slavery & Abolition*, xxvi (2005), 35–54.

Ryden, D. B., *West India Slavery and British Abolition, 1783–1807* (Cambridge, 2009).

——, 'Sugar, spirits, and fodder: the London West India interest and the glut of 1807–15', *Atlantic Studies*, ix (2012), 41–64.

——, '"One of the finest and most fruitful spots in America": an analysis of eighteenth-century Carriacou', *Journal of Interdisciplinary History*, xliii (2013), 539–70.

——, 'The society of West India planters and merchants in the age of emancipation, *c.*1816–35', Economic History Society Annual Conference, 27–29 March 2015 <http://www.ehs.org.uk/dotAsset/e389027d-9708-42cb-a13d-85106e90e947.pdf> [accessed 1 Oct. 2016].

Rubinstein, W. D., *Who Were the Rich? A Biographical Directory of British Wealth-Holders, Vol. I: 1809–1839* (London, 2009).

Samaroo, B., 'Maria Jones of Africa, St. Vincent, and Trinidad', in *Gendering the African Diaspora: Women, Culture, and Historical Change in the Caribbean and Nigerian Hinterland*, ed., J. A. Byfield, L. Denzer and A. Morrison (Bloomington, 2010), pp. 131–43.

Saville, R., *Bank of Scotland: A History, 1695–1995* (Edinburgh, 1996).

Schwarz, S., 'Scottish surgeons in the Liverpool slave trade in the late eighteenth and early nineteenth centuries', in *Recovering Scotland's Slavery Past: The Caribbean Connection*, ed. T. M. Devine (Edinburgh, 2015), pp. 145–66.

Sher, R. B., 'Commerce, religion and the enlightenment', in *Glasgow, Vol. 1: Beginnings to 1830*, ed. T. M. Devine and G. Jackson (Manchester, 1995), pp. 312–59.

Sheridan, R., 'The wealth of Jamaica in the eighteenth century', *The Economic History Review*, 2nd series, xviii (1965), 292–311.

——, 'The wealth of Jamaica in the eighteenth century: a rejoinder', *The Economic History Review*, xxi (1968), 46–61.

——, 'The role of Scots in the economy and society of the West Indies', *Annals of the New York Academy of Sciences*, ccxcii (1977), 94–106.

——, 'The condition of the slaves in the settlement and economic development of the British Windward Islands, 1763–1775', *The Journal of Caribbean History*, xxiv (1990), 121–45.

——, *Sugar and Slavery: An Economic History of the British West Indies, 1623–1775* (Kingston, 2007 ed.).

Skillen, B. S., 'Aspects of the alum mining industry about Glasgow', *British Mining*, xxxix (1989), 53–60.

Slade, H. G., 'Craigston and Meldrum estates, Carriacou 1769–1841', *The Proceedings of the Society of Antiquaries of Scotland* (1984), 481–537.

Slater, T. R., 'The mansion and policy', in *The Making of the Scottish Countryside*, ed. M. L. Parry and T. R. Slater (London, 1980), pp. 223–49.

Slaven, A., *The Development of the West of Scotland 1750–1960* (London, 1975).

Smith, S. D., 'Merchants and planters *revisited*', *The Economic History Review*, lv (2002), 434–65.

——, *Slavery, Family and Gentry Capitalism in the British Atlantic: The World of the Lascelles, 1648–1834* (Cambridge, 2006).

Smout, T. C., 'The development and enterprise of Glasgow 1556–1707', *Scottish Journal of Political Economy*, vi (1959), 194–212.

——, 'The early Scottish sugar houses, 1660–1720', *The Economic History Review*, xiv (1961), 240–53.

——, 'The Glasgow merchant community in the seventeenth century', *The Scottish Historical Review*, xlvii (1968), 53–71.

——, *A History of the Scottish People* (London: Fontana, 1972).

——, Landsman, N., and Devine, T. M., 'Scottish emigration in the early modern period', in *Europeans on the Move: Studies on European Migration, 1500–1800*, ed. N. Canny (Oxford, 1994), pp. 76–112.

Solow, B. L., and Engerman, S. L., 'British capitalism and Caribbean slavery: the legacy of Eric Williams: an introduction', in *British Capitalism and Caribbean Slavery: The Legacy of Eric Williams*, ed. B. L. Solow and S. L. Engerman (Cambridge, 1987), pp. 1–24.

Steele, B., 'Grenada: an island state, its history and its people', *Caribbean Quarterly*, xx (1974), 5–43.

Tann, J., 'Steam and sugar: the diffusion of the stationary steam engine to the Caribbean sugar industry 1770–1840', *History of Technology*, xix (1997), 63–84.

Taylor, M., *The Interest: How the British Establishment Resisted the Abolition of Slavery* (London, 2020).

Thomas, R. P., 'The sugar colonies of the old empire: profit or loss for Great Britain?', *The Economic History Review*, xxi (1968), 30–45.

Timperley, L., *A Directory of Land Ownership in Scotland, c.1770* (Edinburgh, 1976).

——, 'A pattern of landholding in eighteenth-century Scotland', in *The Making of the Scottish Countryside*, ed. M. L. Parry and T. R. Slater (London, 1980).

Titus, N., *Amelioration and Abolition of Slavery in Trinidad, 1812–1834: Experiments and Protests in a New Slave Colony* (Indiana, 2009).

Trainor, R. H., 'The elite', in *Glasgow, Vol. II: 1830–1912*, ed. W. H. Fraser and I. Maver (Manchester, 1996), 227–65.

Turner, M., *Slaves and Missionaries: The Disintegration of Jamaican Slave Society, 1787–1834* (Illinois, 1982).

Vamplew, W., 'Sources of Scottish railway share capital before 1860', *Scottish Journal of Political Economy*, xvii (1970), 425–40.

Wallerstein, I., *The Modern World System II: Mercantilism and the Consolidation of the European World Economy, 1600–1750* (New York, 1980).

——, 'One man's meat: the Scottish great leap forward', *Review* iii (1980), 631–40.

Ward, J. R., 'The profitability of sugar planting in the British West Indies, 1650–1834', *The Economic History Review*, xxxi (1978), 197–213.

——, *British West Indian Slavery, 1750–1834: The Process of Amelioration* (Oxford, 1988).

——, 'The British West Indies in the age of abolition, 1748–1815', in *The Oxford History of the British Empire: The Eighteenth Century*, vol. ii, ed. P. J. Marshall (Oxford, 1998), pp. 415–39.

Watt, D., *The Price of Scotland: Darien, Union and the Wealth of Nations* (Edinburgh, 2007).

Whatley, C. A., *The Industrial Revolution in Scotland* (Cambridge, 1997).

——, *Scottish Society, 1707–1830: Beyond Jacobitism, Towards Industrialisation* (Manchester, 2000).

Whyte, I., *Scotland and the Abolition of Black Slavery, 1756–1838* (Edinburgh, 2007).

Williams, E., *History of the People of Trinidad and Tobago* (New York, 1962).

——, *Capitalism and Slavery* (Chapel Hill, 1944).

Withrington, D. J., 'Education and society in the eighteenth century', in *Scotland in the Age of Improvement*, ed. N. T. Phillipson (Edinburgh, 1996), pp. 169–99.

Zacek, N., *Settler Society in the English Leeward Islands 1670–1776* (Cambridge, 2010).

Zahedieh, N., 'Trade, plunder, and economic development in early English Jamaica, 1655–89', *The Economic History Review*, xxxix (May 1986), 205–22.

——, 'Defying mercantilism. Illicit trade, trust, and the Jamaica Sephardim, 1660–1730', Paper delivered at The British Group of Early American Historians, University of Cambridge, 1–4 September 2016.

——, *Capital and the Colonies: London and the Atlantic Economy, 1660–1700* (Cambridge, 2010).

——, 'Eric Williams and William Forbes: copper, colonial markets, and commercial capitalism', *The Economic History Review*, lxxiv (2021), 784–808.

Websites

Alston, D., and Morrison, D., 'James Dick and the Dick Bequest' <https://www.davidalston.info/documents/james-dick-bequest/james-dick-and-the-dick-bequest-a-legacy-of-slavery-v5.pdf> [accessed 23 Sept. 2021].

Ancestry.com website, 'Slave registers of former British colonial dependencies, 1813–1834' [online database]. <https://www.ancestry.co.uk/search/collections/1129/> [accessed 27 June 2022].

Bellahouston Bequest Fund <https://www.oscr.org.uk/about-charities/search-the-register/charity-details?number=SC011781> [accessed 5 Oct. 2020].

British Library, 'Digitisation of the deed books in St Vincent for the slavery era, 1763–1838', EAP688/1/1/3a: Deed Book 1788 [Part 1], 314. <http://eap.bl.uk/database/results.a4d?projID=EAP688> [accessed 5 April 2017].

Burns, Robert 'Letter LVI – to Dr Moore, Mauchline', 2nd August 1787 <https://www.gutenberg.org/files/9863/9863-h/9863-h.htm> [accessed 19 Jan. 2021].

Church of Latter Day Saints, Family History Library <https://familysearch.org/search/catalog/574884?availability=Family%20History%20Library> [accessed 29 Oct. 2014].

Citizens Financial Group, Inc., and Royal Bank of Scotland Group, 'Historical research report predecessor institutions research regarding slavery and the slave trade' <https://www.citizensbank.com/pdf/historical_research.pdf> [accessed 2 Aug. 2014].

Cooke, A., 'Glasgow West India merchants, 1783–1877', *Kudos Website* <https://www.growkudos.com/publications/10.3366%25252Fjshs.2012.0048/reader> [accessed 29 Aug. 2021].

Legacies of British slave-ownership website <http://www.ucl.ac.uk/lbs> [accessed 23 May 2014].

Measuring Worth 2021 <www.measuringworth.com/ukcompare/> [accessed 29 July 2021].

Mullen, S., and Newman, S., 'Slavery, abolition and the University of Glasgow' <https://www.gla.ac.uk/media/media_607547_en.pdf> [accessed 1 Jan. 2019].

'Narrative by Gilbert Burns of his brother's life' <http://www.robertburns.org/encyclopedia/NarrativebyGilbertBurnsofhisBrothersLife.674.shtml> [accessed 19 Jan. 2021].

Scotland and Glasgow in the records of slave compensation <http://www.ucl.ac.uk/lbs/project/scottishdata.pdf> [accessed 6 Nov. 2012].

Scotland's people website <https://www.scotlandspeople.gov.uk/> [accessed 25 May 2017].

Smith, A., *An Inquiry into the Nature and Causes of The Wealth of Nations* (1776) <https://www.marxists.org/reference/archive/smith-adam/works/wealth-of-nations/> [accessed 31 Aug. 2021]

'The Merchants House of Glasgow: report and consolidated financial statements for the year ended 31 December 2017' <https://www.merchantshouse.org.uk/desktop/web/ckfinder/userfiles/files/MH%20Financial%20statements%202017.pdf> [accessed 4 June 2022].

Transatlantic slave trade database estimates <https://www.slavevoyages.org/assessment/estimates> [accessed 31 Jan. 2020].

Index

absenteeism, 12–13, 25, 34, 36–7, 50–1, 54, 70, 100–2, 130, 147–8, 171, 184, 192, 194, 198, 201, 228–9, 235, 243, 248–9, 254, 258, 296
  differences with West India sojourning, 148
  rates of absenteeism, 171, 201, 235, 243
Alston, David, historian, 249–50
Atlantic slavery economy, 78, 209, 249, 277, 299–301
  complicity of Scottish society, 77, 249, 277, 299
Atlantic commerce, 4, 16, 19, 21, 23, 31–2, 47, 64, 87, 131–2, 194, 197, 252–3, 256, 278, 295
American Revolution (1776), 10–11, 14, 34, 61, 78, 94, 162, 169, 181, 294
American War of Independence (1775–83), 6, 11, 17, 23, 30, 33, 36, 54, 57, 90, 137, 153, 186, 263, 280–1, 293
banking and banks (Scotland), 50, 57, 72, 78–87, 93, 138, 167, 175, 218, 253, 271–2, 280, 295
  capital stock, 72, 83, 93
Bank of Scotland, 82, 175, 253, 272
  importance to West India commerce, 175, 295
  Kilmarnock Banking Company, 175
  provincial banks Glasgow, 50, 72, 79–81, 175, 274
  Royal Bank, 57, 65–6, 78–87, 138, 167, 175, 218, 253, 272, 280, 295

bankruptcy, 36, 58, 65, 97, 101–2, 104, 107–8, 111, 183–4, 187, 195, 197, 220, 253, 256, 261, 263–4
Burnard, Trevor, historian, 5, 11–12, 141, 148–9, 153, 162
Burns, Robert, poet, 147–8, 211
Buchanan, James (1785–1857), colonial sojourner, 130, 200, 202–8, 255
canals, 279–283
Capitalism and Slavery (1944), academic text, 5, 20, 249, 302
capital, 3, 6, 10–11, 14–19, 24–5, 61, 67–70, 73–4, 85–6, 88, 90–3, 100–2, 105, 107, 109–17, 123, 128, 143, 149–50, 154, 157, 159, 164–5, 167–78, 180–1, 198–203, 218, 221–2, 233–6, 238, 241–52, 254–92, 293–302
  sojourning capital (colonial), 123, 157, 164–5, 167–78, 180–1, 198–203, 233–6, 238, 241–52, 296–7
  merchant capital, 3, 14, 18–19, 24–5, 74, 109–15, 249, 254–92, 293–302
  sources of (personal), 3, 6, 41, 67–70, 73, 88, 90–3, 105, 218, 221–2, 241
charity and philanthropy, 15, 51, 63, 125, 177–180, 203–8, 236, 245, 254, 283–90, 292–3, 295–6, 301
  Buchanan's Mortification (James Buchanan, 1785–1857), 203–8
  Bellahouston Bequest, 288–90
  Ewing bequests (James Ewing), 48, 206, 284–8

Churches, 40–1, 46–8, 124, 148, 154, 156, 160, 172, 181, 186, 188, 285–6
  Catholic Church, 214
  Church of England, 154, 186
  Church of Scotland, 40, 47, 124, 285–6
  Episcopal Church, 47–8
  Free Church of Scotland, 48, 284–6
  Scots Kirks in the West Indies, 48, 148, 154, 156, 160, 172, 181, 188
Cooke, Anthony, historian, 24, 27, 53, 262, 264, 275–6, 282
cotton, 1, 7, 13, 17, 19–20, 23–4, 27, 29, 32–4, 52–3, 59, 70, 79–80, 84, 89, 94–6, 99, 105, 112, 117, 137, 150, 172, 187, 189, 191–2, 194–8, 209, 215, 258, 272, 274–81, 291, 294–5, 300, 302
  cotton masters, 29, 52–3, 95, 258, 285–6
  capital stock (firms), 27, 95–6
  importance to Scottish Industrial Revolution, 33, 96, 117, 189, 198, 274–7, 294, 300, 302
  imports and exports, 32–3, 94, 192, 195, 280, 294
  working population (Scotland), 277, 300
coal, 29, 278, 281, 294
credit, 9, 26, 59–61, 65–82, 82–7, 104, 106–8, 112, 115–17, 158, 163, 183, 186, 192, 194–8, 219, 240, 263, 271–4, 277, 279, 281, 291, 293, 295–7
'decline' of slavery-era West India economy, 6, 11–13, 95, 149, 163, 167, 169, 171, 180–1, 213, 299
Devine, T.M., historian, 19–20, 23–4, 27, 36, 51, 58, 67, 123, 243, 264, 267, 275, 282, 298

Draper, Nicholas, historian, 12–14, 25, 87, 187, 235, 259, 297
East Indies, 19, 24, 77, 99, 123, 238, 242, 261, 302
Edinburgh, 1, 50, 52, 77–8, 80–4, 88, 140, 148, 156, 161, 175, 202, 272, 280
education, 14, 26, 29, 41–43, 49, 62–4, 88, 91, 120, 124, 130–3, 145, 150, 159, 161, 178–80, 205–8, 229, 232, 251, 263, 276, 283, 286–8, 296
  mercantile academies, 131–2
  specialist texts for merchants, 63–4
  University, 42–3, 62, 91, 229, 232
'enclave economy' theory, as applied to Scotland, 19
estates (landed), Scotland, 74–8, 263–71, 243–5
estates (plantations), West Indies, 10, 36–7, 45, 59, 79, 100–3, 105, 108, 120, 126, 147, 151, 155, 158–60, 164, 185, 189, 193, 197, 200, 215, 218, 220, 222–6, 237
Ewing, James (1775–1853), West India merchant, 36, 38–9, 43–4, 48, 51–3, 112, 152, 205–6, 254–5, 258–9, 262, 271–2, 284–8, 301, 307
Fedon's Rebellion, Grenada, (1795–1796), 96, 184, 187, 190, 197, 209
Glasgow West India Association, 1, 26, 34, 36–8, 46, 48–50, 53, 57, 59, 61, 66, 80, 86, 97, 113, 119, 219, 303
Glasgow, 1, 22–4, 29, 30–4, 38–48, 49–53, 61, 75–80, 82–7, 109–115, 132–6, 218–20, 253–92, 293–300
  economy, 22–4, 30–4, 61, 75–80, 82–7, 109–15, 132–6, 293–300
  politics, 49–53
  population, 38
  society, 38–48

Greenock, 22, 30, 32, 119, 136–9, 143–4, 246, 280

Hamilton, Douglas, historian, 20, 58–9, 141, 143, 150, 183–5, 208, 245

Highlands, Scotland, 38, 119–121, 126–7, 142–4, 156, 158, 170, 176, 199, 208, 214, 220–1, 228–9, 234, 240–1, 244, 246–51, 254, 287, 299
Highland Clearances, 248–9

Home, Ninian (1732–95), colonial governor and planter, 190–2

industry, and industrial transformation, 1–2, 4–5, 7, 10, 12–14, 16–18, 18–26, 30, 33–4, 38, 95–6
English, 4–5, 7, 10, 12–14, 16–18, 96
Scottish, 18–26, 30, 33–4, 38, 95–6, 111, 115, 128, 169, 177, 189, 243, 248, 274–9, 291–2, 293–5, 297–8, 299–302
Welsh, 7, 16

indenture system, 128–32
Glasgow Atlantic world labour market, 132–6

inventories (confirmation, probate and sequestration), 11, 27, 35, 65, 72–3, 80, 85, 90, 92, 109–11, 113–14, 120, 155–8, 160, 162, 167, 168–72, 174, 185, 198–201, 233–35, 237, 239–52, 255–90, 303–12

Jones, Maria, enslaved woman in Trinidad, 226

Kingston, Jamaica, 48, 66, 94, 97, 119–20, 127, 147–8, 150–2, 154, 156–8, 160–1, 166–7, 169, 172–6, 180, 204, 245

Karras, Allan, historian, 27, 123, 139–41, 149–50, 163

Lamont, John, Trinidad planter, 37, 220–9, 232–3, 235–41, 250, 298

linen, 19, 112, 236, 272, 274–5, 277–9, 294

Liverpool, 15–17, 32, 53, 57, 66, 95, 139, 173–4, 193, 259–60, 291, 293, 297, 299

Livingstone, David, missionary explorer, 300

London 1, 7–8, 12, 14–15, 19, 32, 34, 50, 53, 55, 59, 62, 65–7, 71, 77, 79–80, 82–5, 87–8, 101, 103–5, 115–16, 138, 150, 173–4, 183, 187, 191, 193–4, 238, 248, 254, 259, 263, 297, 299, 302

Macinnes, Allan, historian, 18, 150, 248

Mackillop, Andrew, historian, 18, 123, 242

marriage and marital networks 26, 38–9, 41, 44–7, 49, 54, 67–70, 77, 88, 221, 265, 290

Merchants House (Glasgow) 35, 43–4, 50–1, 53, 112, 203, 205–8, 255, 284–6

merchant firms (Glasgow), 24, 35, 37, 46, 59–62, 67, 72–3, 79–80, 87, 89–109, 132, 152, 187, 192–8, 261–3, 266
capital stock of Virginia and West India firms, 67
family firms, 41, 61–2, 68, 73, 85, 88, 90–3, 159
Jas. & Arch. Smith & Co., West India firm, 103–9
John Campbell senior & Co., West India firm, 29, 37, 46, 61–2, 67, 70–1, 79–80, 84, 96, 109, 119, 132, 137, 187, 191–2, 192–8, 200, 202–3, 261, 280
Leitch & Smith, West India firm, 90–101, 187

migration, 38, 87, 120–2, 124–8, 130, 138-9, 141–4, 189, 212, 221, 246–8, 251, 296

differences in patterns of migration to North America and West Indies, 123–4, 141, 143, 296
effects on local economies, 128, 251
migrants from the Clyde to West Indies 1806–34 (estimates), 141–2
migrants from Greenock to the West Indies 1774–5 (actual), 143–4, 246–8
migrants from Scotland to North America, (estimates), 141
migrants from Scotland to West Indies 1750–1834 (estimates), 141
Migrants from Great Britain to the West Indies 1841 (actual), 138–9,
motives, 124–8, 177
Moncrieff, Robert Scott, agent for Glasgow agency of Royal Bank, 83–5, 138, 218
Pares, Richard, historian, 9–10, 13, 104, 115–16, 271
philanthropy, see *charity and philanthropy*
population, 2, 14–16, 21, 38, 127–8, 141, 144, 150, 153, 188–9, 213, 217–18, 246–7, 250
enslaved people in the British West Indies, 2, 150, 188, 215, 217, 228
estimates of Scots in West India islands, 152–3, 188, 217
Grenada and Carriacou, 188–9
Jamaica, 150, 153
mortality rates of Scots in the West Indies, 127–8
Scotland, 21, 25, 142, 246–7, 250
Trinidad, 213, 215, 217–18, 228
Port of Spain, Trinidad, 211, 218–19
Port Glasgow, 22, 30, 32, 87, 113, 136–9, 195, 216, 221, 236, 246

railways, 13, 24, 115, 117, 173, 177, 204, 206, 279–83, 294
religion, 44, 47, 54, 186, 207, 214–15
Anglicanism, 154, 186
Catholicism, 186, 213–14, 219, 225
Evangelicalism, 48, 286
Scottish Presbyterianism, 44, 47, 54, 148, 154, 188, 198, 214, 297
St George's, Grenada, 94, 98–9, 187–8, 200
Sheridan, Richard, historian, 10–11, 96, 116, 123, 156, 162–3
Scottish
'Agricultural Revolution' 21, 245, 263–71
'Commercial Revolution' 21
'Industrial Revolution' 21–2, 30, 33, 96, 189, 194, 198, 274–9, 291, 293–4, 297, 302
slavery, 1–2, 4–7, 179, 202–3, 223–7
emancipation and compensation 1834, 25
contribution to English Industrial Revolution, 2, 4–7, 12–14
contribution to Scottish Industrial Revolution, 18–22, 24, 293–302
mortality rates in West Indies, 225–6
pro-slavery bodies and arguments, 1, 29, 50, 53, 119, 184, 211, 299
Smith, Adam (1723–1790), economist and philosopher, 9–10, 74, 95, 115–16
Smith, Archibald (1749–1821), West India merchant, 41, 51, 53, 61, 82–7, 89–117, 180, 200, 235, 266, 269, 275, 277, 279, 311
social clubs, 49–50, 54, 293

sojourning, 2, 13, 20, 24–5, 27, 64, 67,
70, 75, 88, 91, 123–4, 128, 143,
148–9, 159, 167–77, 181, 183,
198–203, 229, 233–6, 241–52,
284, 296, 298–9
  economic 'success' rates, 128, 243
  repatriation of wealth from West
    Indies, 163–7, 236–41, 241–52
  wealth levels of Scots in West Indies,
    167–77, 198–203, 233–6, 244,
    284
Scots law (Commissary and sheriff),
58–62, 70, 168, 181
shipping, 32–3, 132, 136–144, 246–7,
279–281
  ships from the Clyde to West Indies
    (estimates), 140
  newspaper adverts, and limitations
    of methodology, 138–9
Stirling, Robert McGregor (d.1832),
colonial sojourner, 229–33
sugar, 2, 4, 7, 9–11, 15, 22, 30–4,
82–3, 100, 102, 138, 185, 189,
215, 223
surname analysis, as a means of
identifying Scots in West Indies,
156–7, 163
tobacco, 2, 15, 17, 19–20, 22–3, 30,
32, 36, 54, 57, 59, 67, 80, 138, 293
Tobago, 37, 122, 127, 129, 140, 142,
185, 189, 214–6, 227, 252
universities, 9, 35, 41–3, 62–3, 77–8,
91, 114, 125, 132, 159, 206, 227,
229, 267, 284, 301
  Anderson's University (University of
    Strathclyde), 62–3, 114, 206
  Old College (University of
    Glasgow), 35, 41–3, 62, 77–8,
    91, 132, 159, 206–7, 229, 267,
    284, 289, 301

Virginia merchants ('tobacco lords'),
Glasgow, 2, 20, 23, 36, 40, 43,
45–7, 49, 54, 59–60, 64, 69, 77–8,
111, 275, 281, 285, 292–3
Wallerstein, Immanuel, sociologist, 3,
18
Watt, James, merchant and inventor, 78
West India merchants, Glasgow, 2–3,
23–6, 29, 32, 38–41, 44, 54, 62–6,
83, 252, 274, 291, 293–4, 302
  education, 41–3
  geographical origins, 38–41
  investments, 263–83
  social rank and mobility, 29, 39–40,
    44, 47, 169, 266–7
  'Sugar Aristocracy', definition of and
    contemporary views, 2–3, 26,
    29, 44, 54, 83, 252, 274, 291,
    293–4, 302
  training, 62–66, 99
  wealth, extent of, investments and
    range, 255–61
Williams, Eric, historian, 5–13, 20–1,
24, 95, 169, 180, 214, 249, 299,
302
wills and testaments, 62, 68, 155, 157,
167–8, 177–9, 202, 236, 238, 242,
255, 283, 290